The Duke of Anjou and the Politique Struggle during the Wars of Religion

MACK P. HOLT

Andrew W. Mellon Faculty Fellow in History
Harvard University

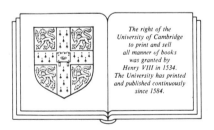

The right of the
University of Cambridge
to print and sell
all manner of books
was granted by
Henry VIII in 1534.
The University has printed
and published continuously
since 1584.

CAMBRIDGE UNIVERSITY PRESS

Cambridge
London   New York   New Rochelle
Melbourne   Sydney

Published by the Press Syndicate of the University of Cambridge
The Pitt Building, Trumpington Street, Cambridge CB2 1RP
32 East 57th Street, New York, NY 10022, USA
10 Stamford Road, Oakleigh, Melbourne 3166, Australia

First published 1986

Printed in Great Britain at the University Press, Cambridge

British Library cataloguing in publication data
Holt, Mack P.
The Duke of Anjou and the politique struggle during the wars
of religion. – (Cambridge studies in early modern history)
1. Anjou, Hercule-François, *Duke of* 2. France –
History – Wars of the Huguenots, 1562–1598
I. Title
944′.028′0924 DC112.A/

Library of Congress cataloguing in publication data
Holt, Mack P.
The Duke of Anjou and the politique struggle during the wars of religion.
(Cambridge studies in early modern history)
Bibliography: p.
Includes index.
1. France – History – Wars of the Huguenots, 1562–1598.
2. Anjou, François, duc d', 1554–1584. I. Title. II. Series.
DC111.H65 1986 944′.029 85–20930

ISBN 0 521 32232 4

CE

Contents

Maps

Preface

At a time when French historical studies on both sides of the Atlantic have come to be dominated by the methods and techniques of the *Annalistes* and their imitators, the appearance of what is an essentially old-fashioned narrative history perhaps needs some explanation. Let me say at the outset that I am one of the keenest supporters of the 'new' social and economic history that is currently *à la mode*; indeed, my next book will be a modest attempt to emulate this kind of history on a small scale. Both types of history have much to offer, however, and they are by no means mutually exclusive. Clearly, events such as the crown's periodic decisions to wage war in the provinces made just as great an impact on the lives of most sixteenth-century Frenchmen as the changing birthrate or climatic transformations over the *longue durée*. Neither kind of history tells the whole story, but each can illuminate the other. Thus, I hope readers who find this study unfashionable may at least find it somewhat useful.

In the spelling of all place names I have followed the usual practice of using an English form if one exists: Brussels, Antwerp, The Hague, Dunkirk, Flushing, etc. If there is no English equivalent, I have used the form currently employed by present-day inhabitants of the place in question: Ieper (rather than Ypres), Mechelen (rather than Malines), Aalst (rather than Alost), etc. A similar practice has been adopted for the spelling of all personal names. If an accepted English form exists, I have used it: Henry III, Philip II, William of Orange, etc. Otherwise, I have used the spelling employed by the person in question.

Comparing sixteenth-century currencies is always a problem. The basic unit of account in France was the *livre tournois*, which was composed of 20 *sous* (and each *sou* consisted of 12 *deniers*). In 1579 the *écu* was introduced as a new unit of account at the rate of 1 *écu* = 3 *livres* = 60 *sous*. To keep all French currency uniform, I have usually converted all figures to *livres* after 1579 (and I have always noted such conversions in the footnotes). The standard English currency throughout the period was the pound sterling of 20 shillings each, while the basic unit of currency in the Netherlands was the gold florin of 20 pattards each. Comparisons are relatively simple for the second half of the sixteenth century, as the *livre tournois* was roughly equivalent to the florin in value, and both were roughly one-tenth the value of the pound sterling. Thus, a general guide for the period is £1 = 10 *livres tournois* = 10 florins.

In France the New Year began on 25 March until 1567, when 1 January was adopted as the beginning of the calendar year. I have converted all dates prior to 1567 to the new style as if the year began on 1 January. Thus, the duke of Anjou's birthday is rendered 18 March 1555, not 1554 as it would have been to his contemporaries. In citing some English sources, however, I have used the form '10 March 1575/6' to refer to the year being observed in England as 1575 and in France as 1576, as England refused to adopt the new-style calendar, with the New Year beginning on 1 January, until much later. Moreover, when Pope Gregory XIII added ten days to the Christian calendar in 1582, many Protestant states (like England) refused to comply. I have nevertheless adopted the Gregorian calendar for all dates after December 1582 when it went into effect, although in citing some English sources I have occasionally used the form '10/20 March 1583/4' to refer to the day observed as 10 March 1583 in England and 20 March 1584 in France.

A number of scholars have very kindly and generously shared their expertise and have made numerous suggestions during the preparation of this book, and I am grateful to them all. *Primus inter pares* is Professor J. Russell Major, who supervised the Emory University Ph.D. thesis from which this book has derived. Without his advice, his encouragement, and above all his friendship, this book would never have been completed. Only his other students (and there are many) can really appreciate what knowing him has meant. Dr Jonathan Powis and Professor Geoffrey Parker have both contributed to this study in countless ways. The former has read virtually every draft of the book (each time adding to its improvement), and has been a constant source of criticism and encouragement. The latter not only corrected a number of errors regarding Anjou's sojourn in the Netherlands, but also kindly introduced me to the archives in Brussels and The Hague, which has substantially strengthened the second half of the book. A number of other scholars have graciously either offered suggestions, answered queries, corrected errors, or read parts of the manuscript at various stages. And, although some of them may not agree with all of my interpretations, their disagreement has made this a better book: Dr Simon Adams, Professor Brian G. Armstrong, Dr Joan Davies, Professor Robert M. Kingdon, Dr H. A. Lloyd, Professor Hugo de Schepper, Professor N. M. Sutherland, Professor K. W. Swart, and the late Dr Frances A. Yates.

I am also grateful to my editors, Professors J. H. Elliott and H. G. Koenigsberger, not only for correcting countless errors and making a number of useful suggestions, but also for setting such high standards of scholarship with their own work. I also wish to thank Richard Fisher and Sarah Barrett of Cambridge University Press for seeing the book through production so conscientiously.

The staffs of the many archives and libraries where I worked were all exceedingly helpful, but I would like to single out especially the staff of the *Cabinet des manuscrits* of the *Bibilothèque Nationale* in Paris, where most of the research for this book was carried out. And I also must thank Emory University for awarding me a graduate fellowship from 1978 to 1981, which enabled me to carry out the bulk of the research. And I am also grateful to the Organized Research Committee of West Texas State University for providing funds to help cover the costs of preparing the index.

The table in Appendix A was first published in my article, 'Patterns of *clientèle* and economic opportunity at court during the Wars of Religion: the household of François, duke of Anjou', *French Historical Studies*, XIII (Spring 1984), 305–22; and I wish to thank the editors of that journal for permission to include it here.

Finally, I wish to thank my wife, Meg, and my parents, all of whom have supported me when I most needed it. They know better than anyone else that I would have never finished this book without their continuous enthusiasm and encouragement. I dedicate it to them.

July 1985, Paris   M.P.H.

Abbreviations

AC	Archives communales
AD	Archives départementales
AGRB	Archives Générales du Royaume, Brussels
MSS Audience	Papiers d'Etat et de l'Audience
Albèri, *Relazioni*	E. Albèri (ed.), *Le Relazioni degli ambasciatori veneti al senato durante il secolo decimosesto*, series i (6 vols., Florence, 1839–62)
AN	Archives Nationales, Paris
ARA	Algemeen Rijksarchief, The Hague
BIF	Bibliothèque de l'Institut de France, Paris
MSS God.	Collection Godefroy
BL	British Library, London
Add. MSS	Additional Manuscripts
Cotton. MSS	Cottonian Collection
Harl. MSS	Harleian Collection
BM	Bibliothèque municipale
BN	Bibliothèque Nationale, Paris
MSS CCC	Collection Cinq Cents de Colbert
MSS Clair.	Collection Clairambault
MSS Dupuy	Fonds Dupuy
MSS fr.	Fonds français
MSS ital.	Fonds italien
MSS n.a.fr.	Fonds nouvelles acquisitions françaises
Cabié	E. Cabié (ed.), *Guerres de religion dans le sud-ouest de la France, et principalement dans le Quercy, d'après les papiers des seigneurs de Saint-Sulpice de 1561 à 1590* (Paris and Albi, 1906)
Catherine de Medici, *Lettres*	H. de la Ferrière and G. Baguenault de Puchesse (eds.), *Lettres de Catherine de Médicis* (10 vols., Paris, 1880–1905)
CODOIN	M. F. Navarrete *et al.* (eds.), *Colección de documentos inéditos para la historia de España* (112 vols., Madrid, 1842–95)

xi

CSPF	*Calendar of State Papers, Foreign*
CSPR	*Calendar of State Papers, Rome*
CSPS	*Calendar of State Papers, Spanish*
CSPV	*Calendar of State Papers, Venetian*
Desjardins	A. Desjardins and G. Canestrini (eds.), *Négociations diplomatiques de la France avec la Toscane* (6 vols., Paris, 1859–66)
De Thou, *Histoire universelle*	J.-A. de Thou, *Histoire universelle* (11 vols., Basel, 1742 edn)
Groen van Prinsterer, *Archives*	G. Groen van Prinsterer (ed.), *Archives ou correspondance inédite de la maison d'Orange-Nassau*, series i (8 vols., Leiden, 1835–47)
Henry III, *Lettres*	M. François (ed.), *Lettres de Henri III, roi de France* (3 vols. to date, Paris, 1959–72)
HMC, *Salisbury MSS*	Historical Manuscripts Commission, *Calendar of the Manuscripts of the Most Hon. the Marquis of Salisbury, K.G., preserved at Hatfield House* (vols. 1–3, London, 1883–90)
Japikse, *Resolutiën der Staten-Generaal*	N. Japikse (ed.), *Resolutiën der Staten-Generaal van 1576 tot 1609* (14 vols., 's-Gravenhage, 1915–70)
Kervijn de Lettenhove, *Huguenots*	J. M. B. C. Kervijn de Lettenhove, *Les Huguenots et les Gueux* (6 vols., Bruges, 1883–5)
Kervijn de Lettenhove, *Relations*	J. M. B. C. Kervijn de Lettenhove and L. Gilliodts van Severen (eds.), *Relations politiques des Pays-Bas et de l'Angleterre sous le règne de Philippe II* (11 vols., Brussels, 1882–1900)
L'Estoile, *Journal*	MM. Brunet *et al.* (eds.), *Mémoires-journaux de Pierre de l'Estoile* (vols. 1–2, Paris, 1888)
Michaud and Poujoulat, *Mémoires*	J. F. Michaud and J. J. F. Poujoulat (eds.), *Nouvelle Collection des mémoires relatifs à l'histoire de France depuis le XIIIᵉ siècle jusqu'à la fin du XVIIIᵉ siècle*, series i (Paris, 1838)
Muller and Diegerick, *Documents*	P. L. Muller and A. Diegerick (eds.), *Documents concernant les relations entre le duc d'Anjou et les Pays-Bas, 1576–1584* (5 vols., Amsterdam, 1889–99)
Nevers, *Mémoires*	Marin le Roy, seigneur de Gomberville (ed.), *Les Mémoires de monsieur le duc de Nevers* (2 vols., Paris, 1665)

Petitot, *Mémoires*	C. B. Petitot (ed.), *Collection complète des mémoires relatifs à l'histoire de la France*, series i (Paris, 1819–27)
PRO/SP	Public Record Office, London, State Papers

Introduction

In December 1576 Queen Elizabeth's principal agent in the Netherlands, Thomas Wilson, proclaimed that the entire fate of Christendom rested in the hands of three men: Don John of Austria, William of Orange, and François de Valois, duke of Anjou.[1] Although he died prematurely only two years later, Don John had already made a name for himself as a military commander at Lepanto. William of Orange led a small group of Dutch provinces in a successful revolt against the mightiest power in Western Europe and, in so doing, established himself as one of the principal heroes of the sixteenth century as well as the *pater patriæ* of the Dutch Republic. What became of the duke of Anjou? All his political and military ambitions ended in tragic failure. He died in 1584 at only 29 years of age and has been largely forgotten ever since. Because all his grandiose dreams ended in frustration and his career was cut short by a premature death, Anjou has been assigned merely a walk-on role on the European stage. After four hundred years of historical writing about the French Wars of Religion, not one biography or major monograph – either serious or popular – has been devoted to the duke of Anjou. This is hardly a just reward for someone who was considered one of the three most important men in all Christendom.

Although Wilson's prognostication proved inaccurate, it is nevertheless an indication that Anjou was a far more consequential figure in the eyes of his contemporaries than his historical press would indicate. Historians appear to have forgotten what Anjou's contemporaries could never ignore, namely that he was destined to become the next king of France. By the late 1570s it was clear that Henry III was unable to produce an heir, a circumstance which left his younger brother, the duke of Alençon and Anjou, as the sole Valois successor to the crown. Thus, his peers viewed him not just as a prince of the blood, but as the future François III. In August 1578, for instance, in commenting upon a possible marriage alliance between Anjou and Queen Elizabeth, Francis Walsingham lamented that it was 'the expectation of the Crowne of Fraunce that is lykely to lyght uppon him which dyfficultye above all others I doe weyghe'.[2] Moreover, for one brief period there was the possibility that he might one day wear the three

---

[1] Kervijn de Lettenhove, *Relations*, vol. IX, pp. 67–8, Wilson to Leicester, 3 December 1576.
[2] Ibid., vol. X, p. 744, Walsingham to Sussex, 18 August 1578.

crowns of France, England, and the Netherlands, a heady prospect upon which his contemporaries commented.[3]

More importantly, because of this prospect Anjou unwittingly became the focus of various political forces within France and abroad, agents who saw in his leadership a possible alternative and escape from the political and religious divisions that plagued Europe in the second half of the sixteenth century. With the belief that religious coexistence was preferable to the ravages of continued civil war and the possible destruction of the state, these political factions turned to Anjou to intervene in their struggles and to fashion a more lasting political solution. Because some form of religious toleration was usually the most visible plank in their platforms, they were later given the pejorative appellation of *politiques* by their more uncompromising and zealous Catholic opponents.[4] First in France, after the St Bartholomew's massacres of 1572, and then in the Netherlands, in the late 1570s and early 1580s, various *politique* factions turned to Anjou for leadership. These were not organized political parties in any modern sense; indeed, their lack of structure and coherence contributed to their lack of success. Moreover, although the duke did share with these factions a general commitment to freedom of conscience (if not necessarily freedom of worship) in religious matters, which made him attractive to many, he unquestionably did not share their political and intellectual aspirations. Thus, Anjou was never really a part of the *politique* movement, much less its self-proclaimed leader. In this sense the *politique* struggle in the latter half of the sixteenth century was a struggle for political and legal recognition of religious coexistence in order to preserve the state. In France this victory was not achieved – and even achieved then only temporarily – until the reign of Henry IV. In the Netherlands the struggle failed as the provinces eventually became permanently divided, largely on account of religious differences. Nevertheless, during his lifetime François de Valois, duke of Alençon and Anjou became the focus of factions from both states, figures who looked to him for an exit from the morass of civil war.

Thus, in 1576 Thomas Wilson had justification enough for bracketing Anjou together with Don John of Austria and William of Orange as the most important figures in all Christendom. That Anjou failed to live up to these expectations, largely due to his own shortcomings and a premature death in 1584, does not alter this fact. The story of this long neglected and oft-maligned prince deserves examination.

[3] See, for instance, Groen van Prinsterer, *Archives*, vol. VI, p. 399, Roch de Sorbiers, seigneur des Pruneaux, to William of Orange, 22 June 1578.

[4] The term *politique* was not really in general use until the mid-1580s, when it was almost always a term of derision used by Leaguers to denounce anyone, Protestant or Catholic, who proposed any form of religious coexistence. The usage here – as a descriptive rather than pejorative epithet applied to figures in the 1570s and early 1580s – is thus anachronistic. I can think of no better alternative, however, and shall employ the term in this fashion throughout this study. Moreover, contemporary works such as Jacques-Auguste de Thou's *Histoire universelle* (first edition 1604–9) quickly adopted this usage of the term by the early seventeenth century, so there is some justification for using the term *politique* in this manner.

Prologue: civil war and the early years of François de Valois, 1555–72

I

When the fourth and last son of Henry II and Catherine de Medici was born in the royal château at Fontainebleau on 18 March 1555, the kingdom of France was at war with Spain, a conflict that had been almost continuous since Charles VIII invaded Italy in 1494. Despite a peace treaty signed by both countries at Cateau-Cambrésis in 1559, this Franco-Spanish rivalry became even more intense towards the end of the sixteenth century. Indeed, it was only after another century of fighting that Louis XIV emerged triumphant over the degenerating Spanish Habsburgs. During the last half of the sixteenth century this rivalry proved to be the most pivotal of all the external factors that permeated the French civil wars. The constant threat of Spanish invasion – from across the Pyrenees or from the Spanish Netherlands – combined with the desire to stay out of another war with Spain at all costs, formed the fulcrum of French foreign policy until the 1590s. The activities of this last Valois prince, the future duke of Anjou, played a critical role in this stormy rivalry. Moreover, in the early 1580s, when he sided with the Dutch rebels in their revolt against Philip II of Spain, this young prince almost singlehandedly brought France and Spain back to the brink of open war.

In addition to the war with Spain there were two other problems which beset the French monarchy in 1555, problems that were never successfully resolved in the duke of Anjou's lifetime. The first was a problem that plagued every early modern European state, namely money. The long and costly involvement in the Habsburg–Valois conflict had almost completely exhausted the financial resources of the French crown by 1555. Indeed, economic necessity rather than a clearcut military victory forced both France and Spain to make peace in 1559. When civil war broke out in France only a few years later, however, the French crown was once more forced to stretch its financial resources to the limit for an extended period of time. Even in the best of times the French monarchy hovered on the precipice of bankruptcy, since there was not yet any systematic, centralized, and state-controlled method of tax collection.[1] In various parts of

---

[1] The first successful attempts to create a more centralized system of tax collection occurred during the reign of Henry IV. See J. Russell Major, 'Henry IV and Guyenne: a study concerning the origins of absolutism', *French Historical Studies*, IV (1966), 363–83.

France taxes were collected by *élus*, tax farmers, royal commissioners, provincial estates, and local *seigneurs*. Unlike England, there was no representative body which met regularly either to coordinate these activities or to assess taxation uniformly over the entire kingdom. This unwieldy system did work up to a point in peacetime, however, as the French state had managed to function after the Hundred Years War without going too deeply into the red. During the sixteenth century, however, the unusual demands of the Habsburg–Valois conflict and the religious wars placed even greater burdens on the royal fiscal system. The French kings resorted to heavy borrowing and deficit spending, and as a result the national debt grew to enormous proportions towards the end of the century, when yearly expenditure exceeded income by two to three fold.[2] Thus, fiscal pressure surrounded the French monarchy throughout the Wars of Religion, and aggravated even further the other major components of civil war.

Finally, the last Valois prince was born into a society that was just beginning to smoulder with the sparks of Calvinism. Protestant churches had already been established in many parts of southern France, and by the year of Anjou's birth there was even one in Paris. That the religious problem had not already broken out into the flame of civil war was largely due to the efforts of Henry II. He considered the new religion heretical and was determined to extirpate it, especially from the capital. The creation of the famous *chambre ardente* in the *Parlement* of Paris and the lesser known presidial courts in the provinces resulted in numerous arrests of Protestants throughout the kingdom. And with the edict of Châteaubriant in June 1551, Henry II progressed from a policy of prohibition and suppression to outright persecution. The new edict not only gave magistrates the right to prosecute practicing heretics, but bound them to search and seek out the more concealed Protestants, even to the extent of searching private homes. The edict forbade reformed teachings to be taught in the schools and universities, and further tightened the censorship laws on printed books. Moreover, Protestants were forbidden to hold any of the major offices of the realm. This was Henry II's rejoinder to the establishment of Calvinist churches in France, and it marked the direction in which the monarchy was moving at the birth of his youngest son, the future duke of Alençon and Anjou.[3] Although the French Protestants, or Huguenots as they were called, were always a minority – never more than one in ten – their fate was not settled during the lifetime of this young prince. Indeed, at his death in 1584 the religious problem was, if anything, worse.

However much Henry II may have thought that he had resolved the above issues by 1559, his solutions were short-lived. The entire nation suffered a

---

[2] David Buisseret, *Sully and the Growth of Centralized Government in France, 1598–1610* (London, 1968), p. 85.

[3] See the useful discussion by N. M. Sutherland, *The Huguenot Struggle for Recognition* (New Haven and London, 1980), pp. 40–8.

serious blow on 10 July 1559 when Henry died from a wound received ten days earlier in a jousting tournament marking the celebration of the peace treaty of Cateau-Cambrésis. At a single stroke the French monarchy was plunged into a crisis of authority, as the rival noble factions at court began vying with one another to dominate the young, inexperienced *dauphin*, now Francis II. In the last years of Henry's reign, one noble faction tended to dominate the king's attention, that led by Francis, duke of Guise, and his brother Charles, cardinal of Lorraine. Since the young *dauphin* had married a niece of the Guises, Mary Stuart, it was only natural that the Guises immediately seized the initiative to dominate the young Francis as well. By acting quickly, the duke of Guise and cardinal of Lorraine seized control of the government. Within days of Henry's death the Guises surrounded a mourning Catherine de Medici and the new king in the Louvre. They immediately occupied the Tournelles, the privileged lodgings formerly reserved for the constable, Anne de Montmorency, and Henry's mistress, Diane de Poitiers. They then assumed control of the *cachet*, took over all foreign negotiations of the crown, and finally consolidated their position by taking control of the army, the church, and the royal treasury. After removing all their opponents from court, they also tried to place their creatures in positions of power in the provinces. The takeover was as complete as it was swift. Within a week of Henry's death the foreign ambassadors at court were quick to acknowledge who controlled the crown – the Guise brothers.[4]

The Guises, of course, justified their actions with assurances that they were merely protecting the king. They also stressed that they favored the continuation of the late king's religious policies. Their actions, however, stirred up vehement opposition. The French Protestants particularly looked to the Bourbon family, headed by Antoine de Bourbon, king of Navarre, to counter the Guises' domination of the crown. Claiming that a regency government was necessary owing to the young king's poor health, they hoped that Navarre, as first prince of the blood, might provide a better alternative. Navarre, however, was either unprepared or unwilling to assume control of a regency government. More to the point, he was absent from court in Guyenne and unable to challenge the Guises. More ambitious, however, was Navarre's younger brother, Louis de Bourbon, prince of Condé. Condé was eager to claim the regency in his brother's name. Indeed, his efforts to do so by force led to the Conspiracy of Amboise in March 1560. The ultimate result of the death of Henry II and the subsequent dominance of the Guises was a crisis of authority. The old and bitter rivalries of the nobility at court were aggravated, with all factions claiming to support the king. The power struggle between the Guises and the Bourbons, with the constable, Anne de Montmorency, caught in the middle, lay at the heart of the crisis. Moreover, this struggle continued throughout the religious wars, as the

---

[4] Ibid., pp. 73–5.

respective sons of the duke of Guise and the king of Navarre re-enacted the scene twenty-five years later in the 1580s.

What made this crisis of authority even more dangerous, however, was that the struggle between the Guises and the Bourbons combined religion and politics. The Guises were zealous Catholics, and had championed Henry II's policies of persecution. Navarre was fairly equivocal in his religious beliefs, though he had often expressed Protestant sympathies and had an outspoken Protestant wife. Condé, on the other hand, was an ardent supporter of the new religion. Thus, the fate of the Protestant church in France became automatically linked to the political struggle at court. The Guises were opposed by those who envied their position at court, as well as by all French Protestants. The Protestants, naturally, looked to the Bourbons for protection against the persecution to which they had been subject for the last decade. The noble rivalry intensified even further after the death of the young Francis II in December 1560, leaving a minor, Charles IX, as heir and the necessity for a formal regency government. The resultant struggle precipitated the French civil wars, or Wars of Religion as they were sometimes called. While there were undeniably strong religious passions on both sides, the conflict began as a struggle for power and authority in the name of religion. Throughout the duration of the civil wars, politics and religion remained so inextricably entangled that even contemporaries found it difficult to distinguish them.[5]

This entanglement of religion and politics also resulted in the politicization of French Protestantism. This may have occurred even had Henry II lived, since many Huguenots were already looking beyond Geneva for physical protection from persecution by 1559. When the prince of Condé organized a conspiracy to unseat the Guises after they seized power, many French Protestants sought Calvin's support for the venture. When he informed them that it was their duty to suffer and die for their faith rather than raise arms, they turned to political leaders in France who could protect them, specifically Condé and Gaspard de Coligny, admiral of France and a nephew of the constable. Thus, French Protestantism emerged in the early 1560s as a religious movement that was led by a strong political element, a political element that never fully merged with the evangelical ideals of Geneva. Indeed, leaders such as Condé and Coligny – and later Henry of Navarre – infused those evangelical ideals with political objectives. In this sense, at least, French Protestantism was both a sociopolitical and a religious force. It explains why many French Catholics referred to the Huguenots throughout the sixteenth century as a 'state within a state'.[6]

Finally, in the background of the entire conflict of faction versus faction and

---

[5] This entire discussion is based on Sutherland, *The Huguenot Struggle*, pp. 63–100, and Sutherland's 'Antoine de Bourbon, king of Navarre and the French crisis of authority 1559–1562', in J. F. Bosher (ed.), *French Government and Society, 1500–1800* (London, 1973), pp. 1–18.

[6] Sutherland, *The Huguenot Struggle*, pp. 97–136, and 'Antoine de Bourbon', p. 9.

religion versus religion stood the queen mother, the widowed Catherine de
Medici. Upon the death of Francis II she lamented to her daughter Elisabeth de
Valois, who had recently married Philip II of Spain to seal the peace treaty of
Cateau-Cambrésis: 'God has taken the king your father away from me, and not
content with that, He has also taken your brother and left me with three small
sons in a kingdom that is completely divided. There is not a single person in
whom I can completely trust who does not have some personal interest at stake.'[7]
As a result Catherine decided to form a regency government herself, in the hope
that neither the Bourbons nor the Guises would be able to control the young
Charles IX. As it happened, she was unable to prevent the religious and political
hostilities from breaking out into civil war. Throughout the next thirty years,
however, the queen mother lurked behind the throne, attempting to provide the
acumen and leadership that her sons so sadly lacked as monarchs. Although the
degree to which she influenced her sons is not always clear, Catherine's power
should not be underestimated. Both as queen and mother, she had every reason
to want to end the political and religious division in France. While she was not
always successful, often because of her own blunders, she spent the rest of her
life trying.

Thus, Catherine's youngest son, the future duke of Alençon and Anjou, was
born and reared in a state that was already in turmoil. He would have to confront
the same difficulties that faced his father and older brothers: financial inadequacy, Spanish hegemony and, above all else, religious and political division at
home. He was only seven years old when civil war broke out in 1562, and the
conflict raged throughout his lifetime. Like his brothers before him, the young
prince played a central role in the wars. Unlike his three older brothers, however,
he never became king of France. This fact haunted him throughout his brief life;
and in many ways the story of the last Valois heir, a dynasty that ruled France for
more than two and a half centuries, is the story of a prince in pursuit of a crown.

II

Very little is known of the early years of the youngest son of Henry II and
Catherine de Medici. He was born at Fontainebleau on 18 March 1555 and
named Hercule.[8] The king honored the constable, Anne de Montmorency, by
making him the godfather. While nothing can be determined about his

---

7 Quoted in Lucien Romier, *Le Royaume de Catherine de Médicis: la France à la veille des guerres de
religion*, 2nd edn (2 vols., Paris, 1922) vol. 1, p. 20.
8 François de Valois's birthdate is usually given as 18 March 1554, but this is clearly the old-style
date. See the letter dated 18 March 1555 from Anne de Montmorency to Antoine à Noilles: 'The
Queen has given birth to a beautiful son, and both mother and child are doing well, thank God.'
Quoted in Francis Decrue, *Anne, duc de Montmorency, connétable et pair de France sous les rois Henri II,
François II et Charles IX* (Paris, 1889), p. 166.

I France during the wars of religion

whereabouts in the first few years of his life, young Hercule probably remained at court near his mother. It was customary for a prince of the blood to be reared and educated at court by women initially, and then, at about the age of seven, to be turned over to a male governor who would then train him to become a young gentleman.[9] It seems probable, then, that the young prince travelled with the court until his father's tragic death in 1559. Along with his three older brothers, he attended his father's funeral at Saint-Denis.[10]

When the Valois court moved to Orléans in 1560 for the meeting of the Estates-General, young Hercule was left behind at the château at Vincennes just east of Paris, along with his brother Alexandre-Edouard (the future Henry III) and his sister Marguerite. Even at this early age the young prince began to develop 'a latent aversion to his brother and a strong affection for his sister', feelings that became more apparent in later life.[11] The three royal children remained at Vincennes until after the death of their brother, Francis II, in December 1560. When the queen mother returned to Paris, they were removed to the Louvre, where they remained until after the Colloquy of Poissy in September 1561. Shortly thereafter, Catherine de Medici separated her three youngest children. Alexandre-Edouard remained at court, while Hercule and Marguerite were sent to the family château at Amboise, where they were looked after by some of the queen mother's ladies-in-waiting. There the youngest Valois prince remained during the opening years of the civil wars until the start of *le grand voyage de France* in the spring of 1564.

Under the pretext of showing him his kingdom, Catherine led the young Charles IX and the rest of the court on a two-year tour of the provinces in March 1564. Departing from Fontainebleau, where the court had resided since the previous January, this royal progress was intended to attract support for the monarchy in the provinces. Moreover, Catherine de Medici intended to call on the local nobility along the way in an effort to quash the traditional tensions between court and country. Thus, with politics underlying the voyage, the court moved slowly southward from Fontainebleau in March 1564, numbering well over 500 persons, and with the entire royal family travelling together.[12]

---

9 Roland Mousnier, *Les Institutions de la France sous la monarchie absolue 1598–1789* (2 vols., Paris, 1974–80), vol. 2, pp. 16–18.

10 Francis Decrue, *Le Parti des politiques au lendemain de la Saint-Barthélemy: la Molle et Coconat* (Paris, 1892), p. 89.

11 Most of the information in this and the preceding paragraph comes from the 'Abrege de la vie du duc d'Alençon' published by Marin le Roy, seigneur de Gomberville, in Nevers, *Mémoires*, vol. I, pp. 69–72 (quotation taken from p. 69).

12 Ibid., p. 70. The principal secondary sources concerning the voyage insist that the young prince did not make the journey because he was too young. See Pierre Champion, *Catherine de Médicis présente à Charles IX son royaume* (Paris, 1937), p. 27; and Victor E. Graham and W. M. Johnson, *The Royal Tour of France by Charles IX and Catherine de Medici: Festivals and Entries, 1564–1566* (Toronto, 1979), p. 6. Both of these sources are mistaken, however. As the following account will demonstrate, young Hercule definitely set out with the rest of the court from Fontainebleau in March 1564. He returned to Paris in the summer because of illness, but rejoined the royal tour the

The itinerary of the voyage was well planned by the queen mother to provide maximum exposure of the young king. From Fontainebleau the court moved southward down the Yonne River to Sens, then overland to Troyes in early April. It was there that Catherine de Medici met with representatives of Queen Elizabeth of England and signed a peace treaty on 11 April.[13] The court then travelled extensively throughout Champagne and Burgundy and arrived in Dijon in May. After a brief stay, the court turned southward via Châlons-sur-Saône and Mâcon and arrived in Lyon on 13 June. The court then rested there for nearly a month before setting off down the Rhône river toward Valence on 8 July.

Somewhere on the journey between Lyon and Valence the young Hercule became very ill, ill enough, in fact, to necessitate sending him back to Paris. Near the town of Roussillon, just south of Vienne, the nine-year-old prince set out northward, accompanied by several secretaries and guards. Details of his illness are vague, although a letter he wrote en route to Paris to François de Montmorency is very informative:[14]

My cousin, since my departure from Rousillon, where I left the Queen my mother, I have set out for this town of Sagonne, where I have spent the last seven days in order to regain my strength. And now before departing I want to write to you to report of my good health, and to say that I do not plan to break my journey until I reach your *gouvernement*, hoping, of course, to keep you informed of my progress along the way. At the same time I hope to hear from you somewhere along the route I shall be taking via Bourges, Orléans, and Fontainebleau. In the meantime I shall tell you, as my godfather Monsieur the Constable assured me upon my departure, that I am to spend a great deal of time with you and my sister, for which I am delighted. I really look forward to having a good time with you two, when I can enjoy your company as much as I like.[15]

The young prince would be plagued by illness and poor health for the rest of his life, and this was the first indication that his body might be as frail as his brother Francis II's had been. Unfortunately, no further details of this particular illness have been found.

Details of the prince's recuperation in Paris are not completely known. He rejoined the court before the completion of the royal tour, but exactly where

following year along the Loire, where he remained with the court for the duration of the journey. For details of the itinerary of the two-year voyage, see the aforementioned works.

[13] N. M. Sutherland, *The French Secretaries of State in the Age of Catherine de Medici* (London, 1962), p. 143.

[14] As the eldest son of Anne de Montmorency (Hercule's godfather), François de Montmorency was governor of the Ile-de-France. He was also married to Hercule's half-sister, Diane de Valois, duchess of Castres, a legitimized daughter of Henri II and a mistress at court. Thus, Montmorency was also Hercule's brother-in-law. (The young prince refers to him as *mon cousin* in the salutation of the letter, as this was the custom of addressing members of the French aristocracy in the period.)

[15] BN, MSS fr. 3410, fol. 25, Hercule de Valois to François de Montmorency, 11 August 1564. This is the earliest piece of correspondence by the young prince that I have been able to locate. It is in the hand of a secretary, M. de Camus, and is signed 'hercules' by the prince in a signature that is virtually printed in large, separated letters.

along the route is not clear. The young Hercule was certainly back with the court in Moulins in February 1566, however. There, just before his eleventh birthday, he was confirmed as a member of the Roman Catholic church by sacrament and renamed François by his mother in memory of his grandfather, Francis I. Moreover, the king awarded him the first portion of his royal *apanage*. Along with several minor seigneuries, he was granted the duchy of Alençon in Normandy from the royal domain.[16] Henceforth, the young prince was known as François de Valois, duke of Alençon. Thus, when the court finally returned to Paris in the spring of 1566 after a two-year absence, the new duke of Alençon arrived with a new name, title, and prestige. Almost nothing else has been recorded, however, of the young prince's activities until after his thirteenth birthday in 1568, when he reached his majority and his public career began. In all likelihood he resided in Paris as his health improved.[17]

In October 1568 Alençon performed his first recorded duty as a prince of the blood. When Charles IX went to Amboise to try to restore the morale of the royal troops after the outbreak of the third civil war, he left the government of Paris in the charge of his youngest brother.[18] That same month the queen mother appointed Jean d'Ebrard, seigneur de St-Sulpice, as Alençon's governor, responsible for his upbringing and education.[19] St-Sulpice had been the French resident ambassador to Spain until October 1565, when he was recalled. Catherine obviously hoped that St-Sulpice's knowledge of diplomatic affairs and activities at court would rub off on her youngest son. The appointment appears to have been an auspicious one, as young Alençon and the veteran diplomat struck up an immediate friendship, despite the fact that St-Sulpice neither wanted the appointment to begin with nor desired to live in Paris.[20] Nevertheless, by 1569 the young duke of Alençon was playing a more active role at court, and as his correspondence shows, he was vitally interested in the religious and political concerns that dominated Europe.

Although Alençon showed concern for one of Coligny's secretaries who was arrested in January 1569 and also expressed an interest in the affairs of William

---

16 BN, MSS fr. 5944, fols. 7–19. Accompanying the grant of the duchy of Alençon was 'jusques à la somme de cent mil livres tournois de revenu par chacun an'. Revenues from the duchy never approached this amount, however. As a result, Charles IX augmented his youngest brother's *apanage* in October 1569 with the counties of Dreux and Sézanne (ibid., fols. 28–31). For more details of the initial grant, however, see BN, MSS fr. 17306, fols 41–50; BN, MSS CCC 81, fols. 65–107; Nevers, *Mémoires*, vol. I, pp. 561–7; and Appendix B.

17 The duke mentioned his improving health in an undated letter to his godfather, Anne de Montmorency: 'My dear godfather, I am sending you this messenger expressly to find out how your gout has been treating you. Please give him the latest news of your health, which I hope is as improved as my own. I love you always. Your godson, Francoys.' BN, MSS fr. 3410, fol. 23. This is the first letter completely in Alençon's hand that I have been able to locate, obviously written some time before the constable's death in November 1567.

18 *CSPF*, vol. VIII, p. 568, Norris to Cecil, 29 October 1568.

19 Cabié, p. 83, St-Sulpice to his wife, 4 October 1568.

20 Ibid., pp. 83, 88, St-Sulpice to his wife, 4 October 1568 and 7 May 1569.

of Orange and the Dutch Revolt even at this early stage of his career,[21] there can be little doubt that he harbored few sympathies for the French Protestants. Like most Catholics, Alençon deemed those who took up arms against the king as rebels and supported all efforts to defeat them militarily.[22] He was jubilant about the royal victory at Jarnac in March 1569, in which his brother Henry, duke of Anjou (Alexandre-Edouard was also renamed, and was awarded the duchy of Anjou in February 1566) led the royal army in a thorough rout of the Huguenots and even killed the prince of Condé.[23] And he threw lavish praise on Henry, duke of Guise, and Charles, duke of Mayenne, when they defended Poitiers against the Protestants later in the year.[24] Moreover, in August 1569 he reiterated his support for the king's efforts to subdue the recalcitrant French Protestants by force: 'Concerning those of the so-called reformed religion who take up arms against the king my brother, there is no doubt whatsoever that the seizure of their homes and possessions is for their own benefit.'[25] It is clear, then, that Alençon placed obedience to the king before religious toleration at this stage of his career. There is no evidence that he had Protestant sympathies or aided them in any way. On the contrary, there is reason to believe that Alençon played a part in raising money from the Catholics in the Netherlands to contribute to the royal cause in France.[26] And he rejoiced at every Huguenot defeat, as he indicated after his brother's great victory at Moncontour in September 1569.[27] So, whatever the duplicity of Alençon's later religious sympathies and political associations, in his early career he was a devout Catholic who opposed those who took up arms against the king.

The young Valois prince's health deteriorated once again in the autumn of 1569, when he contracted a case of smallpox. His doctors wrote to the queen mother on 2 October, to say that he had become ill the night before with a harsh fever and headache. He was unable to sleep for more than an hour at a time, as several pockmarks began to appear on his face and hands. Though more appeared on his legs the following morning, the doctors assured Catherine that they were doing everything in their power to help him recover.[28] Though uncomfortable, Alençon was apparently never near death, and was able to write to the king the same day about such diverse matters as Charles's last letter to him

---

[21] BN, MSS CCC 24, fol. 364, Alençon to the king, 24 January 1569.
[22] BN MSS fr. 3226, fol. 78, Alençon to the duchess of Ferrara, 9 May 1569.
[23] BN, MSS fr. 3205, fols. 76–7, Alençon to François de Montmorency, 13 and 20 March 1569.
[24] BN, MSS fr. 3227, fol. 50, Alençon to the duke of Nemours, 26 August 1569.
[25] BN, MSS fr. 3178, fol. 158, Alençon to Jacques d'Humières, governor of Péronne, 31 August 1569.
[26] Ibid., fol. 162, Alençon to Humières, 1 October 1569: 'Jay eu deux courryers en ung jour po[ur] faire haster les denyers de flandres dont lon a si grand besoing au champ que si promplemen je ny est envoye cela importera grandement aux affaires et service du Roy monseigneur et fre[re] ...'
[27] Ibid., fol. 164, Alençon to Humières, 5 October 1569.
[28] BN, MSS CCC 7, fol. 193, Varade, Vaterre, and Mazille (the duke's doctors) to Catherine de Medici, 2 October 1569.

of 29 September, a sum of money from the *parties casuelles*, and a list of expenses he had sent to the royal treasury.[29] Within six weeks St-Sulpice reported to the queen mother that 'the duke continues to get better and better and can even walk for a few hours every day without the aid of his cane. The pocks still on his face which have not yet dried up worry him more than anything else.'[30] While the young prince recovered soon enough from his infirmity, the disease left him permanently scarred. Nearly every physical description of him in later life refers to his pockmarked face and misshapen features. The viscount of Turenne recorded in his memoirs that Alençon 'had such a severe case of smallpox that it changed him completely rendering him unrecognizable with a completely hollowed-out face, a large and deformed nose, and eyes so red that it made him about the ugliest man one could ever hope to see'.[31] Thus, he recovered from the disease – not always a certainty in the sixteenth century – but the scars remained for the rest of his life.

For the next few years, until the St Bartholomew's massacres in August 1572, Alençon remained in Paris under the guidance of St-Sulpice.[32] He tried to participate in the war effort in any way that he could. While the few duties the king assigned to him were neither difficult nor particularly arduous, they were not unimportant. Whether it was taking charge of a delivery of powder to the arsenal in Paris, or delivering payment to the king's Swiss mercenaries, the young prince was anxious to demonstrate his ability.[33] And his efforts did not go unrewarded, as his brother Henry gave him 80,000 *livres* in 1570 'in gratitude for his services'.[34] While Alençon would have doubtless preferred a military duty, so that he could distinguish himself as Henry had done at Jarnac and Moncontour in 1569, he remained content to serve the king as he was needed, which usually meant behind the scenes.

III

Although precise details of Alençon's early career are incomplete, it is nevertheless important to establish what kind of person he was when he suddenly became more visible in 1572. What was he like, and what did his contemporaries think of him? Who were his friends and enemies at court? How capable was the young prince intellectually? And finally, what was his position at court, both politically and economically, by 1572?

[29] BN, MSS CCC 7, fol. 195, Alençon to the king, 2 October 1569.
[30] Cabié, p. 112, St-Sulpice to Catherine de Medici, 12 November 1569.
[31] Memoirs of Turenne (later duke of Bouillon) in Petitot, *Mémoires*, vol. IX, pp. 66–7.
[32] At Alençon's request, the king appointed St-Sulpice to his privy council in spring of 1569, and in January 1570 named him governor of the duke's *apanage*. Cabié, pp. 86–8, 119–21.
[33] BN, MSS fr. 3178, fols. 167–8, 174, the king to Humières, 26 October 1569, and Alençon to Humières, 31 October and 23 November 1569; and BN, MSS fr. 4632, fols. 140–1, Alençon to Gaspard de Saulx, 22 and 23 March 1570.
[34] Henry III, *Lettres*, vol. I, p. 138, Henry to Alençon, 10 January 1570.

The most famous (and perhaps most extreme) description of Alençon's character comes from the pen of John Lothrop Motley. Motivated by a desire to discredit anyone who impinged on Dutch liberty, Motley left a biting and hostile account:

Francis Duke of Alençon ... was, upon the whole, the most despicable personage who ever entered the Netherlands. His previous career at home had been so flagrantly false that he had forfeited the esteem of every honest man in Europe, Catholic or Lutheran, Huguenot or Malcontent. The world has long known his character. History will always retain him as an example, to show mankind the amount of mischief which may be perpetrated by a prince, ferocious without courage, ambitious without talent, and bigoted without opinions.[35]

To be fair, Motley only followed the lead of some of Alençon's own contemporaries who described him in equally caustic terms: for instance, the Spanish ambassador at the French court in 1571, Don Francés de Alava:

The duke of Alençon counted for little and was a very tricky man. He passed himself off as a Catholic, but in reality he was the leader of the atheists. His governor was St-Sulpice, a man of little substance. When he sat in the council Alençon never listened to [Henry] duke of Anjou and even quarrelled with him. He was unable to speak with intelligence to anyone. Everything that came out of his mouth or any of his followers' was nothing but deception.[36]

More moderate was the evaluation of the Venetian ambassador at court, Lorenzo Priuli:

He is very stable for one so young ... and very liberal, vigilant, and of great spirit. He reads the histories of the great soldiers, ancient as well as modern, and tries to imitate them in every way. He is a Catholic prince, but he also embraces many Huguenots, which he does in order to preserve the state.[37]

One must also keep in mind that an intense hostility and rivalry gradually developed between Alençon and his older brothers, Charles and Henry. As for his rivalry with Henry of Navarre, this only developed later, when both princes resided together at court after 1572. It stemmed from Alençon's personal jealousy, and was exacerbated by the sharing of a mistress: Charlotte de Beaune, madame de Sauve, wife of one of the principal secretaries of state.[38] These personal rivalries are important, because the followers of Charles IX, Henry III, and Navarre rarely wrote or said anything complimentary about Alençon. For instance, the baron de Rosny (the future duke of Sully) recalled in his memoirs

---

[35] John Lothrop Motley, *The Rise of the Dutch Republic* (3 vols., New York, 1858), vol. III, p. 399.
[36] Testament of Don Francés de Alava (1571), printed as an appendix in Champion, *Catherine de Médicis présente à Charles IX*, p. 446.
[37] Albèri, *Relazioni*, vol. IV, pp. 428–9.
[38] David Buisseret and Bernard Barbiche (eds.), *Les œconomies royales de Sully* (vol. I, Paris, 1970), p. 93.

how Navarre once described Alençon to him: 'He will deceive me just as he has deceived everyone who has ever trusted him ... He is so sly and two-faced, his courage is so lacking, and he is so unfamiliar with every kind of virtue, that I do not think he is capable of performing a generous act.'³⁹ It is important, then, to ascertain the particular motives and personal connections of those writers who have left such an unappealing portrait of this Valois prince.

The picture of the young duke that emerges from the correspondence of his governor, St-Sulpice, is less extreme. The former ambassador reveals that Alençon was a normal teenage prince who enjoyed the usual pursuits of those in his exalted position: sports, hunting, falconry, and the company of the opposite sex. Unlike his brother, Henry, Alençon's sexual preferences were never questioned, and he was never accused of being homosexual. Indeed, his appetite for amorous activity was the subject of court gossip by the time he was fifteen. While rumors of his sexual proclivity were doubtless exaggerated, they certainly aroused the ire of the queen mother. St-Sulpice spent much of his time smoothing Catherine's ruffled feathers.

Madame, the many years of faithful service I have rendered to Your Majesty, together with my conscience and the truth which I want to make known, force me to bear patiently the anxiety I received from the letter that you wrote to me concerning the false reports and mischievous inventions which you have heard about Monseigneur the duke's conduct. Thus, so you will understand all the particulars of his behavior, his typical morning is spent dealing with the king's affairs. After mass and lunch, he attends to his studies on the days the council is not meeting ... After that he plays games in the garden or tennis [*jeu de paume*] in the Louvre, or sometimes in the Tuileries when the weather is nice. Sometimes, he goes rabbit-hunting with the dogs in the Bois de Vincennes or near the Château Madrid ... I must confess, Madame, that during Lent he did go to Saint-Pris where some wedding celebrations were going on, but he danced with the same modesty that he would have done in your presence, and there was nothing else for which one could rebuke him. And since Lent I can assure you that he has not seen any women other than madame de Nemours, madame de Nevers, and the constable's wife, who have occasionally come to the Louvre to see him. And I have not seen him speak to any other woman whatsoever!⁴⁰

While many of the rumors about Alençon's sexual activity were just 'false reports and mischievous inventions', as St-Sulpice maintained, there must have been some foundation for them. Apparently his physical deformities did not impede his lovemaking.

Intellectually, however, François de Valois was much less gifted. Although he was obviously literate, he must have received a minimum of formal education. And though Priuli claimed that Alençon read a lot of military history, there is no other evidence that he read much of anything. He spoke no language other than French; and if his correspondence is at all representative of his verbal proficiency, even his French was crude and simplistic. He did make an effort to

---

³⁹ Ibid., pp. 92–3.   ⁴⁰ Cabié, p. 145, St-Sulpice to Catherine de Medici, 14 April 1570.

learn Italian, his mother's native tongue, though there is no evidence that he ever mastered it.[41] His surviving writings, nearly all of it political and personal correspondence, give no indication that he was an original thinker. How ironic, then, that so many of the best minds of the sixteenth century either served in his household or sought his patronage: Jean Bodin, Guillaume Postel, Guy le Fèvre de la Boderie, Jean de la Jessée, Christophe Plantin, Innocent Gentillet, and such famous figures as Brantôme and Ronsard.[42] There is no evidence, however, that Alençon either read or was interested in their works. He inherited none of his mother's and grandfather's artistic sensibilities, and was far more interested in becoming a successful soldier. Unfortunately, he had not even the aptitude for that.

Despite his physical and intellectual deficiencies, the young duke of Alençon occupied a very high position at court, due solely to his rank as first prince of the blood and, after 1574, presumptive heir to the crown. This fact alone ensured that he would enjoy wealth and privilege, though not nearly as much as he would have liked. Nevertheless, one shrewd observer, Etienne Pasquier, called him

a second king who had his own court and favorites, sometimes in a town like Tours, sometimes in other towns throughout his *apanage* ... which was so large that it covered a good part of France. He had his own *chambre des comptes* in Tours and his own exchequer in Alençon which had sovereignty over all legal cases in the duchy, civil as well as criminal. In addition, this prince had jurisdiction over all the bishoprics and abbeys in his *apanage*, so that whomever he selected was named by the pope and appointed by the king, according to the Concordat. All of this grandeur was not as great as the king's, however, which caused still more jealousy.[43]

While Alençon's *apanage* was not this large in 1572, he was still a very wealthy and powerful figure at court in these early years. By 1572 his *apanage* included – in addition to the duchy of Alençon and *seigneurie* of Château-Thierry awarded him in 1566 – the towns and seigneuries of Evreux, Caen, Bayeux, Châtillon-sur-Marne, Epernay, Sézanne, Verneuil, Beaumont-le-Roger, Orbec, Mantes, Meulant, Dreux, and many others.[44] All of these territories generated some annual income, revenues that should normally have been above and beyond what was needed to pay his ordinary expenses. As excessive as his ordinary expenses were (his household wages amounted to 74,850 *livres* in 1571), the annual pension he received from the crown was normally sufficient to cover them. Thus,

---

[41] BN, MSS fr. 26156, fol. 1, a record of payment of 250 *livres* from Alençon to Giacomo Corbinelli for tuition in Italian, 13 June 1570. He was still taking lessons four years later from the Florentine ambassador. See Desjardins, vol. III, p. 920, 26 April 1574.

[42] I hope to examine the duke's relationship with the French intelligentsia in greater detail elsewhere.

[43] Etienne Pasquier, *Lettres historiques pour les années 1556–1594*, ed. Dorothy Thickett (Geneva, 1966), pp. 441–2.

[44] See Appendix B.

the rents and perquisites Alençon received from his *apanage* were all additional incomes.[45]

Pasquier was close to the truth when he referred to the duke of Alençon as 'a second king who had his own court'. As early as 1572, when the duke was only seventeen years old, his household numbered some 262 persons (176 of them nobles) whose combined wages and pensions totalled nearly 78,000 *livres*. With 13 clergymen, 22 gentlemen of the bedchamber, 2 doctors, 3 surgeons, a chemist, 3 barbers, numerous cooks, secretaries, valets, aides, and councillors, the duke's household met his every need.[46] While this cumbersome entourage made for a rather unusual extended household, it continued to expand throughout the duke's lifetime until it reached its peak in the late 1570s and early 1580s, with well over 1,000 officers. Because of its size, his household provided him with a vast *clientèle* system which further increased his power at court. Service in the duke of Alençon's household offered opportunities for advancement for younger sons of the aristocracy, members of the lesser nobility, and some from the bourgeoisie. Thus, the seigneur de St-Sulpice had been Alençon's governor for less than two years when he obtained a position in the duke's household for his eldest son, Henry, as a gentleman of the bedchamber. A year later a second son, Armand, acquired a similar position which paid 500 *livres* per year. Indeed, many of Alençon's most trusted councillors, such as his secretary of finances, Nicolas Hennequin, sieur du Fay, managed to acquire positions in the duke's household for their entire families by the early 1580s. The political implications of such a patronage network are obvious.[47]

François de Valois, duke of Alençon spent his early years in the midst of religious and political conflict. The same problems that confronted his father's generation remained unsolved when the young prince reached adulthood. His early education at court and later tuition by St-Sulpice might have adequately prepared him for a life of service to the crown in normal circumstances. The political and religious strife that dominated Europe in the second half of the sixteenth century, however, tested even the most able. Two events in 1572

45 BN, MSS fr. 23029, fols. 307–8, wage list for 1571; and AN, K 98, no. 30, pension for 1571 showing that Alençon received 64,000 *livres* in 1571 as half his yearly pension (or 128,000 *livres* for the year), which more than offset his high wage bill. For more details about income from Alençon's *apanage*, see Appendix C.

46 BN, MSS Clair. 1216, fols. 112–20. This list for 1572 is the first detailed household expense list, with wages and pensions totalling 77,990 *livres* for the calendar year. For a more detailed analysis of the duke's household see Appendix A.

47 Mack P. Holt, 'Patterns of *clientèle* and economic opportunity at court during the Wars of Religion: the household of François, duke of Anjou', *French Historical Studies*, XIII (spring 1984), 305–22. For some general comments on patronage during the religious wars, see Robert R. Harding, *Anatomy of a Power Elite: The Provincial Governors of Early Modern France* (New Haven and London, 1978), esp. pp. 21–31, 182–9; and Kristen B. Neuschel, 'The prince of Condé and the nobility of Picardy: a study of the structure of noble relationships in sixteenth-century France', (unpub. Ph.D. dissertation, Brown University, 1982), esp. pp. 1–32.

nevertheless forced the young prince onto the European stage, despite his uncertain preparation. First, the queen mother desperately needed a replacement for his brother Henry when the marriage negotiations between Henry and Elizabeth of England broke down because of religious differences. In an effort to continue the negotiations for an Anglo-French alliance, Catherine offered her youngest son as a possible replacement. Secondly, the St Bartholomew massacres of August 1572 changed the course of the Wars of Religion as well as the career of the young Valois prince. From 1572 the duke of Alençon was destined to play a major role in the civil wars at home and in the international conflict in Western Europe.

2

From St Bartholomew's Day to the death of Charles IX, August 1572–May 1574

I

The young duke of Alençon was forced into a more prominent role in the French Wars of Religion in 1572 because of the international rivalry in Western Europe and the religious tension that had built up within France itself. Moreover, both issues fused together in that year and exploded in the most violent series of killings and bloodshed of the entire civil wars: the massacres that began in Paris on 24 August. These massacres were the result of an unsuccessful attempt to assassinate the admiral of France, Gaspard de Coligny, whose efforts to lead a Huguenot army to aid the Dutch rebels in the Netherlands threatened war with Spain. Less directly, the massacres were caused by the serious division between Protestants and Catholics that had precipitated the civil wars a decade before. The French reformed church had certainly grown since the failure of the Conspiracy of Amboise, and this despite the efforts of the theologians of the Sorbonne and the Catholic nobility clustered around the Guises.[1] But in spite of the patronage of many noble families, most notably the Bourbons, in 1572 the Huguenots were still seeking to establish their legal right to worship outside the limited areas that were outlined in the treaty of St-Germain in 1570.[2] In January 1570 Jeanne d'Albret, the widow of Antoine de Navarre, had sought in vain for the maintenance of the reformed religion in all of France, as well as 'the king's protection without exception for all sermons, baptisms, communions, marriages, and all other acts and exercises'.[3] The king and queen mother were well aware of the danger which such a situation might provoke, and they quickly dispersed the queen of Navarre's deputies with a firm reply.[4]

1 Robert M. Kingdon, *Geneva and the Consolidation of the French Protestant Movement, 1564–1572* (Madison and Geneva, 1967), p. 149.
2 According to this treaty the Huguenot nobility could practice their religion in private homes. The rest of the Protestant population was limited to freedom of religion in two towns in each *gouvernement* and four fortified towns. See Sutherland, *The Huguenot Struggle*, pp. 175–7, 358–60.
3 BN, MSS fr. 3239, fols. 11–13, 'Remonstrances au Roy des deputez de la Royne de Navarre en l'an MDLXX'. See also Kingdon, *Geneva and the French Protestant Movement*, pp. 173–6, and Nancy L. Roelker, *Queen of Navarre: Jeanne d'Albret, 1528–1572* (Cambridge, Mass., 1968), pp. 333–5.
4 BN, MSS fr. 3239, fols. 17–22, 'Responce faite par le Roy aux articles presentees a sa Maieste par les deputez de la Royne de Navarre', 4 February 1570.

The cause of the Huguenots received a boost in September 1571, however, when Coligny was recalled to court, apparently in the king's favor.[5] In addition, the negotiations over the winter of 1571–2 between Jeanne d'Albret and Catherine de Medici made the forthcoming marriage of their respective children, Henry of Navarre and Marguerite de Valois (Alençon's sister), a *cause célèbre* for the French Protestants, who hoped the marriage might be followed by recognition of the right to worship anywhere in France. When the queen of Navarre went to Paris to complete her son's wedding plans in May 1572, few suspected what was to follow. Moreover, the Protestants had held a synod at Nîmes only months before and had voted to support Coligny's plea to remain loyal to the king.[6]

The story of the massacres that began in Paris early on Sunday morning, 24 August 1572, and later spread throughout the realm need not be retold here.[7] There is no need to attempt to exonerate the duke of Alençon from this grisly affair, as no-one has ever accused him of taking part. The ringleaders of the conspiracy appear to have been a group of four men: Henry, duke of Anjou; Chancellor Birague; the duke of Nevers; and the count of Retz.[8] Alençon's older brother, Henry, deserves especial blame. Not only was he an instigator of the massacres in Paris, but he wanted to extend the killing to the provinces. He commissioned an agent to write to the governor of Saumur, a small town on the Loire in his *apanage*:

The Admiral and all Huguenots in Paris have been killed, and it is the will of His Majesty that Huguenots everywhere should meet the same end. So, if you have ever desired to serve the king and Monsieur [Henry, duke of Anjou], you must go at once to Saumur with all your supporters and kill any Huguenots you find there ... And having done that, you must go to Angers and help the captain of the château do the same thing there ... You must use the utmost diligence in this affair so as not to lose any time whatsoever.[9]

[5] J. Shimizu, *Conflict of Loyalties: Politics and Religion in the Career of Gaspard de Coligny, Admiral of France, 1519–1572* (Geneva, 1970), pp. 145–52.
[6] Kingdon, *Geneva and the French Protestant Movement*, pp. 197–8.
[7] The literature on the massacres is extensive. The best treatment of the initial massacre in Paris is that of Janine Garrisson-Estebe, *Tocsain pour un massacre: la saison de Saint-Barthélemy* (Paris, 1968), while the international situation that led to the massacre is ably discussed by N. M. Sutherland in *The Massacre of St Bartholomew and the European Conflict, 1559–1572* (London, 1973). In addition, see two useful collections of articles, *Actes du colloque l'Amiral de Coligny et son temps* (Paris, 1974), and Alfred Soman (ed.), *The Massacre of St Bartholomew: Reappraisals and Documents* (The Hague, 1974). And for the provincial massacres, see Philip Benedict, 'The St Bartholomew's massacres in the provinces', *The Historical Journal*, XXI (1978), 205–25.
[8] Félix Rocquain, *La France et Rome pendant les guerres de religion* (Paris, 1924), pp. 123–5; and Joseph de Croze, *Les Guises, les Valois et Philippe II* (2 vols., Paris, 1866), vol. I, pp. 203–5.
[9] Quoted in Ernest Mourin, *La Réforme et la Ligue en Anjou* (Paris and Angers, 1856), pp. 106–7, Puygaillard (an agent of Henry, duke of Anjou) to the count de Montsoreau, governor of Saumur, August 1572. While there is no archival evidence to support the traditional Protestant claim that the crown favored the continuation of the massacres in the provinces, Henry, duke of Anjou apparently did, and he claimed that the king did too.

Though the duke of Alençon was not responsible for any of the violence of the summer of 1572, as a member of the royal family he was nevertheless tainted with the blood of St Bartholomew's Day. This is nowhere more evident than in his first venture onto the European stage as a possible suitor for Queen Elizabeth of England. The same international rivalry that had fomented the attempt on Coligny's life had also provoked both France and England into attempting to cement an alliance against the growing hegemony of Philip II of Spain. Moreover, the negotiations for this alliance had led to suggestions that the English queen might marry one of Catherine de Medici's two youngest sons, either Henry or young Alençon. As incredible as it might seem in the light of their respective ages (Elizabeth was eighteen years older than Alençon), for a short time in 1572 the English queen apparently gave serious consideration to a French marriage. The massacres of 1572, however, seemed to end any interest Elizabeth might have had. Although Alençon denied any complicity in the affair before Elizabeth's ambassador in Paris, Francis Walsingham, and even sent a special agent to England to plead his innocence, the events of 24 August 1572 brought the marriage negotiations to a sudden halt.[10] It is important, however, to reconstruct this brief episode. Not only did it mark Alençon's first venture into European politics; it also marked the beginning of a capricious relationship with Elizabeth, which would culminate a decade later in a more serious courtship that had repercussions all over Europe.

II

Beginning in the late autumn of 1570, the courtship of Queen Elizabeth and Alençon's brother Henry lasted barely a year.[11] It was first proposed by François de Montmorency and some French Protestants in the hope of bringing France and England in closer alliance against Philip II, and was nurtured by Elizabeth and Charles IX for the same reason. With Coligny back in favor at the French court in the autumn of 1571, hopes ran high in both countries. Henry's marriage prospects came to an abrupt end, however, in January 1572. They lapsed, according to the Venetian ambassador in Paris, Sigismondo Cavalli, because of the difference of religion. He suggested that perhaps the duke of Alençon might not be so scrupulous in this respect.[12]

Alençon had been offered as a possible suitor for the English queen much earlier, in fact. The queen mother, perhaps sensing that negotiations were breaking down, suggested it as early as February 1571 to the French ambassador

---

[10] Sir Dudley Digges, *The Compleat Ambassador* (London, 1665), p. 257, Walsingham to Thomas Smith, 24 September 1572; and HMC *Salisbury MSS*, vol. II, p. 33, Maisonfleur to Alençon, 3 December 1572.

[11] This courtship is described by Conyers Read, *Mr Secretary Walsingham and the Policy of Queen Elizabeth* (3 vols., Oxford, 1925), vol. I, pp. 85–175.

[12] *CSPV*, vol. VII, p. 482, Cavalli to the Signory, 25 January 1572.

in London, the sieur de la Mothe-Fénelon.[13] By January 1572 Catherine de Medici was forced to concede to Thomas Smith, a special English agent sent to Paris to negotiate a defensive alliance, that Henry's chances were now slim. Although the queen mother 'wept hot tears' over the failure of this courtship, she was quick to propose young Alençon as a replacement for his brother.[14] Smith, who was more concerned with obtaining a defensive pact with France than a marriage alliance, nevertheless instructed Burghley to urge Elizabeth 'not to procrastinate, as commonly is her wont'. Although Alençon was not as physically acceptable as Henry, Smith explained that the young prince was just as wealthy and was 'not so obstinate, papistical, and restive like a mule as his brother is'. A private interview with Alençon convinced Smith that the marriage would be favorable to England.[15] Even Lord Burghley seemed to support the match, Alençon being less immediately in line to the French throne and more accommodating in religious matters than his older brother.[16] Elizabeth, however, would not be forced into a decision. She urged Smith to get on with the job that he was sent to do, to negotiate a defensive pact with the French king.[17]

Catherine de Medici obviously favored the marriage. She seemed content to follow the advice of her ambassador in England, however, and did not push the Alençon proposal too far at that time. La Mothe-Fénelon had urged her to secure a defensive pact with Elizabeth first; the marriage could then be broached at a later date.[18] As a result, a defensive agreement was finally reached between the two nations in the spring of 1572. The treaty of Blois, as it was called, was signed on 19 April and proved to be a diluted and nearly worthless alliance. Neither side lived up to the vague promise of mutual assistance. Moreover, the trading concessions offered to France were insignificant.[19] The treaty was not without serious political significance, however. At the French court, it seemed to denote a victory for the faction that favored the Huguenots and Coligny more than the ultra-Catholic Guises.[20] For Elizabeth, the treaty signalled French acquiescence over the imprisonment of Mary Stuart, queen of Scotland. More importantly, the treaty indicated the possibility of an Anglo-French alliance against Philip II. With the Dutch rebels having just captured the port of Brill in the Netherlands a few weeks earlier, Philip could have hardly been pleased to see

---

[13] Bertrand de Salignac, sieur de la Mothe-Fénelon, *Correspondance diplomatique*, ed. A. Teulet (7 vols., Paris and London, 1838–40), vol. 7, p. 179, Catherine to La Mothe-Fénelon, 2 February 1571. Catherine suggested Alençon as a replacement for his brother again in July. See ibid., p. 235, Catherine to La Mothe-Fénelon, 25 July 1571.

[14] *CSPF*, vol. x, pp. 9–10, Smith to Elizabeth, 8 January 1572. Also see Shimizu, *Conflict of Loyalties*, pp. 151–2.

[15] *CSPF*, vol. x, pp. 14 and 36, both Smith to Burghley, 10 January and 8 February 1572.

[16] Conyers Read, *Lord Burghley and Queen Elizabeth* (London, 1960), p. 65.

[17] Ibid., pp. 68–71. See also Read, *Mr Secretary Walsingham*, vol. I, pp. 176–7.

[18] La Mothe-Fénelon, *Correspondance diplomatique*, vol. IV, pp. 369–71, La Mothe-Fénelon to Catherine de Medici, 10 February 1572.

[19] Read, *Mr Secretary Walsingham*, vol. I, pp. 176–97.   [20] Ibid., 196.

his two main European rivals join forces, however tenuously.[21] The possibility of combined French and English aid to the Dutch rebels did not escape him either, and he set out to repair the damaged relations between Spain and England, ties that had been so strong only fifteen years earlier when he was Mary Tudor's consort.[22]

It is interesting that so many of Alençon's contemporaries deemed him to be less zealous in his Catholic beliefs than his brother Henry. Indeed, this was specifically what made him more appealing to Smith and Burghley as a suitor for Elizabeth. In the light of his orthodox religious views in his early years, it is perhaps strange that Alençon should be viewed as more moderate in matters of religion than his brother Henry. This attitude was apparently the result of a close personal relationship that Alençon developed with Coligny when the admiral was recalled to court. Coligny had been very friendly to him, and at one time even voiced the hope that Alençon would eventually lean towards Protestantism.[23] Although the two were obviously close, there is no evidence that Alençon was involved in any of the admiral's political activities. Moreover, the duke gave no indication that he was ready to abandon the Roman Catholic church. It is true, nevertheless, that from 1572 Alençon developed the reputation of being more tolerant (or, to his enemies, more duplicitous) than any of his older brothers.

Even after the treaty of Blois of April 1572, Catherine de Medici did not completely abandon hope for a marriage between Elizabeth and her youngest son. When François de Montmorency and Paul de Foix were sent to England in June 1572 to ratify the treaty, they were armed with instructions from the queen mother to make a formal offer of marriage to Elizabeth.[24] Meanwhile, Alençon expressed his own optimism about the match to the earl of Sussex, one of Elizabeth's privy councillors.[25] Once Montmorency and Foix arrived at Dover on 8 June, Lord Burghley initiated lengthy discussions with them and La Mothe-Fénelon. And, although Elizabeth entertained her guests lavishly, she refused to give them a definitive answer concerning the marriage, which greatly irritated the queen mother.[26] Some, such as Francis Walsingham, harbored doubts whether Elizabeth would ever consent to marry such an unhandsome prince, disfigured as he was by smallpox.[27] No-one knew really what Elizabeth

---

21 The significance of the capture of the port of Brill is fully described by Geoffrey Parker in *The Dutch Revolt* (London, 1977), pp. 126–34.

22 See Louis P. Gachard (ed.), *Correspondance de Philippe II sur les affaires des Pays-Bas, 1558–1577* (5 vols., Brussels, 1848–79), vol. II, p. 249, Philip to Elizabeth, 20 May 1572.

23 See A. W. Whitehead, *Gaspard de Coligny, Admiral of France* (London, 1904), p. 244; J. Shimizu, 'Coligny et l'Angleterre, 1545–1572', in *Actes du colloque l'Amiral de Coligny et son temps*, pp. 105–5; and De Thou, *Histoire universelle*, vol. 5, p. 28.

24 La Mothe-Fénelon, *Correspondance diplomatique*, vol. VII, pp. 289–94, instructions to Montmorency and Foix, 25 April 1572.

25 BL, Cotton. MSS, Titus B/vii, fol. 243b, Alençon to Sussex, 12 May 1572.

26 Catherine de Medici, *Lettres*, vol. IV, p. 105, Catherine to Burghley, 27 June 1572.

27 BL, Cotton. MSS, Vespasian F/vi, fol. 107, Walsingham to Burghley, 13 July 1572.

desired, however. Before the French envoys departed for France, she did consent to respond to the offer of marriage within a month.[28]

Elizabeth duly replied on 23 July. She instructed Walsingham to express her goodwill to Catherine and Charles IX, and to tell them that she had carefully considered their offer of Alençon's hand in marriage. Unfortunately, she could not accept it on account of the difference in their ages.[29] True to her equivocal nature, however, Elizabeth sent a second letter to Walsingham four days later, stating that the marriage might still take place if she could see the duke in person.[30] Burghley, it seems, managed to convince her of the wisdom of not shutting the door on the marriage completely.[31] Meanwhile, a confused Walsingham followed his instructions and showed both letters to Charles and the queen mother. In an attempt to keep the negotiations open, Catherine then despatched to England an officer in Alençon's household, the sieur de la Mole.[32] Though La Mole was entertained in much the same fashion as Montmorency and Foix, he made little impression on Elizabeth, who was still vacillating. On 22 August she wrote to Walsingham and asked him to explain that she still had worries over Alençon's religion.[33] Graver difficulties arose a few days later, however, when Elizabeth received Walsingham's report of the massacres in Paris. The massacres were ordered, he noted, by a special commandment of Catherine de Medici and Charles IX.[34]

The immediate impact of the massacres on Alençon's marriage prospects has never been adequately explained. La Mothe-Fénelon reported from London 'how much this news has touched nearly all this kingdom ... and that the matter of Monseigneur the duke has been left hanging in the balance'. Moreover, he believed that the hostility toward France was so great in London that Elizabeth seemed prepared to break off the alliance with France and renew her former ties with Philip II of Spain.[35] The ambassador reported a few days later that Elizabeth reacted very coldly to his lengthy explanation of the massacres; and she was unconvinced by his rationalization that the attempt on Coligny's life was merely to counter an alleged Huguenot attack on the entire royal family.[36] Catherine de Medici was determined to continue the marriage negotiations, however, despite Elizabeth's negative reaction.[37] For his part, the duke of

[28] For a complete summary of their visit, see BN, MSS fr. 3253, fols. 371–409.
[29] BL., Harl. MSS 260, fols. 272–4, Elizabeth to Walsingham, 23 July 1572.
[30] *CSPF*, vol. x, pp. 159–60, Elizabeth to Walsingham, 27 July 1572.
[31] BL., Harl. MSS 260, fols. 277–8, Burghley to Walsingham, 27 July 1572.
[32] Read, *Mr Secretary Walsingham*, vol. I, p. 210; and Martin A. S. Hume, *The Courtships of Queen Elizabeth* (London, 1896), pp. 161–4.
[33] BL., Harl. MSS 260, fols. 287–9, Elizabeth to Walsingham, 22 August 1572.
[34] BL., Harl. MSS 260, fols. 291–2, Walsingham to Smith, 27 August 1572.
[35] La Mothe-Fénelon, *Correspondance diplomatique*, vol. v, pp. 112–15, 115–18, La Mothe-Fénelon to the king and queen mother, 30 August and 2 September 1572.
[36] Ibid., pp. 120–31, La Mothe-Fénelon to the king, 14 September 1572.
[37] Catherine de Medici, *Lettres*, vol. IV, pp. 120–3, Catherine to La Mothe-Fénelon, 11 September 1572.

Alençon despatched Jérôme de l'Huillier, seigneur de Maisonfleur, to express his good intentions to the English queen.[38]

Despite Elizabeth's initial reaction to the massacres, she seemed unwilling to terminate the marriage negotiations completely, perhaps fearing her isolation from both France and Spain. In late September 1572 she instructed Walsingham to discover if the duke was willing to journey to England so that she might see him in person.[39] By early 1573 it was apparent that Alençon was willing to make such a journey, and only awaited the permission of the king.[40] Catherine de Medici urged La Mothe-Fénelon to press upon Burghley and Elizabeth that all reports of Alençon's appearance were exaggerated, as he was 'getting stronger all the time, all grown up, with his face much improved and his beard beginning to grow out, in such manner that he will eventually be as tall and as charming as his other two brothers'.[41] Moreover, in January 1573 Elizabeth despatched a special agent of her own to France, the earl of Worcester, in order to get a more accurate picture of Alençon's appearance and to press the duke to make the trip to England. In a lengthy interview with La Mothe-Fénelon, Lord Burghley made it clear that Elizabeth still harbored some doubts about Alençon's religion, especially after 'the events of France'. Burghley felt that any religious differences could be worked out, however, if only the duke would come to England. The French ambassador concurred that an interview would be in the duke's best interests, 'as many persons have reported only recently that the smallpox had completely obliterated his face'.[42]

New developments soon intervened to complicate matters. When the earl of Worcester arrived in Paris in late January 1573, Alençon was not there. Charles IX had sent his two younger brothers and Henry of Navarre to La Rochelle with an army. Because La Rochelle had been in effective rebellion ever since the massacres, their mission was to bring that city back under royal control. This expedition loomed large in Elizabeth's relations with France because the Protestant leaders of La Rochelle had sought military support from England against the besieging army.[43] And, to complicate matters further, Elizabeth signed a friendship pact with Spain on 15 March. She still sought an interview with Alençon, however, and continued to press Burghley and La Mothe-Fénelon to arrange one.[44] Catherine de Medici responded that the duke was

---

[38] HMC, *Salisbury MSS*, vol. II, p. 23, Alençon to Elizabeth, 23 September 1572.

[39] BL, Cotton. MSS, Vespasian F/vi, fol. 137, Elizabeth to Walsingham, 28 September 1572.

[40] BL, Harl. MSS 260, fols. 385–6, Walsingham to Burghley, 22 December 1572; and PRO/SP 70/126/fol. 6, Alençon to Burghley, 1 January 1573.

[41] Catherine de Medici, *Lettres*, vol. IV, p. 157, Catherine to La Mothe-Fénelon, 23 January 1573.

[42] Ibid., pp. 186–8n., memoir of La Mothe-Fénelon concerning an interview he had with Burghley, January 1573.

[43] Read, *Mr Secretary Walsingham*, vol. I, pp. 253–60; and Wallace T. MacCaffrey, *Queen Elizabeth and the Making of Policy, 1572–1588* (Princeton, 1981), p. 176.

[44] PRO/SP 70/126/fol. 143, Burghley to La Mothe-Fénelon, 28 March 1573. The eight articles of the treaty are printed in Gachard (ed.), *Correspondance de Philippe II*, vol. II, pp. 318–19.

presently engaged and could not go to England until after the capture of La Rochelle.[45] Alençon expressed the same sentiments to Elizabeth himself. He desired to meet her, 'but only after the reduction of this town of La Rochelle, which I hope will soon be in obedience to my lord and brother'.[46]

For Elizabeth it was bad enough that her French suitor was related to the perpetrators of the massacres of the previous summer. It became more than she could stand, however, when Alençon continued to press his courtship while participating in yet more violence against the French Protestants. In June she sent over another envoy, Edward Horsey, to inform Charles and Catherine that she would only continue the marriage negotiations if a more tolerant policy were adopted toward the Huguenots, and if the siege of La Rochelle were lifted immediately.[47] She was persuaded that Catherine and Charles were merely using the Anglo-French marriage to keep English ships out of La Rochelle harbor until the town had capitulated. Thus, on 20 June Burghley informed La Mothe-Fénelon that if peace were not made with the Rochelois soon, Elizabeth intended to provide them with military aid.[48] By this time, however, it was apparent that neither queen had any object in view other than political advantage: the marriage negotiations were simply a façade.[49]

The entire charade became more ridiculous still on 14 August, when La Mothe-Fénelon reported that Elizabeth had had a change of heart and desired an immediate interview with Alençon.[50] Before the queen could change her mind, Burghley and Dale quickly arranged such a meeting, which was scheduled to take place at Dover around the first of September. Catherine de Medici apparently had no intention of sending her youngest son to England, however. She made the startling decision to send the comte de Retz, one of the ringleaders of the massacres, in his place. When Catherine explained to Dr Valentine Dale that Alençon was too ill to travel and that Retz would be his proxy, the English ambassador was dumbfounded. He obviously did not believe the queen mother's 'smooth tale' about Alençon's illness, even though the duke had been ill earlier in the month.[51]

Retz arrived in England in early September and delivered a personal letter of affection from Alençon to the English queen. It is interesting to speculate what Elizabeth thought of this Italian proxy. All of the contemporary chronicles (save

---

[45] PRO/SP 70/127/fol. 55, Catherine to Elizabeth, 26 April 1573; and *CSPF*, vol. x, p. 322, Dale to Burghley, 27 April 1573. (Dr Valentine Dale replaced Francis Walsingham as Elizabeth's ambassador in France in the spring of 1573.)

[46] PRO/SP 70/127/fol. 44, Alençon to Elizabeth, 22 April 1573.

[47] *CSPF*, vol. x, pp. 376–8, instructions to Horsey, June 1573.

[48] La Mothe-Fénelon, *Correspondance diplomatique*, vol. v, p. 353, La Mothe-Fénelon to the king, 20 June 1573.

[49] *CSPV*, vol. VII, pp. 488–9, Cavalli to the Signory, 2 and 12 July 1573.

[50] La Mothe-Fénelon, *Correspondance diplomatique*, vol. v, p. 391, La Mothe-Fénelon to the king, 14 August 1573.

[51] *CSPF*, vol. x, p. 410, Dale to Burghley, 22 August 1573.

one which he is suspected of authoring) incriminate him in the St Bartholomew's massacres.[52] Even had Elizabeth never read these chronicles, it is inconceivable that she was unaware of Retz's reputation. Her private reflections, however, were not recorded. Moreover, Elizabeth treated the count with great pomp and circumstance throughout his visit. Indeed, the only evidence that offers a hint that Elizabeth disapproved of Retz's visit because of his complicity in the massacres is an oblique reference by La Mothe-Fénelon to the king:

> I beseech you, Sire, to thank the ambassador of the said queen by a kind word or some demonstration, as I shall do here in person, for the sincere favor and courteous way in which she has received [Retz] in this kingdom. I can assure you, Sire, that *notwithstanding the things that have happened in France in the last year*, she has asked that he be given the same dignity and respect that was given to MM. de Montmorency and de Foix.[53]

During his interview with Elizabeth, Retz discovered that she still harbored serious doubts about Alençon's appearance. The detailed reports of his misshapen features and pockmarked face had convinced her that she must see her suitor in person. Retz suggested that until Alençon could come to England, perhaps Elizabeth might send a trusted agent and painter to interview him and bring back a portrait. Despite the unfortunate ending of a similarly executed courtship between her father and Anne of Cleves, she agreed to follow the count's suggestion and sent an agent, Thomas Randolph, to France the following month.[54]

The chief stumbling block to the marriage, however, was neither Alençon's appearance nor the difference in age of the two principals. As Retz must have discovered to his dismay, Elizabeth's most serious reservation stemmed from the abominable way in which Charles IX had treated the French Protestants since the massacres of St Bartholomew's Day. Lord Burghley drafted a formal report to present to Retz before his departure, which outlined the chief obstacles to the marriage: Alençon's religion and his participation in the siege of La Rochelle.[55]

Thus, the return of the comte de Retz to the French court on 19 September 1573 marked the end of two years of negotiation for a marriage. While the affair was not completely forgotten, marriage plans were shelved for six years, after which they were to reappear in far more serious circumstances. For two years, however, Catherine de Medici and Elizabeth had used Alençon as a pawn to gain political advantage. At times each seemed genuinely interested in the match, but

---

[52] See the excellent discussion of the massacres and the contemporary evidence by N. M. Sutherland in *The Massacre of St Bartholomew*, pp. 312–37 (and also p. 338 for the incrimination of the comte de Retz).

[53] La Mothe-Fénelon, *Correspondance diplomatique*, vol. v, p. 403, La Mothe-Fénelon to the king, 20 September 1573 (my italics).

[54] *CSPF*, vol. x, pp. 433–4, instructions to Randolph, 24 October 1573. Unfortunately, neither Randolph's report nor the portrait have been located.

[55] Ibid., pp. 379–80, 413, communications from Burghley to La Mothe-Fénelon, June and September 1573.

neither was willing to make a firm commitment. Alençon did, however, get his first taste of international politics, even if only as a go-between. He was disappointed to see the affair end so suddenly in the autumn of 1573, but matters were out of his hands. Nevertheless, he managed to establish a tenuous relationship with the queen of England. And although discussion of marriage was temporarily abandoned, this relationship added further fuel to Alençon's growing reputation as a Protestant sympathizer. Moreover, this brief courtship ultimately blossomed into a more serious romance that occupied the center stage of European politics in the 1580s.

III

Although the duke of Alençon had not been allowed to participate directly in these marriage negotiations, his participation in the royal siege of the Protestant stronghold of La Rochelle did appear to bring them to a close. If there were still slim hopes for marriage after the massacres of 1572, they were surely dashed by Alençon's military involvement against the Huguenots. On the other side of the coin, the marriage talks created serious repercussions in the royal camp outside La Rochelle. Rumors circulated that Alençon was in league with Elizabeth, and that they planned to organize a small military force from the various malcontents and Protestants within the royal camp, rendezvous with an English naval force, and then join the Rochelois in an attack against the king's army. Thus, during the siege of La Rochelle Alençon's name was compromised and he was further linked with the Huguenots and other enemies of the crown. Since the allegations first prompted at La Rochelle continued for the duration of his brief career, it is necessary to examine the role that he played in that operation.

It was hardly surprising when the major center of Calvinism in France rebelled after the atrocities of August and September 1572. This rebellion first became apparent when the city refused to admit its governor, the Catholic Marshal Biron, in September 1572. Preferring to negotiate rather than endure another war so soon after the massacres, the king despatched the Protestant, François de la Noue, to the city to make peace. La Noue was permitted to enter the city in November, but the citizens refused to negotiate with him.[56] Although the Rochelois had no desire to break formally with the crown or to secede from the realm, they had refused to pay either allegiance or taxes to the king since the massacres. In the circumstances Charles had no choice but to force them to submit. On 6 November 1572 he declared war on the fortified city, and ordered Biron to begin the siege the following month.[57]

The siege did not really become effective until early 1573, when the king

[56] Kingdon, *Geneva and the French Protestant Movement*, p. 201; Henri Hauser, *François de la Noue, 1531–1591* (Paris, 1892), pp. 36–44.
[57] Decrue, *Le Parti des politiques*, p. 99.

appointed his brother Henry, duke of Anjou, to lead a large contingent of royal forces to supplement Biron's army. The reinforcements left Paris under Henry's command on 10 January and reached La Rochelle one month later.[58] Most of the important nobles at court were keen to go on the expedition; and they were joined by many of their junior counterparts, who, like Alençon, were getting their first taste of military action. This latter group included Guillaume de Thoré and Charles de Méru – both younger brothers of François de Montmorency – and Henri de la Tour, viscount of Turenne, a nephew of the Montmorency brothers. There was thus a large assortment of nobles included in the royal army: young, old, Protestant and Catholic.[59]

By the time this motley force arrived in La Rochelle in February 1573, mistrust and unrest had already begun to divide them. The military commanders appointed to implement the siege could not agree initially on a workable plan.[60] In addition, some nobles (mainly Protestants, but also some Catholics who were enemies of the Guises) began suggesting ways in which they might covertly aid the Rochelois.[61] And finally, Alençon himself was upset at being excluded from the meetings of the military leaders, and as one of his colleagues noted, 'was most dissatisfied at finding himself in this army without any responsibility whatsoever'.[62] Moreover, the royal army was also faced with rumors that Queen Elizabeth was planning to equip the count of Montgomery with an armada to aid the Rochelois by sea.[63] Henry, duke of Anjou had significant difficulties to overcome if the siege was to be a success.

Partly in an attempt to deprive the malcontent nobles of leadership and partly out of animosity, Henry concocted a scheme to put Alençon and Navarre in charge of an *armée de mer* to combat the English armada. There is little doubt that he simply wanted to be rid of his brother and the Protestant Navarre. Charles IX was furious when he heard of Henry's plan, however, and he scolded him for placing Alençon and Navarre at the head of such a hazardous enterprise.[64] Although Henry agreed to follow the king's orders, the entire episode was an ugly sign of the growing animosity between the king's two younger brothers.

The discord between Henry and Alençon was only the tip of the iceberg, however, as the entire royal camp was fraught with division. Moreover, this

---

58 Etienne Charavay, 'Charles IX, siège de la Rochelle, 1573', *Revue des documents historiques*, III (1875–6), 151.
59 The older nobles are listed in De Thou, *Histoire universelle*, vol. IV, pp. 773–4. A fourth son of Anne de Montmorency did not take part in the siege: Henry de Montmorency, seigneur de Damville, who was governor of Languedoc.
60 Ibid., p. 774.
61 Ernest Lavisse (ed.), *Histoire de France illustrée depuis des origines jusqu'à la Révolution*, vol. 6, part i by J. H. Mariéjol, *La Réforme et la Ligue* (Paris, 1911 edn), p. 138.
62 Memoirs of Turenne in Michaud and Poujoulat, *Mémoires*, vol. XI, p. 10.
63 BN, MSS fr. 3184, fol. 23, Alençon to Damville, January 1573.
64 Charavay, 'Charles IX, siège de la Rochelle', pp. 151–3. See also BIF, MSS God. 256, fol. 83, Henry's reply to Charles, 17 February 1573.

division became polarized around the quarrel of the two royal brothers. For sundry reasons the malcontent nobles had become disenchanted with Charles IX and Henry, duke of Anjou. Navarre and Henry, prince of Condé (son of Louis, prince of Condé) simply wished to escape the jurisdiction of the court and flee to the safety of their followers, where they could publicly embrace Protestantism once again. The Montmorency family was still at odds with the king and Henry for their close association with the Guises since the massacres. Many of the younger nobles, such as Alençon, were dissatisfied with the positions that had been assigned to them. And finally, several of the Protestant nobles had no sympathy for the siege at all and wished to sabotage it.

Unsurprisingly, this disgruntled group turned to the king of Navarre and the duke of Alençon for leadership. Alençon's personal quarrels with his older brothers were well known, and for reasons already discussed he had developed the reputation of a Protestant sympathizer. Having a prince of the blood who was second in line to the French throne at their helm would add authority and a degree of legality to anything these nobles might wish to do. It was logical, therefore, that they should turn to Alençon to join and even to lead them. And that Alençon was concurrently trying to woo Queen Elizabeth made him even more attractive. The outstanding feature of these malcontents, however, was their disunity. Each was at odds with Henry, duke of Anjou and Charles IX for different reasons. And, although religion might appear to have been a common denominator, the quarrels were for the most part personal and political. Furthermore, as the historian De Thou noted, the most powerful of these malcontents – Alençon and Navarre – were at odds with each other. In addition to their personal rivalry, Navarre distrusted some of the officers in Alençon's household, particularly Joseph Boniface, seigneur de la Mole, who he thought was planning to reveal everything to the duke of Anjou.[65] Because of their differences these malcontent nobles never managed to organize themselves into a coherent force capable of opposing the king or aiding La Rochelle. 'In the council they held to decide what measures ought to be taken, opinions became strongly divided', wrote De Thou, 'as is usually the case among men who are all dissatisfied, but for different reasons.'[66] This was hardly, then, a movement of *politiques* who simply sought a peaceful resolution of religious and political differences, as some have suggested.[67] Indeed, it was not a movement at all, but a heterogeneous group of malcontent nobles who harbored various ambitions and who all looked to Alençon and Navarre for leadership.

Despite the malcontents' indecision, rumors of treason and rebellion could be heard throughout the royal camp outside La Rochelle. The chief story was that the malcontents, led by Alençon and Navarre, were in contact with the Protestants inside the city, were in league with the English forces of Mont-

---

[65] De Thou, *Histoire universelle*, vol. IV, p. 787.   [66] Ibid.
[67] See, for example, Decrue, *Le Parti des politiques*.

gomery, and intended to stage a *coup d'état* at the royal camp as soon as Montgomery arrived. The most vicious of the rumors even had it that Alençon and Navarre intended to murder Henry, duke of Anjou.[68] That they planned to take over the royal army in a *coup* is only conjecture, though all the evidence indicates that given the chance they would have done so. And the Montmorencies, including Damville, would probably have helped them, as their hatred of the Guises was still intense.[69] Very little evidence other than that of the memoirists, however, has survived to substantiate the rumors. As a result, it is impossible to know exactly what Alençon and Navarre were planning.

The count of Montgomery, who fled to England after the St Bartholomew's massacres, had organized a plan with English aid for the relief of the siege of La Rochelle.[70] It is difficult to make any connection, however, between Montgomery's plan and the plans of the malcontents in the royal camp. The duke of Alençon became embroiled in the affair because of the activities of two of his agents. The seigneur de Maisonfleur, who was sent to England in late 1572 to plead the duke's case for a marriage with Elizabeth, swore to Lord Burghley that Alençon's life was in danger, and requested that an English ship be sent to pick him up and bring him safely to England.[71] Burghley then contacted Francis Walsingham, who was in Paris on another mission, to see if he could find out anything more about Maisonfleur, specifically if he did in fact represent Alençon. Walsingham then contacted the duke's favorite, La Mole, and discovered that Maisonfleur was Alençon's agent, but was only sent to England to encourage the marriage. He had no authority to do anything else. La Mole did leave some doubt in Walsingham's mind, however, as to what his master's plans really were. Burghley and Walsingham were soon convinced that both Maisonfleur and La Mole had overstepped their authority and were acting on their own initiative. Indeed, the pair so bungled the negotiations that Walsingham decided to ignore them, convinced as he was that they were 'over young and lack experience that were fit to guide a matter of so great weight ... I mean not to deal any further with them unless I see they proceed more orderly.'[72] It is thus difficult to connect Alençon and the malcontents at La Rochelle with Montgomery's scheme. Moreover, François de la Noue, the malcontents' alleged liaison with Montgomery, did his best to prevent an English armada sailing to La

---

68 These rumors appeared in the memoirs of Turenne in Michaud and Poujoulat, *Mémoires*, vol. XI, pp. 10–13, and in the memoirs of the wife of Philippe du Plessis-Mornay in the latter's *Mémoires et correspondance* (12 vols., Paris, 1824–5), vol. I, p. 72. The Venetian ambassador in Paris at the time, Sigismondo Cavalli, also reported these same rumors in his despatches (BN, MSS ital. 1728, fol. 38, Cavalli to the Signory, 20 June 1573).

69 Joan M. Davies, 'Languedoc and its *gouverneur*: Henri de Montmorency-Damville, 1563–1589' (unpub. Ph.D. thesis, University of London, 1974), pp. 123–4.

70 *CSPF*, vol. X, p. 219, Montgomery to Burghley, 24 December 1572.

71 BL, Cotton. MSS, Vespasian F/vi, fol. 226, Maisonfleur to Burghley, 11 December 1572.

72 Quoted in Read, *Mr Secretary Walsingham*, vol. I, p. 248, Walsingham to Burghley, 20 January 1573.

Rochelle. La Noue had little time for the hot-headed Montgomery in any case.[73]

If Alençon and the malcontents did not arrange a league with Montgomery and the English, what were their plans? Again, the evidence is not altogether clear. The most complete account, the memoirs of the viscount of Turenne, is somewhat suspect.[74] According to Turenne, the leaders of the malcontents made a vague plan to seize arms and avenge the injustice of St Bartholomew's Day. There were problems involved in assembling enough men, and in agreeing on a time and date for the execution of the enterprise, and 'these difficulties prevented this plan from being carried out'. As the siege wore on, it soon became apparent that their plan would never work, since too many men had already been killed or wounded. The nobles then turned to La Noue, according to Turenne, and begged him to arrange a rendezvous with Montgomery so they could all flee to England. La Noue talked them out of this foolhardy scheme, for the obvious reason that Elizabeth could not possibly welcome them in England for fear of alienating Charles IX. And 'with this wise advice the game was up ... and all of our designs went up in smoke without any being carried out'.[75]

Unfortunately, there is no way of verifying Turenne's account. Several contemporaries believed his story and some historians have followed suit.[76] The truth of the matter, however, is unclear. It is obvious that some scheme was in the air. Whether it involved aiding the Rochelois, confronting the royal army, or merely seizing arms to demonstrate displeasure at the massacres is unlikely to be revealed. It is true nevertheless that the duke of Alençon associated, or allowed his name to be associated, with a group of malcontent nobles who were considering opposing the royal army and, by association, the king. Alençon's involvement with this group was most likely motivated by 'the dissatisfaction of finding himself in this army without any responsibility whatsoever', as Turenne duly attested.[77] Alençon, however, was clearly implicated.

In the event the malcontents never succeeded in aiding the Rochelois or in disrupting the siege. The citizens of La Rochelle managed to hold out throughout the winter and spring of 1573, despite the arrival of the king's Swiss

---

[73] Hauser, *François de la Noue*, p. 56; and the memoirs of Turenne in Michaud and Poujoulat, *Mémoires*, vol. XI, p. 13.

[74] The memoirs of Turenne need careful treatment. It should be kept in mind that Turenne (as duke of Bouillon) did not write his memoirs until 1610, just before the death of Henry IV and more than thirty-five years after the siege of La Rochelle. And though young Turenne was a supporter of Alençon in 1573, he left the duke's entourage in 1576 to seek his fortunes with Henry of Navarre. As the personal schism between Alençon and Navarre widened after 1576, Turenne became more openly critical of Alençon.

[75] Memoirs of Turenne in Michaud and Poujoulat, *Mémoires*, vol. XI, pp. 11–13.

[76] See, for instance, Mariéjol, *La Réforme et la Ligue*, pp. 138–9; Decrue, *Le Parti des politiques*, pp. 100–4; Hector de la Ferrière, 'Les dernières conspirations du règne de Charles IX', *Revue des questions historiques*, XLVIII (1890), p. 429; and Kervijn de Lettenhove, *Huguenots*, vol. III, pp. 124–53.

[77] Memoirs of Turenne in Michaud and Poujoulat, *Mémoires*, vol. XI, p. 10.

mercenaries on 23 May.[78] This stout resistance, coupled with Catherine de Medici's desire to end the war so that she could concentrate on Anjou's election to the vacant Polish throne, finally forced the crown to capitulate.[79] After much negotiation, peace was finally concluded in July 1573. The principal terms of the peace allowed the inhabitants of La Rochelle, Nîmes, and Montauban to exercise their religion, while the memory of 24 August 1572 was to be extinguished. Apart from freedom of conscience, however, the peace provided little religious freedom.[80] Moreover, the price of war was heavy for both sides. La Rochelle was battered and there were numerous casualties, especially among the royalist forces.[81] And the cost to the royal treasury was more than half a million *livres* per month to maintain the siege.[82]

The duke of Alençon's participation in the siege of La Rochelle cost him credibility with Protestants and Catholics alike. Elizabeth strongly condemned his participation in the military suppression of French Protestants, and the siege hastened the end of their marriage negotiations. At the same time many French Catholics suspected Alençon of attempting to aid the Rochelois. Ironically, Henry, duke of Anjou seemed very pleased with his brother's contribution to the siege.[83] And Charles and Catherine were equally impressed with Alençon's involvement in the peace negotiations, where his close association with many Huguenot leaders proved invaluable.[84] Admittedly, the royal family may have showered Alençon with such compliments so as not to injure the delicate marriage negotiations with Elizabeth, which were proceeding concurrently. Many observers, such as Jacques-Auguste de Thou, were convinced that the marriage talks were just a ruse to keep English aid out of La Rochelle during the siege.[85] In any case, there is no sign of royal displeasure at Alençon's conduct during the entire operation.

After a great deal of bargaining by her agents, Catherine de Medici managed to get her son Henry, duke of Anjou elected to the Polish throne in May 1573. Though Henry did not depart for Poland until December, his election proved vital to the career of his younger brother. With one fewer rival at court, Alençon hoped to establish himself in a more prestigious position. He assumed that he

78 Michael O. H. Lavin, 'Franco-Spanish rivalry from the treaty of Cateau-Cambrésis to the death of Charles IX' (unpub. Ph.D. dissertation, Stanford University, 1956), pp. 577–8.
79 Albèri, *Relazioni*, vol. IV, p. 306; and James Westfall Thompson, *The Wars of Religion in France, 1559–1576*, 2nd edn (New York, 1958), p. 459.
80 For an analysis of the peace terms see N. M. Sutherland, *The Huguenot Struggle*, p. 360.
81 A list of royal casualties is in PRO/SP 70/127/fol. 226.
82 BN, MSS fr. 4554, fol. 92, 'Despense de lex[traordinai]re de la guerre a faire en ce p[rese]nt mois de janvier mv^clxxiij', and MSS fr. 4554, fols. 98–100, 'Estat de la despense que le Roy a ordonee estre faict po[ur] le paiement des compaignies de gens de guerre a pied pour le siege et reduction de la Rochelle'.
83 See Henry's letters of 13 and 26 April and 8 June to Charles IX, 13 April to Catherine de Medici, and 21 and 26 April to Frederick III of the Palatinate in Henry III, *Lettres*, vol. I, pp. 250–72.
84 *CSPF*, vol. X, p. 385, Dale to Elizabeth, 7 July 1573.
85 De Thou, *Histoire universelle*, vol. IV, p. 766.

would inherit his brother's office of lieutenant-general, the highest military rank in the royal army since the death of the constable, Anne de Montmorency, in 1567. His own military inexperience notwithstanding, Alençon fully expected to follow in Henry's footsteps. When these hopes were not immediately realized, he became even more alienated from the king and the queen mother. Once again, as at La Rochelle, there were numerous malcontents who looked to Alençon for guidance and leadership.

IV

The departure of Henry, duke of Anjou for Poland in late 1573 did not alter the struggle for power at the Valois court. Many, including the duke of Alençon, were glad to be rid of him.[86] Nevertheless the divisive conflict between the Guises and the Montmorencies continued to dominate the court. In the eyes of the Guise faction, Alençon had always been associated with the Montmorencies. He was the constable's godson, and was very close to the marshal, François de Montmorency. Moreover, throughout the winter of 1573–4, Alençon made repeated attempts to gain support from the marshal's brother, Henri de Montmorency-Damville, the governor of Languedoc. Damville was uninterested, however, since the Protestants in Languedoc were extremely reluctant to negotiate with the crown.[87] Nevertheless, the Guises had been very suspicious of Alençon's activities since the siege of La Rochelle earlier in the year. By the autumn of 1573, moreover, these suspicions were supported by rumors at court of an impending alliance between Alençon and William of Orange, the leader of the rebels in the Netherlands.

In November 1573 the king received a lengthy despatch from none other than the seigneur de Maisonfleur. This was the same agent whom Alençon had sent to England a year earlier to negotiate his marriage, but who had subsequently joined forces with the count of Montgomery. By the autumn of 1573 he had moved on to Delft in the Netherlands, where he had joined the service of William of Orange. It was as Orange's agent that Maisonfleur wrote to Charles IX and requested that he send the duke of Alençon with a force of French troops to support Orange and the Dutch rebels. Maisonfleur argued that an alliance with the prince of Orange would benefit France by counter-balancing the Spanish military build-up in the Netherlands. Furthermore, Maisonfleur reasoned that, by assisting Orange, Charles would significantly increase the

---

[86] Desjardins, vol. III, pp. 891–2, Alamanni to the grand duke of Tuscany, 22 November 1573.

[87] See the correspondence from Alençon to Damville, all of it requesting money and troops, in BN, MSS fr. 3246, fol. 45, 14 November 1573; MSS fr. 3205, fol. 81, 17 December 1573; MSS fr. 3205, fol. 83, 20 December 1573; MSS fr. 3246, fol. 90, 20 January 1574; MSS fr. 3203, fol. 3, 14 February 1574; MSS fr. 3247, fol. 13, 23 February 1574. Also see Davies, 'Languedoc and its *gouverneur*', pp. 138–9.

chances of a marriage between Alençon and Elizabeth.[88] While there was much
to be said for this approach, the king had no intention of providing the Dutch
rebels with any overt assistance, as the danger of Spanish reprisal was always
present. Money offered a much safer means of aid, since it could be sent secretly.
Whether it was the result of Maisonfleur's appeal or simply a desire to return to
the French policy before the massacres, Charles decided to renew his contributions to the prince of Orange in November 1573.[89]

The court escorted Henry, duke of Anjou to the French border in December,
as he made his way to Poland. The royal entourage was met in the town of
Blamont by Louis of Nassau (Orange's younger brother) and Count Christopher
of the Palatinate (son of the elector, Frederick III). At this meeting the queen
mother gave the two Protestant princes the first instalment of the funds that
Charles had promised Orange.[90] Moreover, in a brief interview with Louis of
Nassau, Alençon agreed to do what he could to aid the Dutch rebels. Nassau was
very optimistic when he reported the meeting to his brother, the prince of
Orange: 'I saw Monsieur, the duke of Alençon, who, while grasping my hand,
whispered in my ear that ... he would do everything in his power to support you.
I know from another source that he is both trustworthy and charitable, which is
no small advantage for us.'[91] More precise details of this interview have not been
recorded, and it is not clear what form of assistance Alençon promised to
provide. The immediate effect of this liaison was that Alençon became even
more alienated from the Guises at court.

The conflict between the Guises and Montmorencies continued to disrupt the
court after Alençon's return from Blamont. Still hoping to acquire the office of
lieutenant-general recently vacated by his brother, the duke turned to his friend
François de Montmorency, who was apparently on close terms with the king.
Though Charles was concerned that 'the greater part of the princes and my
principal ministers and servants are divided and banded against each other', he
declared his confidence in Montmorency and Damville. And it was doubtless
under Montmorency's influence that Charles promised Alençon the office of
lieutenant-general on 25 January 1574.[92] The Guises, who were naturally angry
with the king's decision and jealous of Montmorency's influence, then came up

[88] BN, MSS fr. 17199, fols. 136–40, Maisonfleur to Charles IX, 16 November 1573.
[89] Rumors of French aid to the Dutch had circulated before November 1573. See *CSPF*, vol. X,
p. 431, Henry Killigrew to Burghley, 17 October 1573. The French ambassador at the court of
the sultan of Turkey wrote in May 1574 that Charles IX had been making regular monthly
payments of 100,000 *écus* to the prince of Orange for the last eighteen months, or since November
1572 (see E. Charrière (ed.), *Négociations de la France dans le Levant*, vol. 3 (Paris, 1853),
pp. 477–82). This may have been an exaggeration in order to get the sultan to contribute to the
rebels. It is clear, though, that Charles made some form of payment to Orange in the autumn of
1573. See Groen van Prinsterer, *Archives*, vol. IV, p. 279, Nassau to Orange, December 1573.
[90] BN, MSS ital. 1728, fol. 281, Cavalli to the Signory, 19 April 1574.
[91] Groen van Prinsterer, *Archives*, vol. IV, p. 281, Nassau to Orange, December 1573.
[92] BN, MSS fr. 3247, fol. 1, Charles IX to Damville, 20 January 1574; and Desjardins, vol. III,
p. 897, Alamanni to the grand duke, 26 January 1574.

with a scheme to discredit both the marshal and Alençon. On 16 February 1574, Henry, duke of Guise attacked one of Alençon's gentlemen, the sieur de Ventabren, in the Louvre. He claimed that Ventabren had been hired by Montmorency to assassinate him.[93] Though Ventabren, Alençon and Montmorency appear to be innocent of Guise's charges, the incident was so disturbing that the marshal de Montmorency was induced to leave court. The king never executed his promise to give Alençon the lieutenant-generalcy, and instead offered it to Charles, duke of Lorraine, a cousin of the duke of Guise.[94]

The choice of the duke of Lorraine was apparently the queen mother's, who feared the consequences if her youngest son acquired the power of the lieutenant-general – the *de facto* head of the royal army since 1567, since a new constable had not been appointed after the death of Anne de Montmorency. It had been rumored that Alençon might use the army to keep his brother, now king of Poland, out of France in order that he could assume the crown on the death of Charles IX. The king was so ill by January 1574 that this rumor was more than just a remote possibility. Moreover, the duke of Lorraine was very close to Henry and only distantly in line to the succession. For all these reasons Catherine managed to prevent Charles from appointing Alençon to the office of lieutenant-general.[95]

The possibility of Charles's death occurring while Henry was still in Poland had been considered. Indeed, Charles had issued an edict prior to his brother's departure that spelled out the order of succession very clearly. If the king died without any male children, or if his male heirs died out, in this case the elected king of Poland, duke of Anjou and Bourbonnais, as the nearest in line to the crown, would be the true and legitimate heir, notwithstanding the fact that he was absent or residing outside this kingdom. Only if Henry and all his male heirs died out would the throne pass to the duke of Alençon.[96] Once the edict was registered in the *parlement* of Paris, there could not have been much doubt about the legality of the succession. Legalities mattered little, however, if Alençon, as lieutenant-general, tried to steal the crown from his brother by force. As remote as that possibility was, Catherine did not wish to take any chances. She believed, wrongly as it happened, that the choice of Lorraine would keep Alençon out of trouble and would restore peace to the troubled court.

The departure of Montmorency from court, however, coupled with Lorraine's appointment to the lieutenant-generalcy, only added more fuel to the

[93] Desjardins, vol. III, p. 901, Alamanni to the Grand Duke, 17 February 1574; *CSPF*, vol. x, pp. 468–9, Dale to Burghley, 16 February 1574; and De Thou, *Histoire universelle*, vol. v, p. 31.

[94] Desjardins, vol. III, p. 910, Alamanni to the grand duke, February 1574; and De Thou, *Histoire universelle*, vol. v, p. 31.

[95] De Thou, *Histoire universelle*, vol. v, p. 32.

[96] BN, MSS Dupuy 500, fols. 85–6, 22 August 1573. The edict was signed by the king, Anjou, Alençon, Navarre, the cardinal of Bourbon, the duke of Montpensier and his son the dauphin d'Auvergne, the prince of Condé, the duke of Conti, the cardinal of Vendôme, and the four secretaries of state.

conflict at court. The moderate Protestants and Catholics at court who despised the fanaticism of the Guises could no longer turn to the marshal for leadership. In addition, the younger nobles who had formerly sheltered under the protection of Montmorency had to look elsewhere for support. Thus, immediately after the Ventabren affair a number of disgruntled persons once again turned to Alençon. The duke was approaching his nineteenth birthday in early 1574. Young and ambitious, he had none of the necessary credentials and experience to oppose such a powerful figure at court as Henry, duke of Guise. Nevertheless, Alençon's major asset was his rank as a prince of the blood, which seemed to outweigh all his shortcomings. Nearly every malcontent faction since the Middle Ages had sought the support of royal blood to give its movement a degree of respectability and legality. And as long as Henry, duke of Anjou chose to remain in Poland, Alençon was the highest-ranking prince of the blood resident at court.

As at La Rochelle the previous year, various malcontent nobles turned to the duke of Alençon. While many of them were supporters of the Montmorencies, the only thing common to all of them was a desire to rid the crown of the Guise influence which was responsible for the St Bartholomew's massacres. The author of one pamphlet proclaimed that the fundamental laws of the crown and the ancient liberties of the nobility had been tainted by some enemies of the king who had managed to find their way into the entourage of Catherine de Medici 'without the advice of the princes of the blood and the estates of the kingdom'.[97] It is easy to see how such malcontents might be attracted to Alençon. A legitimate prince of the blood leading a group to purify the monarchy of evil influences had a certain appeal, a fact that attracted many Protestants. Spurned by his brothers and his mother, and overlooked for the lieutenant-generalcy, Alençon was once again only too happy to become the center of attention for these nobles. And according to De Thou, 'he began in earnest to try to stir things up'.[98]

Who were these noblemen who began congregating in the duke of Alençon's apartment after the departure of Montmorency? The best known of the group were the two princes of the blood, Navarre and Condé. Others included Méru, Thoré, the maréchal de Cossé, the seigneur de Montaigu (an agent of Condé's), the comte de Coconas (the captain of Alençon's personal guard), and the duke's favorite, the seigneur de la Mole. The most influential of the group appear to have been Thoré and Turenne, 'who constantly had the ear of the duke of Alençon and filled his head with plots', according to De Thou.[99] Clearly, then, this was for the most part a collection of young nobles who, like Alençon, were trying to promote themselves at court. There was little political acumen and almost no military experience among the group. There was, however, a great

[97] Quoted in Georges Weill, *Les Théories sur le pouvoir royal en France pendant les guerres de religion* (Paris, 1891), p. 122.
[98] De Thou, *Histoire universelle*, vol. V, p. 30.   [99] Ibid., p. 29.

deal of foolhardiness and personal ambition. Thus, it makes little sense to call this coalition a *parti des politiques*.[100] It was far too disorganized to be called a party. Moreover, most of its members had placed their personal ambitions above the well-being of the state. And, although many of them did indeed favor religious coexistence, they were hardly *politiques* in the truest sense of the word.[101]

The court was lodged at St-Germain-en-Laye, just west of Paris, for the winter when new rumors began circulating connecting Alençon and the malcontents with William of Orange. An agent of Louis of Nassau (a former secretary of Coligny named La Huguerie) was known to be in Paris at the time, and there was open speculation that he was conferring secretly with Alençon about aiding the Dutch rebels with French troops.[102] It is impossible to verify whether Nassau's agent made contact with the duke, but this seems likely, in the light of the interview at Blamont only two months earlier. In any case, the Guises became suspicious; they had no intention of seeing Alençon take up the mantle of Coligny, and in February 1574 they did everything in their power to discredit him.[103]

The Guises' worst fears were soon realized. In the middle of the night of 27–8 February the court fled in a great deal of confusion from the château at St-Germain-en-Laye, as a large body of Protestant troops had been spotted gathering in the environs of the château. The aims and intentions of this alleged plot and the details of what happened during that night are not entirely clear. By most accounts it appears that there was an attempt to coordinate uprisings in the provinces with an attempted *coup* at court. The plan was designed to free Alençon and Navarre, who were closely watched at court, presumably so that they could escape to the Netherlands to aid Nassau and Orange. All of the uprisings were apparently intended for 10 March, but the conspirators bungled the timing. The major *faux pas* was committed by the sieur de Chaumont Guitry, a gentleman in Navarre's household, who was supposed to arrive at the château on 10 March with 200 cavalry to aid the liberation of Alençon and Navarre. Unfortunately, Guitry's forces arrived ten days too soon, and put the entire court in a panic. Charles IX feared a conspiracy and, despite his ill health, ordered the court to flee to the safety of Paris that very night. The escape attempt of the princes had failed.[104]

---

[100] As Francis Decrue has done, for example, in his *Le Parti des politiques*, pp. 139–218.

[101] I am aware that this usage of the word *politique* is anachronistic. The term was almost never used by contemporaries until after the revival of the League in 1584. Even then it was always a pejorative term used by radical Leaguers to describe any faint-hearted Catholics who advocated toleration of the Huguenots.

[102] BN, MSS ital. 1728, fol. 211, Cavalli to the Signory, 18 February 1574; and Decrue, *Le Parti des politiques*, pp. 144–5.

[103] Desjardins, vol. III, pp. 901–2, 906–7, Alamanni to the grand duke, 17 February and 5 March 1574; and BN, MSS ital. 1728, fols. 231–3, Cavalli to the Signory, 10 March 1574.

[104] BN, MSS ital. 1728, fols. 231–3, Cavalli to the Signory, 10 March 1574. The various accounts of the spring plots of 1574 provide a variety of detail (especially dates) and interpretation. See the

What was involved in this conspiracy, other than the princes' obvious effort to flee the court, is difficult to determine. The duke of Alençon was definitely involved in its planning, as Guitry produced a patent letter from Alençon for the conscription of troops when he was questioned.[105] Most believed Guitry's declaration that the plot was aimed, not at the king, but at the Guises, and that the conspirators' goal was 'to drive away from court and even kill the Lorrainers, and not to revolt against the service of the king'.[106] The Guises obviously bought Guitry's story, for on the flight back to the capital the cardinal of Lorraine urged Charles 'to spill the blood' of the conspirators.[107] It is also clear that Henry of Navarre was implicated, as Guitry was one of his men. The papal nuncio at court, Salviati, claimed that the conspirators numbered fourteen altogether, including Thoré, La Mole and Turenne. He believed that the marshal de Montmorency knew of the plot but was not involved in its planning or its execution.[108] There is also no evidence that Damville was involved.[109] What is clear, however, is that it was not a conspiracy of Protestants alone. Many Catholics, including Alençon, were involved.[110]

After receiving reports of various Protestant uprisings throughout his kingdom, Charles decided that the court would be safer in the impregnable fortress at Vincennes, on the south-eastern outskirts of Paris. And on 8 March the court adjourned there, accompanied by the king's Swiss guards. When the duke of Alençon was finally questioned in front of Charles, Catherine de Medici, and Chancellor Birague, he claimed that the conspiracy was not aimed at the king but at the Guises, who had prevented him from obtaining a more responsible position in the government.[111] The appointment of the duke of Lorraine as lieutenant-general obviously still stung. Birague declared that Alençon and Navarre had committed treason and should be put to death. Fortunately for the two princes, however, the king and queen mother were unwilling to approve such an extreme measure, and merely placed both princes under heavy guard.[112] On 24 March they were required to sign a loyalty oath, declaring that they were resolved to 'give up our lives and everything that God has given to us, our friends, and servants, for our lord the king for the conservation and maintenance of his crown and state ... and we oppose those

various accounts in J. W. Thompson, *The Wars of Religion in France, 1559–1576*, 2nd edn (New York, 1958), pp. 477–85; Decrue, *Le Parti des politiques*, pp. 139–218; and de la Ferrière, 'Les dernières conspirations', pp. 421–70. I have attempted to piece together my own chronology from the sources.

105 Desjardins, vol. III, p. 909, Alamanni to the grand duke, 11 March 1574.   106 Ibid.
107 Quoted in F. Rocquain, *La France et Rome pendant les guerres de religion* (Paris, 1924), p. 170.
108 *Acta Nuntiaturae Gallicae*, vol. 13, ed. Pierre Hurtubise (Rome, 1975), pp. 794–8, Salviati to Rome, 13 March 1574; and *CSPR*, vol. II, p. 149–50, Salviati to the cardinal of Como, 15 March 1574.
109 Davies, 'Languedoc and its *gouverneur*', pp. 144–8.
110 *Acta Nuntiaturae Gallicae*, vol. XIII, p. 793, Salviati to Rome, 13 March 1574.
111 *CSPV*, vol. VII, pp. 500–3, Cavalli to the Signory, 10 and 17 March 1574.
112 Ibid., p. 504, Cavalli to the Signory, 26 March 1574.

who rebel against him and trouble the peace and tranquility of this kingdom'.[113] It was hoped that the signed declarations of Alençon and Navarre would not only ease the fears of the court but would also put an end to any other plots that might be brewing. The supporters of the two princes, however, were still bent on freeing them from court.

Ever since the court had left St-Germain-en-Laye, Charles had been trying to persuade marshal de Montmorency to return to court. Although it is unclear whether the king felt that Montmorency's presence would put an end to the conspiracies or whether he suspected him and sought his arrest, Charles finally persuaded Montmorency to return to the court at Vincennes in the first week in April.[114] Almost as soon as the marshal arrived, news of a second escape attempt by Alençon and Navarre was somehow leaked to the queen mother. How this plan was leaked out is unknown but, just as at St-Germain-en-Laye, the plot aborted. The Venetian ambassador recorded the details:

A plot was discovered which was supposed to be carried out tomorrow, Easter Sunday, against the Most Christian King, the Queen Mother, and the chancellor. The duke of Alençon was the leader of this plot, together with the king of Navarre and Montmorency ... No one can leave [Paris] as the gates of the city have been closed all day. It is expected that some of the accomplices will be arrested, and I believe that about fifteen have already been captured. These are all only captains and underlings, however, nobody important. A search is underway for the count of Coconas, the former captain of the guard of the king of Poland who left him in disfavor [and has since joined Alençon], but it seems that he has already fled.[115]

Other details of this second plot are unclear. It appears that Alençon and Navarre, once free from the castle at Vincennes, planned to go to Sedan, where they would be met by 300 cavalry under the command of Turenne. La Mole was apparently in charge of getting the princes out of the castle.[116] The king immediately placed the two princes and marshal de Montmorency under an even heavier guard and arrested La Mole and Coconas, among others. The arrests of Thoré, Méru and Turenne were also decreed, but they managed to escape the court as soon as the plot was leaked. Thoré and Méru headed for Strasbourg to join Condé, while Turenne fled to the safety of his estates in Auvergne. In all, about fifty persons were arrested.[117] Rumors began to circulate freely all over the capital, most of them implicating La Mole and Coconas who, along with the two princes, were the alleged ringleaders of the conspiracy. Charles appointed a

---

[113] BN, MSS Dupuy 755, fol. 151, declaration of Alençon and Navarre, 24 March 1574.
[114] Davies, 'Languedoc and its *gouverneur*', pp. 148–9.
[115] BN, MSS ital. 1728, fols. 272–3, Cavalli to the Signory, 10 April 1574.
[116] BIF, MSS God. 291, fol. 100. See also Decrue, *Le Parti des politiques*, pp. 163–79; and Rocquain, *France et Rome*, pp. 172–5.
[117] BN, MSS ital. 1728, fols. 274–8, Cavalli to the Signory, 14 April 1574.

commission to investigate the plot, but as the Venetian ambassador candidly admitted, 'no one knows the truth of all this.'[118]

On Easter Sunday, 11 April, La Mole and Coconas were called before the council to testify what they knew.[119] Christophe de Thou and Pierre Hennequin, two presidents from the *parlement* of Paris, questioned La Mole first. The two magistrates were specifically interested in who was behind the conspiracy, and they speculated that it might be Renaud de Beaune, seigneur de Mende, the chancellor of Alençon's household. La Mole was of little help, however, denying any knowledge of the plot. Coconas gave his testimony the following day and refused to cover up. He told of Alençon's plan to escape to La Ferté, where he had agreed to meet Condé and Thoré with some troops before going on to Sedan, where they hoped to be joined by Louis of Nassau and Count Christopher of the Palatinate. When asked who talked Alençon into all of this, Coconas replied that 'it was the Montmorencies'. Even more startling was Coconas's confession that their intention was 'to destroy the kingdom, and that a secretary named Bodin had told him that they had aid from England and Germany'.[120] This was astounding testimony, and if true, signified a far wider conspiracy than had been suspected. According to Coconas's account the two princes were not going to the Netherlands to join Nassau, but he and Count Christopher were preparing to join them to fight in France. What casts some doubt on this testimony, however, is the fact that both Nassau and Christopher were far away in the Netherlands at the time, fighting the Spanish.[121]

The following day, 13 April, Alençon and Navarre were called in for questioning. Alençon was very intimidated, and repeated his earlier claims that he only meant to escape the court in order to go to the Netherlands. He did, however, implicate La Mole and Coconas, which almost certainly sealed their fate. Navarre was more brazen with the king and the council, perhaps realizing that their status as princes of the blood would ensure their safety. He confessed that he and Alençon were behind the plot, but that they sought their freedom because they feared another St Bartholomew's Day. Moreover, Navarre claimed that Turenne had told him that secretary Villeroy was carrying the order of execution. Thus, they were only trying to escape to preserve their lives. Once

---

[118] Ibid. The commission appointed by Charles IX is in BN, MSS Dupuy 590, fol. 21.

[119] This testimony is in BN, MSS fr. 3969, fol. 24–36, and is printed in Simon Goulart (ed.), *Mémoires de l'estat de France sous Charles Neufiesme* (3 vols, n.p., 1577), vol. III, pp. 208–13.

[120] Goulard (ed.), *Mémoires de l'estat*, vol. 3, pp. 208–13. There is no way of verifying whether this was the famous Jean Bodin, who was attached to Alençon's household at the time, but it would seem probable.

[121] Both Nassau and Christopher were killed in the battle of Mook Heide two days later, on 14 April. See C. V. Wedgwood, *William the Silent: William of Nassau, Prince of Orange, 1533–1584* (London, 1944), p. 138.

again the chancellor begged the king to spill the blood of the two princes, and cited the precedent of Louis XI.[122]

Charles feared the consequences of the princes' deaths, however, especially reprisals from the Huguenots, the German Protestant nobles, and Queen Elizabeth.[123] He decided to spare their lives, and ordered La Mole and Coconas put on trial instead. Their trial on 30 April in the *parlement* of Paris was a brief one. Both were found guilty of *lèse-majesté*, and their execution was ordered for the same afternoon. Alençon tried in vain to save the life of his favorite, La Mole, but the only concession that he could obtain was that La Mole would be put to death in prison instead of being executed publicly. So, on 30 April 1574, the count de Coconas was beheaded and quartered in the Place de Grève, while at the same hour his accomplice La Mole suffered a similar fate in his cell.[124]

By this time Charles IX was near death, 'reduced to skin and bone' according to the English ambassador. He was cheered somewhat to learn of the deaths of La Mole and Coconas, but he was not convinced that their deaths signalled the end of the conspiracy. As a result he arrested the two marshals, François de Montmorency and Artus de Cossé, on 4 May and confined them to the Bastille. Charles further reinforced the guards at Vincennes and refused to allow Alençon and Navarre to go out unattended. The princes made public apologies and asked the king to receive them as faithful servants, but his end was near.[125] Charles died on 30 May, and was mourned by most French Catholics.[126]

As with the first plot at St-Germain-en-Laye, the problem arises as to the nature and extent of the conspiracy. There is no doubt that Alençon and Navarre organized it; they admitted as much. But was their intention to kill the king and steal his throne? Or, as both princes claimed throughout, were they only trying to escape the court and flee to safety or to the Netherlands? Perhaps the most damaging piece of evidence is the report of the Florentine ambassador, Alamanni, of 14 April. He described 'a terrible conspiracy ... against the lives and state of their Most Christian Majesties'. He was convinced that the plot was led by Alençon and Navarre and was 'instigated, animated, and fomented by many of their friends and supporters ... and not without the blessing of the queen of England'.[127] This report is often cited to suggest that Alençon

---

[122] Alençon's testimony is in BN, MSS fr. 3969, fols. 18–24 and Navarre's is in Goulart (ed.), *Mémoires de l'estat*, vol. 3, pp. 219–25. Also see BN, MSS ital. 1728, fols. 274–8, Cavalli to the Signory, 14 April 1574.

[123] BN, MSS ital. 1728, fol. 280, Cavalli to the Signory, 19 April 1574.

[124] 'Procès-verbal de la question et exécution du sieur de la Mole et du comte de Coconas (30 avril)', in L. Cimber and F. Danjou (eds.), *Archives curieuses de l'histoire de France depuis Louis XI jusqu'à Louis XVIII*, series i, vol. 3 (Paris, 1836), pp. 201–21. Also see BN, MSS ital. 1728, fols. 291–2, Cavalli to the Signory, 2 May 1574.

[125] *CSPF*, vol. X, pp. 494–6, Dale to Burghley, 2 and 5 May 1574; and Desjardins, vol. III, p. 928, Alamanni to the grand duke, 24 May 1574.

[126] See the passage in L'Estoile, *Journal*, vol. I, pp. 3–4.

[127] Desjardins, vol. III, pp. 914–16, Alamanni to the grand duke, 14 April 1574.

intended to murder his brother and then steal his crown.[128] It becomes clear when reading through Alamanni's despatches, however, that on 14 April he had not yet learned of the princes' own testimony before the council the previous day. This testimony apparently changed his mind, as he admitted in his next despatch on 22 April. He was satisfied that the princes' main purpose in leaving court was 'to help recover the Low Countries, and afterwards, with the same forces, to help recover that [part of his lands] which the King of Spain had usurped from Navarre'.[129] So it would appear that Alamanni's earlier report of 14 April is not altogether accurate.

The reports of the English ambassador in France, Dr Valentine Dale, put the conspiracy in a different light, although it should be remembered that Dale himself was probably involved. It was his contention that the lives of the princes were in danger, and that they only meant to escape to avoid injury from the Guises.[130] Although there was some truth in Dale's conviction that the Guises desired to see Alençon and Navarre out of the way, it is unlikely that Henry, duke of Guise or the cardinal of Lorraine would have condoned the murder of two princes of the blood. They certainly could have done so on St Bartholomew's night if they had wished. What the Guises probably wanted was to discredit the two princes so much that the king would be forced to imprison them. In any case the evidence concerning the Guises is unclear, and one must ponder Dale's despatches with some reservation.

It seems highly unlikely that the full story of what happened at court in March and April 1574 will ever emerge from the evidence. Those involved had differing ideals. Alençon and Navarre's desire to escape from court, the need for Montmorency to counterbalance the Guises, the ambitions of the younger nobles at court who were seeking their fortunes, and Elizabeth's attempt to aid the French Protestants all involved different aims. The twin plots of the spring of 1574 provided the means toward those ends. As a result, those implicated in the affair each had a different account of what happened. It is unlikely that anyone ever knew the complete story.

Upon Charles's death Catherine de Medici declared herself regent until the new king, Henry III, returned from Poland. She persuaded Alençon and Navarre to sign another declaration of loyalty – although Alençon's true feelings are difficult to assess, since he told the English ambassador that Catherine had forced him to make this declaration.[131] Nevertheless, the death of Charles IX virtually ended the plots to flee from the court, although rumors still abounded

---

128 See Kervijn de Lettenhove, *Huguenots*, vol. III, pp. 312–13.
129 Desjardins, vol. III, p. 918, Alamanni to the grand duke, 22 April 1574. Most of Navarre had been conquered by Ferdinand the Catholic in 1512. Philip II always thought of himself as king of Navarre, and referred to Henry as the prince of Béarn.
130 *CSPF*, vol. X, pp. 486–7, 490, 507, correspondence to Burghley and Walsingham, April and May 1574.
131 Ibid., pp. 518–19, Dale to Burghley, Smith and Walsingham, all 21 June 1574.

that the two princes were making new plans to escape.[132] There is evidence that Queen Elizabeth, through her ambassador in Paris, attempted to assist them in another plot. Lord Burghley had even gone so far as to arrange some money for that purpose.[133] The death of Charles IX, however, changed the duke of Alençon's situation. Some of the responsibility, power and prestige that had for so long eluded him was suddenly his as the presumptive heir to the crown. Until the new king could produce an heir, he was first in line to the throne. With the legitimate king making his way home from Poland, and armed with sympathetic overtures from the queen of England and the prince of Orange, the duke of Alençon was not nearly so pressed to flee the court as he had been a few weeks earlier.

Alençon's capricious relationship with the Huguenots, however, still caused concern. Despite Catherine's repeated announcements to the world that Alençon was assisting her in the regency government and that he fully supported the new king, doubts remained. The duke was implicated in rebellious activities in La Rochelle and at the court. None of those designs succeeded because the conspirators lacked the support, experience and acumen to carry out their plans. Nevertheless, those at court such as the Venetian ambassador recognized the difficult task that Catherine de Medici had undertaken until the new king returned from Poland.

The safekeeping of the duke her son and the king of Navarre is more important than anything else. It is doubtful if anything can be done to prevent their escape, however, especially since everybody knows that they intend to use the first opportunity to do so ... Moreover, I am absolutely sure that the queen of England is doing everything in her power to assist them, and some believe that she was even behind the most recent conspiracy.[134]

If the conflict between the factions of the nobility at court was to be settled, if the hostility between Huguenots and French Catholics was to be tempered, and if the threat of foreign intervention by Elizabeth, Orange and the German princes was ever to be mitigated, it was essential for the new king, Henry III, to return speedily to France, and to make an immediate and resolute attempt to wrestle with the problems that confronted his realm. A forceful and resourceful monarch was sorely needed.

---

[132] Desjardins, vol. IV, pp. 12–13, Alamanni to the grand duke, 8 and 15 June 1574; and *CSPV*, vol. VII, p. 514, Cavalli to the Signory, 16 June 1574.

[133] *CSPV*, vol. X, p. 507, Burghley to Walsingham, 26 May 1574. For other evidence of English aid to the princes' escape attempts, see Desjardins, vol. IV, p. 15, Alamanni to the grand duke, 2 July 1574; and *CSPV*, vol. VII, pp. 516–17, Cavalli and Morosini to the Signory, 15 July 1574.

[134] BN, MSS ital. 1728, fols. 360–1, Cavalli to the Signory, 15 July 1574.

3

War and peace, May 1574–May 1576

I

Upon the death of Charles IX the new king, Henry III, was expected to make a rapid return from Poland to claim his crown. Henry spent the summer months of 1574, however, on a carefree tour of Italy as the court anxiously awaited his arrival.[1] In the meantime Catherine de Medici set up a regency government in Paris. On his deathbed Charles had requested that his mother take control of the government upon his death until Henry returned to France. And with the apparent support of the princes of the blood, the king's council, and the *parlement* of Paris, Catherine took up her responsibilities, 'dropping everything in order to search for peace', as she proclaimed to Henri de Montmorency-Damville.[2] The participation of the duke of Alençon and Henry of Navarre in the regency government was only nominal, and because of their recent activities both princes were treated as virtual prisoners at court. Although Alençon was occasionally allowed to attend meetings of the council, the queen mother moved both princes from Vincennes to her quarters in the Louvre where she could keep a closer watch on them.[3] With the help of the chancellor, René de Birague, she managed to keep a tight rein on the government until Henry III's return.

Catherine hoped that Alençon's new position as heir presumptive might bring him closer to his brother Henry, and possibly deter him from any future dealings with the Huguenots. In June she twice wrote to La Mothe-Fénelon, urging him to impress upon Burghley and Elizabeth that Alençon fully supported the new king.[4] She wanted to continue the friendship with the English queen, but she also wanted it understood that Alençon was no longer to be considered as a ringleader of any malcontent plot in which Elizabeth might want to become involved. Catherine doubtless still hoped that the marriage between Elizabeth and Alençon would take place, but it is difficult to tell how seriously she viewed the match, in the light of the duke's recent involvement in the conspiracies at

---

[1] For Henry's itinerary, see Henry III, *Lettres*, vol. I, pp. 357–77.
[2] Catherine de Medici, *Lettres*, vol. V, p. 5, 3 June 1574.
[3] *CSPF*, vol. X, pp. 512–13, Dale to Burghley, Walsingham and Smith; and Killigrew to Burghley, 7 and 10 June 1574.
[4] Catherine de Medici, *Lettres*, vol. V, pp. 17 and 23, Catherine to La Mothe-Fénelon, 13 and 18 June 1574.

court. Moreover, Elizabeth had procrastinated for so long over the marriage that Catherine had grown rather irritated. 'If she really wants a marriage with my son, the duke of Alençon', she wrote to La Mothe-Fénelon in July, 'then it is about time she made up her mind'.[5]

By the end of the summer, Henry III had decided to return to France to accept his new crown. Although she still had fears that Alençon and Navarre might try to escape, Catherine was determined that they and the rest of the court would go to Lyon to meet Henry. They departed from Paris on 8 August, and Catherine kept both princes in her own carriage for the duration of the journey. 'Her chickens go in coach under her wing', noted the English resident ambassador, Dr Valentine Dale.[6] Henry made his belated entry on 6 September, and one of his first acts was a public show of amity with Alençon and Navarre. On the advice of the queen mother (but against the advice of Birague, the chancellor) Henry granted them the right to come and go as they pleased. Both princes were still closely watched, however.[7]

The king who returned to France in the autumn of 1574 was a changed man, and according to De Thou most Frenchmen were disappointed with him:

It was no longer possible to find in this prince those qualities which had elevated him above the rest, that is to say, his military prowess and warrior courage which was so much admired. Now he never gets on a horse or shows himself to his people as his predecessors have always done ... Ostentation and laxity have replaced the grandeur and majesty which previously distinguished our kings, together with an unfortunate penchant for frivolous living.[8]

His reign would be a troubled one.

The court remained near Lyon for several months after the arrival of Henry III in the autumn of 1574, as the duke of Alençon and the king of Navarre continued to be closely watched. Events elsewhere, however, significantly affected the future of both princes. On 13 November 1574, Henri de Montmorency, seigneur de Damville, issued a proclamation affirming his loyalty to the new king, at the same time listing several grievances against the king's government. Damville had concluded a military alliance with the Protestants of the Midi in April 1574, and in many ways this proclamation voiced the complaints of the Huguenots.[9] Primarily, Damville spoke out against the numerous foreigners who held influential positions in the king's government, and who used their offices to tax the people with new subsidies and imposts. Damville mentioned Birague and marshal de Retz – both Italians – by name.

---

[5] Ibid, p. 50, Catherine to La Mothe-Fénelon, 5 July 1574.
[6] *CSPF*, vol. x, p. 538, Dale to Walsingham, 9 August 1574.
[7] BN, MSS ital. 1728, fols. 397–8, 17 September 1574.
[8] De Thou, *Histoire universelle*, vol. v, p. 101.
[9] BN, MSS n.a. fr. 23488, fols. 111–15, 'Articles de ceux de la religion prethendue reformee assembles a Millaud en avril 1574 presentes au Marechal Damville pour l'associer avec eux'.

Moreover, he believed that these foreigners were fomenting civil strife in France 'under the pretext of religion'. He vowed 'to take up arms against these oppressors and disturbers of the public peace', and sought aid from 'all kings, princes, potentates throughout Christendom'. Furthermore, Damville pleaded for at least limited liberty of conscience, and called for a general church council to settle the religious differences and for the convocation of the Estates-General to enforce such a settlement.[10] An assembly of Protestants and Catholics met at Nîmes the following month, where it was decided to offer political allegiance to the Catholic Damville. He accepted their offer on 12 January 1575 and the assembly drew up a new – and novel – constitution for the province of Languedoc. Now Henry's and Catherine de Medici's worst fears had been realized as Damville vowed 'to take up arms'. This coalition of Catholics and Protestants in Languedoc was a 'state within a state'.[11]

While Damville was negotiating with the Protestants of Languedoc, the prince of Condé spent the winter of 1574–5 in Heidelberg bartering with John Casimir, the youngest son of Elector Frederick III of the Rhenish Palatinate. The Protestant Casimir had befriended Condé as early as 1567, when he offered money and troops to assist Coligny, and in late 1574 he considered aiding the French Protestants once again.[12] Although Frederick III favored cautious diplomacy rather than direct military intervention in France, he did give Casimir 176,735 florins between 1574 and 1576 to recruit mercenaries for Condé.[13] And it should not be forgotten that Frederick also supported his eldest son, Count Christopher, who accompanied Louis of Nassau to Blamont in December 1573 in that curious meeting with Catherine de Medici and the duke of Alençon. In return for their financial and military support, Frederick and Casimir wanted control of the bishoprics of Metz, Toul, and Verdun, occupied by France since 1552. Though Condé could hardly deliver that prize, he promised Casimir just compensation. And, Condé, to strengthen his hand, sent deputies to England to see if Elizabeth would provide any further financial assistance for the French Protestants. The project interested her, and in February 1575 she sent an agent to Heidelberg to discuss the situation with the Elector.[14] This deputy, Thomas Wilkes, was the same agent implicated in Alençon's escapades at court the previous spring. Although Elizabeth would not

---

10 BN, MSS fr. 3239, fols. 69–78, Declaration of Damville, Montpellier, 13 November 1574. For the significance of this document, see the excellent discussion in Janine Garrisson-Estèbe, *Protestants du Midi, 1559–1598* (Toulouse, 1980), pp. 190–1.

11 Garrisson-Estèbe, *Protestants du Midi*, pp. 191–3. Some excerpts from the new constitution are printed (in French) in Gordon Griffiths (ed.), *Representative Government in Western Europe in the Sixteenth Century* (Oxford, 1968), pp. 285–6. Constitutionally, the document was novel in calling for regular meetings (at least once a year) of the provincial estates of Languedoc, with representation of the third estate in twice the numbers allocated to the nobility.

12 Bernard Vogler, 'Le rôle des électeurs palatins dans les guerres de religion en France (1559–1592)', *Cahiers d'histoire*, X (1965), 59.

13 Ibid., pp. 65–7.   14 *CSPF*, vol. XI, p. 15, Instructions to Thomas Wilkes, 16 February 1575.

commit herself to a formal treaty, she did send Frederick 50,000 thalers to assist the French Protestants.[15]

The threat of an alliance between the German princes, Elizabeth, and the French Protestants was not to be taken lightly. It is unclear, however, to what end this Protestant alliance intended to use its military strength in France. At the very least, Frederick, Elizabeth, and Condé hoped to persuade Henry III to grant complete liberty of conscience to his Protestant subjects.[16] It is doubtful whether they considered a direct attack on the new French king, however. It is more likely that they hoped to make their alliance more legitimate by securing the support of a prince of the blood. This Protestant force, with Alençon or Navarre at its head, could then exterminate the Guises, make peace in France, and ultimately drive out the Spanish from the Netherlands. Indeed, there is evidence that the prince of Condé attempted to arrange Alençon's escape from court in early 1575 for this very purpose.[17] Whatever their intentions, Henry III and Catherine de Medici were acutely aware of the danger posed by a large Protestant army on the French frontier.[18] Combined with the hostility toward the government in Languedoc, the forces of Casimir and Condé remained a serious obstacle to peace in France.

While these negotiations were being conducted in nearby Languedoc and Heidelberg, the French court remained in Lyon. In January 1575 the court moved northward to Rheims, where Henry III awaited his traditional coronation. It is difficult to assess how much the duke of Alençon knew of the activities of Damville, Frederick, Casimir, and Condé during that winter, but he was apparently aware of their alliance and of their intention to include him in their plans.[19] His relationship with the Protestants was complicated, however, by the growing enmity that he had developed towards Henry of Navarre. By the time of the king's coronation at Rheims on 13 February 1575, this mutual hostility had become the talk of the court. 'The jealousy of the Duke and the King of Navarre is not yet quenched', noted the English ambassador, Dr Dale, 'and the King would not suffer them to lie in any house but where he lay'.[20] The months of imprisonment together at court had taken its toll. And this personal animosity was no doubt exacerbated by their mutual jealousy over the favors of Charlotte

[15] Vogler, 'Le rôle des électeurs palatins', pp. 65–6; and Read, *Mr Secretary Walsingham*, vol. I, pp. 289–91.

[16] See the letter Frederick III wrote to Henry III on 27 November 1574: 'You have granted them [the Huguenots] nothing as yet, since you have no power over their souls. That is reserved for God alone.' August Kluckhohn (ed.), *Briefe Friedrichs des Frommen, Kurfürsten von der Pfalz* (2 vols., Brunswick, 1868–72), vol. 2, p. 761.

[17] BN, MSS ital. 1728, fol. 522, Morosini to the Signory, 11 January 1575.

[18] See BN, MSS fr. 3388, fol. 7, Henry III to Jacques Viart, 9 January 1575; and L'Estoile, *Journal*, vol. I, pp. 32–3, 53.

[19] *CSPF*, vol. XI, pp. 9–10, [Dale to Burghley], 28 January 1575.

[20] Ibid., p. 13, Dale to Walsingham, 13 February 1575.

de Beaune, madame de Sauve.[21] By June matters had become so heated that John Willes, an English agent in Paris, reported that 'the quarrel between the King of Navarre and the Duke is greater than ever it was, so that one of these days they will cut the throats one of the other'.[22] Thus, whatever the plans of the Protestant alliance to free Alençon from court, there was no mutual conspiracy involving the duke and Navarre. By the summer of 1575 they were so alienated that a mutual escape attempt like that of the spring of 1574 was out of the question. The Venetian ambassador noted in June that 'the hatred between these two princes has reached the breaking point'. They eventually came to blows.[23]

In addition to the bickering of the princes of the blood, the capital of Paris was marked by disturbances outside the court in the summer of 1575. In early July one of the students at the university of Paris was murdered, for reasons unknown, by an anonymous Italian living in the capital. The incident touched off riots and demonstrations in the Latin quarter as the students vowed to avenge the death of their colleague. Within days there was bloodshed. On 6 July the English agent Willes wrote that the students were prepared to kill every Italian in Paris, and that 'they have hurt already three or four'.[24] Before long a mob of 1,500 to 2,000 scholars soon spread the violence to the right bank.[25] The outrage directed towards the Italians in Paris quickly became politicized, as various pamphlets and placards appeared criticizing the Italians in the king's government. Some, like Chancellor Birague, were singled out for special abuse:[26]

> Benefices and gifts, estates and pensions
> Go only to those who by inventions
> Of new taxes and imposts impoverish our France.
> The Italian is especially expert in this art;
> Of all the profits, he gets the largest part;
> We can see with our own eyes that they are ruining France.[27]

---

21 Buisseret and Barbiche (eds.), *Les œconomies royales de Sully*, vol. I, p. 93; and *CSPF*, vol. XI, p. 30, Dale to Burghley, 18 March 1575.

22 *CSPF*, vol. XI, p. 70, John Willes and Dale to Walsingham, both 13 June 1575.

23 BN, MSS ital. 1729, fols. 110–11 and 159, Morosini to the Signory, 1 June and 27 July 1575.

24 *CSPF*, vol. XI, pp. 78, 81, Dale to Burghley and Willes to Walsingham, 3 and 6 July 1575.

25 For estimates on the size of this mob see ibid., pp. 81, 187.

26 A number of Italians who came to France with Catherine de Medici resided at court: the chancellor, René de Birague; Albert de Gondi, count de Retz, who was a marshal of France; Louis de Gonzaga, duke of Nevers, one of the peers of the realm; and a number of bankers such as Ludovico Diacete, Scipione Sardini and Sebastiano Zamette, who had loaned huge sums to the crown throughout the religious wars. They all became the target of anti-Italian sentiment in Paris in July 1575. See Lionello Sozzi, 'La polémique anti-italienne en France au XVIe siècle', *Accademia della scienze di Torino atti*, CVI (1972), 99–190; Myriam Yardeni, 'Antagonismes nationaux et propagande durant les guerres de religion', *Revue d'histoire moderne et contemporaine*, XIII (1966), pp. 273–84; and the wealth of material collected by Pierre de l'Estoile in L.-R. Lefèvre (ed.), *Journal pour le règne de Henri III, 1574–1589* (Paris, 1943), pp. 90–103.

27 Lefèvre (ed.), *Journal pour le règne de Henri III*, p. 90.

Although Birague had been the target of Protestant abuse ever since the massacres of 1572, this bit of doggerel recorded by the Parisian Catholic, Pierre de l'Estoile, is a clear indication of the deep-rooted anti-Italian sentiment that was present in France throughout the Wars of Religion and shared by Huguenot and Catholic alike. Because of a student's murder in 1575, however, this antipathy became focused on the Italians in the government, who were seen to be working in their own interests rather than for the crown and the French nation. The duke of Alençon, disenchanted with his position at court, attempted to use this outburst of anti-Italian propaganda to focus attention on the king's enemies. In this way he hoped to attract support for his own designs, which ultimately involved another escape from court.[28]

By the end of the summer Alençon's fortunes had reached a nadir. He had completely fallen out with his brother Henry, who (like Charles before him) refused to give him the office of lieutenant-general. He was no longer on speaking terms with Navarre. And his hatred of the Guises was further inflamed by the fact that many of their agents were Italians who held offices in the government. For these and perhaps other reasons, Alençon decided to make another attempt to escape in September 1575, this time alone. By early September the entire court was buzzing with rumors of an escape, and Henry and Catherine claimed to have indisputable evidence of it. On 10 September the king arrested three of Alençon's servants, one by the name of Rémy, because he believed that they were preparing to seize a bridge over the Seine at Mantes, just west of Paris, to provide a route of escape for their master.[29] Henry also had reason to believe that the English ambassador might try to aid the duke's flight as in 1574. As a result, he ordered Dale to move his lodgings from St-Germain-en-Laye to somewhere inside the city walls of the capital, allegedly for his own security.[30]

To almost no-one's surprise, Alençon quietly slipped out of Paris at six o'clock in the evening on 15 September.[31] The king immediately assumed the worst – that his younger brother had fled in order to join the Huguenot forces of Condé and Casimir. That same evening he informed the nobility at court of Alençon's escape and read them a letter the duke had left behind, pledging complete obedience to the crown.[32] Henry then made a stirring plea to the nobles gathered there to help him retrieve the fugitive prince as soon as possible.

---

[28] The lengthy despatch of the Venetian ambassador of 5 July gives a complete account of the incident and its aftermath. Morosini went on to say that the murder led to rumors that Birague was unfit for office, although 'tutto che sto rumore era inventione de Mons[igno]r il Duca di Alanson'. BN, MSS ital. 1729, fols. 138–41, Morosini to the Signory, 5 July 1575.

[29] BN, MSS ital. 1729, fols. 221–3, Morosini to the Signory, 11 September 1575.

[30] BN, MSS ital. 1729, fol. 225, Morosini to the Signory, 15 September 1575.

[31] Full details of Alençon's escape can be found in BN, MSS ital. 1729, fols. 238–40, Morosini to the Signory, 16 September 1575 (calendared in *CSPV*, vol. VII, pp. 537–8).

[32] This is almost certainly the letter in BN, MSS fr. 3958, fols. 113–15, Alençon to Henry, September 1575. For Henry's comments to the nobility see Henry III, *Lettres*, vol. II, pp. 240–1.

Most of the nobility remained aloof, however, not wanting to choose sides in what they considered essentially a family dispute. Moreover, as the Venetian ambassador pointed out, there was no guarantee that supporting the king in this quarrel would ultimately be in their best interests.

It is now said that His Highness [the duke of Alençon] has as much as a thousand cavalry with him, or a little less, and more are flocking to him all the time from all parts. This does not bode well for His Majesty [the king], because the major part of the nobility of the realm cannot decide what course to take. Those who take up arms against Monsieur [Alençon], to be sure, will be worse off than those who support him after a settlement is reached, for His Highness will always hold it against them. By contrast, His Majesty will be forced to pardon all those who have demonstrated against him.[33]

Thus, despite the king's appeal, the French nobility were in no hurry to go after Alençon.[34] As a result Henry was forced to appoint a special force under the command of Louis de Gonzaga, duke of Nevers, whose mission was to bring Alençon back to court. Nevers's appointment was met by howls of laughter at court, for he had been nicknamed *le boiteux* ever since he was wounded fighting against the Spanish some twenty years earlier. The limping duke accepted the king's appointment nevertheless, and stoically responded to the derision at court with one of his Italian proverbs: *che va piano va lontano*.[35]

Alençon's flight from court on the evening of 15 September 1575 was surprisingly well planned. As a precaution he arranged for forty or fifty men, all armed and mounted, to meet him outside the gates of Paris to escort him to St-Léger, near Montfort-l'Amaury. He dined there, and then made camp for the night concealed in the forests of Rambouillet. The following morning Alençon and his small band broke camp and headed for Dreux, a small town in his *apanage* about forty miles west of Paris.[36] Upon his arrival he sent a messenger, the sieur de Sourdis, to his mother to inform her of his movements and to assure her of his loyalty to the king. This letter is 'all the proof that you need', he wrote, 'of the affection that I have to serve you and the king'.[37] Most of Alençon's household managed to join him in Dreux within a few days. Thus, the quest to escape from court which had lasted eighteen months finally resulted in success. Although one can only speculate about his true motives for leaving the court, it seems that the political situation there, especially since the return of Henry III, made the coexistence of Alençon, Navarre, and the Guises impos-

---

33 BN, MSS ital. 1729, fol. 255, Morosini to the Signory, 23 September 1575.
34 Henry also wrote to the provincial governors asking for their support. Henry III, *Lettres*, vol. II, pp. 243–4, 16 September 1575.
35 Catherine de Medici, *Lettres*, vol. v, pp. 135–6, Nevers to Henry III, 16 September 1575; and Kervijn de Lettenhove, *Huguenots*, vol. III, p. 550.
36 L'Estoile, *Journal*, vol. I, p. 88.
37 Catherine de Medici, *Lettres*, vol. v, p. 138, Alençon to Catherine, 17 September 1575. See also the undated letter in BN, MSS fr. 6623, fol. 67, Alençon to Catherine.

sible. And as Jacques-Auguste de Thou noted, the beckoning call from Condé and Casimir was too tempting to ignore:

His plan was to place himself at the head of the army on its way from Germany, which he hoped the prince of Condé would allow him to do without any complication. And under the pretext of the public good he intended to advance his own affairs and to obtain a more important position in the state from the king his brother.[38]

II

Upon his arrival in Dreux on 16 September, the duke of Alençon and his confederates immediately began trying to rally support among the local popu- lace. This took the form of an appeal for funds and troops. As was customary among princes of the blood, Alençon issued this appeal in the form of a public declaration, which outlined the ills that afflicted France and suggested some necessary remedies. Issued on 18 September at Dreux, Alençon's declaration purported to be based on the preservation of the ancient laws of the kingdom, 'as they all are', according to the cynical Pierre de l'Estoile.[39] Beginning with the phrase 'the conservation of all kingdoms and domains depends on the observa- tion of the laws', Alençon's declaration does resemble a number of others issued during the fifteenth and sixteenth centuries to attack specific policies of the crown without directly assaulting the king. In particular, there are striking similarities between Alençon's declaration and the one issued by Damville at Montpellier in November 1574. Both urged the removal from court of all foreigners such as the Gondi, Gonzaga and Birague families, as well as the Guises (who were considered foreigners from Lorraine), because they had managed to acquire some of the highest offices in the kingdom. Both also called for a general religious peace until a church council could settle the religious differences, and for the convocation of the Estates-General in order to establish law and order in the kingdom. None of these proposals was novel or particularly revolutionary. Thus, Alençon's declaration at Dreux on 18 September repre- sented a traditional way for a prince of the blood to criticize royal policy.

'The conservation of all kingdoms and domains', Alençon declared, 'depends on the observation of the laws, and by this means peace is maintained among the subjects'.[40] When laws were not enforced, however, kingdoms often fell into ruin and civil war. It was then left to the remedy of God, 'who raises up when it pleases Him, heroic and worthy persons to oppose the tyranny of those who only seek to render all things in disorder'. Alençon further deplored the monopoly

---

[38] De Thou, *Histoire universelle*, vol. v, p. 216.   [39] L'Estoile, *Journal*, vol. I, p. 88.

[40] This declaration, signed by Alençon and dated 17 September 1575 (presumably when it was written), is in BN, MSS fr. 3342, fols. 5–6. The declaration was published the following year as an introduction to the anonymously written pamphlet (actually written by the Protestant Innocent Gentillet), *Brieve remonstrance à la noblesse de France sur le parct de la declaration de Monseigneur le duc d'Alençon* (Paris, 1576).

that these enemies of the crown held on the royal fiscal system, which had resulted in new

taxes, imposts, and subsidies which they invent every day and levy on the poor people, the nobility, and the clergy, all in the name of the king and under the pretext of his service. So much of this profit tends to enrich only a very few persons, nearly all foreigners, who have monopolized the king and the principal offices and governments of the kingdom.

Moreover, Alençon claimed to be responding to those who had sought his help, presumably the Protestant army led by Condé and Casimir:

Seeing this wound grow worse day by day and our own person treated more unworthily than ever, and with so many princes, nobles, clergymen, citizens, and bourgeoisie with their eyes fixed upon us, imploring us to join hands and help them ... we have resolved, without any concern for our own safety, to try to escape from our captivity and to take the public cause in hand, and to oppose the pernicious plans and designs of the enemies of this kingdom.

Furthermore, Alençon was quick to point out that his actions should not be misinterpreted:

We declare that it is our will and intention not to do anything that would undermine the authority of the king our lord and brother, which we desire to increase with all our might. Thus, we are only using our forces ... to chase out the disturbers of the public peace, in order to seek justice for all of the plundering, thefts, murders, and massacres that have been so inhumanely and unlawfully committed and perpetrated in broad daylight.

Like Damville two years earlier, Alençon hoped 'to restore this kingdom to its former splendor, glory, and liberty by a general and free assembly of the three estates of this kingdom, convoked in a secure and free place from which all foreigners would be excluded'. Finally, to ameliorate the religious conflict Alençon professed hope that a church council or the Estates-General would find a lasting solution. Until then, however, he advocated religious toleration to prevent further bloodshed:

To remove all obstacles and to reunite the hearts of all native Frenchmen, we have taken and do take unto our protection and safekeeping everyone, those of one as well as the other religion, praying and exhorting them in the name of God to treat one another as brothers, kinsmen, neighbors, and fellow countrymen.

He sought the support of all princes, lords, nobles, bourgeoisie, towns, communities, and any other subjects of the crown in the 'execution of our so holy enterprise'.[41]

Although Alençon's declaration was couched in tones of support and service to the king, and although he attacked the king's advisors (notably Retz, Nevers, Birague, and above all the Guises) rather than the king himself, there was no

---

[41] BN, MSS fr. 3342, fols. 5–6, Declaration of Alençon, Dreux, 17 September 1575.

53

mistaking his intentions. His support for religious toleration, even on a limited scale, firmly tied him to the cause of the French Protestants. Thus, he unintentionally allied himself with Huguenot resistance theory, which had opposed royal authority ever since St Bartholomew's Day. And there is no doubt that the French Protestants were already advocating theories of resistance by 1575. François Hotman's *Francogallia* (Geneva, 1573) and Theodore Beza's *Du Droit des magistrats sur les sujets* (Heidelberg, 1574), both strong arguments of resistance, had already been published. Moreover, Alençon's declaration made it very clear that he was seeking military and financial support from every quarter; he could hardly have made a more pointed approach to the Huguenots. Therefore, his escape from court and subsequent declaration at Dreux in September 1575 placed the civil wars once more on a knife edge. Were he to go over to the Huguenots and side with Condé and Casimir – and he was clearly in contact with them – the crown itself might be in jeopardy. It was this dangerous situation which prompted the Venetian ambassador's forecast that Alençon's flight from court would lead to 'the complete ruin of this miserable kingdom'.[42]

Having issued his declaration on 18 September, the duke of Alençon set about organizing what few troops he had managed to muster. It is difficult to assess how many men rallied to his call, though most estimates are probably too high. It is unlikely that he had more than 1,000 armed and mounted troops, and even this number is uncertain.[43] In any case, Alençon was in a fairly strong position at Dreux, where he claimed for himself the title of 'The king's governor-general and protector of liberty and the public good of France'.[44] In the first communication to the king since his departure, Alençon assured Henry that all his forces were loyal to the crown.[45] The king was doubtless not convinced.

The duke of Nevers was faced with the daunting prospect of a military confrontation with Alençon if he could not be persuaded to return to court voluntarily. It soon became apparent, however, that the small number of troops the king had assigned to Nevers was no match for Alençon's armed cavalry at Dreux. On 19 September Nevers wrote to Catherine de Medici explaining his predicament, and on the following day he informed Henry III that his mission was impossible without more troops.[46] Moreover, it was reported that many of

---

[42] BN, MSS ital. 1729, fol. 238, Morosini to the Signory, 16 September 1575. For proof that Alençon was in contact with the Protestants after his escape from court, see BN, MSS Dupuy 844, fols. 274–5, La Noue to Alençon, 28 September 1575; and BN, MSS Dupuy 844, fols. 276–7, 'Instruction de Monsieur filz de France unicque du Roy au seigneur de Montagnac gentilhomme ordinaire de sa chambre envoie de sa part vers le roy de navarre et monseigneur le prince de conde', September 1575.
[43] See BN, MSS ital. 1729, fols. 250–1, Morosini to the Signory, 19 September 1575; and *CSPF*, vol. XI, p. 144, Dale to Burghley, 28 September 1575.
[44] *CSPF*, vol. XI, p. 141, Dale to Smith and Walsingham, 21 September 1575.
[45] BN, MSS fr. 6623, fol. 137, Alençon to Henry III, 20 September 1575.
[46] Catherine de Medici, *Lettres*, vol. V, p. 136n.

Nevers's men had abandoned him and taken flight to Dreux to join Alençon.[47] Nevers feared that, unless Alençon were induced to return to court, the future of the Valois dynasty might be in jeopardy. 'The safety of the state depends on the union of the royal family', he wrote to the duke of Montpensier. And if Alençon were to befriend the enemies of the crown, he lamented, 'we are going to fall into real trouble'.[48]

Henry III was also aware of the seriousness of the situation. In order not to alienate his brother further, he sent Alençon all of the latter's gold plate, jewels, apparel, and household goods and allowed the remaining members of his household to join him at Dreux. Moreover, fearing the consequences at home and abroad, Henry specifically refused to declare his brother an enemy of the crown.[49] To have done so would have been an open invitation to the German Protestants, Queen Elizabeth, William of Orange, and perhaps even Philip II to try to lure Alençon into their respective camps. With Nevers unable to bring him back to court, Henry turned to the queen mother. Catherine accepted her responsibility enthusiastically and immediately left Paris to go after her youngest son.

While the queen mother made her way from the capital towards Dreux, however, the duke of Alençon was making preparations to leave. When he heard that his mother was on her way there to see him, he despatched a messenger to explain to her that he was vacating the town 'due to urgent affairs which force me to depart tomorrow with my troops'.[50] By this time word had reached the court that Alençon was leaving Dreux in order to establish a position somewhere on the Loire, and it was rumored that his men had already captured Le Mans.[51] It is impossible to determine Alençon's precise motives for abandoning Dreux. Most probably, he had far fewer men and funds than he pretended. Possibly, he may have feared the retaliation of the duke of Nevers. Or he may have had thoughts of joining the *reîtres* (German mercenaries) of Casimir and Condé. In any case, a fortified position on the Loire would have been a distinct advantage whatever his motives. Catherine de Medici was aware, moreover, of Alençon's anxiety. In order to give herself time to achieve a settlement with him, she asked the king to stop Nevers and his troops from encroaching any further. Thus, on 24 September Henry ordered Nevers not to advance any closer than Chartres while the queen mother and the duke of Alençon were negotiating.[52]

Perhaps thinking that he was being lured into a trap, Alençon was hesitant to meet with his mother. He did not leave Dreux on 24 September as planned, but

47 *CSPF*, vol. XI, p. 141, Dale to Smith and Walsingham, 21 September 1575.
48 Nevers, *Mémoires*, vol. I, p. 85, Nevers to Montpensier, 21 September 1575.
49 *CSPF*, vol. XI, p. 140–1, Dale to Burghley and Smith, both 21 September 1575.
50 BN, MSS fr. 6623, fols. 77–9, Alençon to Catherine, both 23 September 1575.
51 Henry III, *Lettres*, vol. II, p. 254, Henry to Rambouillet, 24 September 1575.
52 Ibid., p. 253, Henry to Nevers, 24 September 1575.

remained there another two days while he decided what to do.[53] Finally, on the 26th he had a change of heart and agreed to meet his mother, travelling directly southward to Cloyes, and eventually reaching the Loire on the 28th. By this time he had already made several requests to his mother, among them the release from prison of two of his followers who had been arrested on 10 September.[54] Alençon had his first interview with Catherine on 28 September in the château at Chambord, just upstream from Blois. At that meeting he insisted that he could not continue the negotiations unless his own supporters and the two marshals – Montmorency and Cossé – were released from prison.[55] Sensing the urgency of the situation, Catherine reported back to the king that very night the demands that Alençon had put to her, and she urged him to accept them and make peace.[56] Apparently the prudence of his mother's advice struck home, for Henry released Montmorency and Cossé on 2 October. He had been holding the elder Montmorency in an effort to exert pressure on the latter's younger brothers, Thoré and Damville, who were negotiating with Condé to bring German troops into France.[57] Placating the duke of Alençon took priority, however. Above all, Henry and Catherine hoped to keep him isolated from Condé and the German *reîtres*. Thus, the king despatched secretary Villeroy to Chambord to inform Alençon that his supporters and the two marshals had been freed. Moreover, Henry granted him the city of Blois as a fortified town.[58]

III

While Henry III and Catherine de Medici attempted to make peace with the duke of Alençon in October 1575, the latter's escape from the court the previous month had already begun to cause consternation abroad. Daniel Rogers, an English agent in the Netherlands, surmised that, because of Alençon's flight, 'the Prince [of Orange] alltogether is bent towards France and persuadeth

---

53 Pierre de l'Estoile was mistaken in reporting that Alençon left Dreux on the 23rd (L'Estoile, *Journal*, vol. I, p. 89). He wrote to the queen mother from Dreux on the 24th and the 25th to express 'le regret que iay daytre parti sans avoir set honneur de vous voir' (BN, MSS fr. 6623, fols. 83–5, Alençon to Catherine, 24 and 25 September 1575).

54 BN, MSS fr. 6623, fols. 67 and 88, Alençon to Catherine de Medici, [26] and 27 September 1575. The two followers in question were the sieur de la Beause and the sieur de St-Rémy. Although the first of these letters is undated, it is clear from the contents when it was written. Also see Henry III, *Lettres*, vol. II, p. 259, Henry to the count de Lude, 28 September 1575.

55 Desjardins, vol. IV, pp. 44–8, Alamanni to the Grand Duke, November 1575; and L'Estoile, *Journal*, vol. I, p. 90.

56 Catherine de Medici, *Lettres*, vol. V, p. 142, Catherine to Henry, 28 September 1575; and BN, MSS ital. 1729, fols. 272–5, Morosini to the Signory, 3 October 1575.

57 Catherine de Medici, *Lettres*, vol. V, p. 146, Catherine to Damville, 2 October 1575; L'Estoile, *Journal*, vol. I, p. 90; and Davies, 'Languedoc and its *gouverneur*', pp. 208–9.

58 Catherine de Medici, *Lettres*, vol. V, p. 147, Catherine to Henry, 5 October 1575; and Sutherland, *French Secretaries of State*, pp. 192–3.

himselfe that the next yeare will make a peace in Fraunce, which will alltogether turn into faurayne wars against the Kinge of Spayne'.[59] Indeed, there were many rumors that Alençon had left the court to lead a French army to the Netherlands to support William of Orange.[60] In England Lord Burghley felt that Henry was too occupied with internal matters to offer any assistance to the Dutch himself, though what Alençon was up to was anybody's guess. Elizabeth was not so certain, however. She sent an agent, Robert Corbett, tó the Spanish governor-general in the Netherlands, Don Luis de Requesens, specifically to warn him of the danger from France.[61]

Alençon's escape from court also aroused concern in Heidelberg at the court of the Palatine Elector Frederick III, who was still cautiously awaiting the outcome of events in France. His son Casimir, however, had no such reservation, and had concluded a treaty with Condé the previous month in which he had promised to provide 16,000 troops to invade France in return for 10,000 thalers per month for the duration of the war. Moreover, Condé promised Casimir the governorship of Metz, Toul, and Verdun upon the conclusion of the conflict.[62] It was a high price for the Huguenots to pay for aid, indeed one they could never afford. The German *reîtres*, however, did seem to offer the best chance for a military victory in France.

As long as Henry III still held the marshal de Montmorency prisoner, he could theaten Damville and Thoré with their older brother's execution if the *reîtres* invaded France. With the release of the two marshals on 2 October, however, this threat was removed. Up until then Alençon had made no positive overtures to Casimir and Condé, although he had contacted them. His financial condition was so deplorable, moreover, that it is unlikely he could have participated in any military exercise in any case.[63] Thus, it was without Alençon's direct support that Thoré led a small band of 2,000 German mercenaries across the French border in early October. This was a far cry from the 16,000 men promised by Casimir, but the ageing Elector was not yet ready to commit himself fully to his son's designs.[64] Henry III, unaware that this small force was unsupported by the remainder of the *reîtres*, sent a royal army under the command of Henry, duke of Guise to ward off the expected assault. The resulting confrontation occurred on 10 October near the Marne River between Damery and Dormans. The duke of Guise's army completely routed the Protestant force, which was unconvincingly

---

59 Kervijn de Lettenhove, *Relations*, vol. VII, p. 592, Rogers to Burghley, 9 October 1575.
60 Kervijn de Lettenhove, *Huguenots*, vol. III, p. 553.
61 Kervijn de Lettenhove, *Relations*, vol. VII, pp. 597–8, and VIII, pp. 8–9.
62 Vogler, 'Le rôle des électeurs palatins', pp. 66–7; and De Thou, *Histoire universelle*, vol. V, pp. 217–18.
63 See his letter to Damville pleading for a loan, in BN, MSS fr. 3331, fol. 36, Alençon to Damville, 4 October 1575.
64 Vogler, 'Le rôle des électeurs palatins', pp. 66–7.

led by Thoré. Many were slain or taken prisoner, and the victory was so complete that Guise let most of the defeated go free.[65]

Although the duke of Alençon's motives are difficult to pinpoint, it seems clear that he was sympathetic to the cause of Thoré, Casimir, and Condé. He was obviously worried when he wrote to Catherine de Medici on 10 October.[66] Many of the aims he outlined in his declaration at Dreux were shared by the Huguenots, but joining a foreign army, presumably to attack the king of France, was a grave step. It is impossible to know Alençon's exact intentions, but the evidence indicates that he was ready to cast his lot with the Protestants.[67] His dire financial position, however, rendered him incapable of doing so.

Essentially, Alençon's plans seem to have gone astray. If he had ever had any overall design when he fled court the night of 15 September, it had most likely been to gather support in his *apanage* from the nobility and the Huguenots. Whether this was done in an attempt to end the civil wars (as he claimed at Dreux) or whether it was simply an act of defiance against the king (as seems more likely) is open to speculation. Alençon doubtless hoped to achieve more recognition at court, acknowledgement that he felt rightly belonged to him as presumptive heir. It is also clear that his conflict with the Guises weighed heavily in his decision to escape. But only a month after gaining his freedom, peace was no nearer at hand. Moreover, the war had escalated into an international conflict involving large numbers of foreign troops. Alençon's most pressing problem, however, was money. He was hard pressed to feed and pay his small following, which the king had ordered to retire to Blois during the negotiations with Catherine de Medici. Indeed, the situation became so desperate that Henry had to issue orders to supply Alençon's men with basic foodstuffs.[68] And although Alençon continued to solicit funds from Protestants and Catholics alike, his position remained precarious at best.[69] He was thus hardly

---

[65] L'Estoile, *Journal*, vol. I, p. 91; and *CSPF*, vol. XI, pp. 164–5, Report from France, 27 October 1575.

[66] BN, MSS fr. 6623, fol. 124, Alençon to Catherine de Medici, 10 October 1575.

[67] The most explicit indication is that after the battle of 10 October, Thoré and his remaining troops (about 500 cavalry) headed for Alençon's camp at Vatan, where they joined forces. See BN, MSS ital. 1729, fol. 340, Michiel and Morosini to the Signory, 28 October 1575; and L'Estoile, *Journal*, vol. I, p. 91 (though the latter grossly overestimates the number of forces that accompanied Thoré).

[68] Henry ordered the mayor and magistrates of Chartres to levy the following on their citizens for Alençon's troops: 30 *muids de Paris* of wheat, 30 *muids* of oats, 300 sheep and 50 cows (one *muid de Paris* was the approximate capacity of one wagonload, or about 2,880 pounds in weight) (Henry III, *Lettres*, vol. II, p. 273, 13 October 1575).

[69] Apart from his requests to Damville, Alençon sought financial support from the duke of Nemours, a zealous Catholic, and from François de la Noue and the Protestants of La Rochelle. See BN, MSS fr. 3342, fol. 4, Alençon to Nemours, 13 October 1575; and BN, MSS fr. 20783, fols. 80–1, Instructions from Alençon to La Noue and the magistrates of La Rochelle, 13 October 1575.

in a position to bargain when the king ordered him and the queen mother to come to terms as quickly as possible.[70]

Serious negotiations between Alençon and Catherine began in late October, and they came to terms fairly swiftly. Because of the obvious threat of foreign invasion, Henry and Catherine offered generous terms: Alençon would receive the fortified towns of Angoulême, Niort, Saumur, Bourges, and La Charité; Condé would receive the fortified town Mézières; Alençon would also receive 2,000 foot, 100 *gens d'armes*, 100 arquebusiers, and 50 Swiss guards; and the Protestants would be granted the free exercise of religion in the areas that they currently controlled.[71] Henry still feared a German invasion, however, and he urged Frederick III of the Palatinate to prevent his son Casimir and Condé from crossing the French border with the main body of the *reîtres*.[72] But by this time the Elector had already made up his mind to support the venture and was financing the *reîtres* with considerable sums.[73]

Based on the agreements of 8 November, a formal treaty was signed by Catherine and Alençon on 21 November in the town of Champigny. The agreement went into effect immediately, and was to last until the feast of St John the Baptist (24 June), or just over six months. In addition to the articles agreed upon previously, the treaty stipulated that each of the fortified towns would be provided with troops to enforce its execution: 600 foot for Bourges, 400 foot for Angoulême, 300 foot for Saumur, and 200 foot each for Niort, La Charité, and Mézières. The free exercise of religion was guaranteed in all areas controlled by the Huguenots. And the *reîtres* were to be paid as soon as they retreated back across the Rhine, with the bulk of the payment of 500,000 *livres* to be turned over to Casimir at Strasbourg or Frankfurt. Moreover, the treaty prohibited the presence of any foreign troops in France other than the king's Swiss guards.[74]

Hardly anyone could be sure if the treaty would last the full six months. First of all, it was uncertain whether Henry would or could pay John Casimir 500,000 *livres* to call off his *reîtres*. 'If you think the *reîtres* will go back without their money', remarked one observer to the queen mother, 'they will never do it'.[75] Thus, a stalemate with the German mercenaries appeared likely. Furthermore, some observers, such as the Venetian ambassador, were sure that the treaty

---

70 Henry III, *Lettres*, vol. II, pp. 268–71, Henry to Catherine de Medici and the Swiss cantons, both 8 October 1575.

71 BN, MSS CCC 7, fol. 625, 'Ce qui a este accorde entre la royne mere du roy et Monseigneur', 8 November 1575.

72 Henry III, *Lettres*, vol. II, p. 296, Henry to Frederick III, 10 November 1575.

73 Vogler, 'Le rôle des électeurs palatins', p. 67; and *CSPF*, vol. XI, pp. 184–6, 'The charge of the whole army prepared by Duke Casimir and levied at the Count Palatine's expenses for the use of the Prince of Condé', 20 November 1575.

74 BN, MSS CCC 7, fols. 667–72, 'Articles de la treve accordée entre la reyne mere et le Duc d'Alençon le 21 novembre 1575', signed by both Catherine and Alençon (and printed in Catherine de Medici, *Lettres*, vol. V, pp. 161–5).

75 Catherine de Medici, *Lettres*, vol. V, p. 169, Monsieur de Schomberg to Catherine, 12 December 1575.

would eventually break down because Henry and Catherine had no real concern to guarantee the privileges granted to the Huguenots. They seemed interested only in separating Alençon from Condé, Casimir, and Thoré.[76] To be sure, Henry and Catherine were coerced into the treaty by Alençon's threat to join the *reîtres*. But whether they intended to renege on the treaty once Alençon was safely back at court is just speculation.

The gravest threat to the peace, however, was still the duke of Alençon. After signing the treaty he sent two of his valets to Condé and Casimir to assure them that he would do everything in his power to see that they were paid. And he mildly chastised Henry and Catherine for not giving proper assurances that they meant to enforce the treaty.[77] More seriously, Alençon was still in great financial difficulty. He could not even afford to pay the messengers who delivered his letters to the court.[78] Moreover, he confided to Damville on 6 December that poverty forced him into signing the treaty and prevented him from joining Casimir and Condé:

My cousin, nothing induced me to concede to the treaty but indigence and a lack of money ... There is nothing more necessary at the moment for the benefit of our affairs than to repay the duke Casimir, and the other princes, colonels, and men of war who have placed the German army at our disposal ... The waters here are so low, however, that I could not pay these porters anything. Otherwise, I would not have troubled you with it. I pray you to pay them whatever you think is reasonable.[79]

It is clear, then, that Alençon was still open to offers from Damville, Condé, and Casimir. Indeed, one of the king's privy councillors, Pomponne de Bellièvre, believed that Alençon was secretly allied with them already.[80] The peace treaty thus remained very fragile. Moreover, the popular reaction to Alençon after the treaty of Champigny was mixed. Many towns, especially those in his *apanage*, received him openly, and he had no need to station garrisons in Dreux, Romorantin, Loudun, Thouars, Melle, and Ruffec.[81] Most of the fortified towns granted to him in the treaty, however, refused to admit his troops.[82] Meanwhile, Alençon further fanned the flames of rumor and suspicion by

[76] BN, MSS ital. 1729, fols. 379–81, Morosini to the Signory, 30 November 1575.
[77] BN, MSS CCC 7, fol. 679, Alençon to Catherine, 25 November 1575; and ibid., fol. 683, Alençon to Henry, 25 November 1575.
[78] See the postscript to both letters cited in n. 77 above.
[79] BN, MSS fr. 3205, fol. 85, Alençon to Damville, 6 December 1575: 'il ny a rien qui m'aye aultant induict et meu a condescendre a la tresve que l'indigence et faulte dargent ... quil ny a rien plus roquia aujourdhuy po[ur] le bien de noz affaires que de rendre le duc Cazemir et aultres princes, collonelz et gens de guerre qui ont miz sur larmee dallemaigne po[ur] no[tr]e service ... les eaues sont si bases ysi que ie point fet baller dargent a ces porteurs sinon pour vous aller trouver a ceste cause ie vous prie de leur fayre baller se que connoytres aytre resonnable'.
[80] BN, MSS CCC 8, fol. 20, Bellièvre to the duke of Mayenne, 16 January 1576.
[81] *CSPF*, vol. XI, p. 208, Report from France, 22 December 1575.
[82] BN, MSS ital. 1720, fols. 390–4 and 461–2, Morosini to the Signory, 16 December 1575 and 30 January 1575/6; and BN, MSS CCC 7, fols. 773–4, Bellièvre to Henry III, 30 December 1575.

negotiating anew with Queen Elizabeth and William of Orange. Elizabeth, it was believed, was willing to deal with Alençon and the Huguenots in an effort to recover Calais and Boulogne. As a result the duke despatched an agent, the sieur de la Porte, to England in late November to solicit financial support.[83] At the same time several agents of William of Orange arrived at the French court to discuss mutual support with the king and Alençon. According to the Venetian ambassador, Morosini, Alençon was offered aid if he would later be willing to lead an enterprise in the Netherlands.[84] What became of these negotiations is unknown, but they doubtless added to the international tension. Above all, it was evident that Alençon's position was of crucial importance to the maintenance of peace in France. As Arnaud du Ferrier, French ambassador in Venice, wrote to Henry III in December 1575, many people were worried about

the numerous forces that the prince of Condé is leading into your kingdom, and the little hope that the said prince will change his mind just because of the present treaty. But all thinking men will sufficiently judge that the reconciliation of Monsieur the duke [of Alençon] is more important to the well-being of your affairs than the damage of the coming of the said prince.[85]

Alençon further inflamed an already deteriorating situation in late December when he claimed that Chancellor Birague had attempted to poison him. He and some friends had become ill after drinking a bottle of wine on the night of 26 December. Because the *sommelier* who served the wine, a man named Blondel, had previously worked for Birague, Alençon concluded that the chancellor had arranged to have him poisoned.[86] Enraged, he wrote to the king the next morning demanding an immediate investigation, and significantly, an end to the Italian domination of the crown.[87] No one was able to discover any evidence of poisoning, but many felt that the Italian faction at court, supported by the Guises since the treaty of Champigny, had designs to harass Alençon at every opportunity. Above all, this faction sought to destroy the recent peace agreement. In January 1576, the English ambassador Dale reported 'a secret league between Guise, Nemours, Nevers, Maine and others of that house, together with the chancellor, against all that would have any peace, and if it should be made, to begin a sharp war afresh'.[88] Morosini spread the net even wider. 'The

---

[83] BN, MSS ital. 1729, fol. 385, Morosini to the Signory, 6 December 1575; and *CSPF*, vol. XI, p. 191, Alençon to Burghley, 28 November 1575.

[84] BN, MSS ital. 1729, fols. 399–400, Morosini to the Signory, 19 December 1575.

[85] BN, MSS CCC 367, fols. 105–6, Du Ferrier to Henry III, 25 December 1575.

[86] Details of the alleged poisoning can be found in Desjardins, vol. IV, p. 54, Alamanni to the Grand Duke, 8 January 1576; L'Estoile, *Journal*, vol. I, p. 110; HMC, *Salisbury MSS*, vol. II, p. 126, Alençon to Dale, 27 December 1575; and BN, MSS ital. 1729, fols. 416–18, Morosini to the Signory, 20 January 1575/6.

[87] BN, MSS fr. 6547, fols. 35–7, Alençon to Henry, 27 December 1575. (This letter is calendared but misdated 1576 in *CSPF*, vol. XI, p. 453).

[88] *CSPF*, vol. XI, p. 233, Dale to Smith and Walsingham, 24 January 1576.

cardinals of Guise and Este, the dukes of Nemours, Guise, and Nevers, the chancellor, the marshal de Retz, and Messieurs Morvillier and Cheverny have banded together in a league to accept neither peace nor a treaty.'[89] Here were the roots of the Holy Catholic League which emerged more than six months later.

Alençon's outrage over the suspected poisoning was so intense that he threatened to call in the *reîtres* himself to clear the kingdom of the crown's enemies. In a fiery letter to the *parlement* of Paris on 9 January 1576, he exclaimed that he would only do so 'with the deepest regret and displeasure, being forced to do this by the enemies of the public repose'. Furthermore, he claimed that he would not call in the *reîtres* to destroy the kingdom, 'but to try to straighten out with force the designs of those who, by their ambition and particular passions, seek to ruin the name and house of Valois'.[90] Thus, Alençon threatened what the king and queen mother feared most: an invasion of German *reîtres* with the duke of Alençon at their head. Henry had already sent his councillor, Bellièvre, to Casimir and Condé's camp near Nancy in Lorraine to discover what state of readiness they were in and, indeed, just how much influence Alençon had with the Protestants. Though he managed to get himself captured by Casimir in the process, Bellièvre sent back several detailed reports to the king in early January. The news was not encouraging:

Sire, I enquired of Monsieur de Schomberg [a French agent in Germany] how long it would be before their [the Protestants'] levies could be ready. He told me that within five weeks these enemy *reîtres* will be well inside your kingdom, and it would seem to be most difficult to prevent them from joining forces with Monsieur your brother ... They have promised that the army of Monsieur your brother will join them, and rumors are circulating here that the duke of Lignys is returning to Germany to make another levy of 6000 *reîtres* ... Monsieur the prince [of Condé] has responded that once having gained control of this army, Monsieur your brother has no intention of losing it.[91]

Henry faced a dire situation. The large Protestant army, which had already crossed the Rhine and was perched on the French frontier, consisted of 9,000 German *reîtres*, 8,000 Swiss mercenaries, 2,000 German foot and 1,000 Walloon foot.[92] Moreover, the duke of Alençon appeared to be on the verge of joining them. Things could thus hardly have been more desperate for the king, when an incident at court exacerbated the situation even more. On 5 February 1576 Henry of Navarre followed Alençon's lead and escaped from court, presumably to join the Protestants. 'One can safely say', Morosini exclaimed that same day, 'that the king is now left completely alone, with the princes of the blood and nearly all the French nobility allied with his brother'.[93]

---

[89] BN, MSS ital. 1729, fols. 447–9, 25 January 1575/6.
[90] Nevers, *Mémoires*, vol. I, pp. 107–9, Alençon to the *parlement* of Paris, 9 January 1576.
[91] BN, MSS CCC 8, fols. IV, 7–8, 10, all Bellièvre to Henry III, 1, 4, and 6 January 1576.
[92] Vogler, 'Le rôle des électeurs palatins', p. 67.
[93] BN, MSS ital. 1729, fols. 471–2, 5 February 1575/6.

Navarre fled Paris with thirty or forty men on the afternoon of 5 February 1576. He headed for the town of Alençon in Normandy, where he would be safe in the duke of Alençon's *apanage*. Although Alençon was spending the winter in the town of Charroux in Poitou (where he claimed to be poisoned), Navarre publicly abjured Roman Catholicism and professed the new religion in the duke's *apanage*. Several days later he departed for his home in Béarn.[94] Thus, the most popular and the most powerful of the Protestant princes appeared ready to join forces with Alençon, Condé, Casimir, and the German *reîtres*. More than ever before, according to the Venetian ambassador, Henry had 'to find some way to satisfy his brother, if that was possible, in order to come up with a peace agreement'.[95]

There were some who doubted whether Navarre and Alençon, who were traditionally hostile toward one another, could put aside their differences in order to join forces. 'Though Monsieur and the king of Navarre have been sending various gentlemen back and forth to one another', reported Morosini, 'they have not yet shown any confidence in each other'.[96] Navarre had the acumen to recognize, however, the political benefits of having Alençon in the Protestant camp. It hardly mattered that the duke had insufficient money, troops, and military experience. Moreover, his small band had not yet even joined Navarre or the *reîtres*.[97] His position as the presumptive heir to the throne simply carried too much political clout to ignore. With the combined Protestant armies behind him, Alençon would easily be 'the most powerful prince in Christendom without a royal crown'.[98]

It soon became clear why Henry and Catherine had struggled so hard to prevent Alençon from joining the Protestants. Within a fortnight of Navarre's escape, a delegation of deputies representing Alençon, Navarre, Condé, and Damville arrived at court with a remonstrance which they presented to the king. This remonstrance of ninety-three articles outlined all the Protestant grievances and the requirements for a general peace. The preface to this remonstrance demonstrated the extent to which the Protestants were willing to allow Alençon to represent them:

Sire, for the conservation of your crown and the pacification of so many troubles and divisions which up until now have torn apart and almost ruined this poor kingdom, Monseigneur your brother has taken under his protection all of your poor and afflicted

---

[94] Buisseret and Barbiche (eds.), *Les Œconomies royales de Sully*, vol. I, pp. 34–5; and De Thou, *Histoire universelle*, vol. V, p. 304, n.1.
[95] BN, MSS ital. 1729, fol. 483, Morosini to the Signory, 12 February 1575/6.
[96] BN, MSS ital. 1729, fol. 487, Morosini to the Signory, 21 February 1575/6; and *CSPF*, vol. XI, p. 264, Dale to Burghley, 8 March 1576.
[97] BN, MSS ital. 1729, fol. 528, 21 March 1575/6.
[98] Buisseret and Barbiche (eds.), *Les Œconomies royales de Sully*, vol. I, p. 35.

subjects, as many from one as the other religion, to reunite them together in union and harmony.[99]

The very first of the ninety-three articles was the most significant, demanding 'the free, general, public, and complete exercise of the Reformed religion … without any modification or restriction to time, place, or person'.[100] The remainder of the remonstrance outlined most of the concessions that Protestants had long sought: the creation of the *chambres mi-parties* in the various *parlements* to provide for an equal number of Protestant and Catholic judges, a number of fortified towns, and payment to the *reîtres*. In addition, the princes insisted that some personal benefits should be included in the peace agreement. Alençon, for instance, requested that the duchy of Anjou be added to his apanage. Navarre sought more rights and local privileges for his possessions in Guyenne. And Condé demanded the town and château of Boulogne.[101]

Above all, the princes negotiated from a position of strength. The king was powerless to oppose the combined Protestant forces, estimated by some to number between 30,000 and 50,000 men.[102] And Henry's own financial position was almost as precarious as his brother's, as he was well aware:

The expenses I have for the upkeep of my numerous forces, even the foreign troops, are so excessive that it is very difficult to maintain them. And if God permits me to make peace in this kingdom, for which I am hopeful, I will need still more money, not only to pay the said foreign troops in my service, but also to pay my brother the duke of Alençon and all those led by the duke of Casimir.[103]

Moreover, the 1,200 Swiss guards that Henry hired after the treaty of Champigny had not been paid, and many had begun to desert. The excessive taxation in the capital, necessitated by the hiring of these guards, further alienated the populace, with many *quartiers* of the city simpy refusing to billet the Swiss.[104] Thus, Henry found himself at a distinct disadvantage in his negotiations with the princes.

By the beginning of April, Henry and Catherine had realized that they would have to separate the duke of Alençon from the Protestants if peace were to be

---

[99] BIF, MSS God. 95, fols. 10–28, Remonstrance presented to the king by the deputies of Alençon, Condé, Navarre, and Damville (autographed by Alençon only), 19 February 1576 (quote on fol. 10).

[100] Ibid., fol. 10.

[101] Ibid., fols. 37–8, Articles from Navarre presented to Alençon and Catherine de Medici, 16 March and 2 May 1576; and ibid., fols. 41–3, articles from Condé presented to the king, 31 March 1576. The king awarded him Péronne instead of Boulogne. The names of the deputies who represented the princes are listed in BIF, MSS God. 71, fol. 153. Also see BN, MSS ital. 1729, fols. 505–7, 27 February 1575/6.

[102] Buisseret and Barbiche (eds.), *Les Œconomies royales de Sully*, vol. I, p. 35; and De Thou, *Histoire universelle*, vol. V, p. 307.

[103] BN, MSS CCC 367, fols. 183–5, Henry III to Du Ferrier, 31 March 1576.

[104] Desjardins, vol. IV, p. 55, Alamanni to the Grand Duke, 29 January 1576; and L'Estoile, *Journal*, vol. I, p. 123.

achieved. Alençon and Condé had recently joined forces for the first time at Moulins, where they were meeting with deputies from Navarre and Damville.[105] The bulk of the *reîtres* were camped nearby along the Allier River between Moulins and the confluence of the Allier and the Loire. Casimir preferred to remain there with his troops rather than go to Moulins with the other princes. He was becoming restless, and vowed 'that he would not be delayed any longer by vain treaties'.[106] Meanwhile, Navarre and his forces were camped in Poitou, as he was hesitant to proceed any farther south towards Béarn in such a critical situation. Moreover, if Casimir began marching the combined Protestant army toward Paris, Navarre had plans to cross the Loire at Saumur and join them just outside the capital.[107] Henry and Catherine were in a hopeless situation.

Alençon issued his second declaration since his escape from court on 9 April in Moulins. He claimed that he was forced to take matters into his own hands because of 'evil ministers and officers of this crown ... who have abused the authority of the king our said lord and brother, against the laws and statutes of this kingdom ... We have decided to exploit the means that God has given us to win by force the peace and tranquility that we could not achieve with reason.'[108] This public declaration confirmed once and for all that Alençon was firmly entrenched in the Protestant camp. The only course of action left to Henry and Catherine, it seemed, was capitulation. The very next day the Venetian ambassador reported that the queen mother was making preparations to go visit Alençon in person in order to offer him a *carte blanche*.[109]

Henry and Catherine spent the next two weeks preparing their responses to the princes' ninety-three articles. When most of the accords and concessions had been worked out, the queen mother departed from Paris on 26 April with the king's responses.[110] They had agreed to meet in the town of Etigny near Sens, in a château called Chestenoy. There, during the last week of April and the first week of May, Catherine and the princes agreed to a general edict of pacification. Virtually all of the princes' earlier demands were conceded, as Henry and Catherine were forced to acquiesce.

The only substantial change from the princes' original list of grievances concerned the very first article pertaining to the free exercise of religion: Henry insisted that the Protestants could not worship within ten leagues of Paris.[111]

---

105 Desjardins, vol. IV, p. 58, Alamanni to the Grand Duke, 10 March 1576; *CSPF*, vol. XI, p. 279, Dale to Walsingham, 25 March 1576; and De Thou, *Histoire universelle*, vol. V, pp. 307–8.

106 *CSPF*, vol. XI, pp. 298, 307, Wilkes and Dale to Burghley, 1 and 10 April 1576.

107 Ibid., p. 305, Dale to Burghley, 6 April 1576.

108 BN, MSS Clair. 633, fol. 287, Declaration of the duke of Alençon issued from the Protestant camp near Moulins, 9 April 1576.

109 BN, MSS ital. 1729, fol. 597, 10 April 1576.

110 BN, MSS fr. 3317, fol. 43, Henry to Humières, 20 April 1576.

111 BIF, MSS God. 95, fols. 50–62, 'Responses faites aux articles presentes par les Deputes de M[onsieu]r d'Alençon, signer et ratifier par le Roy', 2 May 1576. The document is signed by Catherine de Medici, the duke of Alençon, Henry of Navarre, the prince of Condé, John

The princes forced the king to compromise even here, however, and it was agreed that Protestants should abstain from the exercise of their religion only within two leagues of the capital. The resulting edict of pacification, officially known as the edict of Beaulieu, was 'read out and made public in a loud voice and public cry' on 6 May in Etigny and Sens in the presence of the queen mother, Alençon, Condé, Casimir, François de Montmorency, and the nobles of the king's council. And a week later, on 14 May, the edict was registered in the *parlement* of Paris.[112] The sixty-three articles of this edict – which came to be known as 'the peace of Monsieur' because to contemporaries it appeared that it had been forced on the king by the duke of Alençon – marked a watershed in the Wars of Religion. The very generous concessions made to the Huguenots precipitated a strong Catholic reaction. Indeed, after May 1576 the radical Catholic faction led by the Guises became a far more serious threat to the crown than the Huguenots had ever been.

The preface of the edict expressed the king's desire to reconcile his subjects 'in a perfect union and concord and to restore them in peace, tranquillity, and repose'. The edict did pay lip service to the French Catholics. Catholicism was to be restored in areas in which it had been abolished by the Huguenots (article 3), Protestants were to observe all Catholic feast days (article 15), and 'in all acts and public actions where the said [Reformed] religion is mentioned, these words will be used: *religion prétendue réformée*' (article 16). In the main, however, the edict was significant because of the concessions granted to those of this 'so-called reformed religion'. For the first time in the course of the French Wars of Religion the Huguenots were accorded the right of 'a free, public, and general exercise of religion'. Thus, theoretically at least, Protestants could worship freely anywhere in France save within two leagues of Paris and the court (article 4). In addition, the Huguenots won the concession to build churches anywhere in France except within two leagues of Paris (article 8). The famous *chambres mi-parties* were to be created in the eight sovereign courts in order to prevent religious discrimination in cases involving litigants of opposing religions (articles 18–21). Moreover, the edict declared it unlawful for Protestants to be taxed unfairly in Catholic districts (article 47), and it stated that all Frenchmen would be treated equally in the fiscal and judicial courts (article 45). Finally, as Damville had requested at Montpellier in 1574 and Alençon at Dreux in 1575, the edict called for the convocation of the Estates-General within six months (article 58). Although these were easily the most liberal concessions granted to

Casimir, and Henry III. (In a postscript, Secretary Villeroy wrote that the king added his signature on 7 May after it was signed by all the others on 2 May.)

[112] Desjardins, vol. IV, p. 67, Alamanni to the Grand Duke, 17 May 1576; and L'Estoile, *Journal*, vol. I, p. 131. There are numerous MSS copies of the edict of pacification, and it is printed in Nevers, *Mémoires*, vol. I, pp. 117–35, and in E. Haag, *La France protestante* (10 vols., Paris, 1846–59), vol. 10, pp. 127–41. A very useful summary of the edict is in Sutherland, *The Huguenot Struggle*, pp. 228–31, 361–2.

the Huguenots during the course of the civil wars, it must be remembered that they were virtually dictated in arms.[113]

The edict of Beaulieu did not grant any personal concessions to the princes who dictated the peace, however. Alençon was mentioned in article 49, but only to exonerate him of any wrongdoing. The specific concessions to Navarre, Condé, Casimir, and Damville, in fact, were outlined separately in a set of 'secret articles'.[114] These articles were not so much secret as deemed inappropriate for public consumption in the published edict. They, more than anything else, provided ample proof that the peace was forced on the king by the princes. As was true of the main edict, the king and queen mother were careful to let Alençon appear to orchestrate these concessions. Condé was given charge of the *gouvernement* of Picardy, a concession that resulted in great dissatisfaction in this overwhelmingly Catholic district.[115] The articles allowed the princes to settle their financial matters in the Protestant courts at Limousin or La Charité if they so wished. As a necessary concession to remedy the salt scarcity, the king allowed Condé and Damville to fulfill any contracts already made in Languedoc, the richest of France's salt-producing districts. Moreover, the king allowed each of the princes to store 500 *muids* of salt in specified *greniers* in Languedoc for his own use. After six months, all salt that was not stored in these *greniers* would be confiscated by the king.[116] Finally, it was in these 'secret articles' that the king was forced to compromise over the issue of how near Paris Protestantism could be practiced, reducing the restriction from ten leagues to two.[117]

By far the largest personal concessions, however, were granted in neither the edict of pacification nor the 'secret articles'. In separate patent letters, Henry granted to his brother Alençon the rich duchies of Anjou, Touraine, and Berry to add to his *apanage*.[118] In addition to the annual revenues that Alençon would receive from these duchies, Henry awarded his brother an annual pension of 100,000 *écus* (or 300,000 *livres tournois*). Finally, the king granted him the right to make all appointments to offices and benefices in his new duchies.[119] The revenues from the supplement to Alençon's *apanage* were indeed consider-

---

[113] Sutherland, *The Huguenot Struggle*, p. 361.

[114] BIF, MSS God. 94, fols. 2–4, 'Articles secrets qui n'ont pas esté compris dans l'Edict de Pacification, arrester a Ettigny pres de Sens entre le Reine catherine, et le Duc d'Alençon ... 6 mai 1576'.

[115] BIF, MSS God. 94, fol. 3v. Condé had requested Boulogne, but Henry was reluctant to give up such a strategic fortification on the Channel.

[116] BIF, MSS God. 94, fols. 3r–4r.

[117] BIF, MSS God. 94, fol. 4v. Many contemporary observers, such as the Protestant Agrippa d'Aubigné, felt that the edict was of little value without the secret articles. See Agrippa d'Aubigné, *Histoire universelle* ed. A. de Ruble (10 vols., Paris, 1886–1909), vol. v, p. 79.

[118] BIF, MSS God. 316, fol. 79, patent letters of Henry III, May 1576.

[119] De Thou, *Histoire universelle*, vol. v, pp. 311–12. More details on the duke's new lands in his *apanage* can be found in BN, MSS fr. 5944, fols. 71–7; MSS fr. 17306, fols. 51–3; and MSS fr. 23089, fols. 132–6.

able.[120] Equally important, however, was the new title of duke of Anjou, the same prestigious title borne by Henry III before he succeeded to the crown in 1574. Henry and Catherine had recognized, albeit belatedly, the necessity of giving Alençon a position of importance at court. This was the principal reason they allowed him to be recognized as the primary negotiator of the peace edict. And the augmentation of his *apanage* was one of the principal concessions. Thus, Alençon – now called Anjou – emerged as the greatest beneficiary of the edict.

The general edict of pacification, however, appeared to be short-lived. Opposition predictably emerged in the *parlement* of Paris on 30 April, when Henry asked the judges to register a tax edict for funds to pay off the *reîtres* and his own Swiss guards. At the prodding of the king the first and third presidents, Christophe de Thou and Pierre Séguier, finally proposed a new tax to cover the costs of the edict. The *parlementaires* and the people of Paris both grumbled loudly. Placards went up all over the capital in outrage.[121] The edict of Beaulieu itself was only registered in the *parlement* of Paris by a *lit de justice*, and the Guises had to be forced to attend and to swear to uphold it.[122] Indeed, the opposition of the Guises was ominous. The English ambassador noted that 'there is much heartburning touching the execution of this peace. The churchmen and the Guises show themselves open enemies to it, and solicit the towns to make resistance, namely, touching the exercise of religion.'[123] But the Guises had a ready-made following, as it was clear that the populace of Paris was opposed to the edict. Led by the clergy, the Parisians demonstrated vehemently against the

---

[120] For some exact figures see Appendix C.   [121] L'Estoile, *Journal*, vol. I, pp. 127–8.

[122] De Thou, *Histoire universelle*, vol. v, p. 311; and *CSPF*, vol. XI, p. 333. Professor Sarah Hanley comments in her very learned book, *The Lit de Justice of the Kings of France: Constitutional Ideology in Legend, Ritual, and Discourse* (Princeton, 1983), that there were no official *lit de justice* assemblies in the *parlement* of Paris during the reign of Henry III, and by implication, that the sessions of 14 May and 7 June 1576 must have been just ordinary royal *séances*. Jacques-Auguste de Thou, whose father was first president at the time, surely must have known the difference, and he called it a *lit de justice* (cited above). Moreover, Pierre de l'Estoile, who was also familiar with judicial procedure, presents what can only be described as a *de facto* assembly of the *lit de justice*, whether or not it was officially listed as such in the registers of *parlement*: 'Monday, 14 May, the king came to the Palais [de Justice] accompanied by the princes of the blood and the officers of the crown, and the edict of pacification was recognized and published in his presence before the court assembled in red robes … On Thursday, the 7th of this month [of June] the king, accompanied by the princes, lords, and members of his council, came [back] to the Palais to sit in his Parlement, and in his presence the edict creating the new chamber called the "mi-partie" established by the edict of pacification was published. This was so odious to the court, that *if the king had not come there in person, it would never have been published.*' (L'Estoile, *Journal*, vol. I, pp. 131–3 (my italics).) If Professor Hanley is correct (and she has examined the registers of *parlement* in much greater detail than I), it would seem that the mere presence of the king in the court threatened a *lit de justice* and was enough to coerce the judges into action, whether or not all of the royal paraphernalia and rituals of the *lit de justice* were used. That certainly seems to be the case with the registration of the edict of pacification and the edict creating the *chambres mi-parties*, and I have followed the example of De Thou and L'Estoile by calling these sessions *lits de justice*.

[123] *CSPF*, vol. XI, pp. 353–4, Dale to Burghley, 28 May 1576.

king after the edict's registration in the *parlement* of Paris on 14 May, and they even refused him entrance to Notre-Dame.[124]

The malcontent princes and their followers signed an agreement to uphold the new edict of pacification on 18 May.[125] Even Casimir seemed ready to withdraw his *reîtres* and return home when Bellièvre was designated to deliver the first instalment of cash to him in mid-June.[126] But peace was no more than an illusion. The opposition to the new edict was not limited to Paris. Some of the fortified towns which were specified in the edict refused to admit Protestant garrisons as they were required. For instance, one of Etienne Pasquier's most celebrated *plaidoyers* as an advocate in the *parlement* of Paris was in defence of the citizens of Angoulême, one of the fortified towns which refused entry to the new duke of Anjou's troops.[127] Moreover, because they were forced into the edict of pacification, Henry III and Catherine de Medici were slow to uphold it. Indeed, it is not clear whether they ever intended to do so. Several months later Catherine openly boasted to the duke of Nevers that she and the king 'had made the peace in order to get back Monsieur, and not to re-establish the Huguenots, as everybody now realizes'.[128] Henry made similar statements.[129] The incongruously named Peace of Monsieur soon led France back into civil war.

---

[124] L'Estoile, *Journal*, vol. I, p. 131.

[125] BIF, MSS God. 95, fol. 74, Declaration to uphold the edict of Beaulieu, 18 May 1576. There are nearly fifty signatures, including those of all the major participants.

[126] BN, MSS fr. 15904, fol. 111, Anjou to Bellièvre, 15 June 1576; BN, MSS CCC 8, fol. 162, Christophe de Harlay to Henry III, 14 June 1576; Raymond Kierstead, *Pomponne de Bellièvre: A Study of the King's Men in the Age of Henry IV* (Evanston, Illinois, 1968), pp. 39–40; and Vogler, 'Le rôle des électeurs palatins', pp. 66–8.

[127] Etienne Pasquier, *Lettres familières* ed. Dorothy Thickett (Geneva, 1974, pp. 66–70).

[128] This is recorded in the private journal of the duke of Nevers during the meeting of the Estates-General at Blois in 1576–7. Lalourcé and Duval (eds.), *Recueil des pièces originales et authentiques concernant la tenue des Etats Généraux* (9 vols., Paris, 1789), vol. III, p. 18.

[129] Henry III, *Lettres*, vol. III, pp. 135–6, Henry to the sieur d'Abain, 15 January 1577.

4

The Estates-General and the renewal of civil war, May 1576–September 1577

I

The demonstrations made in the *parlement* of Paris and in various *quartiers* of the capital against the edict of pacification in May 1576 were symptomatic of popular feeling in most of France. In towns throughout the realm, local magistrates either ignored or refused to implement the edict, with the town of Péronne in Picardy being the most obvious example. There, the Catholic citizens refused to admit the prince of Condé as their governor, as promised in the secret articles. With nowhere else to turn, Condé was forced to remain with John Casimir and his *reîtres* until the king could work out a compromise or find him another *gouvernement*. Casimir himself was understandably reluctant to withdraw his troops from France without full compensation, and he demanded some of Henry's crown jewels and a few French bishops to serve as hostages until the balance that was owed him was paid. The jewels and the hostages were duly delivered to Casimir in June by Bellièvre along with the first instalment of cash.[1] Thus, despite the newly won freedom of worship, many French Protestants were annoyed that the edict was not being enforced in the months immediately following its registration in the *parlement* of Paris.

For the new duke of Anjou, the religious hostility that swelled after May 1576 remained a peripheral issue, as he gloated over his newly-won recognition and wealth. With the added titles of duke of Anjou, duke of Touraine, and duke of Berry, he set out to take possession of his new duchies at once. On 18 June one of the king's commissioners, the sieur de Richelieu, officially placed the new duke of Anjou in possession of the duchy of Anjou. Two of Anjou's agents, the sieurs de Tilley and Saint-Cerval, presented to the mayor of Angers a letter from their master naming Louis de Clermont, sieur de Bussy d'Amboise, as governor of the duchy.[2] Although Bussy did not arrive in Angers to take up his new post until November 1576, it was already clear that the overwhelmingly Catholic population of Anjou was very suspicious of the edict of pacification, its new duke, and

---

[1] BN, MSS ital. 1729, fols. 759 and 791, Morosini to the Signory, 14 June and 12 July 1576.
[2] AC Angers, série BB 35, fol. 42, Anjou to the Mayor of Angers, 15 May 1576. Also see Desjardins, vol. IV, p. 74, Alamanni to the Grand Duke, 26 June 1576; and Mourin, *La Réforme et la Ligue en Anjou*, p. 137.

its new governor. Indeed, Anjou felt it necessary to spell out to Bussy, in a short treatise on justice in the duchy, that the edict of pacification should be maintained in spite of the religious difficulties.[3] When the new governor did arrive in Angers in November with his garrison of rowdy troops, the citizens were hostile, and the relations between the duchy and its new duke and governor became strained. Bussy offended the town with his personal eccentricities, but above all, with the inordinately high taxation which he levied in order to maintain his undisciplined troops. The testimony of Jacques-Auguste de Thou and Agrippa d'Aubigné is sufficient evidence that Bussy was detested by Protestants and Catholics alike. The Catholic De Thou wrote that from the time Anjou appointed him, Bussy 'was hated by the townspeople and the inhabitants of the entire province because of the exactions and imposts that he levied on his own authority'.[4] The Protestant Agrippa d'Aubigné was equally emphatic, noting 'that any good captain would hope that he joined the side of the enemy'.[5] It was not one of Anjou's more judicious appointments, and the citizens of the duchy of Anjou remained hostile until the detested Bussy was assassinated three years later in August 1579.[6]

Anjou had less trouble governing in the duchies of Touraine and Berry, although the edict of pacification proved impossible to enforce. He nominated Charles de Beauvillier, count of Saint-Aignan, as the governor of Berry, and named one of the captains of his personal guard, the sieur de Droux, as the captain of the Grosse Tour of Bourges.[7] The mayor and magistrates of Bourges willingly acceded to the king's orders to turn over the government of the town to Anjou's nominees. Other towns in Berry, however, such as Vierzon, Mehun, Lignières, Selles, Reuilly, Vouillon, and above all La Charité, proved more recalcitrant. All of them refused to contribute to the donation of accession traditionally given to the new duke of Berry. Moreover, the situation in La Charité was especially sensitive, as its Catholics objected to Anjou's appointment of a Huguenot, Jacques de Morogues, sieur de Sauvage, as governor of the town. As the capital of the duchy, Bourges nevertheless put on a festive face for Anjou's 'joyous and triumphant entry' as the new duke of Berry on Sunday, 15

---

[3] BN MSS Clair. 357, fols. 58–9, 'L'Organisation de la justice dans le duchie d'Anjou', written by Anjou in the summer of 1576. Also see AC Angers, série BB 35, fols. 46–7, Anjou to the citizens of Angers, June 1576.

[4] De Thou, *Histoire universelle*, vol. V, p. 614.

[5] D'Aubigné, *Histoire universelle*, vol. VII, p. 193.

[6] Mourin, *La Réforme et la Ligue en Anjou*, pp. 141–5; and François Lebrun, *Histoire d'Angers* (Toulouse, 1975), p. 57. The fullest account of Bussy's career is still André Joubert, *Un Mignon de la cour de Henri III: Louis de Clermont, sieur de Bussy d'Amboise, gouverneur d'Anjou* (Angers and Paris, 1855).

[7] Most of the information in this paragraph comes from the excellent study by the vicomte de Brimont, *Le XVIᵉ Siècle et les guerres de la Réforme en Berry* (2 vols., Paris, 1905), vol. 2, pp. 124–38. Anjou's new appointee as the governor of Berry, Saint-Aignan, was later replaced by Claude de la Châtre, a future marshal of France under Henry IV. See M. F. Deshoulières, *Un gouverneur de la province de Berry: le maréchal de la Châtre, 1536–1614* (2 vols., Bourges, 1906–7).

July 1576. In an effort to erase its reputation of opposing royal authority since the early 1560s, the citizenry of Bourges welcomed the duke with the traditional triumphal arches, festivals, and tapestries associated with a royal entry. The mayor, local magistrates, and scarlet-robed doctors of the university accompanied Anjou and his entourage in the official procession as the duke claimed possession of his new duchy.[8]

The pomp and circumstance of Anjou's 'joyous entry' into Bourges camouflaged, however, the underlying problems of governing the new duchies and the continued popular opposition to the edict of pacification. Apparently bolstered by Anjou's extended stay in Bourges over the summer of 1576, the Protestants of the town rioted in early August, overturning statues and tearing down crucifixes in the cathedral. The reasons for their discontent are unclear, but their actions brought the religious tensions back to the surface.[9] In the duchy of Anjou some Catholic troops led by the duke of Lorraine, a cousin of the Guises, had taken advantage of Anjou's absence and Bussy's tardiness in claiming his governorship by laying siege to the château in Angers. Anjou desperately sought the king's intervention before hostilities escalated, 'since this could lead to some new disturbance in your kingdom', as he wrote to Henry in July.[10]

Indeed, there was evidence all over France that the new peace was destined to be short-lived. The Catholics at court, who had banded together with the Guises back in January, started organizing leagues and associations throughout the provinces. Their mission was not only to oppose the Huguenot military forces but also to prevent the execution of the recent edict of pacification. 'The Catholics of this kingdom', wrote the Venetian ambassador Morosini, 'are trying to band together to block the execution of the peace and to unite in order to prevent the king from placing new garrisons in some areas'.[11] These associations, especially the one in Picardy which prevented the prince of Condé from assuming his governorship, eventually led to the genesis of the Holy Catholic League, the ultra-Catholic organization led by the Guises that proved to be an even stronger opponent to the crown than the Huguenots after 1584. In 1576, however, the League was just a loose confederation of local associations, 'in appearance founded on the pretext of religion, but in reality on the pretensions of the House of Lorraine', according to Pierre de l'Estoile.[12]

The hostile Catholic reaction to the edict of pacification was further exacerbated by Protestant complaints that the edict was not being enforced in many regions of the kingdom.[13] And rumors abounded that the Huguenots had organized a league of their own in Languedoc and Guyenne to counterbalance

---

8 BN, MSS ital. 1729, fol. 786, Morosini to the Signory, 16 July 1576.
9 Brimont, *Guerres de la Réforme en Berry*, vol. II, p. 136.
10 BN, MSS CCC 8, fol. 252, Anjou to Henry III, 28 July 1576.
11 BN, MSS ital. 1729, fols. 813–14, Morosini to the Signory, 8 August 1576.
12 L'Estoile, *Journal*, vol. I, p. 159.
13 For instance, see BN, MSS CCC 29, fol. 293, Navarre to Condé, September 1576.

the Guise-led Catholic organization. Thus, within months of the edict of May 1576, the king and queen mother found themselves back in the middle of another political and religious conflict, with the Guises on one side and Navarre, Condé, and some of the Montmorencies on the other. Above all, Henry and Catherine hoped to keep Anjou aligned with the crown and out of either camp. In late August they despatched Armand de Gontaut, baron de Biron, to Anjou in hopes of securing his loyalty.[14]

The duke of Anjou was apparently satisfied with his new prestige at court, and seems genuinely to have supported the king and queen mother's efforts to keep the peace. He kept his options open, however, by staying in touch with the Huguenots through the prince of Condé. He urged Condé and Navarre to support the edict of pacification as well as the forthcoming meeting of the Estates-General, which the king had convoked on 6 August to meet in November.[15] Moreover, Anjou refused Condé's request for additional troops to guard the fortified towns of La Charité and Issoire, on the grounds that 'I have not got a single man that I can spare, having only 240 men myself for all the towns in my duchies of Anjou, Touraine, and Berry'.[16] Nevertheless, it is clear that Anjou did not completely write off the possibility of future military involvement with the Huguenots. He wrote Condé in early November that he had already sent some troops to the Netherlands and needed the support of Huguenot-controlled munitions at La Rochelle and Brouage.[17] In addition, he despatched Philippe du Plessis-Mornay on a mission to England in an effort to obtain support from Elizabeth.[18] Although this mission and the expedition to the Netherlands were eventually abandoned, it is clear that Anjou was not bound and fettered by the king and queen mother. For the time being, however, he supported their efforts to maintain peace.

Anjou's interest in the Netherlands deserves careful attention, for Orange had sought his help at least since 1573. Moreover, just after the peace edict had been published in May 1576, Orange and the States of Holland and Zeeland had actually made Anjou an offer of sovereignty in return for military support. As the revolt in the Netherlands had become localized in about twenty towns in Holland and Zeeland since 1572, the prince of Orange had convinced the States of those two provinces that offering their sovereignty to a foreign prince was the only alternative to the complete collapse of the revolt. The first such offer had been made to Queen Elizabeth in November 1575; but she had refused, not wishing to involve England directly. Then, in May 1576, a similar offer was made to Anjou. In return for guarantees against any new taxation or any attempt to inhibit

14 BN, MSS ital. 1729, fols. 815–16 and 824–5, Morosini to the Signory, 8 and 20 August 1576.
15 BN, MSS CCC 29, fols. 283–4, Anjou to Condé, 1 and 30 September 1576.
16 BN, MSS CCC 29, fol. 289, Anjou to Condé, 8 October 1576.
17 BN, MSS CCC 29, fol. 287, Anjou to Condé, 2 November 1576.
18 Du Plessis-Mornay, *Mémoires et correspondance*, vol. II, pp. 79–80, Anjou to Mornay, 30 September 1576.

Protestant worship, the States of Holland and Zeeland offered to make the duke of Anjou their sovereign prince, replacing Philip II of Spain, with an annual subsidy of one million Dutch florins (about a million *livres tournois*).[19] As Elizabeth had done, Anjou turned down their offer, still too flushed with his newly-won prestige in France to worry about the fate of the Dutch rebels.

Nevertheless, all summer rumors circulated in France, England, and the Netherlands that Orange and Anjou had worked out some arrangement for French support of the Dutch rebels. An English agent in the town of Middelburg in Zeeland wrote to Burghley that 'th'arryvall of 4000 Frenchmen from Monsieur are dayly expected'.[20] Similar statements abounded at the French court, especially after the arrival in Paris of the Protestant François de la Noue. Juan de Vargas Mexia, the Spanish ambassador in Paris, was convinced that Henry III intended to send a French army under Anjou's command to fight the Spanish forces in the Netherlands. And Dr Valentine Dale, the English ambassador in Paris, believed that Henry might be willing to support such a venture led by his younger brother just to be rid of him.[21]

All of these rumors reached fever pitch in November 1576 after the attempted *coup* in Antwerp known as the 'Spanish fury'. The Spanish troops, many of them unpaid for more than three years, mutinied and sacked the city. The results of this barbarous attack – 8,000 civilians killed and 1,000 homes destroyed – made it more than ever clear that outside help was needed if the rebels were to succeed.[22] By this time, Anjou had already sent several agents to talk with Orange: the sieur d'Alféran, the sieur de la Beausse, the sieur de Bonnivet, and the sieur de Fonperthuis.[23] These agents expressed Anjou's desire to aid the rebels in any way that Orange saw fit, short of accepting sovereignty. Orange was prudent enough to realize, however, that any promised support from Anjou ultimately depended on the degree to which Henry III would back him. Moreover, the Dutch States-General (the representative body composed of delegates from each of the provincial States) were unwilling to go as far as the States of Holland and Zeeland, and were reluctant to accept Anjou's numerous offers of assistance, though they did not reject him out of hand. In fact, they sent several representatives of their own, the sieur d'Aubigny and the sieur de

---

[19] BN, MSS fr. 3280, fols. 83–6, States of Holland and Zeeland to the duke of Anjou, from Delft, 6 May 1576. I wish to thank Professor K. W. Swart for pointing out this document to me.

[20] Kervijn de Lettenhove, *Relations*, vol. VIII, p. 414, Edward Chester to Burghley, 20 July 1576.

[21] BN, MSS ital. 1729, fols. 862–8 and 871–4, Morosini to the Signory, 22 October and 6 November 1576; and *CSPF*, vol. XI, p. 399, Dale to Burghley, 13 October 1576.

[22] For details of the 'Spanish fury' see Motley, *Rise of the Dutch Republic*, vol. III, pp. 104–21; and Geoffrey Parker, *Spain and the Netherlands, 1559–1659* (London, 1979), pp. 106–21.

[23] In a letter dated 19 October 1576, Orange wrote to Liesfelt (a confidant who was later chancellor of Brabant) that La Beausse had been sent to him from Anjou 'despuis ung mois' (Groen van Prinsterer, *Archives*, vol. V, p. 441). See also the letters from Orange to Anjou and Henry III, both dated 19 October 1576, in ibid., pp. 443–5. (La Beausse, Bonnivet, and Fontperthuis were all chamberlains in Anjou's household at this time).

Mansart, to Blois, where the French court was gathering for the forthcoming meeting of the French Estates-General.[24] In addition, William of Hornes, lord of Hèze, sent one of his secretaries, Henry de Bloeyere, to the French court. Hèze and Bloeyere both had connections with Orange, and were working for a pro-French alliance in the Dutch States-General.[25] From Blois, Bloeyere wrote a letter to the townspeople of Brussels on 25 November urging them to accept Anjou's offers of aid, offers that were 'with the consent of the king, his brother, who told us out of his own mouth that he will never give aid to the said Spaniards'.[26] While Henry may have said as much to Bloeyere, he did not openly support a military campaign to the Netherlands led by his younger brother. On the other hand, Catherine de Medici did write to the Dutch States and thank them for listening to Anjou's offers, an indication that she may have wanted at least to keep the door open for such an enterprise in the future.[27] In the autumn of 1576, however, the problems that forever plagued Anjou's attempt to aid William of Orange were evident. How could Orange convince the other Dutch provinces, still overwhelmingly loyalist, to renounce their particularist tendencies to support Holland and Zeeland, and to adopt the pro-French policy which he felt was vital to the success of the revolt? And how far were Henry III and Catherine de Medici willing to support Anjou's venture? The success of any French involvement in the Netherlands led by Anjou ultimately hinged on these two crucial issues.

The arrival at Blois of the representatives of the Dutch States, and their reception by the king and queen mother, naturally angered the agents of Philip II and the pope. Juan de Vargas Mexia, Philip's ambassador in France, complained vehemently to Catherine de Medici about French interference in the Netherlands, and insinuated that it was in her power to prevent her sons from interfering in Spanish affairs. Catherine curtly informed him, however, that 'her sons had attained the age of twenty-one years and more, and were not now under her government'.[28] The papal nuncio in France, Antonio Maria Salviati, was equally contemptuous of Anjou's repeated offers to aid the Dutch rebels. 'Such offers', he wrote, 'come from a prince who has no following and is in great need of money'.[29] Even Queen Elizabeth, with whom Anjou continued to correspond, was not particularly enamored of French intervention. As De Thou noted, she

---

[24] *CSPF*, XI, 426–7, Dutch States-General to Anjou, 26 November 1576, and instructions to Aubigny, 26 November 1576.

[25] Gordon Griffiths, *William of Hornes, Lord of Hèze and the Revolt of the Netherlands, 1576–1580* (Berkeley, 1954), pp. 32–3.

[26] Muller and Diegerick, *Documents*, vol. I, p. 30, Bloeyere to the 'bons bourgeois' of Brussels, 25 November 1576.

[27] *CSPF*, vol. XI, p. 449, Catherine de Medici to the Dutch States-General, 22 December 1576.

[28] Ibid., pp. 451–2, events in France, probably reported by Sir Amyas Paulet, who replaced Dale as Elizabeth's resident ambassador in France in October 1576 (see ibid., pp. 396–8).

[29] *Acta Nuntiaturae Gallicae*, vol. XIII, p. 532, Salviati to Rome, 24 September 1576.

feared a French-dominated Netherlands even more than Spanish preponderance.[30]

Despite the importance of Anjou's negotiations with the Dutch States and William of Orange, Henry III and Catherine de Medici had a more explosive situation at home to consider during the autumn of 1576: the meeting of the French Estates-General at Blois, scheduled to open in November. Most French Catholics were so *frappés au cœur* by the recent edict of pacification that new hostilities appeared imminent. Anjou, much to Henry's and Catherine's relief, appeared to be supporting royal policy, and he refused to join Condé and Navarre in their boycott of the Estates-General – indeed, he tried to persuade the two to attend.[31] Nevertheless, it is one of the ironies of the French Wars of Religion that the convocation of the Estates-General had been one of the most vocal Huguenot demands since 24 August 1572. When that body was finally convoked in 1576, however, Protestants were on the whole excluded, either by choice or because of Catholic pressure during the election of the deputies. Many Huguenots complained that they were not informed when the elections were to take place.[32] Others protested that recent meetings of the Estates only served particular interests rather than the general welfare of the kingdom. Moreover, it was felt that in many localities Catholics had banded together to exclude Protestants from the Estates in order to renew the war in their absence.[33] As a result, Huguenot leaders like Navarre and Condé either refused to acknowledge the Estates-General as legitimate or simply stayed away. In any case the situation did not bode well. Although Henry III looked forward to the meeting of the Estates because of the possibility it offered to recoup much-needed crown revenue, others saw the renewal of civil war as the only likely result of the meeting. 'The queen mother does not look forward to this convocation', wrote the Venetian ambassador, 'fearing that it might result in the destruction of peace and the repose of this kingdom. The king, however, is of the opposite opinion, believing that he could never fulfill all his needs, and especially his urgent need for money, except in this manner.'[34]

II

The assembly of the Estates-General at Blois in late 1576 was the direct result of article 58 of the edict of pacification of the previous May. And while the convocation of that body was one of the concessions ceded to the Protestant leaders during the negotiation of that edict, by late 1576 Henry III had reasons of

[30] De Thou, *Histoire universelle*, vol. v, pp. 328–9.
[31] BN, MSS CCC 29, fol. 284, Anjou to Condé, 30 September 1576.
[32] Georges Picot, *Histoire des Etats-Généraux ... de 1355 à 1614* (4 vols., Paris, 1872), vol. 2, p. 305.
[33] BN, MSS n.a. fr. 7738, fols. 288–91, 'Protestation faite par ceux de la religion sur la tenue des Estats generaux de France', September 1576.
[34] BN, MSS ital. 1729, fol. 833, Morosini to the Signory, 7 September 1576.

his own to support a meeting of the Estates, an institution that had lain dormant for fifteen years. Above all, there was grave concern for the fiscal stability of the crown. The constraints of more than a decade of civil war had left the treasury nearly barren, a condition not helped by the massive financial concessions made to John Casimir in the edict of pacification. Thus, Henry looked to the forthcoming meeting of the Estates-General for new sources of revenue. On 24 December he wrote to Arnaud du Ferrier, the French ambassador in Venice, of 'the extreme expenses which have plagued me ever since my return to this kingdom [from Poland] and from which I have still not escaped'. He went on to add that he 'hoped that this meeting of the Estates will provide some satisfactory means of remedying the great distress that war has brought to the affairs of this state'.[35]

Anjou played an insignificant role during the Estates-General, where Henry and most of the deputies (though not all of them) decided to renew the civil wars against the Huguenots. Moreover, the deputies at Blois were equally concerned about the disastrous financial condition of the crown. They made various enquiries to Henry and Antoine de Nicolai, the first president of the *Chambre des comptes*, about the crown's receipts and expenses. Because the renewal of war and the crown's fiscal condition played such a crucial role in the remainder of Anjou's brief career, it is necessary to explore briefly what happened at Blois over the winter of 1576–7.

It has already been noted that the election of the deputies to the Estates-General of Blois was largely a Catholic affair. The only Protestant deputy, the sieur de Mirambeau, who represented the nobility of Saintonge in the second estate, departed soon after the meeting opened. Another Protestant, Philippe du Plessis-Mornay, had been elected to represent the nobility of Senlis, but he decided not to serve because of a prior commitment.[36] Thus, from the outset the meeting of the Estates-General was a body that did not really have the interests of the Huguenots at heart.

The deputies began arriving at Blois in mid-November, as the first *séance* was scheduled for 24 November. The king directed the three estates to meet separately in their respective orders, to begin the arduous task of drawing up a general *cahier de doléances* (list of grievances) from the various local *doléances* that each deputy brought with him. Then, at the end of the session, each of the three orders – clergy, nobility, and third estate – would present its general *cahier* and suggestions to the king. Henry naturally hoped that the deputies would be disposed to raise some much needed revenue to ameliorate the crown's financial crisis. He soon discovered to his horror that there was some opposition in the third estate to raising any new revenue for the royal treasury. The famous episode of Jean Bodin's attempt to prevent the renewal of civil war by

---

[35] BN, MSS CCC 367, fols. 324–5, Henry III to Arnaud du Ferrier, 24 December 1576.
[36] Du Plessis-Mornay, *Mémoires et correspondance*, vol. I, p. 109 and vol. II, pp. 79–80.

withholding new funds need not be retold here.[37] Curiously enough, however, there was a similar though less publicized effort in the second estate. Because of the powerful position the nobility still occupied in the government and the military, it was vital for Henry to secure the second estate's support.

On 29 November two members of the king's council, the sieurs de Morvilliers and de Lansac, visited the second estate and urged the nobles to support the king. Later that same day, Pierre de Blanchefort, one of the noble deputies, witnessed a curious incident that caused him to wonder just what the king wanted:

Today I was called to a particular conference at the residence of one of the prelates of this kingdom, along with many others of his rank, plus some other deputies of the nobility, where a certain formula of association was proposed, whose purpose was to break the last edict of pacification and to place the king at war against those of the so-called new religion ... I said that it seemed to me that the king should not be counselled to go to war, because of the recent injuries that the kingdom has suffered, and that whoever desires civil war is ungodly and one should pray for him.[38]

Blanchefort reacted strongly against this proposed Catholic association, and maintained that, ever since the reign of Francis I, the French Protestants had been persecuted 'by edicts and judgments as well as by war'. Yet still the Protestants were strong enough to resist. This was proof enough 'that this method of extermination is not acceptable':[39]

I say to everyone without exception that our sins attract us to these emotions, seditions, and thoughts of war. Should not one hope for peace, which only God can give? Sometimes peace is more important than honor ... Concerning the present formula of association, I say that I cannot sign it and call myself a servant of the king, knowing that war is unjust if it is not conducted and undertaken by the king in his faithful and holy council, which alone has the power to make law and to break and interpret it as necessity dictates.[40]

Blanchefort concluded this episode with the unhappy observation that he was in the minority at this meeting, and his advice was not followed.[41]

[37] For example, see Owen Ulph, 'Jean Bodin and the Estates-General of 1576', *Journal of Modern History*, XIX (1947), 289–96; Martin Wolfe, 'Jean Bodin on Taxes: the Sovereignty–Taxes Paradox', *Political Science Quarterly*, LXXXIII (1968), 268–84; and Julian H. Franklin, *Jean Bodin and the Rise of Absolutist Theory* (Cambridge, 1973), pp. 88–92. See also Picot, *Histoire des Etats-Généraux*, vol. II, pp. 297–572 and vol. III, pp. 1–82; and Edmond Charleville, *Les Etats-Généraux de 1576* (Paris, 1901).

[38] BM Blois, MSS 89, fol. 25r.–v. This is the diary of Pierre de Blanchefort, noble deputy from the *bailliage* of Nivernais and Donsiais. It is important because the *procès-verbal* (official written account of each day's proceedings) of the second estate has not survived. A copy also exists in Paris in BN, MSS fr. 16250; and a very short passage has been printed in Nevers, *Mémoires*, I, 437–9. Few historians seem to be aware of the complete diary's existence, however, and I wish to thank Professor J. Russell Major for pointing it out to me. I have used it extensively in the discussion of the Estates-General that follows.

[39] BM Blois, MSS 89, fol. 25v.   [40] BM Blois, MSS 89, fols. 26v.–7r.

[41] BM Blois, MSS 89, fol. 27r.

Was this the birth of the Holy Catholic League, an effort to organize the opposition to the edict of pacification that was prevalent throughout the kingdom? There had been numerous local bands of Catholics who had reacted against the edict, such as the one in Picardy; but there had not been any organized effort to renew the war. It is unclear whether the association proposed to Blanchefort and other deputies on 29 November was the work of a few zealous Catholics such as the Guises, or the work of Henry's council. Blanchefort seemed convinced that the association was not the work of the council or of the king. Only three days later, however, on 2 December, the king himself sent letters to the royal governors of the provinces: 'I am sending you the articles that I have drawn up concerning the associations which I have mandated to be created in all the provinces of my kingdom.' Henry asked the governors to sign the articles and return them to him within six weeks.[42] These articles were much less explicit than the outline of the association proposed to Blanchefort three days earlier, and contained no reference to uniformity of religion or to the renewal of the war. There was no mistaking Henry's intentions, however, as the articles required each governor to provide troops to serve in any manner that the king saw fit. Moreover, the final clause of the articles of association left the Huguenots in some doubt of Henry's intention to uphold the recent peace edict:

Because it is not our intention to torment in any way those of the new opinion who are willing to honor God, the service of the king, and the welfare and repose of his subjects, we promise and swear to maintain them without investigating their consciences or tampering with their persons, possessions, honors, or families, *provided that they do not violate whatever His Majesty might ordain after the conclusion of the Estates-General.*[43]

This could hardly have comforted the French Protestants.

The three estates continued to meet separately until 6 December, when they assembled in the main hall of the château to hear the opening addresses of the king and the chancellor. Henry's speech was brief and full of the normal exhortations for financial relief. Significantly, he mentioned neither the associations nor the renewal of the war. Birague then took the floor for a lengthy harangue, in which he criticized each of the three estates in turn for allowing the kingdom to slip into such a crisis. He stressed that the only remedy for the ills of the kingdom lay in the union of the estates, and he begged the deputies not to allow divisiveness to creep into their ranks. Finally, he broached the issue of the crown's poverty, which he predictably blamed on the costs of the war and the fiscal irresponsibility of Henry's predecessors. In time of war, he argued, additional revenue was always required, and it was the deputies' duty to provide

---

[42] Henry III, *Lettres*, vol. III, pp. 85–8, Henry to the royal governors (plus the text of the association), 2 December 1576.

[43] Ibid., pp. 88 (my italics).

it. Although he did not explicitly mention the renewal of the war, his meaning was clear: more money was needed to rebuild the royal army.[44]

After the plenary session on 6 December the three estates went back to draw up their respective *cahiers*. Several noble deputies again objected to the renewal of the war against the Huguenots. The sieur de Mirambeau, the lone Protestant deputy, appeared before the king on 11 December to complain of rumors of a second St Bartholomew's massacre within the next fortnight. Henry assured Mirambeau that this was not the case, and he promised to send a special despatch to all the provincial governors 'to assure the Huguenots that he meant them no harm'. What Henry actually sent to the provincial governors was a copy of the articles of association.[45] Moreover, the Protestant Mirambeau was not the only dissenter in the second estate. The very next day the baron de Senecey, who had been elected to preside over the meetings of the nobility, also said that he thought it imprudent to renew the war to ensure the uniformity of religion.[46] Though the question of religion was not put before the second estate for a vote for several more days, the king must have been unnerved to find the president of the nobility speaking out against enforcing the uniformity of religion.

On 19 December the religious issue was finally debated and presented for a vote in the second estate. The clergy had already routinely passed an article mandating the uniformity of religion, and the heated debate in the third estate was only just beginning. By a voice vote, a majority of the noble deputies decided in favor of maintaining only one religion in the kingdom. The Protestant Mirambeau immediately got up and opposed this decision, claiming that it was contrary to the wishes that the king expressed in the last edict of pacification. While it is unclear how large the majority was, Blanchefort tells us that other deputies rose after Mirambeau and also spoke out against the decision: Louis de Bueil, sieur de Racan, deputy from the *baillage* of Touraine and Amboise; the sieur de Landigny, *sénéchal* and deputy from Angoumois; the seigneur de Poussay, deputy from the *baillage* of Estampes; and the sieur de la Mothe-Massilly, deputy from the *baillage* of Autun. In addition, Pierre de Blanchefort himself opposed the majority decision and urged his colleagues to consider 'the maintenance of the edicts which His Majesty had made to pacify his said subjects'. All of the deputies in the second estate who had voted against the article on the uniformity of religion then signed a declaration urging the king 'to maintain his subjects in peace'. Unfortunately, Blanchefort did not say how many deputies this entailed.[47] To be sure, it was probably only a small minority of nobles, but this minority grew as the meeting wore on. Meanwhile, after dinner on 22 December the king and his council declared that the articles of

[44] Lalourcé and Duval (eds.), *Recueil des pièces originales*, vol. II, pp. 43–9, 50–68.
[45] Ibid., vol. III, p. 12, private diary of the duke of Nevers.
[46] Ibid., p. 13.
[47] BM Blois, MSS 89, fols. 62v.–4r. Also see *CSPF*, vol. XI, p. 451, events in France, 24 December 1576; and De Thou, *Histoire universelle*, vol. V, p. 343.

association were to be recognized throughout the kingdom of France, and, in conjunction, that uniformity of religion was to be observed for a trial period of six months. Thus, the die seemed cast for a conflict over religious toleration as well as the king's finances.

Significantly, the duke of Anjou attended this meeting of the king's council on 22 December, where (according to Nevers) he consented to the associations and the uniformity of religion. Moreover, the council decided that Anjou should present an official harangue to the king before the full meeting of the Estates-General to demonstrate his obedience and devotion.[48] Thus, Anjou made a complete *volte-face* on the religious issue only six months after the edict of pacification. Many of his Protestant contemporaries accused him of religious insincerity, and cursed him for using the Huguenots to achieve his own ends. The Protestant historian, Agrippa d'Aubigné, was especially indignant. 'Monsieur, once back at court, suddenly abandoned the affairs of the Huguenots', he noted. 'He often said that in order to hate the Huguenots he had to get to know them better.'[49]

Anjou was neither the first nor the last sixteenth-century figure to be chided for placing political gain above religious consistency. The principal charge that can be levelled against him in late 1576 is that he appears to have abandoned his previously-held position favoring religious toleration. By December 1576 Anjou apparently felt sufficiently recognized and rewarded at court to throw in his lot with the king's council and to declare himself in favor of the association and the uniformity of religion. While this appeared to be outright deceit in the eyes of the Huguenots, it was the most lucrative path for him to take in terms of political self-interest. He had sided with the Huguenots in the first place in order to advance his own ambitions and because he had felt snubbed at court, not because he condoned their rebellion against the crown. That situation changed with the edict of pacification. With his new income titles and perquisites, Anjou sold out his former allies in order to support the king. Moreover, the public mood all over France was hostile to the peace edict. The king, his councillors, and most of the deputies at Blois were bent on renewing the war. Anjou can hardly be faulted for not going out on a limb to side with those few *politiques* such as Jean Bodin in the third estate and Pierre de Blanchefort in the second estate. The time for the *politique* cause clearly had not yet arrived. In any case, Anjou's *volte-face* was apparently not as straightforward a betrayal as D'Aubigné implied. There is evidence that he had to be coerced into signing the articles of association, and that he only assented to renewing the war against the Huguenots 'with some difficulty'.[50]

Most deputies appeared to be far more concerned with the state of the king's

[48] Lalourcé and Duval (eds.), *Recueil des pièces originales*, vol. III, pp. 22–3.
[49] D'Aubigné, *Histoire universelle*, vol. V, pp. 116–17.
[50] *CSPF*, vol. XI, p. 475, events in France, 3 January 1577.

finances than with religious uniformity. Nearly every local *cahier* that has survived included attacks on financial abuses, the sale of offices, and the unhealthy state of the French fiscal system. In an attempt to demonstrate his extreme need and to prove that he had not been wasteful, the king sent the first president of the *Chambre des comptes*, M. de Nicolai, to give a summary of his finances to each of the estates on 31 December. Nicolai argued that most of the crown's financial miseries were inherited from Henry II, Francis II, and Charles IX, and that Henry was doing everything in his power to ameliorate the situation.[51] Moreover, the king welcomed twelve deputies from each estate to come and inspect his books. There were skeptics, such as Jean Bodin of the third estate. In his private journal Bodin related that 'it was impossible to learn the truth about the state of the finances, since M. the President [Nicolai] presented only a summary, and many thought that his summary was not the whole truth'.[52] Bodin's suspicion was confirmed by no less a source than the duke of Nevers, a member of Henry's council, who reported that the king ordered Nicolai 'to present only a summary of the finances to the deputies of the Estates to prevent them from getting to the bottom of the matter'.[53] While Nicolai did not exaggerate the crown's poverty (debts totalled 101,000,000 *livres*, according to Blanchefort), it is obvious that he was covering something up.[54]

The twelve deputies chosen from each estate to examine the records of the *Chambre des comptes* returned more convinced than ever that Nicolai had not told them the whole truth.[55] Henry continued to lobby for more funds, however, and on 26 January 1577 he sent several members of his council – Chancellor Birague, the cardinal of Bourbon, the duke of Nevers, and Jean de Morvilliers – to visit each of the estates for this expressed purpose. In the chamber of the clergy, the royal contingent requested a subsidy of 200,000 *livres* per month for six months. In the second estate the cardinal of Bourbon reminded the nobles that it was their duty to serve the king with their arms, for that was why they were given their privileges. In the third estate the king's men argued strongly for an immediate subsidy of two million *livres*, to be levied within two months so the king would apprehend the 'disturbers of the public repose'. The deputies of the third estate responded coolly that 'His Majesty in his patent letters did not

---

[51] Lalourcé and Duval (eds.), *Recueil des pièces originales*, vol. II, p. 145 and vol. III, pp. 218–19; and BM Blois, MSS 89, fols. 85v.–6r.

[52] Lalourcé and Duval (eds.), *Recueil des pièces originales*, vol. III, p. 298, private diary of Jean Bodin.

[53] Ibid., p. 44, the diary of Nevers: 'Le roi a ordoneé au President Nicolay de déclarer sommairement les affaires des finances aux Députez des Estats pour ne leur faire entendre le fond d'icelles.'

[54] BM Blois, MSS 89, fol. 124v. This figure is confirmed in Picot, *Histoire des Etats-Généraux*, vol. III, p. 3.

[55] BM Blois, MSS 89, fols. 105r.–11v.

mention the aid of 2,000,000 *livres* which he is now seeking, but only to put forth the complaints and grievances of the people and to give him advice'.[56]

When none of these advances produced any result, Henry decided that it was time for Anjou to put in his personal appearance before the deputies, as the council had decided earlier. Hence, Anjou, accompanied by the duke of Guise, made a brief visit to each of the estates on 30 January. Because the clergy seemed the most adamant about renewing the war, Anjou visited them first and asked them to supply 400 foot and 100 horse for the king's service, which they agreed to consider. In the second estate he reminded the nobles that it was their duty to support the king in this time of need. To incite others to follow his example, Anjou offered his services for the war and agreed to pay his own expenses. He urged the nobles present to serve the king free of charge for six months as an expression of their loyalty. Finally, he made the public gesture of reconciliation with the crown that Henry had wanted, and he proclaimed himself free of the Huguenot taint that had clouded his Catholic zeal. He vowed to strive for the uniformity of religion in France and urged the nobles to do likewise 'by association or any other means'.[57]

Again, it is difficult to assess Anjou's personal motives. Was he persuaded by the king to perform as a royal lobbyist, or had his position on religious toleration and the renewal of the war really altered radically? When Henry asked his council members to submit written advice on the matter of the renewal of the war against the Huguenots, the duke of Anjou's response was not exactly a vote of support for war:

Since all these persons on the council are so much more experienced in matters of state, are so much more knowledgeable, and some have even served in the military, they are all so much better qualified than I to counsel you wisely. So, I hope that you will understand that, after these men, not only can I add nothing, but just following in their footsteps without stumbling will be all that I can manage.

Anjou went on to advise his brother to deal with Navarre, Condé, and Damville frankly and openly. If the war was to be resumed, they should be made aware that Henry did not intend to permit any religion other than Roman Catholicism to be practiced. Above all, Anjou reiterated that it was the principal duty of every Frenchman to obey the king, which he hoped his own recent behavior had demonstrated.[58] Whatever Anjou's personal feelings on the renewal of war, Henry and Catherine had been correct in their assumption that the large

---

[56] Lalourcé and Duval (eds.), *Recueil des pièces originales*, vol. II, pp. 164–5 and vol. III, pp. 258–60; and BM, Blois, MSS 89, fols. 143v.–4r.

[57] Lalourcé and Duval (eds.), *Recueil des pièces originales*, vol. III, pp. 84–5, diary of Nevers; BM Blois, MSS 89, fols. 147r.–50r.; BN, MSS fr. 3958, fol. 144, 'Acte par lequel il apert que Monsieur frere du Roy fut en la chambre de la noblesse aux estats priant ladite noblesse de le vouloir imiter en cette action', 30 January 1577; and Nevers, *Mémoires*, vol. I, pp. 444–5.

[58] Nevers, *Mémoires*, vol. I, pp. 234–7, 'Advis de Monsieur'.

concessions made to him in the edict of pacification would win back his loyalty. And though his support for the renewal of the war was perhaps not as strong as the Guises', Anjou faithfully supported his brother the king throughout the assembly of the Estates-General, and tried to persuade the deputies to provide the crown with more revenue.

The three estates finally completed their general *cahiers* and submitted them to the king on 9 February 1577. Although their work was finished, Henry asked them to remain in Blois to await his response. Moreover, the envoys that Henry had sent to Navarre, Condé, and Damville in an effort to attract their support were expected back in a day or two.[59] The king was disappointed in the three *cahiers* that were presented to him, however. Although each estate subscribed to the uniformity of religion, and by implication the renewal of the civil wars, none was willing to provide the financial support needed for such a venture.[60] At the end of his rope and willing to try anything, Henry reconvened the three estates on 20 February, and suggested that the crown's financial situation was so grave that emergency measures were called for: specifically, an alienation of 300,000 *livres* from the royal domain.[61] The clergy and nobility seemed willing to go along with the idea, but only due to the urgency of the situation. The third estate stood firm, however, and forced Henry to abandon the scheme.[62]

On 28 February, when many of the deputies had already begun to depart, Louis de Bourbon, duke of Montpensier, made one of the most moving speeches of the entire meeting. One of the most ardent persecutors of the Protestants in the 1560s, Montpensier had just returned from a visit with Henry of Navarre, whom he had been trying to persuade to come to the Estates-General in Blois. His speech to the remaining deputies came as something of a surprise:

I believe, gentlemen, that there is not one of you doubts the zeal and devotion I have always displayed for the advancement of God's honor and for the support of the Roman Catholic Church ... Nevertheless, when I consider the evils which the recent wars have brought us, and how much this division is leading to the ruin and desolation of this poor kingdom ... and the calamities such as those which I saw on my journey here, of poor people immersed in poverty without hope of ever being able to raise themselves from that state except by means of peace ... I am constrained to advise their Majesties to make peace ... being the only remedy and best cure that I know of for the evil that has spread all over France ... I do not mean to give the impression that I favor any other but the Roman Catholic religion, but I would advise the toleration and sufferance of those of the new opinion for a short time ... until by means of a council, another meeting of the estates, or any other means, their Majesties having thus reunited and reconciled their subjects, God

---

[59] Lalourcé and Duval (eds.), *Recueil des pièces originales*, vol. III, p. 330; and BM Blois, MSS 89, fol. 163r.–v.

[60] The three *cahiers* are printed in Lalourcé and Duval (eds.), *Recueil des cahiers généraux des trois ordres aux Etats-Généraux* (4 vols., Paris, 1789), vol. II, pp. 1–122 (clergy), 122–83 (nobility), and 184–355 (third estate).

[61] Lalourcé and Duval (eds.), *Recueil des pièces originales*, vol. II, pp. 370–1.

[62] Ibid., pp. 372–3.

can bless us with only one religion, the Roman Catholic faith held and followed by all previous kings, and in which I protest to live and die.[63]

Thus, the duke of Montpensier, one of Henry's most influential councillors, adopted the *politique* viewpoint of opposing the renewal of the war. The king and the deputies were clearly shocked by his change of heart.

Moreover, on the same day as Montpensier's speech, a group of noble deputies presented a remonstrance to the king protesting against the decision of their order to support the renewal of the war. This remonstrance makes it clear that there was a strong faction in the second estate, similar to the more publicized group led by Jean Bodin in the third estate, that opposed the king's decision to resume the war against the Huguenots. Pierre de Blanchefort recorded this remonstrance in his journal:

It is highly desirable for all the people of France to live in one Roman Catholic and apostolic religion, under which they remain in your obedience. And it is true that when people have only one religion, a king is better obeyed and served. But as the people are subject to kings, so are kings subject to God ... And one of the greatest afflictions occurs when the people are torn apart, as when the children of one house at the wish of their father are banded together one against the other ... The war is so entirely contrary to the establishment of proper order and the increase of your grandeur ... Your Majesty will be aware, however, that we by no means approve of the so-called reformed religion ... but we beseech you very humbly, Sire, to believe that anyone who favors civil war is ungodly. And also, please take notice of two maxims: the first, that the peace of your subjects depends on the union of the princes, and secondly, that violence eventually leads to self-destruction ... We have no other goal than your service and grandeur, for which we shall always sacrifice our lives and means.[64]

No fewer than twenty deputies of the second estate, more than one-fourth of the seventy-five nobles who signed the general *cahier* on 9 February, added their signatures to this remonstrance.[65] It was given to Montpensier to present to

---

[63] Ibid., pp. 210–13.   [64] BM Blois, MS 89, fols. 193v.–7r.
[65] The signatures are listed in BM Blois, MSS 89, fols. 196v.–7r. The twenty deputies were M. de la Chapelle Lozières, deputy from Quercy; M. de St-Vainssan [St-Vincent], deputy from Rouerges; M. de la Huillières, deputy from Comminges; M. de Blanchefort, deputy from Nivernais; M. de Ponteville, deputy from Picardy; M. de Baranau, deputy from Armagnac; M. de Cabanes, deputy from Auvergne; M. de Roux, deputy from Provins; M. de la Rocque, deputy from Montpellier; M. de Lassegnan, deputy from Toulouse; M. de Moretz, deputy from Nemours; M. de Landigny, deputy from Angoumois; M. de Maintenon, deputy from Chartres; M. de Misery, deputy from Auxois; M. de Campandau, deputy from Lauraguay; M. de Rochefort, deputy from Berry; M. de Racan, deputy from Touraine; M. de la Roche, deputy from Brittany; M. de Pignan, deputy from Calais; and M. d'Escars (whom I have been unable to trace, since he arrived late and is not included in the lists of deputies in Lalourcé and Duval or in Blanchefort's diary. It seems unlikely, however, that he was a member of the famous d'Escars family of Guyenne, which was zealously Catholic and later supported the League). It is interesting to note that nine of these deputies came from the south – Guyenne or the Midi – areas of the greatest Protestant strength. Five others were from the Loire region, where most of the fighting took place during the spring of 1576. It is also interesting to note that MM. de Racan

the king, doubtless because of the sentiments he expressed in his own speech earlier in the day. Henry received it graciously, but noted that he was bound to follow the advice of the majority of the second estate and of his council, which was to renew the war.[66]

Thus, by the beginning of March 1577 when the meeting of the Estates-General came to an end, Henry III found himself in an awkward position. The majority of the deputies favored his policy to renew the war, but there was division in the second and third estates. Moreover, none of the three estates was willing to provide new revenue to carry out this policy. And although the majority of his council strongly favored the return to civil war, the duke of Montpensier made a strong appeal for peace. Even Catherine de Medici began to waver. Whereas in early January she had advocated sending troops to the Midi to bring the Huguenots to submission, by late February she had begun to lean toward a more peaceful solution.[67]

Finally, the support of the duke of Anjou, for whose allegiance Henry had issued the previous edict of pacification in the first place, was only lukewarm. Although the Huguenots believed otherwise, Anjou had no firm ideological ties to the pro-war party at court. While he worked for acceptance of royal policy during the Estates-General, this was mainly due to the great rewards heaped upon him after the recent peace edict, rather than to a serious desire to exterminate the Protestants. In short, he sold out to further his own ambition. As his earlier career indicated, he was quick to jump at any chance of recognition and prestige. Once the king offered him the chance to head the royal army against the Huguenots (at Catherine's suggestion), he quickly accepted it.[68] Doubts remained, however. According to Nevers, when Anjou was asked after Montpensier's speech on 28 February if he really favored the renewal of the war, he replied 'that because of his lack of experience he could not really offer any advice; but since everyone else was so resolved to permit only one religion, he was unable to do anything about it'.[69] For the moment, however, Anjou appeared to be placated, and willing to serve his brother in the royal army. It is unfortunate that he chose not to champion the *politique* cause and fight for the maintenance of the recent edict of pacification, but peace supporters were in a distinct minority.

(Touraine) and Rochefort (Berry) were members of Anjou's household in 1576, chamberlain and gentleman of the bedchamber respectively (see Nevers, *Mémoires*, vol. I, pp. 578, 588). One can only speculate whether Anjou was upset to find opposition to the king within his own household or, intriguingly, whether they represented Anjou's true position on the renewal of the war and religious toleration.

[66] BM Blois, MSS 89, fols. 198r.–9r.

[67] BN, MSS ital. 1729, fols. 967–8 and 983, Morosini to the Signory, 21 and 25 February 1576/7; and Nevers, *Mémoires*, vol. I, p. 72. For Catherine's earlier views see Catherine de Medici, *Lettres*, vol. v, pp. 234–5, Catherine to Henry III, 2 January 1577.

[68] This was first suggested by Catherine in her advice to the king on 2 January 1577; Catherine de Medici, *Lettres*, vol. v, pp. 234–5.

[69] Nevers, *Mémoires*, vol. I, p. 174.

Thus, in March 1577 France appeared to be back on the road to civil war. The king's council, a majority of the deputies at Blois, and indeed many Frenchmen favored such a policy. Unfortunately, Henry III did not have the financial resources necessary to defeat the Huguenots.

III

The decision taken by the king at Blois to revoke the edict of pacification of May 1576 led directly to the sixth civil war. Henry had been forced into the Peace of Monsieur and thus made to suffer its predictable consequences. He doubtless preferred peace to war, but the edict of May 1576 did not bring peace. Thus, throughout the meeting of the Estates-General Henry found his authority threatened by the growing menace of the Catholic League. This is why he tried to initiate his form of association and was forced to abandon the edict of pacification. He reasoned that a return to civil war was the only means of maintaining his authority in the kingdom.[70]

Even though the Protestants had already begun to re-arm, Henry's lack of money to carry out the war meant that a quick settlement was almost inevitable. Why did the king hastily declare his intentions to renew the war before securing the necessary finances from the Estates-General to do so? The pressure from the League was one factor, but the simplest explanation seems to be that he never considered the possibility that the deputies at Blois would not grant him the funds that he requested.[71] Once he had committed himself to war, he was forced to make the best of the situation. This meant, of course, that Henry was eventually forced to back down somewhat from his militarist stance. On 1 March he explained his position before the council:

Gentlemen, each of you has seen how hard I have tried to honor God and how much I have wanted only one religion in my kingdom. Needless to say, I have even solicited the deputies of the three estates and have asked them to vote for religious uniformity, in the belief that they would help me carry out this holy resolution. But seeing what little money they have given me, I have little hope of executing my intentions, which I want each of you to understand . . . I do not consider myself a failure if, for the present, I do not speak out in favor of permitting only one religion in my kingdom, because I simply do not have the means to do it.[72]

This change of heart was welcome news to Catherine de Medici and to the duke of Montpensier, who had been urging the council to abandon plans to renew the war. It was too late, however. Catholics and Protestants alike were already re-arming, and hostilities were virtually inevitable. The militarist Catholics on the council demanded that a royal army be formed with whatever

---

[70] See Sutherland, *The Huguenot Struggle*, pp. 248–68.   [71] Ibid., p. 249.
[72] Nevers, *Mémoires*, vol. I, pp. 176–7.

emergency funds could be mustered in order to meet the expected Huguenot offensive. In order to maintain his authority and to regain the initiative following the humiliating edict of pacification, Henry was forced to comply.

Henry's compliance was made easier by the reconciliation of Henri de Montmorency-Damville in early March. Damville's position in Languedoc was crucial, and it came as a surprise when he broke his alliance with the Protestants in the Midi and declared his allegiance to the crown.[73] To secure his brother's loyalty, Henry made Anjou the head of the royal forces as the queen mother had suggested. As in the negotiations for the Peace of Monsieur, the duke had only the appearance of leadership. He had little military experience, and the real command of the royal forces was given to the duke of Nevers, seconded by the dukes of Guise and Mayenne. Anjou seemed satisfied with the title of commander, and the arrangement did not appear to bother Nevers or Guise. The problem still remained, however, of finding sources of revenue to pay for this army.

Henry determined that he needed at least 2,000,000 *livres* to maintain his forces. He hoped to get 1,200,000 of it from forced loans on the fortified towns and the rest from the *taille*. He also hoped for an additional 1,000,000 *livres* from the ordinary tithe of the clergy.[74] This was wishful thinking, as one by one the towns which were asked for loans either begged for exemption, were slow to pay, or refused outright.[75] With the small funds that he could muster Henry did manage to turn out a considerable force (at least for a month or so) under the nominal command of the duke of Anjou, and he decided that its first mission would be to lay siege to the Huguenot stronghold of La Charité on the Loire. This royal army consisted of 20 companies of *gens de guerre*, 60 companies of infantry, 24 pieces of assorted artillery (18 cannon and 6 smaller guns), and powder and shot for 10,000 discharges.[76] Unfortunately, Henry was unable to keep this army in the field for longer than a month. 'Please do the best that you can to ensure that our *deniers* are used sparingly', he lamented to Nevers in April, 'for as you know, they are hard to come by, especially as the infantry must be paid in cash'.[77]

Meanwhile, as the court departed from Blois and moved to Chenonceaux for the spring, the royal army began to assemble at La Chapelle-d'Angillon, just north of Bourges, in preparation for the siege of La Charité. As Anjou and

[73] Desjardins, vol. IV, p. 117, Saracini to the Grand Duke, 11 March 1577. Complete details of Damville's reconciliation are explained in Davies, 'Languedoc and its *gouverneur*', pp. 221–37.

[74] Henry III, *Lettres*, vol. III, p. 171, Henry to Matignon, 2 March 1577.

[75] For instance, see Henry's letters to the magistrates of Paris, Rouen, and Angers, in ibid., pp. 193, 202–3, 224–5, March and April 1577.

[76] BN, MSS fr. 3337, fols. 13–17, 'Estat particulier des forces ... qui sont destinees pour la charité', March 1577.

[77] Henry III, *Lettres*, vol. III, p. 215, Henry to Nevers, 13 April 1577. Also see BN, MSS CCC 8, fol. 378v., Henry to Anjou, 13 April 1577.

Nevers waited for the arrival of Guise and several other noblemen, food and provisions in the royal camp began to run out. On 21 April, Anjou despatched a messenger to inform the king that neither the money which was promised to pay the infantry nor the food and wine which was promised by the city of Orléans had arrived. Anjou begged the king for an immediate delivery of wheat to feed his men. Henry replied that, regrettably, it was necessary 'to order the local inhabitants to furnish your army with such quantities of bread ... due to the scarcity caused by the war'.[78] It was one of the few cases when a besieging army was worse off than the inhabitants of the city under siege. The royal army still had plenty of fire power, however. And it was this ample supply of shot and powder, especially for the large cannons, that persuaded Nevers to go ahead and begin the siege in late April before supplies were completely exhausted.

There is no doubt that Nevers was in charge of the royal forces rather than Anjou. Not only did Nevers make this explicit in his memoirs, but all of Henry's instructions concerning strategy and policy were directed to him.[79] Moreover, Henry instructed Nevers to keep Anjou well out of the way once the shooting started:

I am very distressed to hear that my brother and some of the princes and principal noblemen who are with him are regularly exposing themselves to every sort of danger like common soldiers. I fear some sinister or irreparable accident, so please instruct my brother from now on to be more careful ... It is not proper for the head of an army, especially a person of such quality and respect, to expose himself to such hazards.[80]

The siege commenced on 25 April, and the royal guns pounded the city for seven days. Finally, the municipal leaders capitulated on 2 May. It was a complete and total victory for Anjou and Nevers, as their troops suffered hardly a casualty. Unfortunately, they could not prevent their hungry and unpaid troops from pillaging the conquered town. In a virtual mutiny reminiscent of the 'Spanish fury' in Antwerp in November 1576, the entire city was sacked.[81] Henry was nevertheless pleased with the success of the siege, and expressed his congratulations to his brother, whom he urged to come to Chenonceaux for a victory celebration.[82] Anjou arrived back at court a few days later and was treated like a conquering hero. The king honored him with a *fête* and made sure that he received all the credit for the royal victory. Moreover, in the heat of celebration it was decided to continue the offensive against the Huguenot strongholds. And, as

78 BN, MSS CCC 8, fols. 382–3, memoir from Anjou to the king, 21 April 1577. Henry received it and made his responses in the margin (which are written in Secretary Villeroy's hand) on 27 April.
79 Nevers, *Mémoires*, vol. I, p. 289; Henry III, *Lettres*, vol. III, pp. 246–7, 251–2, both Henry to Nevers, 10 and 13 May 1577; and Desjardins, vol. IV, pp. 118–19, Saracini to the Grand Duke, 8 May 1577.
80 Henry III, *Lettres*, vol. III, p. 226, Henry to Nevers, 26 April 1577.
81 L'Estoile, *Journal*, vol. I, pp. 187–8.
82 BN, MSS fr. 3337, fols. 19–20, Henry to Anjou, 3 May 1577.

Anjou informed the duke of Nevers on 8 May, their next target was the city of Issoire in Auvergne to the south.[83] By this time the royal forces were severely depleted, numbering only about 5,000 men.[84] Nevertheless, the siege of Issoire began when Anjou rejoined the army on 28 May. On the following day, the leaders of the town were asked on four separate occasions to surrender to the royal army. After the last refusal a herald was despatched inside the town with a message for its governor, the marquis de Chavignac: 'If you do not recognize the king as your sovereign, you will be battered by thirty pieces of artillery and you will be put to the sword without any mercy.'[85] Chavignac replied that surrendering to the besiegers would be in violation of the edict of pacification of May 1576; thus the town stood firm. Hoping that the destruction of Issoire would discourage other recalcitrant Protestant strongholds from resisting, Henry instructed Anjou to make the town pay for its disobedience. 'I hope that God will soon bless you with the same success that you had at La Charité', he wrote, 'and that those [in Issoire] will be punished for their rebellion as they deserve'.[86] Despite a vigorous defense, two weeks of heavy fighting forced the town to surrender on 12 June, and the king's wishes were duly carried out. The soldiers burned down every Protestant house in the city, and raped or violated numerous women and girls. As De Thou noted, 'most of the town and all its riches were reduced to cinders'.[87] Historians have always blamed Anjou for the terrible destruction at Issoire, especially since many contemporaries did likewise.[88] Henry's instructions show otherwise, however. Moreover, it is clear that, according to the contemporary conduct of war, the inhabitants chose their own fate by not surrendering when given numerous opportunities to do so.

In early July, Anjou was again called to court for a second round of celebrations, as the royal army, now numbering fewer than 2,000 men, headed westward from Issoire toward Périgueux. The court, which had moved to Poitiers, gave Anjou another hero's welcome on 19 July.[89] Meanwhile, the king's army struggled through Limousin as Nevers complained of being out of ammunition. Moreover, his men no longer had the will (or so he believed) to continue the fight.[90] When the city of Limoges offered Nevers 30,000 *livres* to

---

83 BN, MSS fr. 3337, fol. 36, Anjou to Nevers, 8 May 1577.   84 BN, MSS CCC 8, fol. 402.
85 Quoted in Albert Longy, *Histoire de la ville d'Issoire* (Clermont-Ferrand, 1890), p. 182. Longy provides (pp. 179–204) a full account of the siege taken from a contemporary manuscript.
86 Henry III, *Lettres*, vol. III, p. 277, Henry to Anjou, 4 June 1577.
87 L'Estoile, *Journal*, vol. I, p. 190; and De Thou, *Histoire universelle*, vol. V, p. 373.
88 Longy, *Histoire de la ville d'Issoire*, p. 194. Agrippa d'Aubigné is a typical contemporary example; see his *Histoire universelle*, vol. V, pp. 232–3.
89 PRO/SP 78/1/fols. 1 and 20, Paulet to Walsingham, 10 and [28] July 1577; BN, MSS fr. 3337, fol. 91, Henry to Nevers, 12 July 1577; and BN, MSS ital. 1730, fol. 96, Lippomano to the Doge, 22 July 1577.
90 BN, MSS fr. 3337, fol. 98, Nevers to Henry III, 16 July 1577; and ibid., fol. 100, Henry III to Nevers, 17 July 1577.

refrain from billeting his troops there, the king urged him to accept.[91] After more complaints, Henry was forced to tell Nevers that the treasury was empty and that the troops could not be paid. Ultimately, he had to recall his loyal servant and the remnants of the royal army to court.[92]

La Charité and Issoire had been captured in the preceding three months, but the remaining Protestant strongholds were left untouched. Moreover, Henry of Navarre and the prince of Condé were still at large, with the majority of the Huguenot forces. When they captured Brouage on the coast and began to receive aid from Elizabeth in August, Henry had no choice but to come to terms. Secretary of state Villeroy, who had been negotiating with Navarre since early June, finally concluded a peace treaty that was acceptable to both parties in mid-September. Known as the peace of Bergerac (where it was negotiated), this settlement was issued by the king as the edict of Poitiers on 17 September 1577. Considering the circumstances of its negotiation, the edict was predictably similar – often word for word – in form and content to the previous edict of May 1576. The one major difference was that the general freedom of worship outside Paris was restricted to one town in each *bailliage* and *sénéchausée*. Thus the peace of Bergerac was in many ways a compromise between the extreme positions that the crown had taken, first in the liberal edict of pacification of May 1576, and then the repressive policy that was adopted during the meeting of the Estates-General. More importantly from Henry's point of view, the edict of Poitiers outlawed all leagues and associations throughout the kingdom.[93]

The duke of Anjou's career had taken an unusual twist between May 1576 and September 1577. Although Navarre had always been rather lukewarm toward him, Anjou had emerged from the Peace of Monsieur as the champion of toleration and an ally of the French Protestants. Less than a year later, however, he lobbied for the renewal of the war in the Estates-General and was named as the titular head of a royal Catholic army whose mission was to ransack and destroy Protestant strongholds. Because of his association with events at La Charité and Issoire he had quite a different reputation by September 1577, especially in the Huguenot camp. Despite the fact that he had little to do with the actual sieges and nothing to do with the pillaging that followed, La Charité and Issoire remained millstones around his neck for the rest of his life. Philip Sidney pointed to it as the main flaw in Anjou's career when he wrote his famous letter to Queen Elizabeth in 1579 denouncing Anjou as a possible suitor.[94] And historians have continued to blame him for those atrocities.[95]

91 BN, MSS fr. 3337, fol. 115, Henry III to Nevers, 21 July 1577.
92 BN, MSS fr. 3337, fols. 124–5, both Henry III to Nevers, 24 and 25 July 1577.
93 See Sutherland, *French Secretaries of State*, pp. 197–200 for the negotiation of the peace, and the same author's *The Huguenot Struggle*, pp. 270–3, 362–3 for the terms of the peace.
94 Katherine Duncan-Jones and Jan van Dorsten (eds.), *Miscellaneous Prose of Sir Philip Sidney* (Oxford, 1973), p. 48.
95 See, for instance, Motley, *Rise of the Dutch Republic*, vol. III, p. 340.

What this chapter has attempted to demonstrate is that Anjou's *volte-face* on the matter of religion between May 1576 and September 1577 was much more a matter of political expediency than of ideological betrayal. The desire for recognition, prestige, and furthering his own career were his motives and, in fact, were what persuaded him to side with the Protestants in the first place upon his flight from court in September 1575. Indeed, throughout this period Anjou never once swayed from Roman Catholicism or even intimated that he was considering doing so. It should also be noted that, throughout the period from May 1576 to September 1577, the duke kept close contact with the Dutch rebels, who continued to pursue him even during the sieges of La Charité and Issoire. The atrocities in those two cities apparently did not significantly damage his reputation in the Netherlands.[96] And it was no coincidence that, for the rest of his brief career, Anjou was as involved in the Dutch revolt as he was in the French religious wars.

Finally, a nascent *politique* movement emerged during the meeting of the Estates-General at Blois. A significant number of deputies in the second and third estates vehemently opposed the majority decision to renew the war against the Huguenots, and stressed that peace was more vital to the kingdom than religious uniformity. Because of his recent association with the Protestants before May 1576, his long association with the Montmorencies, and the fact that Jean Bodin – the vocal *politique* leader in the third estate – was a member of his household, the duke of Anjou has often been associated with this group. It has been demonstrated, however, that this was not the case. While Anjou's personal feelings were somewhat equivocal and difficult to pinpoint, he clearly saw his political future in the royalist camp. There is no evidence to indicate that he was even approached to support the *politique* cause. Sadly, that cause had to wait another fifteen years or so before discovering its champion.

[96] See Muller and Diegerick, *Documents*, vol. I, pp. 47–9; and BN, MSS ital. 1730, fols. 158–9, Lippomano to the Doge, 23 October 1577.

5

Overtures from the Netherlands, September 1577–January 1579

I

The ink was barely dry on the edict of Poitiers when international tensions and domestic hostilities threatened once again to break up the delicate peace settlement that Henry III and Catherine de Medici had worked so hard to achieve. The revolt in the Netherlands intensified over the summer, when Philip II's governor-general, his half-brother Don John of Austria, violated the pacification of Ghent by seizing the citadel of Namur on 24 July.[1] As a result, the Dutch States-General doubled their efforts to attract the support of the duke of Anjou to their cause. Two Dutch agents, Aubigny and Mansart, were once again despatched to France in October 1577 for this purpose. The issue was complicated, however, by the efforts of the duke of Guise to aid Don John with troops, munitions, and supplies. Guise met Don John in late September and offered to send him whatever forces he could muster from those released by the peace of Bergerac. The States pleaded with Henry III not to allow Guise to aid Don John, while at the same time Aubigny and Mansart presented Anjou with a gift of three Flemish tapestries from the States.[2] Anjou, who was visiting his sister Marguerite in La Fère at the time, diplomatically refused the tapestries at Henry's request. Nevertheless, he reiterated to the Dutch that he had always favored their cause and would continue to support them. For the moment, he promised to do his best to dissuade the duke of Guise from assisting Don John of Austria.[3] Thus, the spectre of two French forces joining the Dutch revolt on

---

[1] The pacification of Ghent was a pact signed in November 1576, between the rebel provinces and those still loyal to Spain, to exclude all Spanish troops from the Netherlands. Signed four days after the 'Spanish fury' at Antwerp, it temporarily united all seventeen provinces. The text of the pacification is printed in English in E. H. Kossmann and A. H. Mellink (eds.), *Texts concerning the Revolt of the Netherlands* (Cambridge, 1974), pp. 126–32. For the background to the pacification, see Parker, *The Dutch Revolt*, pp. 177–8.
[2] Muller and Diegerick, *Documents*, vol. I, pp. 56–7, Dutch States to Henry III, 14 October 1577; ibid., pp. 59–65, instructions from the States to Aubigny and Mansart, 18 October 1577; ibid., pp. 70–2, Aubigny and Mansart to the States, 23 October 1577; Kervijn de Lettenhove, *Relations*, vol. IX, p. 518 and vol. X, pp. 12, 20–1, all Davison to Walsingham, 15 September and 12–17 October 1577; Desjardins, vol. IV, p. 132, Saracini to the Grand Duke, 22 October 1577; and *CSPR*, vol. II, p. 344, Newsletter from Brussels, 27 October 1577.
[3] Muller and Diegerick, *Documents*, vol. I, pp. 74–6, Anjou to the States, 25 October 1577.

opposite sides haunted Henry and Catherine de Medici throughout the autumn of 1577, as the fragile peace of Bergerac quickly faded from memory.

Henry was in a treacherous position. He naturally opposed any aid to Don John, especially if it came from Guise. Though Spain and France were not at war in the 1570s, the Franco-Spanish rivaly that was renewed in 1494 was a factor that engulfed French policy throughout the civil wars. Thus, it was only natural that Henry should refuse to support Philip's governor-general in the Netherlands. By aiding the Dutch rebels, however, Henry ran the risk of incurring Philip's wrath and drawing France into an unwanted war with Spain. As a result, in the autumn of 1577 Henry made every effort to persuade Philip's ambassador in Paris that he did not intend to support any enterprise in the Netherlands, ultimately declaring it illegal for any of his subjects to participate in the Dutch revolt.[4] Moreover, to demonstrate his sincerity, Henry suggested that Anjou might marry the Spanish infanta, Philip's eleven-year-old daughter, Isabella Clara Eugenia. No-one seemed to take Henry seriously, however, least of all Philip. Nevertheless, in November Henry despatched a secretary to Madrid, a man named Gassot, to discuss the marriage and to attempt to appease the growing Spanish anger over French involvement in the Netherlands.[5]

Despite Henry's efforts to the contrary, the duke of Anjou kept up his dialogue with William of Orange and the Dutch States throughout the autumn of 1577. This was partly to further his own cause, but also to keep abreast of the changing situation in the Netherlands. After Don John's capture of Namur and attempted seizure of Antwerp, there was ready agreement among the deputies of the States-General, that he ought to be recalled by Philip II. Deciding upon a replacement, however, was another matter. The deputies were generally divided between the supporters of Orange, for the most part from Holland and Zeeland, and the more conservative Catholics from the southern provinces. The latter group was led by the duke of Aerschot, stadholder of Flanders, and the count of Lalaing, governor of Hainaut, two of the most powerful and prestigious nobles in the entire assembly. They managed to procure the election of the archduke Matthias, brother of Emperor Rudolf II and nephew of Philip II, as Don John's successor in August 1577, before the deputies of Holland and Zeeland had arrived in Brussels. Matthias was the choice of the conservative nobles because he was a Habsburg; they thought that his election was less likely to be construed as an assault upon the sovereignty of Philip II, whom they still acknowledged. The expected power struggle between Matthias and Orange never developed,

---

[4] Joseph Lefèvre (ed.), *Correspondance de Philippe II sur les affaires des Pays-Bas, 1577–1598* (4 vols., Brussels, 1940–60), vol. I, pp. 110–11, Maximilien de Longueval, sieur de Vaulx (a Spanish agent in Paris) to Philip, 4 November 1577.

[5] Ibid., 132, Vaulx to Philip, 22 November 1577; BN, MSS ital. 1730, fols. 169–70, Lippomano to the Signory, 22 November 1577; and Kervijn de Lettenhove, *Relations*, vol. X, p. 97, Davison to Walsingham, 18 November 1577.

however. When Matthias arrived in the Netherlands in October to take up his new position, the prince of Orange so charmed the twenty-year-old archduke that he made Orange his deputy and chief adviser. Before long the prince of Orange was the *de facto* head of the government.[6]

Aubigny and Mansart, the two Dutch agents still in Paris, reported that Matthias's arrival in Brussels could jeopardise the possibility of French aid, as Anjou might be offended. Anjou was obviously jealous, but he informed Orange and the States that he would continue to support them.[7] The States replied that they were touched by Anjou's pledges of support; but as long as Philip II observed their ancient rights and liberties, they wanted to remain obedient to him. Thus they could hardly refuse to accept one of his relations by blood as their new governor-general.[8] By this time Anjou was growing insecure, and decided to send another agent to the Netherlands to see if he could work out a deal of his own with some of the Catholic provinces in the south. This agent was Claude de Mondoucet, who had frequently served as Henry III's representative in the Netherlands.[9] About this same time Philippe de Croy, duke of Aerschot, and several other Catholic nobles who opposed Orange in the States became disenchanted with Matthias, and wanted to come to a private agreement with the duke of Anjou, without the knowledge of either Orange or the States-General.[10] This news must have got back to Anjou, because when Mondoucet arrived in Brussels in early December he expressed the duke's dissatisfaction with the election of Matthias.[11] The prince of Orange, who feared the consequences if some of the southern provinces began negotiating with Anjou independently, deputized Aerschot and the other nobles as agents of the States-General on 24 December. He asked them to meet with Mondoucet and report back whatever he had to say. Unfortunately, there are no records of what transpired at that meeting. Mondoucet did appear before the States on 9 January 1578, however, and relayed Anjou's expressions of goodwill. The deputies thanked him and

---

6 This entire paragraph is based on the discussion in Parker, *The Dutch Revolt*, pp. 183–6.

7 Muller and Diegerick, *Documents*, vol. I, p. 83, Aubigny and Mansart to the States, 3 November 1577; and Groen van Prinsterer, *Archives*, vol. VI, pp. 242–6, Anjou to the States and to Orange, 12 and 16 November 1577.

8 Muller and Diegerick, *Documents*, vol. I, pp. 97–8, States to Anjou, 18 November 1577. Matthias made it known as early as October 1576 that he wanted the position. See Parker, *The Dutch Revolt*, p. 184.

9 The sieur d'Alféran, who had been commuting back and forth between Anjou and the Dutch States for over a year, informed the States that Mondoucet was on his way to Brussels in late November. See J. B. Blaes (ed.), *Mémoires anonymes sur les troubles des Pays-Bas, 1565–1580* (5 vols., Brussels, 1859–66), vol. 2, pp. 338–9, States to Anjou, 29 November 1577.

10 Or so claimed Orange in December 1580 in his 'Apology', printed in Jean du Mont (ed.), *Corps universel diplomatique du droit des gens* (Amsterdam and The Hague, 1728), vol. 5, part i, p. 400.

11 Groen van Prinsterer, *Archives*, vol. VI, pp. 265–6, Cornelius van der Straten to Orange, 10 December 1577; and Kervijn de Lettenhove, *Relations*, vol. X, p. 158, Davison to Walsingham and Wilson, 12 December 1577.

promised to despatch three agents to the duke to discuss the situation further. Nothing more was agreed, however.[12]

Anjou was growing increasingly restless. Not only had the Dutch States turned to the archduke Matthias, they also signed an alliance with Queen Elizabeth of England on 7 January 1578.[13] The situation deteriorated further when the troops of Don John of Austria, still Philip's official representative in the. Netherlands, routed the army of the States at Gembloux on 31 January. On 13 February Spanish troops moved closer to Brussels and captured the town of Leuven, only fifteen miles away. The following day Matthias, William of Orange, and the deputies of the States abandoned Brussels and fled to the security of Antwerp. Apparently, Anjou decided that his moment had arrived and he could wait no longer. On the same day, 14 February 1578, he suddenly departed from the court in Paris and went to his *apanage* in Angers to begin raising troops to lead to the Netherlands.[14]

Anjou's flight from court in February 1578 is usually portrayed as the result of the heady events in Paris in January and February prior to his departure. During those months, Henry's and Anjou's *mignons* waged one of the most spectacular battles ever witnessed at court. On 10 January, 300 of Anjou's *mignons*, led by the infamous Bussy d'Amboise, went to the king's apartment and challenged his *mignons* 'to fight it out to the death'.[15] Memoirists in Paris such as Pierre de l'Estoile duly recorded these events, and they have been cited by historians ever since. The general consensus is that a quarrel of the severest intensity between the two royal brothers was fought out by their respective *mignons*, which ultimately forced the duke of Anjou to flee from court in a state of pique.[16] To be fair, most contemporary observers believed the same thing. The Florentine ambassador Saracini noted that 'the quarrels of Bussy are bound to lead to a new row between the king and Monsieur, his brother. The latter is not only resolved to withdraw from court, but this morning, together with all his followers, he saddled his horses and prepared to set out for Tours.'[17] Perhaps because he was so circumspect about his plans, or indeed had no plans until the last moment, few were aware at the time that Anjou had withdrawn from court to make preparations to go to the Netherlands. The feud at court in January and February 1578 certainly produced a propitious moment to depart, but it seems

---

[12] Japikse, *Resolutiën der Staten-Generaal*, vol. I, p. 299 and vol. II, p. 52; and Muller and Diegerick, *Documents*, vol. I, pp. 103–4, deputies from Ieper to the magistrates of Ieper, 9 January 1578.

[13] This treaty is printed in Kervijn de Lettenhove, *Relations*, vol. X, pp. 219–21.

[14] Muller and Diegerick, *Documents*, vol. I, p. 106, n.1.

[15] L'Estoile, *Journal*, vol. I, p. 230.

[16] See, for instance, Mariéjol, *La Réforme et la Ligue*, p. 193; Joubert, *Un mignon de la cour de Henri III*, pp. 103–17; and Jean Héritier, *Catherine de'Medici* (London, 1963), pp. 364–6.

[17] Desjardins, vol. IV, p. 140, Saracini to the Grand Duke, 6 February 1578. Also see ibid., pp. 143–9, Saracini to the Grand Duke, 12 and 15 February 1578; L'Estoile, *Journal*, vol. I, pp. 231–6; and BN, MSS ital. 1730, fols. 233–5, Lippomano to the Signory, 15 February 1577/8.

clear that his negotiations with Orange and the Dutch States over the winter of 1577–8, and the setbacks that the States suffered at the hands of the Spanish army in January 1578, lay behind his decision to leave the court.

This conclusion seems warranted for several reasons. First of all, upon leaving the court Anjou despatched two additional agents to the Netherlands, M. de la Fougère, one of his *maîtres d'hôtel*, and a secretary named Harengier.[18] Having offered his services to the States for months, Anjou was impatient, and hoped that La Fougère could convince them to issue him an official invitation. Secondly, his agents already in Brussels contacted the deputies from Hainaut, who were already disposed toward a French alliance. In Mons, Mondoucet and Alféran outlined Anjou's promise of support to the States of Hainaut, remarking that 'at present he has better means and is freer to assist you because of his departure from court several days ago'.[19] Finally, in a letter to Mondoucet in early March, Anjou himself cautioned that the deputies of the States-General 'had certainly better weigh my offer and consider it carefully, since I departed [from court] more for their regard than for any other reason'.[20]

The details of Anjou's flight on the night of 14 February are of no special interest.[21] Fearing that his brother might instigate some new trouble, the king despatched the secretary Villeroy and the queen mother the next morning to go after Anjou, who had escaped to the safety of his *apanage* in Angers. Both Henry and Anjou made an effort to ensure that public opinion would not interpret the escape as a signal to renew the civil wars. Anjou wrote a lengthy letter to the *parlement* of Paris in which he voiced the traditional expressions of loyalty to the crown. He claimed that he had no intention of joining the Protestants to stir up new troubles, and moreover, that he felt that the decision taken by the deputies at Blois to return to one religion ought to be enforced. Thus, he hoped that the judges would not interpret his actions as being in any way detrimental to the king.[22] Anjou also wrote to Damville, Navarre, and Condé to assure them that his flight from court was in no way similar to his last escape in September 1575. He informed them that, on the contrary, he would be very upset if they used his escape as a pretext to renew the war, and he urged them to uphold the last peace edict.[23] Henry III made similar declarations of amity with his brother to all the foreign diplomats at court and to his ambassadors abroad. Fearing the consequences if other European powers thought that Anjou was on the loose again, he

---

18 Muller and Diegerick, *Documents*, vol. I, p. 107n.
19 Blaes (ed.), *Mémoires anonymes*, vol. II, p. 367, Mondoucet and Alféran to the provincial states of Hainaut, 27 February 1578.
20 Ibid., p. 370, Anjou to Mondoucet, 10 March 1578.
21 For details see Desjardins, vol. IV, pp. 145–6, Saracini to the Grand Duke, 15 February 1578; BN, MSS ital. 1730, fols. 233–5, Lippomano to the Signory, 15 February 1577/8; L'Estoile, *Journal*, vol. I, pp. 235–6; and Kervijn de Lettenhove, *Huguenots*, vol. V, pp. 3–12.
22 BN, MSS fr. 6547, fols. 28v.–35r., Anjou to the *parlement* of Paris [February 1578].
23 BN, MSS fr. 3420, fol. 1, Anjou to Damville, 24 February [1578]; Cabié, p. 392, Anjou to Condé, 21 February 1578; and Cabié, pp. 393–2, Anjou to Navarre, 24 February 1578.

tried to maintain the appearance of harmony at court. And when Villeroy and the queen mother returned to Paris in early March, they also repeated Anjou's vows of loyalty and devotion.[24] The majority of those at court, however, remained suspicious and did not know what to make of recent events.[25]

Anjou's flight to Angers was his first visit to that city since becoming the duke of Anjou nearly two years earlier. Unfortunately, most of the rowdy *mignons* who had caused so much trouble at court earlier in the year accompanied him, which rather dampened his 'joyous entry'. One of the king's officials in Angers complained of numerous abuses caused by 'these companies [of soldiers] who are stationed in this region, something that pains me very much ... I can truthfully tell you, Sire, that your poor region of Anjou is completely ruined.'[26] Perhaps the worst incident occurred when the bishop of Angers, Guillaume Ruzé, honored Anjou as the duke with a dinner and banquet. Several members of Anjou's household and personal guard became unruly, aided by large quantities of the local wine. They insulted the bishop and soon began swearing and fighting among themselves. Before long furniture, food, silver plate, and some of the rowdies themselves were tossed out of the windows of the banquet hall. Although some local inhabitants – such as M. de Louvet, an officer in the presidial court in Angers – did not hold Anjou personally responsible, the duke encountered a great deal of hostility because of such acts. And despite the fact that it was blown out of proportion, incidents such as the 'defenestration of Angers' strongly influenced the way many provincials perceived the court during the Wars of Religion.[27]

Meanwhile, Anjou was still trying to negotiate a treaty with the Dutch States. Tired of waiting for a formal invitation, he decided to negotiate separately with the provincial States of Hainaut, who had long shown an interest in him. On 28 March, Anjou despatched Roch de Sorbies, seigneur des Pruneaux, and Antoine de Silly, count de Rochepot, to the Netherlands with an offer of his own. He instructed the two agents to negotiate only with the count of Lalaing, who was governor of Hainaut and leader of that province's delegation in the States-General. Anjou offered to lead an expedition of French troops to Hainaut in return for several fortified towns on the frontier. He insisted that one of these should be the crucial fortification at Mons, but in return he promised to provide 10,000 foot and 2,000 horse for two months. Moreover, he swore not to interfere

[24] See, for example, BN, MSS CCC 367, fols. 466–7, Henry to Arnaud du Ferrier, 18 February 1578; Henry III, *Lettres*, vol. III, p. 471, Henry to Michel de Castelnau, sieur de Mauvissière, 15 February 1578; and BN, MSS ital. 1730, fols. 244 and 256–9, Lippomano to the Signory, 25 February and 6–16 March 1578.

[25] See, for instance, *CSPF*, vol. XII, pp. 515–18, Paulet to the secretaries, 1 March 1578; and Cabié, p. 393, Villeroy to St-Sulpice, 25 February 1578.

[26] BIF, MSS God. 259, fol. 117, Du Bellay to Henry III, 17 March 1578.

[27] See J.-F. Bodin, *Recherches historiques sur l'Anjou* (2 vols., Angers, 1847), vol. 2, pp. 121–2 (although the author seems unaware that the bishop's predecessor, Gabriel Bouvéry, died in 1571); and Mourin, *La Réforme et la Ligue en Anjou*, pp. 153–8.

with the exercise of the Protestant religion in the province, and vowed to uphold the pacification of Ghent.[28]

Meanwhile, Anjou had to contend with the opposition of the king and queen mother, who were trying to avoid a war with Spain. They maintained their denials of aiding Anjou's enterprise to the Spanish ambassador in Paris, Juan de Vargas Mexia. Moreover, when Bernardino de Mendoza stopped off in Paris on his way to London to serve as Philip's resident ambassador in England, Henry informed him that Anjou would not dare disobey him by leading an expedition to the Netherlands. When Mendoza reached London, however, he found out otherwise. He discovered that not only had Anjou been negotiating with Orange and Lalaing, but he was also on the brink of leading a French army to Hainaut to oppose the Spanish troops of Don John and Alexander Farnese, prince of Parma.[29] This was exactly the impression that Henry and Catherine had worked so feverishly to avoid. The queen mother spent several weeks with Anjou in Angers trying to get him to change his mind about going to the Netherlands, but she was not entirely convinced by his promises of loyalty to the king. Catherine and Henry decided, in fact, to send a representative of their own to Orange in an effort to convince him that they opposed Anjou's plans.[30] All of their efforts proved to be in vain, however. Rochepot and Pruneaux continued to negotiate with the States of Hainaut, while the duke of Anjou began raising an army.

The Parisian diarist Pierre de l'Estoile recorded that toward the end of April Anjou 'raised several companies of infantry and cavalry from all the lands in his *apanage* to go to Flanders in aid of the States'.[31] How did he accomplish this? The conscription of troops is one of the relatively unexplored areas in this period, and little is known about the methods used to raise an army.[32] It appears that Anjou appointed some of the officers in his household who were already in his pay to fill the principal officer positions in the regiments. While a list of his officer corps for 1578 has not survived, this is the pattern that he followed in 1581 when he raised an even larger force to relieve the siege of Cambrai.[33]

[28] Muller and Diegerick, *Documents*, vol. I, pp. 124–9, instructions to Rochepot and Pruneaux, 28 March 1578.
[29] *CODOIN*, vol. XCI, pp. 195–6, 211, both Mendoza to Philip, 4 and 31 March 1578.
[30] Kervijn de Lettenhove, *Relations*, vol. X, p. 410, Davison to Leicester, 12 April 1578.
[31] L'Estoile, *Journal*, vol. I, p. 254.
[32] But for the earlier period, see Philippe Contamine, *Guerre, état et société à la fin du Moyen Age* (Paris and The Hague, 1972). On the Spanish side see I. A. A. Thompson, *War and Government in Habsburg Spain* (London, 1976), pp. 103–45; and Geoffrey Parker, *The Army of Flanders and the Spanish Road, 1567–1659* (Cambridge, 1972), pp. 35–48. On Huguenot recruiting, see two useful articles in *Archiv für Reformationsgeschichte*, XLVII (1957), 64–76, 192–215, by J. de Pablo; and Steven M. Lowenstein, 'Resistance to absolutism: Huguenot organization in Languedoc, 1621–22' (unpub. Ph.D. dissertation, Princeton University, 1972), pp. 218–36. Finally, some very general remarks about early modern recruitment are in André Corvisier, *Armées et société en Europe de 1494 à 1789* (Paris, 1976), pp. 52–74 and 143–8.
[33] The officer lists for 1581 are printed in Muller and Diegerick, *Documents*, vol. IV, pp. 101–4; and *CSPF*, vol. XV, p. 288.

Moreover, in the spring of 1578 Anjou appointed Bussy d'Amboise, a rather unfortunate choice, to take charge of his troops. Thus, most of the officers in Anjou's army were as young and inexperienced as he, and they were entrusted with the job of recruitment. By issuing patent letters to each of them, Anjou authorized them to raise 'under our name the levy of one company of French infantry, numbering 200 of the most experienced and best *arquebusiers* that you can find'. These letters specifically stated that the duke was raising men to take to the Netherlands and not to fight in France, 'we having been sought out and requested by the gentlemen of the States-General and other particular persons, villages, towns, and inhabitants of the Netherlands to assist, succor, and aid their enterprise'.[34] Unfortunately, the patent letters provide no indication how the troops were paid. By all appearances most of the recruits were from the lower orders of society, and were both inexperienced in war and highly undisciplined. In May the king had to send four companies of royal infantry to St-Denis, just north of Paris, to prevent one of Anjou's regiments from terrorizing the town and ransacking the basilica. As Pierre de l'Estoile noted, 'this was a bad start and a sinister omen for the prosperity of such an enterprise'.[35]

Hoping to dissuade her recalcitrant son, Catherine de Medici set out once again for yet another interview with Anjou in early May. She caught up with him at Bourgueil, just east of Saumur, and lectured him on the dangers that would befall the kingdom if he should carry out his threat to lead a French army to the Netherlands. After showing him letters from Don John, Philip II, and Juan de Vargas Mexia, she assured him that his actions would force Philip II to declare war on France.[36] Anjou responded that it was hardly his fault if the Dutch rebels turned to him for help and offered to give him several fortified towns. He did promise, however, not to do anything contrary to the king's wishes, or that would endanger the peace in France. This was of small comfort to Catherine. And while the king's council decided in May that it would be imprudent either to assist Anjou or oppose him openly, Henry and Catherine made it clear that they would try to throw every obstacle in his way.[37]

Meanwhile, Rochepot and Pruneaux finally made an agreement with the States of Hainaut at Mons on 7 May.[38] The States-General as a whole, however,

---

[34] AN, K 1548, no. 99, 'Patente donnée par le duc d'Alençon aux capitaines de son armée', from Alençon, 16 June 1578. Also see BN, MSS ital. 1730, fols. 373–8, Lippomano to the Signory, 25 June 1578.

[35] L'Estoile, *Journal*, vol. I, p. 255.

[36] Catherine de Medici, *Lettres*, vol. VI, pp. 21–6, memoir of Catherine's interview with Anjou, May 1578. Juan de Vargas Mexia was clearly suspicious of French motives, despite Henry's and Catherine's repeated statements of opposition to Anjou's enterprise in the Netherlands. See Lefèvre (ed.), *Correspondance de Philippe II*, vol. I, pp. 273, 277, 280–2, 286, and 288–90, all Vargas Mexia to Philip II, 7–30 May 1578.

[37] BN, MSS fr. 3300, fol. 29, promise made by Anjou to the queen mother at Bourgueil, 9 May 1578; and BN, MSS ital. 1730, fol. 353, Lippomano to the Signory, 26 May 1578.

[38] Muller and Diegerick, *Documents*, vol. I, pp. 167–70, resolution of the States of Hainaut, 5–7 May 1578.

were still split. By this time Anjou had retired to his *apanage* of Alençon in Normandy, where he despatched another agent, M. de Dammartin, to the States-General in late June, to try to iron out the difficulties.[39] He also sent a few troops to Mons to display his goodwill. Hoping that the States as a whole would recognize his sincerity, he sent 2,500 foot and 500 horse under the command of the sieur de Saint-Léger on 10 June. On 5 July Henry ordered all bridges across the Seine to be garrisoned and mandated that no one was to cross the river without his permission. Two days later the king reiterated his proclamation forbidding anyone to enter military service without his consent, under pain of death and confiscation of property.[40] It was too late, however. The expeditionary force under the command of Saint-Léger had already crossed the Seine near Mantes, and Anjou and his household were not far behind. On 8 July 1578 the duke despatched a messenger to Paris to inform the king that, as a prince of France, he could not ignore the numerous pleas of assistance that he had received from the Netherlands. Thus, he was setting off that very day towards Picardy and eventually Mons. 'This news has caused a sensation in Paris', noted the Spanish ambassador. 'The king and his mother were very affected by it, and it is claimed that Henry III is even ill.'[41]

II

Accompanied by only ten members of his household, the duke of Anjou rode through Picardy, and eventually arrived in Mons in the province of Hainaut on 12 July. The following day he wrote to William of Orange, announcing that he had come to the Netherlands 'to assist, help, and aid the gentlemen of the States-General of this country in their just quarrel'.[42] And despite the fact that his agents had still reached no formal agreement with the entire body of the Dutch States, Anjou expressed an immediate willingness to get on with the job, as he informed them in another letter the same day. He noted that the main body of his army was on the way and would arrive shortly, and he hoped that they would send him some deputies so that they could work out a formal agreement.[43] The deputies of the States-General, however, were not overly impressed with Anjou's allegedly good intentions. Until his army arrived, they were unwilling to put as much faith in him as had the States of Hainaut. They decided to refer the matter to the council of state, and only 'after conference and communication

39 Ibid., pp. 176–85, response of Anjou's envoys to the proposals of the States-General, 9 and 15 May 1578; and ibid., pp. 304–6, remonstrance of Dammartin to the States-General in Antwerp, 25 June 1578.
40 Ibid., p. 272, Anjou to Rochepot, 10 June 1578; and BN, MSS ital. 1730, fols. 380–8, Lippomano to the Signory, 5 and 7 July 1578.
41 Lefèvre (ed.), *Correspondance de Philippe II*, vol. I, pp. 324–5, Vargas Mexia to Philip, 10 July 1578. Also see *CSPV*, vol. VII, p. 580, Lippomano to the Signory, 9 July 1578.
42 Groen van Prinsterer, *Archives*, vol. VI, pp. 404–6, Anjou to Orange, 13 July 1578.
43 Muller and Diegerick, *Documents*, vol. I, pp. 332–4, Anjou to the States, 13 July 1578.

2   Provinces of the Netherlands during the revolt

with them' did they even agree on 17 July to send two representatives to Mons to acknowledge Anjou's arrival.[44] Moreover, many of the Netherlanders were equally dubious. 'He has written to the States, the prince of Orange, and the magistrates of this city, claiming that his men, numbering 2,000, are on the way to aid them', noted one observer in Antwerp, 'but I do not see it'.[45]

Of course, Anjou's credibility depended on his ability to raise the army that he had promised. And, as usual, his primary obstacle was a paucity of funds. Thus, to raise more revenue Anjou applied to the king for permission to alienate or sell the rights to certain sources of income from his *apanage*, a widespread practice whereby one could acquire substantial amounts of immediate cash in return for giving up lesser (albeit regular and continuous) income over the longer term. This was a privilege that was regularly given to princes of the blood, and it should not be seen as an attempt by Henry III to aid and support his brother's activities in the Netherlands. Thus, on 24 July Anjou's permission to alienate funds from his *apanage* was registered in the *parlement* of Paris. The royal patent letter stated that the duke could 'sell, alienate, or transfer the title of any office created by his council or by his other attorneys ... either from his original *apanage* or any supplement to the same, up to the amount of 12,000 *livres tournois* of revenue'.[46] Anjou doubtless sold the rights to this annual income of 12,000 *livres* for ten to fifteen times its face value. Though even this amount was not enough to pay for his army, it nevertheless led to rumors that Henry and Catherine were secretly aiding him.[47] Despite the alienation from Anjou's domain, however, it seems clear that the king and queen mother were both firmly opposed to his venture in the Netherlands for the present.

The wrangling in the Dutch States was finally resolved by Orange, who reasoned that it would be better to draw Anjou into the service of the States as a whole than to leave him in the hands of the States of Hainaut and the Catholic faction of Lalaing. Thus, on 19 July, just one week after his arrival in Mons, the States-General despatched Philippe de Croy, duke of Aerschot and stadholder of Flanders, to Mons to welcome Anjou and to request that he come to terms for a treaty as soon as possible.[48] This was exactly what Anjou had been waiting to hear. On the 23rd he wrote back to the States saying that he would send several deputies within twenty-four hours with 'full and comprehensive power' to complete the negotiations already commenced, 'since I do not want to waste any

---

[44] Japikse, *Resolutïen der Staten-Generaal*, vol. II, p. 66.

[45] AN, K 1544, no. B 43[71], anonymous letter from Antwerp, 16 July 1578.

[46] BN, MSS fr. 5944, fols. 91r–5v, patent letter of Henry III, 14 July 1578, registered in the *parlement* of Paris (despite strong objections) on 24 July 1578.

[47] Charles Piot and Edmond Poullet (eds.), *Correspondance du Cardinal de Granvelle (1565–86)* (12 vols., Brussels, 1877–96), vol. 7, p. 159, Granvelle to Philip II, 17 September 1578; and AN, K 1544, no. B 43[74], Vargas Mexia to Philip II, 27 July 1578.

[48] Blaes (ed.), *Mémoires anonymes*, vol. II, pp. 318–20, n.2, States to Anjou, 19 July 1578. Also see Kervijn de Lettenhove, *Relations*, vol. X, p. 618, Cobham and Walsingham to Wilson, 20 July 1578; and Parker, *The Dutch Revolt*, p. 191.

time needlessly in the ruin of your country'.[49] Within the week the sieur de Rochepot arrived in Mons with all the troops he was able to muster, estimated to be about 3,000 men – far short of what was promised.[50] Nevertheless, for the first time it appeared that all the considerable obstacles that stood in the way of an alliance between Anjou and the States might be overcome.

On 7 August 1578 Anjou despatched Bussy d'Amboise and François de la Noue to discuss the religious situation with William of Orange.[51] And on 13 August Anjou finally reached an agreement with the States-General: Anjou was to provide the States with 10,000 foot and 2,000 horse for three months, he was given the title of 'Defender of the liberty of the Netherlands against the tyranny of the Spanish and their allies', and he was asked to solicit Elizabeth to join him and the States in a 'firm and indissoluble alliance'. Anjou was prohibited from playing any role in the administration or government of the Netherlands, and was not allowed to make a separate agreement with any town, province, or individual in the Netherlands without the consent of the States. For his part, Anjou was awarded the fortified towns of Le Quesnoy, Landrecy, and Bavay; and the States named him as their first choice as successor to Philip II should they ever decide to replace Philip as their sovereign. Finally, Anjou was required to recognize the rights, privileges, and liberties of all towns that were placed in his protection. The States commissioned the Antwerp printer, Christophe Plantin, to publish the treaty, and in a matter of weeks it was circulated in the major towns of the Dutch provinces in revolt.[52]

Thus, a formal alliance between the duke of Anjou and the Dutch, which had been in serious negotiation since 1576, was finally consummated with this treaty on 13 August 1578. Curiously, however, the nature of Anjou's commitment to the States, and theirs to him, was not clearly spelled out. He was given no political power, which the treaty clearly indicated rested with the States-General, the Council of State, and (theoretically at least) with the archduke Matthias. Moreover, Anjou's military power depended entirely on the number of forces that he himself could levy and pay. Indeed, it is clear that the meaningless title bestowed upon him was chosen primarily because it carried no connotations of authority. It is interesting that the possibility of replacing Philip II as the sovereign prince was broached in the treaty, and that Anjou was the first choice

---

[49] Blaes (ed.), *Mémoires anonymes*, vol. III, pp. 16–17, n.3, Anjou to the States, 23 July 1578.
[50] Kervijn de Lettenhove, *Relations*, vol. X, pp. 653, 673, Davison to Wilson and Burghley, 28 and 31 July 1578.
[51] BN, MSS fr. 3277, fols. 54–8, Anjou to Bussy, Orange, and the States, all 7 August 1578. Also see Desjardins, vol. IV, p. 186, Saracini to the Grand Duke, 10 August 1578.
[52] BN, MSS fr. 5138, fols. 57–60, 'Traité entre Monsieur le Duc d'Anjou et les estats generaux des pays bas, 13 aoust 1578'. The treaty is printed in Du Mont (ed.), *Corps universel*, vol. V, part i, pp. 320–2, and it is calendared in Muller and Diegerick, *Documents*, vol. I, pp. 408–14. The original printed edition is *Accord et Alliance faicte entre Monseigneur le Duc d'Anjou, Alençon, &c, d'une part: & les prelets, nobles & deputez des provinces & villes representans les Estatz generaulx des pays bas, d'autre part* (Antwerp, Christophe Plantin, 1578).

as Philip's successor. An anonymously written pamphlet first circulated the revolutionary idea of replacing Philip with Anjou in June 1578. Its author argued that Philip had become a tyrant, having reneged on the *Blijde Inkomst* (joyous entry), the oath to uphold the liberties and privileges of the Dutch provinces which he swore upon his installation as the duke of Brabant.[53] It was equally clear, however, that if the States should designate Anjou as their sovereign prince as the pamphlet argued, it would have been a very narrowly defined form of sovereignty. Therefore, not only was Anjou given little power or authority in the treaty signed on 13 August; the deputies of the States-General never intended it to be otherwise, even if the duke were chosen to replace Philip II.

Anjou's negotiations with Orange, which had been handled by Bussy and La Noue in Antwerp, placed even more restrictions on him and ensured that he would not exploit the religious divisions in the various provinces. On 18 August Anjou was made to swear to guarantee the rights of all Protestants in the Netherlands, and he also promised not to initiate any attempt to get those provinces which did not tolerate Calvinism to separate from the others.[54]

The reaction at the French court to the treaty was one of alarm. Henry had already despatched Pomponne de Bellièvre to Antwerp at the beginning of August in an effort to block the negotiations between Anjou and the States, though De Thou claimed that it was only 'to have a ready excuse to justify himself to Philip II'.[55] Moreover, the main body of Anjou's troops, still stationed on the frontier in Picardy and Champagne, was terrorizing the countryside in those provinces as the soldiers were forced to billet themselves on the local inhabitants until their first pay arrived. This resulted in numerous popular uprisings against the troops' presence, which disturbed Henry.[56] These acts did apparently prevent the 3,000 or so men Anjou had with him at Mons from deserting, however. An English agent in Antwerp reported that they were 'afraid to retorne home least they should [be] ... slaine ... by the parsons [persons] who are in armes all the frontier over to revenge themselves of the spoils, villanies, and outrages done by these souldiers in coming hitherwardes'.[57] Moreover, Anjou's camp was in complete disarray, visited by plague, famine, and mutiny. A severe outbreak of the plague forced him to flee from Mons to the safety of a palace outside the city walls, and in fact, reduced the main body of his forces on the frontier to about 4,000 men, 'the rest being either dead or scattered', according to Lippomano.[58]

---

53 This pamphlet is entitled *Lettre contenant un avis de l'estat auquel sont les affaires des Pais-bas* (June 1578) and is printed in English translation in Kossmann and Mellink (eds.), *Texts concerning the Revolt*, pp. 152–4.

54 Muller and Diegerick, *Documents*, vol. I, pp. 424–6.

55 De Thou, *Histoire universelle*, vol. V, p. 499. Also see BN, MSS ital. 1730, fols. 313–14 and 395, Michieli and Lippomano to the Signory, 26 August and 3 October 1578.

56 BN, MSS fr. 15905, fol. 110, Henry III to Bellièvre, 14 August 1578.

57 Kervijn de Lettenhove, *Relations*, vol. XI, p. 61, Davison to Walsingham, 21 October 1578.

58 BN, MSS ital. 1730, fol. 479, Lippomano to the Signory, 26 October 1578.

Thus, the duke of Anjou's expedition to the Netherlands began to go awry almost from the moment he arrived in Mons. The king had still not given him permission to bring the main body of his troops across the frontier. Moreover, he had been pleading with Henry for weeks to allow some new recruits in Lyonnais and Burgundy to have free passage in France to Franche-Comté, where he doubtless planned to cut off the supplies and munitions of Don John's army along the 'Spanish Road'.[59] The king, however, continued to deny him any firm support. When Henry despatched an agent to Anjou in September to reprimand him for his troops' behavior, it was reported back to the court 'that Monsieur is very unhappy with the Most Christian King, seeing as how he has received neither money nor anything else he has asked of him'.[60] Anjou's lack of finances became even more acute when he made the mistake of appointing the chancellor of his household, Renaud de Beaune, bishop of Mende, to collect the revenue from the alienation of income from his *apanage* that the king had approved back in July.[61] Although Anjou was unaware of it at the time, his chancellor was lining his own pockets with those funds, and he had to be dismissed several years later.[62] Finally, Anjou's support in the States-General began to deteriorate rapidly. The provinces of Holland, Zeeland, Friesland, Gelderland, and Utretcht wanted to pull out of the States and govern themselves independently, but still with the counsel and favor of the prince of Orange. The provinces of Hainaut and Artois, however, preferred to maintain their Catholic uniformity of religion and their obedience to Philip II, as long as he recognized their privileges and liberties. Moreover, a portion of the city of Ghent separated from everybody and put itself under the protection of John Casimir.[63] Thus, whatever hopes the deputies of the Dutch States had that Anjou might render them service soon vanished, as his political, financial, and military position began to disintegrate.

Perhaps the most explicit sign of Anjou's weak position in the Netherlands was the refusal by the three fortified towns awarded to him in the treaty of 13 August to admit him or his troops.[64] Le Quesnoy, Landrecy, and Bavay were all French-speaking towns and predominantly Catholic. Nevertheless, they refused to submit to the duke of Anjou, and informed the States that they would rather return to the authority of Philip II than submit to the French.[65] Moreover, the magistrates of Le Quesnoy were particularly outraged by

---

[59] BIF, MSS God. 259, fol. 143, Anjou to Henry, 2 October 1578.
[60] BN, MSS ital. 1730, fol. 289, 9 September 1578.
[61] BN, MSS fr. 5944, fols. 96–9, patent letter of Anjou to Renaud de Beaune, 16 November 1578.
[62] On Beaune's embezzlement and subsequent dismissal, see L'Estoile, *Journal*, vol. I, pp. 355–6; F. J. Baumgartner, 'Renaud de Beaune, Politique Prelate', *Sixteenth Century Journal*, IX (1978), 101; and Holt, 'Patterns of *clientèle*', pp. 316–17.
[63] BN, MSS ital. 1730, fol. 481, 26 October 1578.
[64] Blaes (ed.), *Mémoires anonymes*, vol. III, pp. 85–7.
[65] Louis Gachard (ed.), *Actes des Etats-Généraux des Pays-Bas, 1576–1580* (2 vols., Brussels, 1861–6), vol. II, p. 29, 'Articles pour induire ceux de Landrecies et du Quesnoy à recevoir les gens du duc d'Anjou', September 1578.

the great and cruel atrocities that the French have committed and commit daily, such that, if they ever managed to enter this town, they would slit the throats of all the inhabitants and sack the city. They already demonstrated this a few days ago when they passed through some villages in this provostship, having pillaged and plundered them like enemies, raped the women and young girls, killed many of the inhabitants, and even ransacked a number of churches.

They ultimately begged the States to find some other town to give to Anjou.[66] The magistrates of Landrecy voiced similar sentiments.[67] In addition, many towns were simply unwilling to give up their political independence by submitting to the directives of the central government, whether that be from the States-General or from Madrid.[68] Above all, Anjou had to come to grips with the fact that the Netherlanders, whether Flemish or Walloon, were as opposed to an invasion of French troops as they were to the Spanish.

When Anjou's fortunes were at their lowest in the autumn of 1578, he decided to turn to Queen Elizabeth once again and reopen their dormant marriage negotiations. Partly to avert her son's attention from the Netherlands and partly to attract English support should Spain declare war on France, Catherine de Medici had been pressing for a renewal of the marriage negotiations since late summer.[69] Moreover, Anjou's treaty with the States explicitly stated that he should arrange an alliance with Elizabeth. So, in response to all of these pressures, it is hardly surprising that he turned to Elizabeth when his expedition in the Netherlands soured.

Elizabeth had long followed Anjou's progress in the Netherlands, since events there affected England. Her basic desire had always been a non-threatening or neutral government in the Netherlands that remained under Philip II's sovereignty but with some degree of religious toleration. The means by which she thought she could most easily accomplish this, however, changed with each new crisis. Primarily she favored any solution that brought peace, and for England this meant peace in the North Sea. While her religious and dynastic policies ultimately led her to oppose Philip II in the Netherlands, she by no means favored a French-dominated Netherlands. Thus, while she tacitly encouraged Anjou's efforts to defeat Don John of Austria, she made repeated attempts to ensure that the Dutch provinces did not pass from Spain into the hands of the

---

66 Blaes (ed.), *Mémoires anonymes*, vol. III, pp. 368–9, governor, mayor, provost, and magistrates of Le Quesnoy to the States, 19 September 1578.
67 Ibid., p. 366, magistrates of Landrecy to the States, 15 September 1578.
68 See Guy Malengreau, *L'Esprit particulariste et la Révolution des Pays-Bas au XVIᵉ siècle, 1578–1584* (Leuven, 1936), p. 128. Also see Parker, *The Dutch Revolt*, p. 201.
69 See, for example, Catherine de Medici, *Lettres*, vol. VI, pp. 36–7, Catherine to Walsingham, 13 September 1578; ibid., pp. 50–3, 111–12, Catherine to Henry III, 2 and 4 October and 8 November 1578; and ibid., pp. 112–13, Catherine to Queen Elizabeth, 9 November 1578.

French king.[70] Indeed, when the Dutch States-General made their first serious overtures to Anjou and Henry III in 1576, Elizabeth threatened to aid Don John if the French intervened on the side of the rebels. Thomas Wilson, her agent in Brussels, expressed her fears. 'I would bee sorie that Flanders showlde stande in neede of Fraunce', he wrote, 'for that wer to committe the sheepe to the government of the wolfe'.[71]

Elizabeth did sign an agreement with the States on 7 January 1578, whereby she promised to provide them with military support and a loan.[72] Although the troops did not arrive until 1585, she was willing to lend the Dutch 20,000 pounds sterling (about 200,000 *livres tournois*) to pay for John Casimir's mercenaries, albeit under stringent conditions. In the spring of 1578, when the negotiations between Anjou and the States were at their peak, Elizabeth instructed William Davison to hand over the loan of £20,000 only if the deputies agreed to break off all talks with Anjou, and only if they agreed not to make any peace settlement without her consent.[73] Davison met with Orange in Antwerp on 17 May, and the prince explained the dilemma of the States. They desperately needed Elizabeth's money, but they could hardly afford to break off talks with Anjou at such a delicate stage. When Davison presented the conditions for the loan to the States on 20 May, he urged them to forget Anjou and rely on Elizabeth as a more trustworthy ally.[74] When the deputies replied on 24 May, they evaded Elizabeth's conditions by proclaiming that they had not yet concluded anything with Anjou. Therefore, they could in good conscience accept her loan with its conditions.[75]

Elizabeth strongly rebuked Davison for allowing Orange to take advantage of her. She despatched Lord Cobham and Francis Walsingham to Orange and the States in June, both to explain her own position more clearly and to find out the true intentions of the States. Cobham, an elderly conservative in religious matters, and Walsingham, a younger Puritan, seemed an odd couple. They had been primed by Lord Burghley for over a month, however, to deal with William of Orange or Don John of Austria, whichever was necessary. In her instructions the queen told them to explore 'to what end Monsieur's offers do tend, whyther to abuse the Estates or to ayde them, and how lykely it is that he shall not become the absolut lord'. Above all, they were to commit England to Dutch assistance as

---

[70] For Elizabeth's policy toward the Dutch rebels, see the very contrasting views of R. B. Wernham, *Before the Armada: The Emergence of the English Nation, 1485–1588* (New York, 1966), pp. 324–72; and Charles Wilson, *Queen Elizabeth and the Revolt of the Netherlands* (London, 1970), pp. 1–85.

[71] Kervijn de Lettenhove, *Relations*, vol. IX, p. 117, 132, both Wilson to Walsingham, 30 December 1576 and 2 January 1577 (quotation from p. 132).

[72] The text of the agreement is ibid., vol. X, 219–21, 7 January 1578.

[73] Ibid., pp. 468–9, instructions from Elizabeth to William Davison, 15 May 1578.

[74] Ibid., pp. 481–2, proposition of Davison to the States, 24 May 1578.

[75] Ibid., pp. 490–1, States to Davison, 24 May 1578.

a last resort.[76] Thus, Cobham and Walsingham arrived in Antwerp on 28 June hoping to head off the alliance between Anjou and the States before French troops arrived in the Netherlands. But by that time, Anjou's small expeditionary force was already on the march, and the duke himself arrived in Mons only a fortnight later.

Thus, it was to a rather reluctant Elizabeth that Anjou turned in the autumn of 1578. He had attempted to maintain good relations with her ever since his arrival in Mons. He sent Dammartin and Alféran to Antwerp to meet Cobham and Walsingham and despatched another envoy, M. de Bacqueville, to England in July.[77] Elizabeth was still unsure of Anjou's motives, however, especially since the reports from Cobham and Walsingham indicated that the Dutch were getting desperate. 'Thys pepell, to put awaye the yowke of Spayne', Cobham wrote in September 1578, 'will take them sellfes to enye prynce or master'.[78] Elizabeth was obviously distressed by the alliance between Anjou and the States, and she rebuked Cobham and Walsingham for allowing those negotiations to proceed so far – even though it was far too late to halt the talks by the time they arrived in Antwerp.[79] As for marriage, however, she preferred to keep her options open. Those at the English court who favored an Anglo-French marriage – and Lord Burghley and the earl of Sussex were nearly alone in that respect – tried to show Elizabeth 'the benyfytes that might grow by this maryage at this tyme, and the perrelles that would follow yf she maryed not att all'. The queen was receptive to the idea, but she told Anjou's agent in England, M. de Bacqueville, that she 'wold never marry with any person whom she shuld not first hir self see'.[80]

Philip II, who perhaps had more to fear from an Anglo-French marriage than anyone, remained quietly confident that any such union was out of the question. He felt that Elizabeth was only bluffing, and that all talk of marriage would soon 'go up in smoke'.[81] While it may be argued that Philip's assessment was more or less accurate, the 'business of marriage' was not nearly as innocent as he pretended to Mendoza. When Bacqueville returned to his master, who was still outside Mons, in September with the news that Elizabeth would never marry anyone without first seeing him, Anjou decided to sound her out on the matter. He announced in October 1578 that until he was able to cross the channel for a personal visit himself, he was sending over Jean de Simier, master of his

---

[76] Ibid., p. 507, instructions from Elizabeth to Cobham and Walsingham, 2 June 1578. Also see Wilson, *Queen Elizabeth and the Revolt*, pp. 65–7.

[77] *CSPF*, vol. xiii, pp. 88–97, miscellaneous despatches of John Sommers and Thomas Wilson, 25–8 July 1578.

[78] Kervijn de Lettenhove, *Relations*, vol. x, pp. 811–12, Cobham to Burghley, 9 September 1578.

[79] Ibid., p. 767, Elizabeth to Cobham, 29 August 1578.

[80] Ibid., pp. 774, 800–1, Sussex and Burghley to Walsingham, 29 August and 8 September 1578.

[81] *CODOIN*, vol. xci, pp. 286, 296, both Philip to Mendoza, 19 September and 15 October 1578 (quotation from p. 286).

wardrobe, to display his good intentions.[82] By this time Catherine de Medici had managed to convince Henry III that a trip to England was perhaps the best way to lure Anjou out of the Netherlands. In December the king despatched the sieur de Dinteville with fifty armed men to find Anjou and inform him of his and the queen mother's intentions. The duke was to be reminded that he was the king's only brother and, as such, was still loved and respected. Furthermore, Anjou was to be made fully aware that Henry and Catherine supported his marriage plans and wished to contribute some money to help finance Simier's voyage. Above all, however, Henry instructed Dinteville to inform Anjou that, because of the Protestant uprisings in the provinces of Normandy and Burgundy, the duke was needed at home to help maintain the peace.[83] Simier had just departed from Paris on 12 December with full powers to negotiate and conclude a marriage. So, although appearances indicated that Anjou was seriously pursuing the marriage, no one could predict what he was going to do. 'Now', wrote the Venetian ambassador Lippomano, 'everyone waits for the outcome of this negotiation'.[84]

The duke of Anjou, in fact, departed from the vicinity of Mons on 26 December 1578 and headed southward, though his departure had little to do with the king's admonishments or the prospect of an English marriage. His unpaid troops had been deserting him for nearly two months, and they were ravaging the countryside as they made their way back to France.[85] Moreover, he had little political support in the Dutch States-General. The three months that he had contracted to assist them were up, and he had no further motivation to remain. The lack of financial resources and outbreaks of the plague, however, were the underlying causes of his departure. The beleaguered Pomponne de Bellièvre, who had been keeping Henry and Catherine de Medici informed of Anjou's movements for six months, made them aware of the duke's plight and urged them to send him enough money to get back to court safely. Anjou, who had only advanced as far south as Condé, barely ten miles from Mons, was very grateful. He urged Bellièvre, however, to find his chancellor, Renaud de Beaune, who was supposed to be raising funds from his *apanage*. The money was vital, Anjou wrote, 'as I cannot leave here without it'.[86] When Bellièvre queried Beaune about the matter, the bishop feigned ignorance and urged Bellièvre to persuade the king to assist Anjou.[87] Thus, the duke of Anjou slowly made his way back toward the court in January 1579, dependent on Bellièvre's good offices and the king's generosity.

Right up until the end, however, Anjou claimed that he had acted in the king's

[82] Ibid., p. 295, Mendoza to Philip, 11 October 1578; and Desjardins, IV, 208, Saracini to the Grand Duke, 25 October 1578.

[83] BN, MSS Dupuy 537, fols. 119–22, instructions of Henry III to Dinteville, 13 December 1578.

[84] BN, MSS ital. 1730, fols. 501–2, Lippomano to the Signory, 12 December 1578.

[85] Desjardins, vol. IV, p. 210, Saracini to the Grand Duke, 4 November 1578.

[86] BN, MSS fr. 15905, fol. 258, Anjou to Bellièvre 12 January [1579].

[87] Ibid., fol. 273, Beaune to Bellièvre, 1 February [1579].

best interests. Despite all the attempts of Catherine de Medici and the secretaries to dissuade him from his enterprise, and despite the threat of provoking a war with Spain, Anjou still put on a face of loyalty and devotion to the French crown. He expressed these sentiments on 5 January 1579 in a letter written to Secretary Villeroy, the person who had pleaded with him more than any other, save the queen mother, not to go to the Netherlands. Anjou explained that he decided to go to the Netherlands because he was asked to do so, and once there he 'found that their cause was a worthy one and should be supported by those of a gentle and generous heart'. Moreover, he emphasized 'how useful these provinces could be to France'. He insisted that the only thing to which he aspired was the king's good graces, and he hoped that Villeroy would persuade him 'that nothing guides my actions but the welfare of his kingdom and his personal contentment, which are inseparable'. Anjou regretted that he could not return directly to court, but certain persons close to the king still opposed him. Moreover, many of the king's men were still hostile to several members of his household, hostilities that flared up a year earlier in the *querelle des mignons*. Thus, Anjou lamented that at court he was 'regarded by everyone as a common criminal'.[88]

So, despite the fact that he had defied Henry's orders ever since he left court in February 1578, Anjou still justified his enterprise in the Netherlands. His arguments do not sound particularly convincing, though, to be fair, his claims that his intervention in the Dutch revolt might prove beneficial to France were true enough. He was less sensitive than the king and the queen mother, however, to the possibility of a war with Spain. They were unwilling, at least without a firm alliance with Elizabeth, to back Anjou even tacitly because of such a threat. This is what made the resurrection of the marriage negotiations with Elizabeth, dormant since 1573, so significant. A firm commitment from her, which a marriage would necessarily ensure, might make Anjou's enterprise in the Netherlands more palatable and less of a risk. His brief venture over the summer and autumn of 1578, however, had no such guarantee.

Finally, Anjou's brief encounter at Mons was plagued by his complete ignorance of the constitutional complexities of the Netherlands. Ultimately, he failed to realize that by 1576 the Dutch States-General had begun the revolutionary process of wresting away the principal powers of government from Philip II. In the century prior to that date, the States had been convoked about 150 times, but with decreasing frequency – indeed, rarely since 1559. Moreover, their powers were severely restricted. Their main function was to grant taxation for the government to levy through the provincial estates and towns. They did have the right to submit grievances before consenting to fiscal demands, but in Philip's view they could neither legislate nor meet on their own authority. After the 'Spanish fury' in Antwerp in November 1576, however, a radical trans-

[88] BN, MSS Dupuy 137, fols. 13–18, Anjou to Villeroy, 5 January 1579.

formation began. The States began to legislate, negotiate with foreign powers (like Anjou), raise and finance their own army, and decide when and how often they should meet. By 1581 it was decided that Philip II had reneged on his oath to uphold the rights, privileges, and liberties of the provinces – the oath of the *Blijde Inkomst* – and the States chose a replacement. And by 1590, the deputies of the States felt that a figurehead prince was no longer necessary, and they proclaimed that they were the sovereign body of the country. When Anjou signed a treaty with them in 1578, this revolution was already well under way. Sadly, he had little understanding of its consequences.[89]

Having said that, the States-General were sorely handicapped by their own composition. Having wrested away the principal powers of government, the Dutch deputies were neither prepared nor able to govern effectively. This was in large part due to the particularism of the individual provinces. In an effort to avoid greater taxation, many provinces sent delegations to the States-General only rarely, feeling that their own provincial States tended sufficiently to their needs. Moreover, a unanimous vote was required by all the delegations that did attend before any decision was binding (although each delegation decided by majority vote). Should any province decide not to abide by these decisions, there was little that the deputies of the other provinces could do. More serious, however, was the fact that the deputies had to refer back to their own constituencies, the provincial States, before any financial matter could be settled. This made for a long and arduous process, as Anjou discovered for himself. It also made for very inefficient government in the midst of a war. By far the greatest obstacle, however, was the self-interest of each province. None was willing to sacrifice its own interests for the good of the whole. They were all reluctant to vote a single penny that was not earmarked for local purposes. Indeed, many provinces adopted the same suspicious attitude toward the States-General as they had shown toward the Habsburg government.[90] Again, Anjou only learned this through experience.

Anjou's gravest error, however, and a blunder he perpetrated for the rest of his life, was his misconception that the States intended to offer him some power and authority along with his titles and offices. It is clear that this was never the case. Quite possibly he was aware that he was being given no authority in the Netherlands, and had hopes of acquiring some once installed there. His later career would support this hypothesis, but it is impossible to confirm. In any case, Anjou returned to France in January 1579, his retreat having been forced on him by his unstable economic and political situation. But with Simier still in London and Pruneaux still in Antwerp, he returned with high hopes of another, more successful attempt to secure a crown in both England and the Netherlands. Unfortunately, he had no conception of the role that Orange and the States intended him to play. Moreover, he may have missed the last chance of holding the Protestant and Catholic provinces together.

[89] This paragraph is based on Parker, *The Dutch Revolt*, pp. 179–80, 242–3.   [90] Ibid., p. 201.

6

Civil war, marriage, and more overtures from the Netherlands, January 1579–December 1580

I

The duke of Anjou's slow retreat from Mons towards Paris in January 1579 was in part prompted by the volatile and uncertain condition of the government in the Netherlands, over which he had no control. The death of Don John of Austria in October 1578 resulted in the appointment of Alexander Farnese, prince (and later duke) of Parma, as Philip II's new governor-general. Philip II, naturally, never recognized the Dutch States-General's preference for the archduke Matthias for the position. When Don John, on his deathbed and stricken with the plague, requested that Parma succeed him, Philip consented. As far as Anjou was concerned, however, the major cause of the political instability in the Netherlands was the disintegration of the States-General. By late 1578, Holland and Zeeland had virtually withdrawn from the States and formed a state within a state. Always very independent, the States of these two provinces opposed giving freedom of worship to Catholics, despite the fact that Catholics were still a large majority there. In town after town they replaced Catholic magistrates with Calvinists by force. Moreover, they never recognized the authority of either Don John or Matthias. This new Calvinist aggressiveness, however, alienated many of the Catholics in the southern French-speaking provinces. Shocked by the violence in the city of Ghent, the provinces of Walloon Flanders, Hainaut, and Artois refused to contribute to the general war effort of the States-General in the autumn of 1578. Frightened by this new outbreak of iconoclasm, they felt that safeguarding their property and defending their Catholic religion were more urgent objectives than fighting the Spanish.[1] This explosive situation left Anjou completely isolated. 'What I fear more than anything else', Parma wrote to Philip II in November 1578, 'was that the Walloon and Catholic provinces would unite and align themselves with the duke of Anjou and the French. This often frightened me, but now I see that they will

---

[1] See Parker, *The Dutch Revolt*, pp. 189–94; Malengreau, *L'Esprit particulariste*, pp. 80–2; and the useful article by Alistair Duke and Rosemary Jones, 'Towards a reformed polity in Holland, 1572–1578', *Tijdschrift voor Geschiedenis*, LXXXIX (1976), 373–93. Obviously, the eventual split did not coincide with the linguistic split, and in the north there were other languages spoken besides Dutch. See Parker, *The Dutch Revolt*, pp. 35–6, 240–1.

not possibly do it'.[2] After towns like Le Quesnoy and Landrecy began to complain of the atrocities of his troops, the Catholics of French-speaking Hainaut – the only enthusiastic supporters that Anjou had in the States-General – quickly abandoned him. Further burdened by his financial deficiencies, he really had no choice but to return to France in early 1579.

Coupled with the Calvinist iconoclasm in the cities, the atrocities of Anjou's troops forced some of the nobles in the southern Walloon provinces to turn to the prince of Parma for protection.[3] With the aid of the seigneur de la Motte, the governor of Gravelines who had earlier sold out to Don John, Parma won over the count of Lalaing and his half-brother, Emmanuel-Philibert de Lalaing, baron of Montigny.[4] Others quickly followed suit during the months of November and December 1578. The result of the defection of the southern provinces was the union of Arras, which was formed on 6 January 1579 by the Walloon provinces of Hainaut and Artois and the towns of Douai, Lille, and Orchies, who had all agreed to come to terms with Parma. In return for the restoration of law and order, the States of the Walloon provinces agreed to maintain their loyalty to Philip II and not to tolerate Calvinism. Moreover, they agreed to accept Parma as governor-general, provided that all Spanish and other foreign troops were evacuated from the Netherlands.[5] Paralleling the union of Arras, several northern provinces signed a union of their own at Utrecht on 23 January. Deputies from Holland, Zeeland, Utrecht, Gelderland, and the Ommelanden of Groningen (the province but not the city of Groningen) agreed to provide mutual assistance and defense in case of attack; and in matters of war and peace they agreed to act 'as if they were but one province'.[6]

Unlike the union of Arras, the union of Utrecht made no mention of the sovereignty of Philip II or the maintenance of Catholicism. Indeed, in the matter of religion the right of each province to govern itself was explicitly safeguarded. The leaders of both unions were unaware in 1579 that they had taken the first step toward a permanent division of the Netherlands, since they were still unwilling to admit that a total victory was impossible. Nevertheless, the unions of Arras and Utrecht made it clear for the first time that permanent division was a possible solution to the revolt. For this reason both unions were unacceptable to

---

[2] Louis Gachard (ed.), *Correspondance d'Alexandre Farnèse, prince de Parme, gouverneur général des Pays-Bas, avec Philippe II, dans les années 1578, 1579, 1580 et 1581* (Brussels and Ghent, 1853), p. 399, Parma to Philip II, 27 November 1578.
[3] Ibid., p. 411, Parma to Philip II, 16 December 1578.
[4] Kervijn de Lettenhove, *Huguenots*, vol. V, pp. 319–24.
[5] The members of the union of Arras signed a formal treaty with Parma called the treaty of Arras on 7 May 1579. It is printed in French and Dutch in Du Mont (ed.), *Corps universel*, vol. V, part i, pp. 350–5, and in English translation in Herbert Rowen, *The Low Countries in Early Modern Times* (New York, 1972), pp. 261–6.
[6] The union of Utrecht is printed in French and Dutch in Du Mont (ed.) *Corps universel*, vol. V, part i, pp. 322–8, and in English translation in Rowen, *Low Countries in Early Modern Times*, pp. 68–74 and in Kossmann and Mellink (eds.), *Texts concerning the Revolt*, pp. 165–73.

the moderate, Catholic majority in the States-General, who hoped for an honorable compromise with the king and certainly for a united Netherlands.[7] In any event, the duke of Anjou's departure from Mons in January 1579 coincided with significant milestones in the revolt of the Netherlands. While the unions would have doubtless been formed anyway, the presence of his French troops in the summer and autumn of 1578 hastened their creation.

As Anjou slowly made his way back home in the early months of 1579, Henry III and Catherine de Medici had high hopes for an extended period of peace. With the queen mother busy in south-western France trying to restore the obedience of many recalcitrant Protestant communities, Henry wrote in mid-February that he was more hopeful than ever of restoring order to his kingdom:

I hope that I shall soon have the means, God willing, to re-establish peace in my kingdom, of which I am now more hopeful than ever. This is as much because the queen my mother has written me that she has been in conference at Nérac with the king of Navarre since the fourth of this month, for which she promises favorable results, as it is because I am assured that my brother the duke of Anjou, having returned to my kingdom, will help me execute my intention in this respect, as he has promised me and has always said and demonstrated that he was willing to do.[8]

While Anjou was in the Netherlands in the latter half of 1578, Huguenots in Guyenne, Languedoc, Provence, and Dauphiné remained in arms, and Henry found the peace of Bergerac as impossible to enforce among the Protestants as the peace of Monsieur was among the Catholics. Through the efforts of Catherine de Medici, however, a truce was signed at Nérac in February with Henry of Navarre and the prince of Condé 'to facilitate the execution of the last edict of pacification made in the month of September 1577, and to clear up and resolve the difficulties which have since arisen and still hinder the intentions and designs of that edict'.[9] Thus, with Anjou back in France and the Huguenots apparently obedient once more, Henry had reason for optimism.

Pomponne de Bellièvre, the faithful councillor who had served as a go-between for Henry and Anjou when the latter was in the Netherlands, was called upon once more to escort the duke into Paris from his *apanage* in Normandy. Though Henry apparently believed the many good reports of his envoys who had told him of Anjou's intentions to serve the crown, he instructed Bellièvre to keep his brother away from certain enemies who might try 'to disturb the affairs of this kingdom in order to increase their own passions'. Catherine, who was still in the south, wrote to Bellièvre to impress upon him the importance of his mission. The reconciliation of the king and Anjou, she wrote, was one of the 'most important

---

[7] Parker, *The Dutch Revolt*, p. 194.
[8] BN, MSS CCC 367, fol. 607, Henry III to Arnaud du Ferrier, 15 February 1579.
[9] Quoted from the preamble to the treaty of Nérac, which is printed in E. Haag, *La France Protestante*, (10 vols., Paris, 1846–59), vol. X, pp. 159–67. For a summary see Sutherland, *The Huguenot Struggle*, pp. 274–5.

affairs that the king, my lord and son, currently faces, and one of the most necessary'. When Anjou finally arrived in Paris on 16 March, there were great displays of friendship, loyalty, and devotion between the two royal brothers; and Catherine made every effort to perpetuate this impression of unity and harmony.[10] The duke remained in Paris for five days of 'continuous festivities and celebrations, with great jubilation all over the court', before departing once more for his *apanage* in Alençon, there to await the arrival of the queen mother from the south. He vowed to return to Paris only if the king granted three concessions: that he be allowed to enter the court with his full guard, that several of his favorites (including Bussy, Simier, and La Châtre) be admitted to the king's privy council, and that he be given a grant of 100,000 *livres*. 'Although these are important demands and pose some difficulty for him', wrote the Venetian ambassador, 'the king nevertheless has such a strong desire to satisfy his brother and completely win him over, with the tranquillity of the kingdom depending on it, that he will soon concede this and everything else besides'.[11] Anjou thus found himself in a strong bargaining position.

Although Catherine de Medici was still in the south trying to sort out the problems of the Huguenots in Provence and Dauphiné, she had not abandoned her efforts to secure a marriage alliance with Elizabeth. Like Henry, the queen mother wanted to placate Anjou in every possible way to prevent him from turning to the Protestants once more. After his brief visit with the king in March, Catherine urged him to accept Elizabeth's invitation for a personal interview:

I am certain that she will not be so ill-advised as to allow you to return discontented, for she realizes the wrong that she would commit by abusing the brother of such a great king as the king of France. The sooner the interview can take place the better . . . I am sure that the king will do everything in his power to help you, but you must consider that he does not have all the means that you both would like to assist your visit, seeing how the Estates have persuaded him to cut back on expenses. In order to placate them, he has had to cut out a lot of things.[12]

Nevertheless, Catherine informed Henry that the recent truce signed with the Huguenots at Nérac greatly facilitated Anjou's marriage plans, and she urged him to support the match.[13]

Jean de Simier remained in England throughout the spring of 1579, trying to arrange an interview between Elizabeth and his master. The English queen was obviously fond of Simier, which spawned numerous rumors that he was nothing more than a proxy lover. Despite such publicity, however, Simier made known

[10] BN, MSS fr. 15905, fols. 4–6, instructions of Henry III to Bellièvre, 3 March 1579; Catherine de Medici, *Lettres*, vol. VI, pp. 300, 318, Catherine to Bellièvre and Damville, 14 and 24 March 1579. See also Desjardins, vol. IV, pp. 252–4, Saracini to the Grand Duke, 20 and 25 March 1579.
[11] BN, MSS ital. 1731, fols. 9–11 and 21, Lippomano to the Signory, 21 March and 6 April 1579.
[12] Catherine de Medici, *Lettres*, vol. VI, p. 316, Catherine to Anjou, 24 March 1579.
[13] Ibid., pp. 319, 322, 25 March and 11 April 1579.

Anjou's wishes for an interview to the inner members of Elizabeth's privy council: Burghley, Sussex, Walsingham, and Leicester. From late March until early May, Simier presented Anjou's conditions for a marriage: that he be crowned king of England rather than just consort, that he have joint authority with Elizabeth over the royal estate, and that he be given an annual pension of £60,000 (about 600,000 *livres*) for his maintenance. While some members of Elizabeth's privy council were willing to grant these concessions, the chancellor of the exchequer, Sir Walter Mildmay, strongly objected to the last of them. He protested that Anjou was already one of the wealthiest men in France because of his vast *apanage*, 'which beeinge true he nedeth no supplie of the Queene, speciallie such a one as the Crowne of Englande cannot beare'.[14] Mildmay was not alone in his protests, and the negotiations broke down chiefly because Elizabeth's councillors were divided. Although Burghley and Sussex strongly supported the match, Walsingham, Leicester, and Mildmay vehemently opposed it. Francis Walsingham outlined the major objections in a treatise entitled 'A Consyderation of the dyseased State of the Realme, and how the same may in some Kynde of Sort be recovered'.[15] His objections focused on several key issues: the succession problem, how marriage to a Catholic would affect the religious settlement, and how the marriage would affect English foreign policy. First of all, Walsingham believed that a marriage with Anjou would not alter the succession problem. It was uncertain whether Elizabeth, at age 45, could safely conceive and bear a firstborn child. Walsingham went on to describe the efforts already afoot to marry the young son of Mary Stuart to some great noble family 'in respect of the expectation of this crown'. Secondly, the Puritan Walsingham strongly objected to Anjou's religion. With memories of papist plots all too fresh, it was easy to couch his religious prejudices in terms of national security interests and the stability of the religious settlement. Finally, Walsingham distrusted France, and French political aims. Should Anjou succeed his brother as king of France – a likely prospect, he thought – or should he and Elizabeth produce a single heir, he feared for the future of England's political independence. Moreover, it was his opinion that England should avoid entangling alliances with any Catholic power, and indeed, should encourage Protestant insurrection in those nations.

In rebuttal, William Cecil, Lord Burghley, outlined his own 'Obyectyons to be made ageynste the Queen's marryage with the Duke of Alençon, withe the awenswers to every [one] of them ... with a note of the benefyts [that] maye growe by the marryage, & of the perrells [that] maye growe by lacke of the marryage'.[16] Burghley deftly answered each of Walsingham's objections, in

---

[14] Quoted in Stanford E. Lehmberg, *Sir Walter Mildmay and Tudor Government* (Austin, 1964), p. 159.

[15] BL, Harl. MSS 1582, fols. 46–52. This important tract is unpublished, though a useful summary is provided in Read, *Mr Secretary Walsingham*, vol. II, pp. 14–18.

[16] HMC, *Salisbury MSS*, vol. II, pp. 239–45.

some instances with logic that was difficult to counter. Concerning the succession, Burghley argued that God would not possibly leave such a union childless, and that it was thus pointless to worry about the succession. He was equally sure that God would protect the life of the queen in childbirth. Moreover, he argued that the dangers of childbirth were 'by God's ordynaunce comon to the sexe, and not particular to her Majestie, and yf all wemen should forbere marryage for that respecte ther showld be no posteryte'. As for religion, Burghley saw no reason why Anjou and those French Catholics who lived with him at court could not worship as they pleased in private, without infringing on the religious settlement. Finally, Burghley countered Walsingham's most convincing objection – the fears of what might happen if Anjou should become the next king of France – with mere conjecture. Though he happened to be correct, Burghley was one of the few contemporaries in 1579 who doubted that Anjou would succeed his brother. 'It maye be', he wrote, 'that the Duke shall never be Kynge of Fraunce, and yf he be yet it is not lyke to be over hastely, & therfor no present perrell but futuer & accydentall'. After countering each of Walsingham's objections to the marriage, Burghley appended what he thought were the major benefits likely to result from the marriage. The most significant of these was the effect that an Anglo-French marriage would have on Spanish hegemony in Europe, as Burghley expected Henry III to join Anjou and Elizabeth in aiding the Dutch rebels. It was the first clear statement that supporting the revolt in the Netherlands was one of the objectives of the marriage for both parties.

The polarization of opinion of Elizabeth's privy councillors left the situation hopelessly unresolved, and it was decided that nothing more could be accomplished until the duke of Anjou came to England for a personal interview. Meanwhile, Simier tried to remain optimistic. Nevertheless, when he wrote to the sieur des Pruneaux, Anjou's agent still in Antwerp, in mid-April to report on his negotiations, he was not as hopeful as he had been when he arrived in England a few months earlier. 'I began to negotiate the articles of marriage between Monseigneur our master and the queen of England', he wrote, 'on the 5th of this month. I have been very hopeful, but I will wait until the curtain is drawn, the candle snuffed, and Monsieur is in bed [with the Queen] before saying any more. Only then will I speak with assurance.'[17]

Anjou returned to Paris on 26 April to confer with the king and his council about a possible voyage to England to meet Elizabeth. Henry was very supportive of the voyage, and even offered to escort his brother to Calais. Anjou despatched an officer from his household, the sieur de Bainville, to the queen mother, who was still in the south, to inform her of developments and to seek her advice.

---

[17] PRO/SP 78/3/fols. 41–2, Simier to Pruneaux, 12 April 1579: 'Jey ay toute bonne esperance, mes den dyre davantage jatandre que le rydeau soit tyre, la chandelle estainte et mons[ieu]r couche et lors jen parleray avec bonne assurance.'

Bainville relayed to her Simier's negotiations of the preceding few months, and the precise issues that divided Elizabeth's privy councillors. Catherine was strongly in favor of the voyage, and she urged Anjou to let Elizabeth set the time and place.[18] With the support of both the king and the queen mother, Anjou remained in Paris throughout May and June awaiting word from Elizabeth. It was a peaceful spring, the first in France for a number of years, and observers at court were particularly struck by the unusually close relationship between Henry and Anjou.[19]

On 29 June the English ambassador in Paris, Sir Amyas Paulet, informed Anjou 'that he might perchance have occasion to dispatch shortly into England', and a week later Walsingham sent Anjou a safe-conduct for the journey.[20] When the king made Anjou a grant of 600 *écus* (1,800 *livres*) later in the month, it appeared that the voyage across the Channel was at hand.[21] Opinion in England was less certain, however. In London the bookmakers were giving odds of two to one against Anjou's visit and three to one against the marriage. Francis Walsingham concurred with the bookmakers, and felt certain that Henry and Catherine would not allow Anjou to make the voyage. 'But matters of love and affection be not guided by wisdom', he noted.[22]

The international significance of the Anglo-French courtship was recognized by Pruneaux in Antwerp. On 3 August he sent Anjou a synopsis of events in the Netherlands, and reported that the Spanish had captured several fortified towns between Brussels and Antwerp. Moreover, he had learned that Philip II was making every effort to become the king of Portugal, the former king having died childless. 'It seems to me', Pruneaux went on, 'that you must advance the English marriage now more than ever, if that can be done. All of the talk here is about the interview.'[23] Pruneaux had already despatched the sieur d'Harengier to Paris in mid-July to discover what progress had been made.[24] He was unaware, however, that on the very day that he wrote to his master on 3 August, Anjou had departed from Paris and headed for Boulogne. Pruneaux received the news from Harengier, who wrote to him from Paris that Anjou had departed for England 'in the same fashion as his voyage to Flanders one year ago'. He was accompanied by fewer than a dozen members of his household, and was expected back within a

---

18 *CSPF*, vol. XIII, pp. 499–500, Amyas Paulet to Elizabeth, 28 April 1579; and Catherine de Medici, *Lettres*, vol. VI, pp. 488–91, Anjou's instructions to Bainville and Catherine's reply, 23 May 1579.
19 BN, MSS ital. 1731, fol. 55, Lippomano to the Signory, 20 May 1579.
20 *CSPF*, vol. XIV, pp. 3, 8, Paulet to Elizabeth, 4 July 1579, and safe-conduct for Anjou, 6 July 1579.
21 AN, K 100, no. 49, donation from the king, 15 July 1579.
22 Quoted in Read, *Mr Secretary Walsingham*, vol. II, p. 19.
23 Muller and Diegerick, *Documents*, vol. III, p. 116, Pruneaux to Anjou, 3 August 1579.
24 *CSPF*, vol. XIV, p. 17, Paulet to Walsingham, 14 July 1579.

fortnight, whether an agreement with Elizabeth was reached or not. 'Meanwhile', Harengier went on, 'everybody here just waits'.[25]

II

Though the duke of Anjou departed from Paris on 3 August and reached Boulogne in just a few days, his journey was delayed by bad weather in the Channel. As a result he did not arrive at Greenwich until 17 August. Because of recent propaganda spread by the Puritans, Elizabeth hoped to keep his visit secret from the population at large. Therefore, Anjou travelled incognito as the seigneur du Pont de Sé. His first meeting with the English queen was an amicable one, according to observers, and Elizabeth was pleasantly surprised to discover that all the reports of his pockmarked visage were exaggerated. They spoke in French, as Anjou knew neither English nor Italian. Strangely, Anjou never met with the privy council. The duration of his short visit was spent either at Greenwich or at Richmond Court, attending numerous balls, dances, dinners, and parties. He departed on 29 August, less than two weeks after his arrival, apparently as taken with Elizabeth as she was with him. It was an uneventful visit and the marriage was hardly discussed. Many on the French side remained optimistic, however. Though no promises of marriage were exchanged, Anjou was encouraged.[26]

The principal significance of Anjou's brief fortnight in England lies in the hostility to, and popular reaction against, the match that it provoked in England. Bernardino de Mendoza, the Spanish ambassador in England who was always prone to exaggeration, wrote on 25 August that several opponents of the marriage were plotting to do something about it. Apparently Leicester, the earl of Pembroke, Lord Henry Sidney, and a few relatives (Philip Sidney probably among them) had been meeting to decide what to do about the marriage issue. According to Mendoza they were encouraged by the fact that 'the people in general are threatening to revolt over it'.[27] The English populace was so aroused largely because of a pamphlet published that same month by John Stubbs.[28] Stubbs was a zealous Puritan from Norfolk, whose religious convictions as much as anything else prompted the pamphlet, which William Camden described as

[25] Muller and Diegerick, *Documents*, vol. III, pp. 119–20, Harengier to Pruneaux, 7 August 1579. Anjou clearly believed that the marriage would benefit his affairs in the Netherlands. See ibid., pp. 74–7, Anjou to Pruneaux, 11 June 1579.
[26] The best accounts of the visit are in ibid., pp. 128–30, Castelnau to Pruneaux, 31 August 1579; BN, MSS fr. 15973, fol. 173, Castelnau to Henry, [1] September 1579; ibid., fol. 178, Castelnau to Henry, 4 September 1579; and *CODOIN*, vol. XCI, pp. 416–18, Mendoza to Philip II, 25 August 1579. Also see Kervijn de Lettenhove, *Huguenots*, vol. V, pp. 390–3.
[27] *CODOIN*, vol. XCI, p. 417, Mendoza to Philip II, 25 August 1579.
[28] For details of Stubbs's life, see the *Dictionary of National Biography*, vol. XIX, pp. 118–19.

'written against the marriage with a stinking stile'.[29] Although Anjou's visit had been expected in England for months, Stubbs had no idea that his tract would appear just a week or so before he arrived. Thus, when his *Discoverie of a Gaping Gulf whereinto England is like to be swallowed by an other French marriage, if the Lord forbid not the banes, by letting her Maiestie see the sin and punishment thereof* (London, 1579) was printed on 6 and 7 August, it was read at court with more than passing interest.

The *Gaping Gulf* included many of the same arguments put forth by Francis Walsingham in his own discourse against the marriage, although Stubbs couched everything in unashamedly Puritan language. 'It is a sin, a great and mighty sin', he wrote, 'to couple a Christian lady, a member of Christ, to a prince and good son of Rome, that anti-Christian city'. Moreover, this particular prince was from France, 'a den of idolatry, a kingdom of darkness, confessing Belial and serving Baal'.[30] Stubbs answered with a vengeance those supporters of the marriage who argued that it would prove beneficial to the French Huguenots. 'This man is a son of Henry the Second, whose family, ever since he married with Catherine of Italy, is fatal, as it were, to resist the gospel.'[31] Moreover, Stubbs maintained that Anjou would have doubtless participated in the planning and execution of the St Bartholomew's massacres in August 1572 with his brothers, except for the fact that 'he was not old enough to execute anything'.[32] To be fair, Anjou's *volte-face* with the Huguenots after the peace of Monsieur contributed to that impression:

He was content to be used to pull towns out of Protestants' hands, and in wars against them, namely in La Charité and Issoire, where, after his revolt, he committed such abominable cruelties and beastly disorders as, if he now meant never so good faith and had never so honest a mind in these matters, yet is it not like that this man's foul hands should lay one stone of God's church.[33]

Stubbs concluded that the duke had no justification for coming to England 'unless he had some extraordinary purpose and some Italian quintessence of mischief meant to be compassed against the Church of Christ'.[34]

Stubbs was also cognizant of the dangers if Elizabeth married 'the brother of childless France'. Should Henry die soon after the marriage, Stubbs feared that either Elizabeth would have to go to France with her husband, whereby England would be ruled by a viceroy, or else she would remain in England and rule 'diminished in sovereignty', as Anjou governed her and her state. In either case Stubbs viewed England as the slave and France the master.[35] Moreover, he felt that French domination of England would not be remedied even if the marriage

---

29 William Camden, *The Historie of the Most renowned and Victorious Princesse Elizabeth, Late Queene of England* (London, 1630), book iii, p. 9. 'Stinking' is probably a printer's error for 'stinging'.
30 Lloyd E. Berry (ed.), *John Stubbs's Gaping Gulf* (Charlottesville, 1968), pp. 6–7.
31 Ibid., pp. 21–2.
32 Ibid., p. 24.   33 Ibid.   34 Ibid., p. 29.   35 Ibid., pp. 48–50.

produced offspring, which he doubted because of Elizabeth's age and Anjou's health. In any event, if only daughters were produced, he felt that they would doubtless be married to Frenchmen and their offspring would be reared under Roman Catholicism. Should Anjou and Elizabeth have but a single son, he would surely return to France and rule England through a viceroy. Finally, if there were two or more sons, Stubbs predicted civil war as the inevitable result of disagreement among the brothers. In short, Stubbs was convinced that 'the Frenchman's marriage is most dangerous to this realm'.[36]

There is no doubt that the *Gaping Gulf* was circulated and read in a very short time. That its publication coincided with Anjou's visit, which was no longer a secret after his return to France, doubtless helped sales. Unfortunately for Stubbs and his printer, Hugh Singleton, Elizabeth was not amused and on 27 September she condemned the pamphlet as libelous and treasonous. Because Stubbs had so aroused popular feeling against the marriage, she also prohibited the possession of the *Gaping Gulf* and ordered the lord mayor of London to collect and burn all copies.[37] Moreover, Stubbs was rewarded for his efforts by being brought to trial for sedition, along with the printer Singleton, and William Page, a London gentleman who purchased fifty copies of the pamphlet and sent them to Cornwall to be circulated among his friends.[38] Justice was swift, and on 30 October Stubbs and Page were convicted and sentenced to lose their right hands as punishment (Singleton was fortuitously acquitted). Stubbs was convicted rather ironically under a statute passed in the reign of Mary to prohibit similar seditious writings against her consort, Philip II of Spain. When one of the lawyers hearing the case protested that this particular statute applied only to Mary's reign and became void on her death, Elizabeth immediately sent him to the Tower. Thus it is clear that the queen demanded Stubbs's conviction.[39]

The sentence was duly carried out by the sheriff of Middlesex in the marketplace at Westminster on 3 November. Stubbs courageously mounted the scaffold and managed to utter a pun: 'Pray for me, now my calamity is at hand.' Then, but only after three blows, his right hand was severed at the wrist. He stood up at the block, doffed his hat with his left hand, and cried out, 'God save the Queen!' The stunned onlookers then watched Stubbs collapse and faint. When William Page suffered the same fate, he raised his bloody stump and cried out, 'I have left there a true Englishman's hand.' The scene was recorded by enough eyewitnesses to be credible, including William Camden, who noted that the crowd was unusually moved by the proceedings. 'The multitude standing about', he wrote, 'was altogether silent, either out of horror of this new and unwonted punishment, or else out of pitty towards the man being of most honest

36 Ibid., pp. 51–6.
37 For the *Gaping Gulf*'s impact on public opinion, see *CODOIN*, vol. XCI, pp. 430–1, Mendoza to Philip II and Zayas, 25 and 29 September 1579; and BN, MSS ital. 1731, fols. 233–4, Lippomano to the Signory, 23 October 1579.
38 Berry (ed.), *Gaping Gulf*, p. xxvi, introduction. 39 Camden, *Historie*, book iii, p. 10.

and unblameable report, or else out of hatred of the marriage, which most men presaged would be the overthrow of Religion'.[40]

Stubbs was no fanatic. He simply dared to put into print what many Englishmen were already thinking. The prolamations of Stubbs and Page at the block were especially apposite, as they linked freedom of speech and the press with loyalty to the crown. Thus, they viewed themselves as patriots rather than traitors. As one English historian has recently pointed out, Stubbs was but one in the long tradition of Wentworth, Prynne, Hampden, Pym, and Cromwell. By an incredible irony, Stubbs lost his right hand just a few yards from the spot where, seventy years later, the cause of that long tradition exacted a greater trophy, the head of Charles I. In 1579, however, John Stubbs's *Gaping Gulf* was a harbinger of popular hostility toward the Anjou marriage, and one that Elizabeth could hardly ignore.[41]

Had Stubbs's tract been the only opposition to the marriage, Elizabeth could probably have procrastinated long enough to ride out the storm. Intense hostility to the match at court, however, made such a scheme impossible. Although Leicester, Pembroke, Sidney, and the others who met on 25 August to discuss the marriage probably had no intention of inciting popular insurrection as Mendoza implied, they did organize their efforts to oppose the match at court. They decided, in fact, to present a private statement against the marriage to the queen. The result was the famous letter written to Elizabeth by Philip Sidney 'touching her marriage with Monsieur'.[42] Though Sidney was a well known opponent of the Anjou marriage by the autumn of 1579 when the letter was written, it was almost certainly his uncle, Robert Dudley, earl of Leicester, and his future father-in-law, Francis Walsingham, who came up with the idea and urged him to write it.[43] Sidney's letter contained many of the arguments of the *Gaping Gulf*, which Sidney doubtless read, and the two have often been compared. Sidney's letter was a different form of propaganda altogether, however. Whereas Stubbs's tract was written to arouse public opinion, Sidney's letter was meant only for the eyes of the queen, the privy councillors, and several close friends. It seems to have been designed especially for the propaganda campaign waged by Walsingham in the council. Thus, Sidney's letter was a much more politicized statement of opposition to the marriage than the *Gaping Gulf*.

---

[40] Ibid. Also see Berry (ed.), *Gaping Gulf*, pp. xxxiv–vi.

[41] A. G. Dickens, 'The Elizabethans and St Bartholomew', in Soman (ed.), *The Massacre of St Bartholomew*, p. 70. See also Wallace T. MacCaffrey, *Queen Elizabeth and the Making of Policy, 1572–1588* (Princeton, 1981), pp. 243–66, who demonstrates that the *Gaping Gulf* was 'just the tip of the iceberg', as virtually every segment of the English population opposed the marriage.

[42] I have cited the edition of Philip Sidney's 'Letter to Elizabeth' in Duncan-Jones and Van Dorsten (eds.), *Miscellaneous Prose of Sir Philip Sidney*, pp. 33–57.

[43] Roger Howell, *Sir Philip Sidney, the Shepherd Knight* (London, 1968), pp. 67–8. There is some evidence that Sidney was forced to write the letter. See Hubert Languet's letter to Sidney of 22

Like Stubbs, Sidney played on the religious issue. He urged Elizabeth to consider the consequences of a marriage with a Roman Catholic, and especially how it would affect the English people:

How their hearts will be galled, if not alienated, when they shall see you take to husband a Frenchman, and a Papist, in whom, howsoever fine wits may find further dangers or painted excuses, the very common people will know this: that he is the son of the Jezebel of our age; that his brother made oblation of his own sister's marriage, the easier to make massacres of all sexes; that he himself, contrary to his promise, and against all gratefulness, having had his liberty and principal estates chiefly by the Huguenots' means, did sack La Charité and utterly spoil Issoire with fire and sword. This I say, even at the first sight, gives occasion to all the true religions to abhor such a master, and so consequently to diminish much of the hopeful love they have long held to you.[44]

Thus, Sidney (like Stubbs) tried to tie Anjou to the St Bartholomew's massacres and attempted to make him solely responsible for the atrocities of La Charité and Issoire. Moreover, he held Anjou guilty by association of the sins of Charles IX, Henry III, and Catherine de Medici.

Sidney then took a more effective line of attack by pointing out Anjou's personal deficiencies:

His inconstant attempts against his brother; his thrusting himself into the Low Country matters; his sometimes seeking the King of Spain's daughter, sometimes your Majesty; are evident testimonies he is carried away with every wind of hope, taught to love greatness any way gotten, and having for the motioners and ministers of his mind only such young men as have shown they think evil contentment a sufficient ground of any rebellion; whose age gives them to have seen noe other commonwealth, but in faction; and divers of which have defiled their hands in odious murders. With such fancies and favourites, is it to be hoped for that he will be contained within the limits of your conditions? Since, in truth, it were strange, he that cannot be contented to be second person in France and heir apparent [*sic*], would come to be the second person in England, where he shall pretend no way sovereignty.[45]

Sidney was open-minded enough to admit that there were political advantages to the marriage, as well as hope for a successor. Moreover, he openly refused to dwell on Anjou's poor health. There was one major drawback to the marriage as Sidney perceived it, however, which outweighed the advantages. This was the fact that Anjou was French 'and desiring to make France great: your Majesty English, and desiring nothing less than that France should grow great'.[46]

Philip Sidney's battle against the Anjou marriage was much more tactful and eloquent than Stubbs's. Indeed, there is no evidence to indicate that Elizabeth

October 1580 in S. A. Pears (ed.), *The Correspondence of Sir Philip Sidney and Hubert Languet* (London, 1845), p. 187.
[44] Sidney, 'Letter to Elizabeth', p. 48.
[45] Ibid., pp. 49–50. Anjou was the heir presumptive and not the heir apparent.
[46] Ibid., pp. 52, 56.

ever held Sidney in disfavor because of his letter. The long-held belief that Sidney's absence from court in 1580 was due to the letter has been thoroughly demolished.[47] Moreover, the letter must have been effective. While it is not known for certain exactly when the letter was composed and circulated, there was mounting opposition in the privy council by the beginning of October 1579. Elizabeth summoned the council for a special meeting on 2 October at Greenwich, in order to consider the marriage and offer advice. She doubtless hoped that the council would endorse the match, thus making it easier for her to present a Catholic prince to a Protestant nation.[48] The council, which sat for five days 'from eight in the morning until seven in the evening without leaving their places' according to Mendoza, had decidedly turned, however, towards the position of Leicester and Walsingham. Of all the councillors present, only Lord Burghley and the earl of Sussex favored the match.[49] The councillors were mindful of Stubbs's fate, however, and they chose not to reveal their near unanimity on the subject. Instead, they informed Elizabeth on 8 October that they were grateful that she was of a mind to marry, and they, of course, would support her in whatever she decided. But even this was not quite what the queen wanted to hear. As poor Burghley, who had supported the marriage all along, recorded, 'Her Majesty's answers were very sharp in reprehending all such as she thought would make arguments against the marriage'.[50]

Thus, the innocent visit of the duke of Anjou to England for a brief fortnight in August 1579 stirred up a tempest of protest against his proposed marriage to Queen Elizabeth. Despite the queen's efforts to bridle the opponents of the marriage, opposition continued to mount in the autumn, and she found herself in the unenviable position of being thwarted by her own privy council. And the reaction to the *Gaping Gulf* indicates that most Englishmen probably opposed the marriage as well. Moreover, even English Catholics, who might have been expected to support the match, found Anjou too fickle and self-serving. Those recusants who sought foreign support looked to Spain rather than to France. As Sir Henry Cobham later remarked, 'our English Romanists ... presuppose that Monsieur seeks nothing but his own preferment'.[51] The marriage was not entirely abandoned by either side, however, due to other mitigating factors, chiefly Anjou's continued involvement in the Netherlands. It was nevertheless apparent for the duration of their alleged courtship that there was mounting opposition to the marriage in England. Ultimately, this proved impossible to overcome.

---

47 Ibid., pp. 34–5, introduction.
48 W. MacCaffrey, *Queen Elizabeth and the Making of Policy*, pp. 249–66.
49 *CODOIN*, vol. xci, pp. 434–5, Mendoza to Philip II, 16 October 1579. Also see the proceedings of the council in HMC, *Salisbury MSS*, vol. ii, pp. 267–71.
50 HMC, *Salisbury MSS*, vol. ii, 273, Message delivered from the privy council to Elizabeth by Lord Burghley, 7–8 October 1579.
51 *CSPF*, vol. xv, p. 511, Cobham to Walsingham, 3 March 1582. Also see John Bossy, 'English Catholics and the French Marriage, 1577–81', *Recusant History*, v (1959), 2–16.

III

Upon his return to Paris at the beginning of September 1579, the duke of Anjou was greeted with the news that his long-term favorite, Louis de Clermont, Bussy d'Amboise, had been murdered while he was in England. Bussy, who had been governor of the duchy of Anjou since 1576, was never a popular figure there because of his all too frequent attempts to raise taxes, as well as his heavy-handed means of collecting them. It was not a taxpayer, however, but a nobleman, the seigneur de Montsoreau, who assassinated him at the château de Coutancière near Saumur on 19 August 1579. The circumstances surrounding the murder have never been adequately explained. Some accounts say that it was because Bussy was having an affair with Montsoreau's wife, while others say that the motives were political. In any event, Anjou had recently fallen out with his former favorite, and was apparently unconcerned when he learned of his death.[52]

The duke of Anjou arrived back in Paris late in the evening of 3 September, and the following morning went to see the king. Anjou described his sojourn in England and, according to the Venetian ambassador, reported that Elizabeth had promised him financial aid for his enterprise in the Netherlands.[53] This may have been just conjecture on Lippomano's part, although Burghley had given earlier indications that the Anjou–Elizabeth courtship was not totally unrelated to affairs in the Netherlands. In any case, both Anjou and Henry appeared to be optimistic about the trip to England and confident that the proposed marriage would take place in the near future, despite the opposition across the Channel.[54]

Anjou left Paris in late September to await the arrival of the queen mother in his *apanage* in Alençon. Catherine, who had been in the south for more than a year, was expected back at court in October or November, and the king instructed Anjou to meet her and escort her back to Paris. Fearful that Anjou's departure might be interpreted as another royal row, Henry made every effort to assure those not at court that he and his brother had never been on better terms.[55] Unfortunately, Anjou contracted a severe case of diarrhea (*un dévoyement d'estomac*) in early November and was forced to retire to his château at

[52] De Thou, *Histoire universelle*, vol. V, pp. 614–15; L'Estoile, *Journal*, vol. I, pp. 321–3; and Desjardins, vol. IV, pp. 263–4, Saracini to the Grand Duke, 24 August 1579 (although the claims of De Thou and others that Henry and Anjou conspired to have Bussy killed are a little far-fetched).

[53] BN, MSS ital. 1731, fol. 164, Lippomano to the Signory, 4 September 1579; ibid., fols. 246–7, same to same, 6 November 1579; and *Acta Nuntiaturae Gallicae*, vol. VIII, pp. 516–17, Anselmo Dandino to Cardinal di Como, 11 October 1579.

[54] BN, MSS fr. 15973, fol. 178, Castelnau to Henry, 4 September 1579; BN, MSS CCC 367, fol. 721, Henry to Arnaud du Ferrier, 9 September 1579; and Muller and Diegerick, *Documents*, vol. III, pp. 158–9, Anjou to Champvallon, 3 November 1579.

[55] For instance see BN, MSS fr. 3344, fol. 24, Henry to Montpensier, 30 September 1579; and BN, MSS CCC 367, fol. 740, Henry to Arnaud du Ferrier, 9 October 1579.

Château-Thierry northeast of Paris.[56] He was thus not present when the queen mother arrived back at court in mid-November, and this spawned further rumors that he had fallen out with the king yet again. In fact, Anjou was somewhat upset that Henry had still not executed his promise to make him the lieutenant-general of the realm, and he did not return to court until December, despite numerous attempts by the queen mother to persuade him otherwise.[57]

In November, however, Anjou was contacted at Château-Thierry by an agent of the prince of Parma, who offered to make a deal to bring the war in the Netherlands to a quick conclusion. Anjou thought that Parma's desire to end the war was laudable, but he was suspicious of his motives. He informed the agent that, in any case, he could do nothing without conferring with 'the princes, princesses and others of his allies and confederates'.[58] Before he returned to Paris, Anjou wrote to William of Orange, the Dutch States-General, and for the first time, the members of the union of Utrecht. He made it clear that he had no intention of coming to terms with Parma. 'You had better take care', he cautioned the States, 'that you are not deceived under the pretext of peace offerings, as you surely will be if you fall for the subtle promises of the enemies'.[59]

Why the sudden interest of Philip and Parma in negotiating a peace? The situation in Portugal doubtless played a major role. When the childless king of Portugal, Dom Sebastian, was killed in the battle of Alcázarquivir in August 1578, his aged uncle, Cardinal Henry, succeeded him to the throne. As Henry was not expected to live long, a fierce struggle had already begun over the succession. Philip II, who probably had the best claim, decided to shift much of the manpower and most of the resources used to wage the Netherlands campaign to Portugal in order to secure his claim to the Portuguese throne. There was thus an urgent need to make peace in the Netherlands in order to facilitate the removal of most of the Spanish army.[60] Another factor that has received less attention, however, was the Anjou–Elizabeth marriage project. Just one year earlier Philip had written off the marriage as mere fancy and bluff.[61] Anjou's brief visit to England, however, forced Philip to take the match more seriously. Moreover, those on the Spanish side began to suspect that Elizabeth and Anjou were interested in more than marriage. Mendoza wrote to Philip on

---

56 BN, MSS CCC 367, fol. 772, Henry to Arnaud du Ferrier, 11 November 1579.

57 *Acta Nuntiaturae Gallicae*, VIII, 552–4, Dandino to Como, 4 and 6 December 1579; and *CSPV*, VII, 662–3, Lippomano and Priuli to the Signory, 19 November and 4 and 6 December 1579.

58 Muller and Diegerick, *Documents*, vol. III, pp. 159–61, Anjou to Pruneaux, 15 November 1579.

59 Ibid., pp. 163–7, Anjou to the States and the union of Utrecht, both 29 November 1579; and Groen van Prinsterer, *Archives*, vol. VII, pp. 161–2, Anjou to Orange, 29 November 1579.

60 G. Parker, 'Spain, her enemies and the Revolt of the Netherlands', *Past and Present*, 49 (1970), 87; idem, 'Why did the Dutch Revolt last eighty years?', *Transactions of the Royal Historical Society*, 5th series, XXVI (1976), 59; and A. W. Lovett, 'Some Spanish attitudes to the Netherlands, 1572–78', *Tijdschrift voor Geschiedenis*, LXXXV (1972), 29–30.

61 *CODOIN*, vol. XCI, p. 296, Philip to Mendoza, 15 October 1578.

16 October that Simier and Elizabeth 'still continue in negotiations to unite with France in order to obstruct Your Majesty in Portugal'.[62] Philip's ambassador in Paris, Juan de Vargas Mexia, believed that Anjou and Elizabeth doubtless planned to interfere in the Netherlands as well. 'The marriage contemplated by the duke of Anjou with Elizabeth', he wrote to Philip in January 1580, 'has no other goal but to tear away Flanders from Spain, with the help of England. French Catholics and Protestants are in agreement on this point.'[63] Thus, Anjou's projected marriage with Elizabeth, and the threat of Anglo-French military assistance to Portugal and the Netherlands, was another reason why Philip and Parma sought to make peace in late 1579.

The popular hostility to a French marriage continued to mount in England. In February 1580, Henry III expressed his growing concern to his ambassador in London, Michel de Castelnau, sieur de Mauvissière. 'I am well aware of the intrigues which are perpetrated to retard the marriage of my good sister and cousin, the queen of England, and my brother the duke of Anjou', he wrote, 'and it should not be doubted that such things are done expressly by the Puritans and other enemies of the said marriage, not only to retard it but to destroy it any way they can'.[64] Henry was correct in his assessment. Elizabeth had sent Simier back to France in late November 1579 with a promise that she would marry Anjou, but only if she could get her people to support the match. If she proved unable to win them over within two months, her promise to marry would be null and void. Simier had no choice but to agree with this proposal, an ingenious plan to maintain her authority in the council without alienating the Puritans.[65] As more than two months had elapsed since Simier's return without any response from Elizabeth, Henry had every reason to suspect that men such as Stubbs and Sidney had sabotaged the marriage.

Meanwhile, in the Netherlands, William of Orange spent the winter of 1579–80 trying to convince the deputies of the Dutch States-General that Anjou's aid was vital to the success of their cause. In January 1580 the deputies finally agreed on certain conditions that must be met if they were to negotiate another treaty with Anjou. First of all, the duke had to assure them that his brother Henry would support his enterprise, specifically by providing 8,000 foot and 2,000 horse. Anjou was required to uphold all of their ancient rights, franchises, privileges, and liberties, as well as the *religionsvrede*, or religious settlement that was established in each province. He must be guided in all his activities by a council composed mainly of Netherlanders. And finally, the States promised to provide him with 160,000 *écus* (480,000 *livres*) per month 'in order

[62] Ibid., p. 435, Mendoza to Philip, 16 October 1579.
[63] Lefèvre (ed.), *Correspondance de Philippe II*, vol. I, p. 733, Vargas Mexia to Philip II, 6 January 1580.
[64] BN, MSS CCC 473, fols. 15–17, Henry III to Castelnau, 8 February 1580.
[65] HMC, *Salisbury MSS*, vol. II, pp. 275–6, certificate signed by Simier, 24 November 1579.

to make war'.[66] Anjou readily agreed to the conditions, and urged the deputies to go back to their respective provincial States to inform them of their negotiations and to conclude a formal treaty.[67]

More significant, perhaps, were the efforts of François de la Noue, Philippe du Plessis-Mornay, and Henry, prince of Condé. These three Huguenots made significant contributions to winning over the towns of Ghent and Cambrai to Anjou's cause. Indeed, primarily due to the groundwork laid by Mornay, the city of Ghent was the first town or province to withdraw its sovereignty from Philip II and offer it to Anjou since the overture from Holland and Zeeland in 1576, which it did on 18 February 1580. It was not a unanimous decision, as, of the tripartite council which governed the town, only the tradesmen and weavers supported Anjou. The bourgeois members refused to offer sovereignty to anyone.[68] Although Anjou was offered only limited powers and was required to maintain the religious status quo in the town, the resolution taken by Ghent was nonetheless significant. Hubert Languet, who was living in Antwerp at the time, remarked upon it to his friend, Philip Sidney. 'What inconsistency is this of the men of Ghent!', he wrote. 'A year ago they were cutting in pieces the name and character of Anjou with the bitterest abuse and most slanderous lampoons: and his envoys were driven from the city at night with ignominy. They even formed designs upon his life; and yet now they are the first with their votes to give over the sovereignty of the country to him.'[69] Moreover, the provincial States of Flanders, who were meeting in Ghent, followed suit on 22 February. As Ghent had done, they gave Anjou only limited powers, and failed to spell out their conception of sovereignty very clearly.[70] Finally, François de la Noue and the prince of Condé negotiated a treaty with the town of Cambrai on 24 February. While the magistrates there did not offer Anjou any form of sovereignty, they did offer their allegiance, and allowed him to establish a garrison there under Condé's command.[71] Why did the deputies from Flanders and the magistrates of Ghent and Cambrai – many of whom were Calvinists – suddenly decide to support a French Catholic prince? The reasons are not absolutely clear, but the fear of reprisals from the Catholic malcontents of the union of Arras was probably the principal motive. And the assurances of Protestants like Mornay, La Noue, and Condé doubtless contributed to the decision.

As the duke of Anjou spent the late winter and spring of 1580 in his *apanage* in

---

66 Muller and Diegerick, *Documents*, vol. III, pp. 222–5, propositions of the States to Anjou, 13 January 1580 (with his responses in the margin, dated 12 February 1580).
67 Ibid., pp. 225–6, Anjou to the States, 12 February 1580.
68 Ibid., pp. 235–40, 'Résolution des trois membres de la ville de Gand concernant l'acceptation conditionelle du duc d'Anjou comme protecteur et souverain', from Ghent, 18 February 1580.
69 Pears (ed.), *Correspondence of Sidney and Languet*, p. 174, Languet to Sidney, 27 February 1580.
70 Muller and Diegerick, *Documents*, vol. III, pp. 245–8, Anjou to the Four Members of Flanders, 10 March 1580.
71 Ibid., pp. 241–4, treaty made by La Noue and Condé with the town of Cambrai, 24 February 1580.

Angers watching his star ascend in the Netherlands, his attention was diverted by more explosive matters in France. The king's lieutenant-general in Guyenne, Armand de Gontaut, baron de Biron, refused to honor some of the concessions that the queen mother had granted to the Huguenots in the truce signed at Nérac in February 1579. As a result, many Protestants throughout the Midi began to re-arm in the spring of 1580. By mid-April the situation had become so alarming that Catherine feared violence was likely to break out in the region. She notified the king that 'those of the so-called reformed religion are taking up arms everywhere'.[72] Under the pretext that he never received the *sénéchaussées* of Quercy and Agenais as part of the promised dowry of his wife Marguerite de Valois, Henry of Navarre raised a Huguenot army and made preparations to lay siege to the town of Cahors in Quercy. Thus, what became dubbed by the memoirists as the *guerre des amoureux* marked the renewal of the civil wars. When Navarre's forces finally captured Cahors on 5 May, many Catholics were massacred, their churches razed, and their homes burned. 'The town was captured and pillaged', noted the historian De Thou, 'with endless cruelty'.[73]

With the rebellious provinces in the Netherlands making overtures to Anjou through Huguenots such as Mornay, La Noue, and Condé, Henry and Catherine were naturally concerned that Anjou might be persuaded to renew his former ties with the French Protestants. Secretary Villeroy was despatched to Anjou on 5 May, the very day Cahors was taken, to find out what it would take 'to keep Monsieur satisfied'.[74] The result of the visit was that Anjou promised to mediate with Navarre and the Huguenots to restore peace in the Midi in return for the lieutenant-generalcy of the realm, the one office that had eluded him since the death of Charles IX in 1574. With the Protestants in arms in the south, Henry and Catherine had no option but to accept Anjou's terms. They were careful, however, to impose some conditions of their own which limited the powers of the office. Anjou was not allowed to raise money outside his *apanage*, open the royal *cachet* letters, or do virtually anything without the consent of the king's council. Moreover, Henry, duke of Guise was named as the deputy lieutenant-general to ensure that Anjou did not abuse the office. Anjou accepted these restrictions and agreed to try to restore peace in the Midi, which satisfied the king.[75]

Some observers at court were justifiably cynical about the king's decision to employ Anjou to restore peace in the Midi. 'Monsieur his brother', wrote the Venetian ambassador, 'wants peace, not caring how it is achieved, in order to

---

[72] Catherine de Medici, *Lettres*, vol. VII, p. 245, Catherine to Henry III, 16 April 1580.
[73] De Thou, *Histoire universelle* vol. VII, p. 6.
[74] BN, MSS ital. 1731, fols. 336–7, Priuli to the Signory, 6 May 1580. Also see Sutherland, *French Secretaries of State*, p. 213.
[75] Desjardins, vol. IV, p. 309, Renieri to the Grand Duke, 9 May 1580; BN, MSS CCC 368, fols. 83–4 and 102–4, Henry to Arnaud du Ferrier, 11 May and 6 June 1580.

make war abroad'.[76] Certainly, Anjou had been warned for months by Pruneaux and others that his enterprise in the Netherlands was jeopardized by war in France. 'I deplore our miseries and calamities [in France]', wrote Philippe du Plessis-Mornay in March 1580, 'but more than this I fear another drawback, that these [Dutch] provinces cannot be assisted if this continues'.[77] Moreover, this was the same message sent to Anjou by the provincial States of Flanders, who despatched two deputies to France in April to sign a formal treaty of sovereignty with the duke. 'There is nothing more prejudicial to this negotiation', the deputies cautioned Anjou, 'than seeing the forces of France banded together against one another. We beseech His Highness to employ all his credit and authority with the parties involved, and especially with the king, in order to stop this war. If it continues, it is not necessary to doubt that the assistance to these provinces would be broken off.'[78] The warnings of the Flemish deputies were all the more apposite because they were shared by the States-General as a whole. The Dutch States had been monitoring Anjou's situation very closely and owing largely to Orange's efforts earlier in the year, they were considering making a formal treaty with him.[79] Indeed, François de Provyn and Noel de Caron, the two deputies of the States of Flanders who were despatched to the duke of Anjou, found him very well disposed toward their cause. Moreover, they were hopeful that the States-General would soon make a formal treaty with him.[80]

Provyn and Caron, in fact, wrote to the States and asked them to send their own deputies to the duke as soon as possible. They noted that the large number of troops that Henry III had allowed Anjou to raise was intended for the Netherlands:

What he [Anjou] has not wanted to declare openly as yet is that the assistance which he is preparing is for Your Lordships, and according to our calculations, the total comes to more than ten thousand foot and three or four thousand horse. This is not counting the nobles who have resolved to follow him, which we gather will be a considerable number. It is even confirmed that the *prince dauphin* [François de Bourbon, dauphin d'Auvergne and son of the duke of Montpensier], brother of madame the princess of Orange, will accompany him.[81]

The two Flemish deputies thus painted a very attractive picture of the duke of Anjou, which must have made a favorable impression in the States.

The possibility of the Dutch States withdrawing their sovereignty from Philip

---

[76] BN, MSS ital. 1731, fol. 362, Priuli to the Signory, 12 July 1580 (incorrectly dated 1 July 1580 in *CSPV*, vol. VII, p. 641).

[77] Muller and Diegerick, *Documents*, vol. III, p. 282, Mornay to Pruneaux, 29 March 1580; and ibid., p. 273, Pruneaux to Anjou, 22 March 1580.

[78] Ibid., p. 304, States of Flanders to Anjou, April 1580.

[79] Groen van Prinsterer, *Archives*, vol. III, pp. 242–3 and 256–7, both Orange to Pruneaux, 2 and 15 March 1580.

[80] Muller and Diegerick, *Documents*, vol. III, p. 322, Provyn and Caron to Pruneaux, 6 June 1580.

[81] Ibid., pp. 323–30, Provyn and Caron to the States-General, 7 June 1580 (quotation from p. 328).

II and offering it to the duke of Anjou emerged from the negotiations in progress since 13 January 1580, when the deputies were asked to present the matter to their respective provinces.[82] In the interim the prince of Orange tried to overcome all opposition. He argued that the provinces of the Netherlands had always obeyed their natural prince and were content to do so, 'provided that they could be treated like loyal subjects and vassals, and not like slaves of some cruel and foreign tyrant'. He maintained that Philip II had abused their rights and privileges, in addition to overturning the religious settlement in some provinces. Thus, the regrettable result was that they were forced to turn to another prince.[83] These arguments eventually persuaded a majority of the deputies, who had been conferring with their constituencies since January. And on 24 June 1580 the Dutch States-General adopted twenty-seven articles upon which to base an agreement with the duke of Anjou. Although any decision taken by the States was theoretically unanimous, the deputies from Gelderland, Tournai, Utrecht, and Brabant had not been given authority by their respective provincial States to make a treaty with Anjou, and therefore had to abstain.[84] Especially significant were the reasons which prevented the deputies from Brabant from supporting the articles. Above all, they were shackled by the opposition of the local magistrates of Antwerp, the major city of Brabant and the *de facto* capital of the Netherlands. Economic factors outweighed political considerations, as the magistrates of the city council feared that a break with Spain would deal a mortal blow to the city's thriving commerce.[85] Antwerp's hostility to Anjou seriously weakened the decision of the States to offer him a treaty.

The discussions at Tours between Anjou and the Flemish deputies during the summer of 1580 did not go unnoticed by Elizabeth. Alarmed by what appeared to be the likely prospect of French intervention in the Netherlands, she despatched a special envoy to Tours in early July, Sir Edward Stafford. She hoped that Stafford could revive the flagging marriage negotiations, but more importantly, she wished to be kept abreast of the discussions between Anjou and the Dutch. If Elizabeth had any hope of dissuading Anjou from his enterprise by proffering marriage, she was quickly disappointed. By the time Stafford arrived at Tours, Anjou was more determined than ever to bring the wars in France to a quick halt in order to negotiate a treaty with the Dutch States-General. Moreover, on 16 July the king gave Anjou 20,000 *écus* (60,000 *livres*) which the queen mother had promised him several months earlier, a monthly stipend 'to cover the expenses of his travels and other necessities', and permission to raise

---

[82] Japikse, *Resolutiën der Staten-Generaal*, vol. III, p. 47; and Gachard (ed.), *Actes des États-Généraux*, vol. II, p. 322.

[83] Groen van Prinsterer, *Archives*, vol. III, pp. 230–42, Orange to Lazarus de Schwendi, baron de Hohenlansberch, March 1580 (quotation from p. 232).

[84] Japikse, *Resolutiën der Staten-Generaal*, vol. III, pp. 48–9; and Muller and Diegerick, *Documents*, vol. III, pp. 351–7.

[85] Muller and Diegerick, *Documents*, vol. III, pp. 357–8n.

200 horse in each territory of his *apanage*.[86] While this was ostensibly to enable him to make peace in France, it could hardly have gone unnoticed by the Flemish agents in Tours. Anjou was growing impatient, however, and was unaware of the difficulties that Orange faced in getting unanimous consent for an agreement in the States. 'You know that there is nothing more important than time', Anjou anxiously wrote to Pruneaux in July. 'But even in the complexity of the present circumstances, I tell you that whatever has been proposed by the gentlemen of the States-General has taken so long in coming that I no longer know what to think.'[87]

Try as he might, William of Orange was unable to achieve unanimity in the States-General on the treaty with Anjou. The States of Utrecht refused to enter into any treaty without first consulting the other provinces of the union of Utrecht. The States of Gelderland, meanwhile, raised the intriguing question of whether they ought to offer sovereignty to Anjou without first formally withdrawing it from Philip II.[88] Despite the opposition of the magistrates of Antwerp, however, the States of Brabant reluctantly agreed to support the majority on the condition that Anjou sign a preliminary agreement with them promising never to burden the city of Antwerp with troop garrisons. Thus, on 11 August 1580 the States passed a resolution to make Anjou their 'prince and lord', adopting the articles already agreed upon on 24 June.[89] The resolution was supported by a strong majority, but it was not unanimous. Only the deputies from Brabant, Flanders, Holland, Zeeland, Malines, Friesland, and the Ommelanden of Groningen voted for it. Despite a lack of unanimity, the deputies felt justified in taking such action, 'having found it inconvenient to delay the execution of the said resolution of our said provinces any longer'. Moreover, the deputies from the remaining provinces (Tournai, Tournaisis, Utrecht, and Overijssel) 'are still discussing the matter' and were expected to follow suit shortly.[90]

The States appointed a commission to go to France to negotiate the treaty with Anjou. It was headed by Philippe de Marnix, seigneur de St Aldegonde, and included the Flemish deputies already in Tours, Provyn and Caron.[91] On 24 August they sailed down the mouth of the Schelde from Antwerp to Flushing. From there they traversed the North Sea, went through the straits of Dover,

[86] BN, MSS fr. 15536, fols. 71–3, 'Articles donnez par le duc d'Alençon au Roy pour avoir augmentation des finances et de gens de guerre avec l'advis du conseil et les apostilles du Roy contenant sa volonté escrits de la main de Mr de Villeroy', 16 July 1580. This is a request for money and troops presented by Anjou to the king's council. Beside each request Villeroy has written in the margin the action taken by the king and his councillors.

[87] Muller and Diegerick, *Documents*, vol. III, p. 374, Anjou to Pruneaux, 16 July 1580.

[88] Ibid., pp. 379–81, 423–6, resolution of the States of Utrecht, 22 July 1580, and resolution of the States of Gelderland, 14 August 1580.

[89] Ibid., pp. 399–407, articles adopted by the States for a treaty with Anjou, 11 August 1580.

[90] Ibid., pp. 415–16, preamble to the instructions to the deputies of the States chosen to go to Tours to make a treaty with Anjou, 12 August 1580.

[91] The instructions to the commission are ibid., pp. 417–23.

sailed up the Seine, and finally arrived at Rouen on 27 August.[92] The sieur des Pruneaux, who accompanied them, must have been pleased to see his months of negotiation come to fruition.

IV

The deputies of the States-General arrived in Tours on 6 September, and had their first audience with the duke of Anjou on the following day in his château of Plessis-lès-Tours just outside the city. They were pleased to report back to Antwerp that Anjou was readying his forces on land and sea and apparently had the consent of his brother the king, although Henry was still unable to support him openly.[93] In their first session of business on 12 September the deputies encountered Anjou and several members of his council. Present were the marshal de Cossé; the marquis d'Elbeuf; the baron de Fervacques, governor of the duchy of Alençon; M. de la Reynie, keeper of Anjou's seals; Claude de la Châtre, governor of the duchy of Berry; M. de la Fin, governor of the duchy of Touraine; the viscount de la Guerche; M. de Combelles; the sieur de Méru; and the sieur de Mauvissière, *premier maître d'hôtel*.[94] The Dutch delegation consisted of Philippe de Marnix, seigneur de St Aldegonde; Jean Hinckaert; André Hessels; Francois de Provyn and Noel de Caron, the Flemish deputies already present; Jacques Tayaert; and Gaspard de Vosbergen. For five days the two delegations discussed article by article, sometimes word by word, the proposals that the States-General had voted to present to Anjou. Their five-day debate was so crucial to understanding what each side hoped to gain from the alliance that it is necessary to examine it in some detail.[95]

It was hardly an auspicious start when Anjou's councillors balked at the very first article, which read 'that the States will accept His Highness as prince and lord of the said provinces with such titles as duke, count, marquis, lord and any others that his predecessors possessed'.[96] La Reynie wanted to substitute 'will elect, will name or will appoint' for 'will accept'. This was doubtless to give the impression that Anjou was invited to come to the Netherlands and did not foist himself upon the States. Moreover, Anjou's men insisted on adding the word 'sovereign' to the title of 'prince and lord'. They were clearly aware that the lack

---

[92] Ibid., pp. 437–8, 440–3, Dutch deputies to the States, from Flushing and Rouen, 24 and 27 August 1580.

[93] Ibid., p. 454, Dutch deputies to the States, 10 September 1580.

[94] Gachard (ed.), *Actes des Etats-Généraux*, vol. II, p. 376.

[95] A complete record of these negotiations was left by the Dutch deputies in their report to Orange and the States-General. It is printed in Louis Gachard (ed.), *Correspondance de Guillaume le Taciturne* (6 vols., Brussels, 1850–7), vol. IV, pp. 421–72, 'Rapport fait au prince d'Orange et aux Etats Généraux par les ambassadeurs qu'ils avaient envoyés au duc d'Anjou', 12–17 September 1580. This 'Rapport' forms the basis of the discussion which follows.

[96] All quotations from the articles presented to Anjou (i.e., those voted by the States on 11 August 1580) are from Muller and Diegerick, *Documents*, vol. III, pp. 400–7.

of any specified powers could work against Anjou once he arrived in the Netherlands. Also, it can hardly be considered an unreasonable request, since Philip II, whom Anjou was replacing, had always been regarded as the sovereign of the Netherlands. The Dutch deputies were not about to lose the initiative, however. They attempted to evade the issue by claiming that the word 'sovereign' had no equivalent in the Dutch language (despite the fact that the articles presented to Anjou were in French). And technically, they were correct, since (as in English) the French word was simply adopted. They replied that the only real equivalents in their language were either *genadighe heere* or *geduchte heere*. Moreover, they felt that the addition of the word 'sovereign' was unnecessary. If it was interpreted to mean simply *opperste heere*, first or highest lord, then that was already implied in the title 'prince and lord'. But if it was interpreted as the holder of absolute power, the deputies claimed that they were prevented by 'their laws, customs, and privileges' from making any such concessions. Try as they might, the French councillors were unable to persuade the deputies. The only concession that Anjou was allowed, in fact, was that the words 'with the same superiorities and pre-eminences' were appended to the final clause. Thus, the final draft of the first article read 'that the States will elect and will name, and do elect and do so name His Highness as prince and lord of the said provinces, with such titles as duke, count, marquis and any others, with the same superiorities and pre-eminences that his predecessors possessed'.[97] It was a significant moment, as both the Dutch deputies and the French councillors were fully aware that Anjou was being offered the titular sovereignty of the Netherlands under far more onerous conditions than applied to his predecessors, Charles V and Philip II. Indeed, the different concepts of sovereignty remained a constant source of irritation throughout the duration of the alliance, as the States soon discovered.[98]

A second major issue of contention between Anjou's councillors and the Dutch deputies was article vii, which required Anjou to assemble the States-General at least once a year. 'In addition', stated the article, 'the said States have the power to convoke themselves as often as they find it necessary for the affairs of the provinces'. As in article i, Anjou was shocked to discover that as 'prince and lord' he did not have the sole responsibility of convoking the States-General. Once again the deputies resorted to the argument of their ancient customs and privileges, which precluded anyone from holding the sole power to convoke the States. To make their point more explicit, they insisted on amending the original article to read 'that the said States have the power to convoke themselves as often

[97] Compare the articles presented to Anjou (cited in footnote 96 above) with those finally accepted, which are in Muller and Diegerick, *Documents*, vol. III, pp. 469–79.

[98] Professor Gordon Griffiths has suggested that Jean Bodin, who was one of Anjou's *maîtres de requêtes*, was responsible for raising the issue of sovereignty with the Dutch deputies. See Griffiths (ed.), *Representative Government in Western Europe*, p. 314. The 'rapport' of the Dutch deputies does not show that Bodin was even present, however, so his participation must be questioned.

as they find it necessary for the affairs of the provinces, *following their ancient privileges*.[99]

The fiercest argument, however, was reserved for articles xv and xvi. It is no coincidence that these two articles were the cornerstone of the entire alliance as far as the Dutch were concerned, as they required Henry III to support his brother openly and to declare war on Philip II. Article xv read 'that the king of France will declare the king of Spain and his allies as his enemies and will make war against them, on land and sea, and he will give his brother sufficient means to maintain these provinces against the said king of Spain, or any other enemy of these provinces, forever'. 'To such end', read article xvi, 'the kingdom of France and these provinces will remain allies forever, making war by common consent against all those who attack either one or the other. It is well understood, however, that these provinces will never be incorporated into the crown of France.' This was a difficult pill for Anjou and his councillors to swallow. While they would have doubtless welcomed Henry's open support and the defensive alliance that was stipulated in article xvi, they realized that Henry could never make such declarations. They argued that this was a treaty between the States and the duke of Anjou, not the king of France. Moreover, Anjou's councillors pleaded that they had no authority to speak for the king. The deputies of the States responded that these provisions were not intended for the sole benefit of the Dutch provinces, but were meant to ensure the safety of the duke as well. Anjou's councillors persisted, however, and maintained that it would be impossible to obtain such concessions from Henry. Moreover, with the Protestants still in arms in the Midi, the king was in no position to declare war on Spain even if he was of a mind to do so. The deputies of the States were equally adamant, however, and insisted that they were not empowered to sign a treaty without assurances of Henry III's support. It was a stalemate, and for a while it looked as if the entire treaty might break down over these two articles.

Fortunately, both sides realized the importance of what was at stake and were willing to compromise. The deputies of the States said that they would be willing to sign a treaty if Anjou promised to obtain the king's support himself. The treaty still depended on assurances from Henry III, they insisted, but they were willing to leave that to Anjou to work out in due course. This was only marginally more acceptable to the French councillors, but they reluctantly agreed to go along, provided that the final draft did not require Henry to declare war openly on Philip II. With this compromise an agreement was reached. The final draft of article xv read 'that His Highness will guarantee and require the king of France to aid him and his heirs with sufficient forces and means to support him, together with the provinces contracted in his obedience, against all enemies, whether it be

---

[99] Compare the original article with the final version in Muller and Diegerick, *Documents*, vol. III, pp. 402, 472 (my italics).

the king of Spain or anyone else'. Article xvi stated that after Anjou was installed in the Netherlands, 'he will ensure that the kingdom of France and the said provinces will ally themselves together and that they will always remain allies, making war by common consent against all those who attack either one or the other. It is well understood, however, that these provinces will never be incorporated into the crown of France.'[100] To make sure that Anjou did not renege on his promise to obtain Henry's support, the deputies included a proviso at the end of the treaty which stipulated that its ratification by the States-General hinged on a public declaration of support by the king. Thus, the burden was still on Anjou to guarantee the execution of the treaty.[101]

The last major issue of contention between the two sides was article xxvi concerning the loyalty oath, commonly called the *Blijde Inkomst*, which Anjou was required to swear upon his installation. The article mandated that 'His Highness and his successors will be required to make the solemn and accustomed oath in each province, in addition to the general oath that must be made to the States to observe this treaty. If His Highness or his successors contravene this said treaty in any point whatsoever, the States will be absolved and discharged from all obedience, loyalty, and fidelity.' What particularly galled Anjou and his councillors was that the treaty included a proviso for his removal from office before he had even accepted that office. The deputies assured Anjou that the States had no intention of revoking their obedience for technical violations of the treaty or for reasons that were beyond Anjou's control. Moreover, they replied that they were forced to withdraw their obedience from Philip II not for individual violations, 'but for an entire reversal of all justice, equity and policy, and the total subversion, ruin and desolation of their provinces'. Because of past experience, they argued, they simply wanted to avoid the possibility of another tyrant. Furthermore, the deputies pointed out that the States 'hoped that His Highness would not make any difficulty in assuring them in this regard, and would demonstrate by his agreement that he desires to be their good guardian and protector'. Anjou's councillors, especially La Reynie, persisted with their arguments, and claimed that the entire article was insulting. The deputies remained unwilling to compromise on this issue, however. 'We persisted in this', they wrote in their report to Orange and the States, 'claiming that we have no power to change it, and since it was an ancient privilege, of which the people guard more closely than any other, we cannot and we dare not change anything whatsoever'.[102] Anjou and his councillors were once again forced to concede when it was pointed out that the installation oath, or *Blijde Inkomst*, itself

---

[100] Again, compare the original and final drafts, ibid., pp. 404, 474–5.   [101] Ibid., p. 478.
[102] This and the preceding quotes are from Gachard (ed.), *Correspondance de Guillaume le Taciturne*, vol. IV, pp. 454–6, 'rapport' of the Dutch deputies.

contained a similar provision for removal from office.[103] Thus, article xxvi of the treaty was left unchanged.[104]

When all the reservations had been ironed out (and there were many technical difficulties in addition to those just outlined), both sides agreed on a final draft of the treaty on 17 September, after five long days of negotiations. The Dutch deputies, however, addressed one final issue to Anjou that was excluded from the treaty: the city of Cambrai. The town of Bouchain had recently fallen to Parma after a siege, which threatened the city of Cambrai. Because Cambrai had already sworn its loyalty to Anjou independently of the States-General, the deputies hoped that Anjou would demonstrate his willingness to serve them by sending some immediate aid to Cambrai, to serve as an example of his intentions.[105] This Anjou promised to do, and on 19 September 1580 he and the seven Dutch deputies signed the treaty of alliance. Whether or not they were aware of it at the time, they had just performed perhaps the single most revolutionary act of the entire Dutch revolt.[106]

The States-General's rejection of Philip II was indeed a revolutionary step.[107] Although it could be argued that offering their allegiance to another prince was less radical than setting up a republic or constitutional monarchy, the novelty of the treaty with Anjou should not be underestimated. Despite all the allusions to the ancient rights and privileges of the States, which the deputies continually pointed out to Anjou's councillors at Plessis-lès-Tours, there never was any privilege that gave the States the right to choose another prince. Even the relevant clause of the *Blijde Inkomst* which relieved them of their duty to obey a prince who had violated his installation oath said nothing about choosing a replacement. Moreover, the deputies conveniently ignored a vital phrase in that clause which implied the opposite:

And should it be that we, our heirs or successors, should by our own action or that of others violate [the above listed privileges] in whole or in part, in whatsoever manner, we consent and concede to our aforesaid prelates, barons, knights, cities, franchises and to all our other subjects aforesaid, that they need not do us, our heirs or successors any services, nor be obedient to them in any other things we might need or which we might request of them, *until such time as we shall have corrected the mistaken course hitherto pursued toward them, and have completely abandoned and reversed it.*[108]

[103] This section of the *Blijde Inkomst* is printed in Griffiths (ed.), *Representative Government in Western Europe*, pp. 346–50.

[104] See the original and final versions (which are identical) in Muller and Diegerick, *Documents*, vol. III, pp. 406–7, 477.

[105] Gachard (ed.), *Correspondance de Guillaume le Taciturne*, vol. IV, p. 458, 'rapport' of the Dutch deputies.

[106] The final draft of the treaty is printed in Muller and Diegerick, *Documents*, vol. III, pp. 469–79.

[107] This point is forcefully made by H. G. Koenigsberger, 'Why did the States General of the Netherlands become revolutionary in the sixteenth century?', *Parliaments, Estates and Representation*, II (1982), 103–11.

[108] From the *Blijde Inkomst* printed in Griffiths (ed.), *Representative Government in Western Europe*, p. 348 (my italics).

It could be argued that Philip II had had plenty of time to ameliorate his mistaken course. Nevertheless, the revolutionary nature of the treaty between Anjou and the States was evident in the very first article, which stated that 'the States will elect and will name, and do elect and do so name His Highness as prince and lord of the said provinces'. In one swift stroke they metamorphosed the hereditary duchies of the old Burgundian Netherlands into an elective prince-dom.[109]

The treaty was also revolutionary in another, albeit related, way. It is clear that the conditions imposed upon Anjou by the deputies at Plessis-lès-Tours were much harsher than those imposed upon his predecessors, Charles V and Philip II. The well worn argument about ancient privileges was used time and again to exact one concession after another from the duke. There was never an ancient constitution which stipulated that ultimate sovereignty rested with the States-General or even the individual provinces, as the deputies implied in article i. Moreover, with these same ancient privileges the deputies propagated the revolutionary notion (revolutionary to Philip II at least) that they could convoke and assemble themselves on their own authority. Thus, the deputies of the States created an ancient constitution from their own historical myth, which they used most effectively to their advantage during the negotiations. In many ways the treaty with Anjou was a far more revolutionary document than the more celebrated 'declaration of independence', which the States used the following July to withdraw their sovereignty from Philip II.[110]

The remaining details of the treaty stipulated that Anjou had to accept the religious settlement that each province had worked out for itself (article xii). The maverick provinces of Holland and Zeeland were bound by the treaty only in matters of war or other inter-provincial affairs (article xiii). In order to carry out the war the States agreed to furnish Anjou with an annual pension of 2,400,000 florins (one florin was roughly equivalent to one *livre tournois*), an enormous sum that the States were never able to pay (article xvii). The States also retained the power to expel all foreign (including French) troops whenever they thought it necessary (article xxii). Finally, Anjou was required to find some satisfactory means of contenting archduke Matthias, who still lurked in the background as

---

109 Even the States recognized that Philip had inherited the Dutch provinces, which they later admitted in their act of abjuration, 26 July 1581. See Kossmann and Mellink (eds.), *Texts concerning the Revolt*, p. 226.

110 It has been claimed by one historian that Anjou was encouraged by Orange to accept the Dutch treaty as it stood, despite his many reservations. In a letter dated 31 July 1580 the prince allegedly advised the duke of Anjou to accept whatever conditions were offered to him, no matter how onerous, as the duke could then seize power by force once installed in the Netherlands. See Kervijn de Lettenhove, *Huguenots*, vol. v, p. 527. This letter is an obvious forgery, however, and Orange never expressed any such idea. The letter was probably the doing of Anjou's camp, and is a further expression of his dissatisfaction with the terms of the treaty. A fuller examination of this evidence will appear in the forthcoming biography of William of Orange by Professor K. W. Swart, who kindly shared this information with me.

governor-general (article xxvii).[111] Thus, it was clear that the treaty signed at Plessis-lès-Tours hinged on two key issues. From the Dutch point of view, the success of the treaty depended on whether Henry III fully supported his brother. From Anjou's point of view, success hinged on his ability to live with the onerous conditions imposed by the deputies, as well as on the 2,400,000 florins per year they promised him. Because neither Henry nor the deputies were willing to act until the other had made a guarantee, Anjou's mission was almost defeated from the start. Nevertheless, on 25 September 1580, an optimistic and perhaps naive duke wrote to the States-General in Antwerp accepting their terms. 'At the risk of losing my life', he wrote, 'I will undertake to restore your former and ancient liberties, to maintain your state, laws, privileges, and customs, and to protect, defend, and secure your lives, property, and families'.[112] These were stirring words and exactly what the States had hoped to hear. But could Anjou deliver what he promised?

v

Because of the importance of his negotiations with the Dutch States-General in the summer of 1580, the duke of Anjou had neglected the responsibility that the king had given him to establish peace in the Midi. It was clear that if he ever hoped to have his brother's support, and if he was ever to raise a sizeable army to take to the Netherlands, peace must first be established in France. Therefore, Anjou departed from Tours in late September and headed for Guyenne to discuss terms with Henry of Navarre. He reported to the States in early October that peace in France was at hand, 'realizing that establishing peace in this kingdom was the only means by which we could bring our other enterprises that concern you to a head'.[113] Anjou had already despatched the marshal de Cossé to the king with the same message, in an attempt to win royal support for his venture in the Netherlands. Although Henry informed Cossé that he did not intend to stand in Anjou's way, the first priority was peace in the Midi. Henry therefore despatched Villeroy and Bellièvre to conduct the peace negotiations.[114] These negotiations, which took place at Cognac, were completed in a matter of weeks. This was largely due to Villeroy's diplomatic skills and the constant complaints of the Dutch deputies, who protested at Anjou's delayed departure for the Netherlands.[115]

Thus, another in the series of peace treaties in the French Wars of Religion was signed in the town of Fleix, just west of Bergerac on the Dordogne River, on 26 November 1580. The treaty of Fleix merely confirmed the earlier agreements

[111] The following spring the States paid Matthias a small sum to resign. See Parker, *The Dutch Revolt*, p. 197.
[112] Muller and Diegerick, *Documents*, vol. III, p. 508, Anjou to the States, 25 September 1580.
[113] Ibid., p. 516, Anjou to the States, 4 October 1580.
[114] BN, MSS ital. 1731, fols. 406–7, Priuli to the Signory, 3 October 1580. See also Sutherland, *French Secretaries of State*, p. 213.
[115] See a typical complaint in Muller and Diegerick, *Documents*, vol. III, pp. 563–4, Dutch deputies to Anjou, from Tours, 10 November 1580.

of Poitiers (September 1577) and Nérac (February 1579), and like them, the principal differences centered on the choice of fortified towns for the Huguenots and the administration of justice.[116] Because the peace of Fleix was so crucial to Anjou's enterprise in the Netherlands, it was significant that Sir Edward Stafford, the agent of Queen Elizabeth, and Philippe de Marnix, the leader of the Dutch delegation in France, were present at the signing ceremony. Anjou had invited all the Dutch deputies from Tours to join him in Fleix for the signing, but they complained that they were still waiting for Henry III's confirmation of support for the treaty with the States. Henry had not yet made such a guarantee, and all but Marnix politely refused Anjou's invitation.[117] The king was extremely pleased with Anjou's efforts to bring peace to the Midi, however.[118] And it came as no surprise when just after Christmas he decided to proclaim his support for his brother's expedition to the Netherlands. As outlined in the treaty between Anjou and the States, Henry made a general promise to promote and sustain Anjou's enterprise on 26 December:

I will aid and assist you with all my power, and I will join, league, and associate myself with the provinces of the Netherlands that have contracted with you, once they have effectively received and admitted you to the lordship of the said provinces, following your request to me. I hope that God will have the goodness to restore my kingdom to peace before then.[119]

Henry's promise of support clearly fell far short of what the States had hoped for. The treaty of Plessis-lès-Tours explicitly stated that the treaty would not be ratified in Antwerp without the expressed support of the king, and yet Henry refused to offer that support until after his brother was already installed as Philip II's successor. Moreover, Henry implied that the implementation of the Peace of Fleix was a priority in any case.[120] Surprisingly, however, a stalemate was avoided. Perhaps sensing that this was the most that they could expect from the French king, the States ratified the treaty shortly thereafter, on 30 December 1580. The deputies managed to save face by declaring that the treaty would only take effect after Henry made a more public declaration of support for his

116 See Sutherland, *The Huguenot Struggle*, p. 277. The original forty-seven articles of the Peace of Fleix signed by Anjou and Navarre on 26 November (and later by the king) are in BIF, MSS God. 96, fols. 154–60.
117 Muller and Diegerick, *Documents*, vol. III, pp. 569–70, Marnix to the States, from Fleix, 21 November 1580.
118 See, for instance, BIF, MSS God. 260, fol. 59, Henry to Anjou, 5 November 1580; and BN, MSS fr. 15563, fols. 200–1, Catherine and Henry to the secretary Villeroy, 7 and 8 November 1580.
119 Kervijn de Lettenhove, *Huguenots*, vol. v, p. 599, Henry III to Anjou, 26 December 1580. Kervijn de Lettenhove has misdated this document as 26 November 1580. From other evidence, especially the timing of the States-General's ratification of their treaty with Anjou (30 December 1580), it seems clear that Henry's promise of support was made on 26 December. I am grateful to Professor K. W. Swart for pointing this out to me.
120 The Dutch deputies were concerned about this, but realized that there was little that they could do. See their 'rapport' in Gachard (ed.), *Correspondance de Guillaume le Taciturne*, vol. IV, p. 467.

brother.[121] Thus, Anjou found himself caught in the middle of a complex and still unresolved web of intrigue spun by the States-General and his own brother. For the moment, however, the alliance appeared secure.

How far did Henry III and Catherine de Medici really intend to support Anjou's activities in the Netherlands? Henry's tenuous promise of support naturally gave credence to speculation at court that he planned to assist his brother's enterprise. The Venetian ambassador, for instance, speculated that, under the guise of a reward for helping with the peace negotiations at Fleix, Henry might aid Anjou with a monthly pension of 100,000 *livres*.[122] Moreover, in November Henry did give Anjou permission to alienate a further portion of the income from his *apanage* in order to raise needed revenues. As a result, Anjou managed to sell the rights to 25,000 *livres* of annual income for twelve times its face value, or 300,000 *livres*. When this transaction came before the *parlement* of Paris, it was registered only with reservation, and with the stipulation that the money was to be used only for an emergency.[123] It is equally clear, however, that Henry had no intention of aiding or assisting his brother with immediate support in the Netherlands. The situation in the Midi was still explosive, and Henry wanted Anjou to remain in Guyenne for at least two more months to help implement the peace. He made this clear to the sieur de la Fin, an agent whom Anjou had despatched to the court asking for more money to raise troops. Furthermore, the king instructed La Fin to tell Anjou 'that it would be impossible to assemble at present, in this season, the forces that would be necessary [to relieve Cambrai], in addition to the paucity of means available to do it'.[124] Although Anjou consented to the Henry's request to remain in Guyenne for another two months, the door was still open for aid from the king in the future. For the moment, however, Henry was more concerned with keeping the peace in the Midi than with making war abroad.

The position of the queen mother was less ambiguous. Above all else she feared a reprisal from Spain. Her fears appeared justified, as Spanish agents all over Europe were predicting that Anjou's treaty with the Dutch States would eventually lead to war between France and Spain. Don Bernardino de Mendoza, Philip's ambassador in London, feared that Elizabeth was also involved because of the suspicious nature of Edward Stafford's mission to France in the autumn of 1580. 'The object of this [mission] is decidedly to break with Your Majesty', he

---

[121] Muller and Diegerick, *Documents*, vol. III, pp. 621–3, act of ratification of the treaty made at Plessis-lès-Tours by the Dutch States-General, 30 December 1580.

[122] BN, MSS ital. 1731, fol. 460, Priuli to the Signory, 28 December 1580.

[123] BN, MSS fr. 5944, fols. 104v.–11v., 114v.–17v. and 125r.–8v. (I have converted the figures in the MSS from *écus* to *livres tournois* at the rate of 1 *écu* to 3 *livres*.)

[124] BIF, MSS God. 327, fols. 173–4, instructions of Henry III to M. de la Fin touching the matter of Cambrai, 31 December 1580.

wrote to Philip, 'and to strike a blow in the Netherlands'.[125] In any case, Catherine was justifiably concerned that Anjou's activities might lead to a disastrous war with Philip II, and she made every effort to dissuade him from continuing with his plans. On 23 December she sent Anjou a lengthy letter that outlined her feelings on the subject. As she also despatched copies to Villeroy and Bellièvre, who were still with Anjou in Guyenne, there is little doubt that it represented her true sentiments:

I will begin by telling you, my son, that no mother who has ever desired the union and welfare of her children, as I surely do even more than the preservation of my own life, has been more relieved and contented than I with the complete satisfaction that the king has had with you and your laudable behavior in this pursuit and negotiation of peace ... But having heard from M. de la Fin that you have despatched M. de Fervacques with charge to assemble all the forces that he can muster in order to go relieve the town of Cambrai, that you have written to all your servants to mount their horses, and that you now demand the king to help you in this matter with men and money, I must confess that my joy has changed to utter perplexity. Moreover, I have no doubt whatsoever that this project will not only deprive you of the glory and recognition that you have earned by your service to the king and this kingdom in the matter of the said peace, but it will also ruin the House [of Valois], bring you public hatred and ill will, and completely destroy this state. In short, it will leave me the most distressed and troubled mother who was ever born ... The king your brother has always told you that he truly desired to contribute to your grandeur and advancement. But this was something that he could not do until he had first restored peace to his kingdom ... We have too much proof of the lack of respect and obedience that those of the new religion in the provinces of Dauphiné and Languedoc, including the king of Navarre, have for the king to be sure of their faithfulness before their promises are executed and completely carried out. I still have all too recent memories of their behavior on this count ... Moreover, my son, do not you find it pertinent that you and the king your brother should undertake this war against the most powerful prince in Christendom, before you have even ascertained for sure the will and friendship of your neighbors, especially those who have a vital interest in the hegemony of the said Catholic King, such as the queen of England and the German princes? ... You tell us that you have given your word to those of Cambrai and that you are thus obliged to help them, they having thrown themselves into your arms. My son, you made all those negotiations without us, to my great regret, and it does not follow that you should place this kingdom in danger, destroy it, and displease the king your brother simply to keep your word. And no matter how much you owe this honor to your position as brother of the king, you are nevertheless his subject and you owe him complete obedience. Moreover, you ought to give priority to the welfare of this kingdom, which was inherited from your predecessors and of which you alone are the presumptive heir, and place it above every other consideration.[126]

---

[125] *CSPS*, vol. III, p. 52, Mendoza to Philip, 16 October 1580. Other Spanish agents felt the same way. See Lefèvre (ed.), *Correspondance de Philippe II*, vol. II, p. 87, Parma to Philip, 16 November 1580; and ibid., p. 90, Diego Maldonado to Parma, from Paris, 21 November 1580.

[126] Catherine de Medici, *Lettres*, vol. III, pp. 304–9, Catherine to Anjou, 23 December 1580 (quotations from pp. 304–5 and 308). See also Catherine's letter of 4 January 1581 to Bellièvre

Catherine was clearly opposed to Anjou's designs in the Netherlands. Above all else his enterprise threatened war with Spain, which she believed would be disastrous, with France still beset with the problem of the Protestants in the Midi.

Despite her vast experience and political acumen, the queen mother never had complete control over the policies of her sons. Although some observers were convinced that 'she is without doubt the master of this ship', appearances were sometimes deceiving.[127] Moreover, the king had been so duplicitous in the whole affair that Catherine was hardly sure what his intentions were. In January 1581 she sent him a despatch as lengthy as the one she sent to Anjou a month earlier. The tone and message were identical, as she cautioned him 'that you have neither the means nor the will to enter into a war against the king of Spain, knowing that it would be the ruin of this kingdom'.[128] Catherine never trusted Anjou, nor the favorites who surrounded him. Heretofore, however, she had more or less managed to keep Henry III in line and out of trouble. That situation had now altered. Although Henry continued to express his innocence of any knowledge of Anjou's activities in the Netherlands, for the first time Catherine had good reason to suspect otherwise. Moreover, the king's trusted councillor, Pomponne de Bellièvre, had recently shifted course and had begun to counsel Henry to support his brother's enterprise. Bellièvre, like Villeroy, had desperately tried to dissuade Anjou from his venture for months, but had come to the conclusion that the duke was not going to be talked out of it. If Anjou insisted on going ahead with his plan to relieve Cambrai, Bellièvre thought it might be wise to support the venture. 'If he loses the battle', he wrote to Catherine from Coutras, 'everything is lost for him and the Netherlands'. A further consideration, or so Bellièvre thought, was that Anjou and his band of rabble-rousers might be less of a nuisance abroad than at home.[129]

At the end of 1580 Anjou remained steadfast in his desire to lead an army to the Netherlands to relieve Cambrai, and ultimately to assume the titles that the Dutch States had recently bestowed upon him. Although he promised the king to remain in Guyenne for another two months, this was as much due to an attack of jaundice that he suffered in December 1580 as to any ardent desire to implement the peace of Fleix.[130] Furthermore, he had already despatched a

---

and Villeroy, ibid., p. 314. For further examples of Catherine's opposition, see ibid., pp. 318, 330–3.

[127] Lefèvre, *Correspondance de Philippe II*, vol. I, p. 754, Juan de Vargas Mexia to Philip II, 16 February 1580.

[128] Catherine de Medici, *Lettres*, vol. VII, pp. 341–4, Catherine to Henry III, January 1581 (quotation from p. 341).

[129] Ibid., pp. 453–5, Bellièvre to Catherine, 11 December 1580 (quotation from p. 454). Also see Edmund H. Dickerman, *Bellièvre and Villeroy: Power in France under Henry III and Henry IV* (Providence, RI, 1971), pp. 95, 107–8; Kierstead, *Pomponne de Bellièvre*, p. 42; and Sutherland, *French Secretaries of State*, pp. 215–16.

[130] For a report on his illness, see Catherine de Medici, *Lettres*, vol. VII, p. 455, Bellièvre to Catherine, 20 December 1580.

small troop of cavalry toward Cambrai under the command of Antoine de Silly, count de Rochepot, and was firmly committed to his enterprise. Bellièvre was certainly correct in thinking that Anjou was not about to be talked out of his venture in the Netherlands. What were Henry and Catherine to do? Villeroy summed up everyone's frustration in a letter to Bellièvre. 'No one knows which saint to invoke or what decision to take', he lamented, '[and] their majesties are in great distress about it'.[131]

---

[131] BN, MSS fr. 15905, fol. 640, Villeroy to Bellièvre, 24 December 1580; quoted in Sutherland, *French Secretaries of State*, p. 215.

7

Ménage à trois: Elizabeth, Anjou, and the Dutch Revolt, January 1581–February 1582

By the beginning of 1581 events in Western Europe had escalated to such an extent that the activities of the duke of Anjou began to take on added significance. In January 1580 the aged Cardinal Henry of Portugal died after having named Philip II as his successor. Philip was unable to take possession of his new crown, however, except by conquest. Led by the veteran duke of Alva, the Spanish army invaded Portugal and captured Lisbon in late August. The significance of Philip's annexation of Portugal was twofold. With the addition of the Portuguese coastal salt deposits, the Azores, and above all the Portuguese overseas empire, Philip strengthened his already formidable position as the most powerful prince in Western Europe. To the other European nations, especially the smaller Protestant states, the Spanish goal of a *res publica christiana* became all the more real. On the other hand, because Philip was required to keep his army in Portugal throughout 1581 in order to hold on to his newly acquired crown, the military strength of the Spanish army in the Netherlands was severely weakened. The Spanish and Italian units of Philip's army had been withdrawn completely, and the few troops that remained did not receive regular pay. With the growing threat of Spanish hegemony of Europe, the withdrawal of the 'army of Flanders' to Portugal thus presented Queen Elizabeth and Henry III with a golden opportunity to interfere in the Netherlands on the side of the rebels. Hence, Anjou's treaty with the States could hardly have come at a more auspicious moment. Moreover, it was no coincidence that in early 1581 the Elizabeth–Anjou marriage project, which had lain dormant since the harsh outbursts of Stubbs and Sidney in 1579, was resurrected. In a final desperate attempt at marriage, Anjou tried in vain to overcome the English opposition to the match. It became clear, however, that the only *raison d'être* for the marriage talks was the revolt of the Netherlands. While English and French councillors argued endlessly over the details of the marriage contract, the principals used the entire charade to pour English money into Anjou's enterprise in the Netherlands. This episode is the story of the present chapter.

I

Despite his preoccupation with Portugal, Philip II did not completely ignore the Netherlands. In March 1580, upon the recommendation of Cardinal Granvelle, he offered a reward of 25,000 *escudos* (about 70,000 *livres tournois*) to anyone who assassinated William of Orange.[1] In reply, Orange issued his famous 'Apology' in December 1580. In a stinging diatribe Orange launched vicious accusations aimed at denigrating Philip's honor, morality, and competency. Moreover, he tried to justify the Dutch provinces' decision to withdraw sovereignty from the Spanish king.[2]

Orange began by addressing the charges that Philip had levelled against him. Without 'this jumble of impudent and malign slanders', he declared, 'this ban would be only a whiff of smoke'.[3] Then he got to the heart of the matter, and boldly declared that Philip had overstepped his bounds and had reneged on his installation oath, the *Blijde Inkomst*:

They will reply that he is a king, and I will reply that here I do not know this title of king. He may be a king in Castile, Aragon, Naples, the Indies and wherever he commands according to his own pleasure; if he wants, he can be a king in Jerusalem or even a peaceful ruler in Asia and Africa. But in this country I know only of a duke and a count whose power is limited by the privileges which he swore at his Joyous Entry.[4]

Thus, Orange's 'Apology' tried to maintain the fiction that, despite the revolutionary offer of sovereignty to the duke of Anjou, it was Philip who had broken his oath of loyalty to the Dutch provinces, and not the other way round. The revolutionary process which began at Plessis-lès-Tours was crowned several months later when the States-General officially withdrew from Philip II the sovereignty that they had already offered to the duke of Anjou.[5]

Faced with the increasing prospect of a war with Spain, Henry III and Catherine de Medici decided in January 1581 to reopen the marriage negotiations with Elizabeth in the hope of securing an alliance with England. 'After the repose of my kingdom', Henry wrote to his ambassador in England on 20 January, 'there is nothing in this world that I desire more than the contentment, grandeur, welfare and advancement of my said brother with the said queen of England'.[6] Henry proceeded to foster this relationship by choosing a council of nobles to send to England in an attempt to get Elizabeth to sign a marriage contract with Anjou. This all happened so suddenly, in fact, that Jean Baptiste de Tassis, Philip's new ambassador in France, complained vehemently to Henry

---

[1] The proscription or ban against Orange is printed in Rowen, *Low Countries in Early Modern Times*, pp. 77–9.

[2] Orange's 'Apology' is printed in full in Du Mont (ed.), *Corps universel*, vol. v, part i, pp. 384–406. The most significant selections have been translated in Rowen, *Low Countries in Early Modern Times*, pp. 80–91, and in Kossmann and Mellink (eds.), *Texts concerning the Revolt*, pp. 211–16. I have cited the Rowen translation.

[3] Rowen, *Low Countries in Early Modern Times*, p. 84.   [4] Ibid., pp. 85–6, 88.

[5] The Act of Abjuration was adopted by the States-General at The Hague on 26 July 1581, and applied to all provinces not members of the union of Arras. It is printed (in French and Dutch) in Du Mont (ed.), *Corps universel*, vol. v, part i, pp. 413–21, and in English translation in Kossmann and Mellink (ed.), *Texts concerning the Revolt*, pp. 216–28.

[6] BN, MSS fr. 3307, fol. 29, Henry to Castelnau, 20 January 1581.

and Catherine. First of all, he had intercepted a letter from the sieur de Roche-pot which proved conclusively that Anjou was assembling troops to lead to Cambrai. Moreover, Tassis wanted to know why Anjou insisted on further alien-ating Philip II with the renewed talk of marriage to a heretic. Catherine assured Tassis that both she and Henry were opposed to Anjou's excursion to Cambrai, but declared that the marriage was another matter. 'Rather than question whether my son would withdraw from our religion', she protested to the ambas-sador, 'I would hope on the contrary that he might bring the queen back into the fold'.[7] Tassis did not believe a word of this, nor did he put much faith in Henry and Catherine's claims that they were trying to discourage Anjou's enterprise to Cambrai. He later wrote to Parma that 'these are always the same old words'.[8]

By the end of February Henry had finished selecting the nobles for the com-mission he intended to send to England. It was an experienced group, led by the count of Soissons and the duke of Montpensier. Other members of the commis-sion included the *prince dauphin* of Auvergne, marshal de Cossé, the sieur de Lansac, the sieur de Carrouges, the sieur de la Mothe-Fénelon (former ambas-sador to England), Michel de Castelnau, sieur de Mauvissière (present ambas-sador in England), Barnabé Brisson (a president in the *parlement* of Paris), Claude Pinart (a secretary of state), the sieur de Marchaumont (a member of Anjou's household), and Jacques de Vray, sieur de Fontorte (one of Anjou's secretaries of finances).[9] Henry empowered the commission to negotiate a mar-riage contract based on the agreement worked out by Jean de Simier and Eliza-beth in November 1579. It was significant, however, that the commissioners were not given the authority to negotiate a treaty or defensive alliance between the two countries.[10] Although such an alliance was one of the principal reasons which prompted Henry to renew the marriage negotiations in the first place, he clearly felt that Elizabeth could not be trusted to uphold her promises simply because of a piece of paper. After all, she had been promising the Dutch rebels financial support for years – support that would never materialize until 1585. Thus, the marriage was seen on the French side as the only guarantee that Eliza-beth would uphold her end of a dual alliance or defensive pact.

Meanwhile, Anjou continued his preparations to relieve Cambrai. In Feb-ruary he despatched Pruneaux once again to the Dutch States-General, and appointed the marquis de Fervacques as the commander of his army until he could arrive in person.[11] Fervacques led Anjou's small band, probably no more

---

[7] Catherine de Medici, *Lettres*, vol. VII, pp. 353–5, Catherine to St-Gouart, 8 February 1581.

[8] Lefèvre, *Correspondance de Philippe II*, II, 130.

[9] BN, MSS fr. 3308, fol. 48, Commission sent to England by Henry III to negotiate a marriage contract between Queen Elizabeth and the duke of Anjou, 28 February 1581.

[10] BN, MSS fr. 3308, fol. 1, powers of the commissioners, 28 February 1581.

[11] Muller and Diegerick, *Documents*, vol. IV, pp. 1–6, Commission of Pruneaux, 18 February 1581; ibid., pp. 6–8, Fervacques to the magistrates of Bruges and Franc, 19 April 1581; and *CSPF*, vol. XV, p. 43, Russell to Walsingham, 4 February 1581.

than 2,000 men, to the village of Bray-sur-Somme near Péronne, only 'four leagues from the enemy'.[12] At this stage Anjou's army was woefully under-manned, and was certainly nowhere near the estimated strength of 6,000 foot and 2,000 horse predicted by an English agent.[13] In fact, an anonymous observer from Parma's camp noted on 3 April that 'the French troops that are assembling on the outskirts of Amiens to go to Flanders number at most about 1,200 foot, 300 horse including the valets, and 300 mounted *arquebusiers*'.[14] Anjou was thus desperately in need of aid, from both his brother and Elizabeth.

Many observers at court had begun to wonder if the king planned to aid his brother secretly if he could not do so openly. Lorenzo Priuli, the Venetian ambassador, realized that the English marriage was central to the entire enterprise, however, and noted 'that the king of France will not make up his mind until these negotiations with England are resolved'. Moreover, Priuli went on to say that Anjou's principal interest in the marriage was to secure support for the Netherlands:

Although Monsieur appears resolved to stand by his promise [to marry], he has told the king and his mother that he made this promise and committed himself only because he needed the support and help of the queen of England in his Flemish affair, vital assistance which the king would not give him. This proves that the break-up of the marriage would not upset him, provided that he got the necessary support for his expedition to Flanders.[15]

The view of the Venetian ambassador is corroborated by a letter that Elizabeth herself wrote to Anjou in April 1581. She feared that the marriage might never take place because of popular opposition, doubtless recollecting the outbursts of Stubbs and Sidney in 1579. 'But, if you do not find these difficulties too great', she went on, 'the enterprise of Flanders will give enough shade to cover up all opposition, and that fact should content you enough to reach an agreement in these negotiations'.[16]

The king's commissioners arrived in England and had their first audience with Elizabeth and her council on 24 April.[17] In the end, both the count of Soissons and the duke of Montpensier were too ill to travel, and Montpensier's son, the *prince dauphin* of the Auvergne, was put in charge of the French delegation. Moreover, the sieur de Marchaumont had been sent ahead to act as personal agent for the duke of Anjou, the same role that Jean de Simier had filled for so long throughout 1579. Marchaumont was unable to accomplish much, however, before the rest of the commissioners arrived. Although most of

12 Muller and Diegerick, *Documents*, vol. IV, pp. 6–8, Fervacques to the magistrates of Bruges and Franc, 19 April 1581.

13 *CSPF*, vol. XV, p. 43, Russell to Walsingham, 4 February 1581.

14 Muller and Diegerick, *Documents*, vol. IV, p. 12, anonymous agent of Parma, 3 April 1581. These were in addition to the troops being raised by Rochepot (see L'Estoile, *Journal*, vol. II, p. 1).

15 BN, MSS ital. 1732, fols. 9–11, Priuli to the Signory, 22 March 1581.

16 HMC, *Salisbury MSS*, vol. II, p. 495, Elizabeth to Anjou, [April] 1581.

17 *CODOIN*, vol. XCII, p. 16, Mendoza to Philip, 4 May 1581.

Elizabeth's privy councillors were willing to discuss a defensive pact with France, none – apart from Burghley and Sussex – was interested in the marriage. They remained unmoved as Barnabé Brisson delivered a harangue on 29 April extolling the advantages of the marriage. Moreover, he explained that Henry III had only empowered them to negotiate a marriage contract; thus, they could hardly discuss a treaty.[18] Francis Walsingham, one of the principal opponents of the marriage, replied the next day that there were two overriding reasons why he thought that 'the marriage proceeding could not but be greatly to the discontent of the subjects of this realm'. First of all, he described the trouble that was currently being caused by Jesuits, who were advocating disobedience to the queen. As a Catholic, it was felt that Anjou's presence in England would only encourage such treason. Secondly, Walsingham did not want to involve England in a war with Spain should Anjou's activities in the Netherlands cause Philip II to declare war on France.[19]

Walsingham's speech clearly proves that Henry was right to fear that Elizabeth would never fully support France in a war with Spain without the marriage. Understandably, however, Elizabeth and her councillors did not want to be drawn into such a war if they could help it, and they continued to press for a defensive alliance rather than a marriage contract. Even Lord Burghley, who had valiantly tried to keep the marriage talks alive, was forced to admit that it was more prudent to negotiate a defensive alliance before proceeding with the marriage.[20] Thus, there appeared to be a virtual stalemate. Elizabeth's councillors had no desire to negotiate a marriage, while the French commissioners did not have the authority to negotiate a defensive pact. A crisis was averted, however, when a somewhat farcical agreement was reached on 11 June. A marriage contract was signed by both sides that was so general and vague that it satisfied neither delegation. Indeed, most of the significant details of the contract were reserved for private negotiation between Elizabeth and Anjou.[21]

Unsure of Elizabeth's support, Henry and Catherine spent the entire spring of 1581 attempting to discourage Anjou from making his journey to Cambrai. The duke proved as stubborn as ever, however, and both the king and queen mother began to fear the consequences of such an enterprise. Catherine was very upset that Anjou had abandoned his peacekeeping duties in the south in order to raise troops for the relief of Cambrai.[22] Henry was equally disturbed, especially since the Huguenots were 'reacting very coldly to the execution and establishment of

[18] BN, MSS fr. 3952, fols. 20–5, 'Harrangue prononcee a Londres au conseil prive d'angleterre par messire Barnabe Brisson president au Parlement de Paris le [vingt] neufiesme jour d'avril 1581'.
[19] CSPF, vol. xv, pp. 142–3, draft of speech delivered to the commissioners in Walsingham's hand, 30 April 1581.
[20] Ibid., p. 174, memorandum in Burghley's hand, 16 May 1581.
[21] A copy of the contract dated 11 June 1581 is in BN, MSS fr. 3308, fols. 44–8. It has been printed in Du Mont (ed.), Corps universel, vol. v, part i, pp. 406–9.
[22] BN, MSS fr. 15906, fol. 402, Catherine to Bellièvre, 29 April 1581.

my edict of pacification'.[23] While there was some talk at court that Henry would support his brother's mission because Cambrai was such a vital fortification on the frontier, the king gave no such indication. Moreover, when Anjou at last departed from the Midi and headed north in early May, Henry sent the queen mother after him in one last attempt to dissuade him from his journey.[24]

During their brief meeting on 10–11 May, Catherine discovered that she was unable to prevent Anjou from going to the Netherlands, and that there was little that she and the king could do, short of force, to change his mind.[25] Moreover, on 20 May Anjou issued a declaration to the *parlement* of Paris, seeking the support of the king and his council for his venture. He explained that his decision to accept the offer of the Dutch States should not be interpreted as a sign of disloyalty to the king. On the contrary, he insisted that the relief of Cambrai was vital to the defense of the French frontier:

I have voluntarily seized the opportunity presented by the city, citadel, and region of Cambrai, as well as the provinces of Brabant, Flanders, Holland, Zeeland, Malines, Friesland, and the Ommelanden, who, after long deliberation and the universal consent of all their people, towns, estates, and communities, threw themselves into my arms and asked me to take them under my wing in a just and legitimate rulership, and to defend them from the tyranny and unjust oppression which they have suffered for many years. I have not done this for my own particular glory, but, realizing that such an enterprise was necessarily related to the service of the king my lord and brother, I have done it for the conservation of his state and the augmentation of his crown, staking out for France this admirable and vast frontier, garrisoned with some of the most important fortified towns and provinces in the world.[26]

Anjou also wrote to the chancellor of his household, Christophe de Thou, who was also the first president of the *parlement* of Paris. 'You see how I am treated', he wrote, and urged his chancellor to spell out his true intentions to the court.[27] Though the judges replied respectfully, Anjou's activities clearly concerned them.[28]

The queen mother returned to the court on 24 May and explained to the king the futility of her visit. She was especially worried because Anjou was still 'so discontented'.[29] The king still seemed firmly opposed to Anjou's designs, however, and he confided to Bellièvre that he was as worried as Catherine. 'I am

23 BN, MSS CCC 368, fols. 250–1 and 276–7, both Henry III to Arnaud du Ferrier, 2 May and 19 June 1581.
24 BN, MSS ital. 1732, fols. 43–4, Priuli to the Signory, 6 May 1581.
25 BN, MSS ital. 1732, fol. 54, Priuli to the Signory, 2 June 1581; and *CSPF*, vol. xv, p. 176, Cobham to the secretaries, 18 May 1581.
26 BN, MSS Dupuy 87, fols. 127–9, Anjou to the *parlement* of Paris, 20 May 1581.
27 BN, MSS Dupuy 569, fol. 22, Anjou to Christophe de Thou, sieur de Cély, 20 May 1581.
28 BN, MSS fr. 6547, fols. 74v.–84r., remonstrance of the *parlement* of Paris to Anjou, [May or June] 1581.
29 BN, MSS ital. 1732, fols. 54–5, Priuli to the Signory, 2 June 1581.

completely resolved', he wrote, 'not to assist him in any way whatsoever, but, on the contrary, to hinder with every possible means the levies of *gens de guerre* that he has mandated'.[30]

In early June it was estimated that Anjou's forces totalled no more than 3,000 foot and 200 horse. Moreover, the duke was having problems raising new recruits.[31] Most of the men who had flocked to his banner were young Catholic noblemen who had volunteered.[32] As always, the main problem was a lack of money. Nevertheless, by early July Rochepot and Fervacques had managed to add a number of new recruits to the army, which was assembling at Château-Thierry in Anjou's *apanage*, north-east of Paris on the Marne River. While it is difficult to estimate exact numbers, estimates of 14,000–15,000 were surely exaggerations.[33] Fewer than 10,000 is probably more accurate, as the surviving officer lists indicate.[34] The lack of sufficient financing was not Anjou's only military concern, however. A noticeable deficiency was the absence of officers with military experience. 'It is hard to say if it [the relief of Cambrai] will succeed', noted Priuli, 'since Anjou does not have any experienced officers, even if he has some who are deemed to be brave'.[35] Of all his officers, only the marshal de Cossé and Claude de la Châtre had any significant military experience or training. Most were about Anjou's age (or younger) and had seen only limited combat action, such as at La Rochelle in 1573 or La Charité and Issoire in 1577. For many of them, the proposed journey to the Netherlands was their first real taste of war.

It has already been pointed out that the recruitment of troops in the early modern period is a subject that needs further study, and little is known about the methods employed to raise Anjou's army. Most of his recruiting was done by individual captains. Anjou invited various nobles and gentlemen – many from his own household – to serve as his officers, and they in turn raised their own

---

[30] BN, MSS fr. 15906, fol. 429, Henry III to Bellièvre, 27 May 1581.

[31] BN, MSS ital. 1732, fol. 57, Priuli to the Signory, 2 June 1581.

[32] BN, MSS ital. 1732, fol. 75, Priuli to the Signory, 18 June 1581: 'essendo la maggior parte di quelli che la vanno à servire gentilhuomini voluntarii et cattolici'. This would appear to contradict Professor Geoffrey Parker's suggestion that Anjou led a 'Huguenot army' to the Netherlands in 1581, but the religious affiliation of the troops is difficult to pinpoint because of the lack of documentation. See Parker, *The Army of Flanders*, p. 243.

[33] These estimates were made by the English and Venetian ambassadors in France, Cobham and Priuli respectively. See *CSPF*, vol. XV, p. 266, Cobham to Walsingham, 14 July 1581; and BN, MSS ital. 1732, fol. 98, Priuli to the Signory, 13 July 1581.

[34] There are two similar lists of officers in Anjou's army, in Muller and Diegerick, *Documents*, vol. IV, pp. 101–4, and *CSPF*, vol. XV, p. 288. There are a total of 47 officers on the lists. Even if each officer captained a full company, which is unlikely, the total would amount to fewer than 10,000 men (a company normally consisted of 200 men). Moreover, one list indicates that after Orange's forces were added in, Anjou commanded a total force of 8,000 foot and 3,000 horse (Muller and Diegerick, *Documents*, vol. IV, p. 104). Thus, he almost certainly commanded fewer than 10,000 men of his own.

[35] BN, MSS ital. 1732, fols. 98–9, Priuli to the Signory, 13 July 1581.

companies.[36] He also tried to persuade the various towns, duchies, and seigneuries in his *apanage* to contribute troops, but these efforts did not prove very fruitful. The outright refusal of the city of Angers, for example, was probably a typical response.[37] Finally, Anjou hired 1,000–2,000 German mercenaries to swell his ranks.[38] Although it would be impossible to estimate exact numbers, his army had obviously grown since the first of June. Indeed, Henry was so worried that he issued an edict forbidding anyone to leave the kingdom of France without his permission, upon pain of death and confiscation of property.[39]

By July the signs of war were so ominous that both Henry III and Elizabeth began to reconsider their earlier rigid positions regarding the marriage and Anjou's enterprise to Cambrai. Neither of them wanted a war with Spain, yet it appeared that Anjou's venture would take place without their permission. Because he could not stop his younger brother, Henry began to worry about Anjou's security, fears that were underlined by his brother's ill-led and underpaid troops. Since Anjou was the only Valois heir to the crown, his loss could prove harmful to the internal stability of France. For these reasons, Henry considered offering his brother aid for the first time. If Anjou was determined to make his voyage, Henry reasoned that he might have no other option but to support it to ensure his brother's safe return.[40]

Elizabeth had similar fears. She still hoped for an alliance without a marriage, but reasoned that if England was going to be dragged into a war with Spain in any

36 A typical invitation is that issued to Guy de Laval, who commanded a company of cavalry raised in Brittany. BN, MSS fr. 3348, fol. 1, Anjou to Guy de Laval, sieur de Boisdauphin, 15 May 1581. Also see Muller and Diegerick, *Documents*, vol. IV, p. 102.

37 AC Angers, série BB 36, fols. 339–44, Registers of the Hôtel-de-ville d'Angers, May–June 1581. Also see BN, MSS fr. 3177, fols. 243v.–5v., 'Declara[ti]on et protestation de Monseigneur frere du Roy sur la levee des trouppes po[ur] flandres'.

38 BN, MSS ital. 1732, fol. 75, Priuli to the Signory, 18 June 1581.

39 Ibid. Even the fullest account of Anjou's military activities, a journal written by the captain of his light cavalry, Claude de la Châtre, does not say how Anjou raised his forces. See BN, n.a. fr. 4709, fol. 7: 'Je ne dirai point ici les traveses et oppositions qui se presenterent en l'assemblement de ces forces et ce qui se traita durant les mois de juin et juillet parce que cella n'apartient à ce discours, tant y a que surmontant touttes difficultés S[on] A[ltesse] arriva à Chateau-Thierry où sad[ite] armée commença fort à s'engrossir.' This journal of Claude de la Châtre, baron de Maisonfort (and later marshal of France under Henry IV) was entitled 'Relation du voyage du Duc d'Anjou au Pays-Bas, Mal-entendu d'Anvers 1583' and was written as an apology of Anjou's actions in the 'French fury' at Antwerp on 17 January 1583. He wrote it to present to the Dutch States-General, hoping they would excuse Anjou of any blame in the affair; and it is therefore necessary to treat La Châtre's judgment with extreme caution. Nevertheless, it is the fullest military account of the venture, and provides many useful details about Anjou's army that are not recorded elsewhere. This journal should not be confused, however, with La Châtre's description of the siege of Cambrai, which is printed in Muller and Diegerick, *Documents*, vol. IV, pp. 102–3, 166–73, 200–7, and entitled 'Lettre de Monsieur de la Châtre, en forme de discours'. Both documents are very useful, and I have referred to them in the discussion that follows despite their obvious flaws and bias.

40 BN, MSS ital. 1732, fols. 155–6 and 163–4, both Priuli to the Signory, 28 July and 7 August 1581.

case, she might be better off assisting Anjou. This might at least give her some degree of control over his actions. She hastily despatched John Sommers to Henry and Francis Walsingham to Anjou to see if their positions on the marriage had changed since the visit of the French commissioners to England. Their first task was to see if Henry would sign an offensive and defensive treaty, after which she would consider the marriage – the same position which she had rigidly held for months. Sommers had an audience with the king on 10 July in which he relayed Elizabeth's instructions. Henry responded that he would be more than willing to negotiate a treaty with Elizabeth, and would provide 'soldiers, artillery, powder, shot, munitions, and anything else that was necessary'. He added, however, 'that everything depended on the said marriage and would be completed only after the consummation had taken place'.[41]

Elizabeth had given Walsingham slightly different instructions. Initially, he was to try the same tactic as Sommers and insist on a treaty before the marriage.[42] If that failed, however, she urged Walsingham to make Anjou understand that she might be willing to help finance his expedition to Cambrai secretly, in effect making an unofficial treaty with Anjou rather than an official one with Henry. 'You shall say', read Walsingham's instructions, 'that it may be reasonably conjectured by them that though we will not give him any aid openly ... we may so temper our actions that he may in secret sort be relieved of us, and that without open note to breed either a war or great offence to our subjects'.[43] This was a considerable compromise from Elizabeth's earlier position, and it underlined the fact that the marriage was just a façade to disguise English aid to Anjou's venture in the Netherlands.

Walsingham had his interview with Anjou at La Fère-en-Tard, just north of Château-Thierry, on 2 and 3 August. He relayed his first set of instructions, and the duke predictably replied that the treaty was not possible until a date had been set for the marriage. The following day the viscount de Turenne, one of Anjou's military captains, approached Walsingham and frankly described the miserable state of the French army. He pleaded with Walsingham for English support, without which the duke's project was bound to fail.[44] Walsingham had not yet revealed his full hand, and he wanted to discuss the matter with Cobham and Sommers in Paris before disclosing that Elizabeth was prepared to do exactly what Turenne had requested. He was already on his way to Paris, in fact, when Catherine de Medici arrived in La Fère for a final attempt to dissuade Anjou from his journey. Walsingham was called back, and the three of them had a long

---

[41] BN, MSS fr. 3307 fols. 32–4, Henry to Castelnau, 12 July 1581.
[42] *CSPF*, vol. xv, pp. 273–4, instructions to Walsingham, 21 July 1581.
[43] Ibid., p. 281, 'Certain later degrees of proceeding, if the former cannot take place', 22 July 1581. Also see Wallace MacCaffrey, 'The Anjou match and the making of Elizabethan foreign policy', in Peter Clark, A. G. R. Smith, and Nicholas Tyacke (eds.), *The English Commonwealth, 1547–1640* (New York and Leicester, 1979), pp. 72–3.
[44] Sir Dudley Digges, *The Compleat Ambassador* (London, 1665), pp. 367–8.

discussion on 5 August. Catherine was obviously desperate, and wanted to send Bellièvre to Parma to negotiate a truce. Whether she was serious or was simply using this as a ploy to discover Elizabeth's true intentions is difficult to tell. In any case, nothing was settled, and Walsingham departed for Paris once more on 8 August.[45]

On 11 August Walsingham wrote to Lord Burghley and recommended that the queen send Anjou the 100,000 *écus* (300,000 *livres*) which Turenne had requested a week before. 'I beseech you to procure her Majesty's speedy resolution to the Viscount of Turenne's proposition for the 100,000 crowns, without which I fear we shall find some stay in the treaty. I would be very sorry that so small a sum employed to so good purpose should be stuck at.'[46] By this time Henry III had reached the same conclusion. In a personal letter to Villeroy he related his personal feelings on Anjou's venture, noting 'that by covert means one should and could assist him'.[47] Most of the king's council were of a like mind, not wishing to leave Cambrai in Parma's hands nor to risk the lives of Anjou and so many of the French nobility.[48] Thus, in mid-August Henry secretly sent his brother 90,000 *livres* to assist his venture.[49] He almost certainly had mixed feelings about it, but probably realized that there was little else he could do in the circumstances.

By this time Anjou and his forces had departed from Château-Thierry. They arrived in the vicinity of Cambrai on 17 August and camped at an abbey two leagues outside the city. That same day the English agent, John Sommers, having departed from Paris the day before, caught up with the duke and asked for an audience. Sommers had been despatched by Cobham and Walsingham to see if Anjou's position regarding the marriage had changed. In three separate meetings on 17 and 18 August, Sommers was encouraged to learn that the duke was not as insistent on the marriage as Henry had been. The looming battle with Parma naturally diverted Anjou's attention, and he was adamant to know what assistance was being offered by Elizabeth in return for her desired treaty. Sommers replied that he was not empowered to negotiate any financial aid, but that the matter would be put before Elizabeth 'with speed'.[50]

Meanwhile, at six o'clock in the evening of 18 August, Anjou's army entered

---

45 See Read, *Mr Secretary Walsingham*, vol. II, pp. 64–6.
46 *CSPF*, vol. XV, p. 289, Walsingham to Burghley, 11 August 1581.
47 Catherine de Medici, *Lettres*, vol. VII, p. 389, Henry to Villeroy, August 1581.
48 BN, MSS ital. 1732, fol. 186, Priuli to the Signory, 14 August 1581.
49 PRO/SP 78/10/122/fols. 308–35, 'Estat abregé de la Recepte et despense faicte en lextraord-in[air]e de la guerre de Monseigneur depuis le premier jour de may mil v^c quatre vingtz un que son Altesse dressa l'armee pour le secours de Cambray jusques au dernier jour doctobre mil v^c quatre vingtz trois'. This is a copy of all Anjou's receipts and expenses of his Dutch venture from May 1581 to October 1583. It was given to Burghley by one of Anjou's financial secretaries, which explains its location in the PRO in London.
50 *CSPF*, vol. XV, pp. 294–5, Sommers's negotiation with Anjou, 17–18 August 1581; and Read, *Mr Secretary Walsingham*, vol. II, pp. 72–3.

the citadel of Cambrai without a shot being fired. It was a splendid irony that, despite all of Henry and Elizabeth's concerns about a war with Spain, Parma's troops were so depleted that they meekly retreated at the first approach of Anjou's recruits. The baron de Rosny (later duke of Sully), who was getting his own first taste of war, later related that 'Monsieur was given an overwhelming reception in Cambrai by the overjoyed inhabitants of the town and sieur d'Inchy, their governor, which was evidenced by a magnificent entry with guns, clanging bells, bonfires, feasts, and banquets'.[51] In the midst of the celebration, however, it was apparent that Anjou could not follow up his victory without further financial aid. He was not yet aware of Elizabeth's willingness to assist him, and on 19 August he wrote to the prince of Orange of his plight. Without further troops and money, he argued, Orange and the States would have to content themselves with the capture of Cambrai. His men could advance no farther.[52] Moreover, Anjou reminded the deputies of the States-General – who had not yet advanced him a single pattard – of their promised 2,400,000 florins per annum to maintain the war. 'I have sent word to you', he pleaded, 'of the extreme expense that I have incurred in levying and maintaining this army, which was done as much in your interest [as mine]. It is very important that I get assistance and aid from you as soon as possible, in the form of money as well as provisions.'[53] The condition of Anjou's army after the relief of Cambrai was thus cause for concern. Without immediate aid, his continuation as an ally of the Dutch States-General was in jeopardy.

Anjou's pleas of poverty to Orange and to the States were more than empty words. The commander of the duke's light cavalry, Claude de la Châtre, kept a record of the campaign, and there is no doubt that most of the army was ready to return home immediately because of lack of pay, food, and water. Although Anjou and his personal guard remained in the city after the flight of Parma, the greater part of the French army camped outside in several small villages. La Châtre and his company stayed in a village 'without water or any other provisions whatsoever'. He added that

what went on the rest of that day and all the following day [18 and 19 August] inside the city, I do not know, but I well know that this stay of three or four days with such great hardship for those lodged in this camp caused a great deal of grumbling among the troops, both cavalry and infantry, and was the main cause of the break-up of the army.[54]

La Châtre pointed out that it was a journey of more than two leagues to the

51 Buisseret and Barbiche (eds.), *Œconomies royales de Sully*, vol. I, pp. 100–1. Also see Anjou's own description in BN, MSS Dupuy 569, fol. 28, Anjou to Christophe de Thou, sieur de Cély, 19 August 1581.
52 Gachard (ed.), *Correspondance de Guillaume le Taciturne*, vol. IV, p. 296, Anjou to Orange, 19 August 1581.
53 Muller and Diegerick, *Documents*, vol. IV, pp. 164–5, 199–200, both Anjou to the States, 19 and 26 August 1581.
54 Ibid., pp. 171–2, 'Lettre' of La Châtre.

nearest water, and that his cavalry's horses were dying of thirst at an alarming rate.[55]

The army being thus useless ... the troops began to get angry and desired to return to France. As soon as I realized this, I went to find His Highness in the abbey and told him that he had better look after his affairs, that his army was beginning to beat a retreat back to France. Having lost their original ardor during the last few days, and being volunteers without pay or contract, it appeared that they would scatter at any moment.[56]

The international reaction to Anjou's victory at Cambrai was predictable. Philip II was naturally furious. Moreover, Cardinal Granvelle was adamant that Henry and Catherine were behind the entire operation. 'If we want to amuse ourselves with words', Granvelle wrote to Margaret of Parma, 'I hardly know what one would call a declaration of war if this is not it'.[57] Henry III, however, rather naively believed that all of his denials of complicity and his attempts to hinder Anjou's enterprise would somehow count for something. 'I cannot believe', he wrote, 'that all this will put me at war with the Catholic king, who has seen what step I march to'.[58] The most significant reaction, however, was Elizabeth's. As Burghley explained to Walsingham on 24 August, £30,000 was already on its way to Anjou from the queen.[59] Remarkably, the money was delivered almost immediately. Lord Henry Seymour landed at Boulogne on 29 August and delivered £15,000 to Anjou on 1 September. The remaining £15,000 was paid by Jean du Bex before the end of the month.[60]

Although Elizabeth's £30,000 alleviated Anjou's most pressing needs, his overall financial state was still far from sound. The grant did cause him to consider, however, whether his greatest source of assistance might not lie across the Channel. He was doubtless grateful for the 90,000 *livres* provided by his brother, but it was much less than he expected. Moreover, Elizabeth had given him a sum more than three times greater. Ironically, all of the difficult negotiations between Henry and Elizabeth over whether the marriage or the treaty should be enacted first proved not to matter. Elizabeth opted for a third course, to aid Anjou in the Netherlands covertly without a treaty or a marriage. As both the treaty and the marriage were proving impossible, perhaps Elizabeth also felt that a little monetary support might give her some degree of control over Anjou's enterprise in the Netherlands. Anjou, for his part, had never made it a secret that financial support was his primary concern. Thus, it could hardly have come as much of a surprise when the French ambassador and the sieur de Marchaumont, who was still representing Anjou in England, announced later that month that Anjou would be arriving in London shortly for a second

[55] Ibid., p. 201.   [56] Ibid., p. 205.
[57] Groen van Prinsterer, *Archives*, vol. VIII, p. 11, Granvelle to the duchess of Parma, 3 September 1581.
[58] BN, MSS CCC 368, fols. 310–11, Henry to Arnaud du Ferrier, 23 August 1581.
[59] Digges, *The Compleat Ambassador*, p. 397, Burghley to Walsingham, 24 August 1581.
[60] PRO/SP 78/10/122/fols. 308–35.

interview with the queen.[61] The king and queen mother's hopes for a marriage were raised once again, and so perhaps were Anjou's. The marriage remained just a smoke-screen, however. It was not given up altogether, at least on the French side, but it continued to be subordinate to the main issue. 'The primary object of his visit is to ask for money', noted Bernardino de Mendoza, 'and the queen is inclined to give it to him'.[62]

II

Elizabeth's £30,000 allowed Anjou's diminishing forces to capture Cateau-Cambrésis and several smaller towns in September 1581, but was not enough to do more than delay the inevitable break-up of his army. Almost immediately after the capture of Cambrai unpaid troops began to desert and make their way back to France, billeting themselves on the civilian population as they went. Henry III received a letter from a worried agent in Mons, which had recently defected to Parma: 'The arrival of Monsieur and his army has . . . stirred up these people, in the towns and countryside alike, so that a Frenchman cannot show his face here without endangering his life.'[63] By late September it was reported that Anjou had departed from the region of Cambrai and was heading westward toward the Channel, with only his household and 200 horse.[64]

The Dutch States-General commissioned Philippe de Marnix, seigneur de St Aldegonde (who had helped to negotiate the treaty with Anjou at Plessis-lès-Tours) to go after the duke and ask him to remain in the Netherlands. When Marnix caught up with him in the village of Le Catelet on 7 September, he apologized profusely for the States' delay in providing financial support. He begged Anjou's forgiveness, and assured him that the States intended to assist him as they had promised, but said that, because of the war, it had proved impossible. Anjou, who was ill at the time, seemed to be understanding. Although as Marnix reported back to Orange and the States, everything still depended on money:

The duke responded that he was convinced of the goodwill of the States, but that it had been impossible, because of this [lack of money], to prevent his army from disbanding, even though he had paid the volunteers considerable sums. That being the case, he felt that he was too undermanned to continue his enterprise along the original course and that he was now forced to withdraw to look for some alternative . . . and that it was impossible to hold his volunteer army together over the winter, which would needlessly add enormous costs.[65]

[61] *CODOIN*, vol. XCII, p. 130, Mendoza to Philip, 1 October 1581.
[62] Ibid., p. 155, Mendoza to Philip, 29 October 1581.
[63] Muller and Diegerick, *Documents*, vol. IV, p. 215, Blatier to Henry III, 27 August 1581.
[64] BN, MSS ital. 1732, fol. 201, Priuli to the Signory, 20 September 1581.
[65] Muller and Diegerick, *Documents*, vol. IV, p. 237, report of Marnix on his visit with Anjou, 17 September 1581.

Anjou suggested that his remaining troops join ranks with the forces of the States, which would be enough to occupy the enemy over the winter. Then, in the spring, Anjou would return to the Netherlands at the head of a new and more powerful army. The duke then despatched Marnix back to the States to tell them that 'it was their own fault that he was prevented from leading all of his forces to them [now]; and in order not to ravage the countryside needlessly, he thought it better to disband them for the present'.[66] Marnix's report naturally upset the deputies of the States, who suspected that, having once departed for England, Anjou might not return. The council of state begged him on 26 September to attend the next meeting of the States-General and to swear the loyalty oath of the *Blijde Inkomst*. He was needed immediately, they insisted, as Parma had recently laid siege to Tournai. They even promised him 50,000 florins, half of which Marnix delivered to the duke by mid-October. By that time, however, Anjou had already reached St-Valéry-sur-Somme on the Channel coast. His mind was made up.[67]

Meanwhile, Henry III and Catherine de Medici, with their hopes for the marriage raised once again, did what they could to foster the match. They each had a private interview with Francis Walsingham before he departed for England in mid-September. In a meeting in the Tuilleries on 30 August, Catherine tried to appeal to Walsingham's known anti-Spanish sentiments. Although he had consistently opposed the marriage, he was known to favor giving support to the Dutch rebels and to Anjou's own enterprise. Catherine told him that Henry had not only been providing troops for Dom Antonio in Portugal for over a year, but that he was also giving his brother assistance in the Netherlands, 'there being no better way to humble the king of Spain'. While they had no desire to enter into a war with Philip II, she felt that it would be in the best interests of both France and England 'to find some means of re-establishing the Dutch in their liberties'.[68] On 10 September Henry met with Walsingham, who made one last attempt to fulfill the instructions that Elizabeth had given him: to secure a league with France without the marriage. It was no use, however, as Henry refused any league except by means of marriage.[69] Both Henry and Catherine still felt that the marriage was the best way to guarantee Elizabeth's support for Anjou, especially as Henry had finally provided some token support of his own. Moreover, he had come to believe that all of Europe would benefit from a Spanish defeat in the Netherlands. 'The forces of the prince of Parma are forever at Tournai, though they have not yet accomplished much on account of the season', Henry wrote in late autumn. 'And I now see more than ever that all

---

66 Ibid., pp. 237–8.
67 Ibid., pp. 239–45, council of state to Anjou, 26 September 1581; ibid., pp. 249–51, same to same, 13 October 1581; and ibid., pp. 251–2, Anjou to the council of state, 20 October 1581.
68 Catherine de Medici, *Lettres*, vol. VII, pp. 492–7, summary of Catherine's conversation with Walsingham, 30 August 1581.
69 BN, MSS fr. 3307, fols. 41v.–2r., Henry to Castelnau, 11 September 1581.

things there are leading to war, for which I am distressed, fearing that it could light a fire which will consume all of Christendom.'[70] Finally, the king had another reason for supporting the marriage, as he related to his ambassador in England on the eve of his brother's voyage across the Channel. He considered Anjou 'not only as a brother, but like a son. Since God has not yet graced me with any children, he is my one and only heir.'[71]

The duke of Anjou crossed the Channel and landed at Rye on 31 October. He was accompanied by several gentlemen from his household, and significantly, by Philippe de Marnix, who was still trying to get him to return to the Netherlands. On 1 November Anjou arrived in London, and from there went on to Richmond Palace.[72] Henry III despatched secretary Pinart to England on 15 November to express his official support for the marriage. Pinart carried two letters from Henry to Elizabeth. One was a simple statement of support for the match in the hand of the king. The other was an official patent letter in which Henry promised to sign an offensive and defensive alliance with Elizabeth under whatever terms she wished, after the consummation of the marriage. Moreover, Henry promised Elizabeth that he would pay for half of Anjou's costs in the Netherlands if she would pay for the other half.[73] This was further than Henry had ever committed himself in support of his brother. Although Henry may never have intended to execute this daring promise, it was nevertheless another indication that the marriage was just a vehicle by which to aid the Dutch rebels.[74]

Mendoza's assertion that the primary purpose of Anjou's visit was to secure more money from Elizabeth appears to have been borne out by events.[75] Within a fortnight of his arrival, Anjou and Elizabeth issued reciprocal declarations of friendship. Styling himself the 'protector of Cambrai', Anjou vowed to defend Elizabeth from all enemies and to maintain their longstanding friendly relations. The queen followed with a similar declaration concerning the duke. On 14 November the two signed a formal pact, which was about as close as they could get to an offensive and defensive alliance. Elizabeth pledged to maintain and support Anjou in the Netherlands, and in return Anjou promised not to make any agreement with Philip II or Parma without her approval. Significantly, the marriage was not even mentioned.[76]

[70] BN, MSS CCC 368, fol. 367, Henry to Arnaud du Ferrier, 9 November 1581.
[71] BN, MSS fr. 3307, fol. 45, Henry to Castelnau, 31 October 1581.
[72] CODOIN, vol. XCII, pp. 162–5, Mendoza to Philip, 2 and 7 November 1581; and CSPF, vol. XV, p. 357, Walsingham to Villiers, 10 November 1581.
[73] BN, MSS fr. 3307, fols. 47v.–9r., Henry's instructions to Pinart and his patent letter to Elizabeth, both 14 November 1581.
[74] Although Henry clearly supported the marriage, he was still prudent enough to ask Castelnau to keep an eye on Anjou in England, and especially to make sure that Protestants such as Marnix and Du Plessis-Mornay did not lure him into some dangerous Protestant league. BN, MSS fr. 3307, fol. 45v.
[75] CODOIN, vol. XCII, pp. 155, 176, Mendoza to Philip, 29 October and 11 November 1581.
[76] BIF, MSS God. 74, fols. 185–91, Declarations and pact between Anjou and Elizabeth, 14 November 1581.

Also of interest was an unusually detailed memorandum presented by Francis Walsingham to the queen in November. It did not concern the marriage issue, but dealt with the necessity of supporting Anjou in the Netherlands. In short, Walsingham surmised that the Dutch rebels could not hope to hold out against Parma without foreign assistance. Therefore, Elizabeth had to decide whether it would be better if the Netherlands were to be ruled by Spain or by the duke of Anjou. Walsingham's choice was clear, and he tried to persuade Elizabeth that Anjou was the lesser of two evils. He admitted that the duke might prove to be no better sovereign than Philip II, but 'present griefs being dangerous are to be preferred before conjectural doubts of future diseases'. In any case, Walsingham felt that Anjou was a prince 'that yieldeth to a toleration of religion'. His long memorandum made it clear that the Puritan faction of Elizabeth's privy council that so ardently opposed the marriage was in favor of supporting Anjou in the Netherlands. Whether Walsingham delivered his memorandum because of the recent siege of Tournai, or simply to distract the queen's attention from the marriage, is not altogether clear. As he himself noted, however, it was the best way to avoid the popular upheaval that accompanied the duke's last visit to England. 'If an overt war may be avoided', he concluded, 'and that it shall suffice to give some support underhand, then shall it be expedient for avoiding of the grief of the subjects'.[77]

It would appear from all accounts of Anjou's visit, however, that the flame of marriage was suddenly rekindled. On 22 November while the court was at Whitehall to celebrate Accession Day, an incident sparked off new rumors of the match:

On the 22nd at eleven in the morning, while Anjou and the queen were strolling through the gallery accompanied by the earl of Leicester and Walsingham, the French ambassador entered and said that he wanted to write to his master, who had ordered him to find out from the queen's own mouth what she planned to do concerning the marriage with his brother. She responded: 'You can write this to the king, that the duke of Anjou will be my husband.' At the same moment she kissed Anjou on the mouth and gave him a ring which she took from her finger as a token of her pledge. Anjou then gave her one of his own in return. A short while later the queen called the ladies and gentlemen who were present in the hall to the gallery, and repeated to them in a loud voice, in front of Anjou, what she had previously said. This delighted all of the French delegation, and Anjou immediately despatched a gentleman to his brother with the news.[78]

There was no mistaking Elizabeth's intention. 'The standers by tooke it that the marriage was now contracted by promise', as William Camden noted. 'Some

[77] BL, Harl. MSS 1582, fols. 38–41, 'Whether it be good for her Majesty to assist the Duke of Anjou in the Low Countries, November 1581. Sir F. W.' A summary of this document is in Read, *Mr Secretary Walsingham*, vol. II, pp. 91–4.

[78] *CODOIN*, vol. XCII, pp. 193–4, Mendoza to Philip, 24 November 1581. Similar accounts were recorded by Marnix in Muller and Diegerick, *Documents*, vol. IV, pp. 258–60; and Camden, *Historie*, book iii, pp. 7–8.

leaped for joy, some were astonished, and some were cast down with sorrow.'[79] It is equally clear, however, that this was just a charade designed for public consumption. The very next day Elizabeth privately informed Leicester, Hatton, and Walsingham that she had no intention of marrying. Anjou's reaction to the queen's *volte-face* seems to indicate either that he was aware of her game or that he did not much care about the marriage anyway. According to Mendoza, he accepted the news very calmly, *con gran blandura*, and with little show of emotion.[80] Camden noted, however, that Anjou was later heard to utter one or two quips about 'the lightness of women and the inconstancy of I[s]landers'.[81] Elizabeth's display on the 22nd was clearly just a ruse, in all probability designed to pressure Henry III into the treaty that she had long desired.[82] And she later told Sussex (who, with Burghley, was the lone supporter of the match on the council), that she hated the idea of marriage more and more every day.[83]

The initial French reaction was just what Elizabeth had hoped for. The Florentine ambassador in Paris reported that upon reading the letter carrying the news of 22 November, Henry III shouted 'that he was the king of France and his brother the king of England, which would be a thorn in the leg of the king of Spain'.[84] He had despatched Pinart to Elizabeth the week before, however, and was content to wait and see how she responded to his offers. Once Pinart arrived, it became clear that little progress would be made. Henry's bountiful offer to pay for half of Anjou's expenses in the Netherlands was contingent on the consummation of the marriage. Thus, Elizabeth's sleight of hand with the ring on 22 November was insufficient. Moreover, her ploy provided Anjou with ample reason to remain in England throughout the winter rather than return to the Netherlands, as Marnix continually begged him to do.[85] Indeed, Marnix informed the Dutch council of state on 10 December that Anjou had no immediate plans to leave England for the Netherlands. 'I believe it will be a long time', he wrote 'as he would certainly desire to go there with some means, which is the cause of his delay'.[86]

So Elizabeth was forced to entertain and provide for Anjou and his retinue over the winter of 1581–2. The public example made of John Stubbs two years earlier obviously achieved the intended results, for there were no popular outbursts against Anjou's visit on this occasion, despite the fact that hostility to

[79] Camden, *Historie*, book iii, p. 8.
[80] *CODOIN*, vol. xcii, p. 198, Mendoza to Philip, 4 December 1581.
[81] Camden, *Historie*, book iii, p. 8.
[82] Not only did Mendoza suspect this (see *CODOIN*, vol. xcii, pp. 194–6), but Elizabeth's instructions to Cobham confirm these suspicions (*CSPF*, vol. xv, p. 388, Elizabeth to Cobham, November 1581).
[83] *CSPS*, vol. iii, p. 252, Mendoza to Philip, 29 December 1581.
[84] Desjardins, vol. iv, p. 412, 26 November 1581.
[85] *CSPF*, vol. xv, pp. 495–6.
[86] Muller and Diegerick, *Documents*, vol. iv, p. 263, Marnix to the council of state, 10 December 1581.

the marriage was as strong as ever. Moreover, this time Elizabeth countered with some propaganda of her own at court. Painters such as Nicholas Hilliard were invited to capture Anjou's likeness on canvass.[87] And musicians such as William Byrd and John Dowland were asked to compose some special scores to commemorate the duke's visit.[88] All this attention certainly flattered Anjou, and he reciprocated by giving Elizabeth a large cache of jewelry.[89] By Christmas, however, it was clear that the queen did not intend to marry. The hostility to the match first made manifest in 1579 had obviously taken its toll. Moreover, Anjou had further alienated the English Catholics during his visit. Thirteen recusant clerics and a legate had been sentenced to death for treason just prior to his visit. When the Spanish ambassador Mendoza pleaded with him to intervene with the queen to spare the life of one of the thirteen, the Jesuit Edmund Campion, the duke refused to lift a finger. Campion became a Catholic martyr upon his execution on 1 December 1581.[90]

In refusing the marriage, Elizabeth had no other option but to give Anjou the financial assistance that he came for. In any case, her task was made easier by the fact that Henry III had just sent his brother 150,000 *livres*.[91] On 15 December Elizabeth decided to give (or technically lend) Anjou £60,000 (about 600,000 *livres*). Half of this large sum would be given to Anjou within a fortnight after his departure from England. The remainder would be paid two months after that.[92] Anjou was grateful, though rightfully dubious that Elizabeth would ever provide him with more than half a million *livres*. Thus, on 31 December he asked Burghley if he could have £10,000 immediately, or at least before he left England. Elizabeth had no option but to comply, and on 1 January her agent Horatio Palavicino turned over £10,000 (about 100,000 *livres*) to Anjou.[93]

Thus ended the saga of the Elizabeth–Anjou courtship, always more a

87 Roy C. Strong, *Portraits of Queen Elizabeth I* (Oxford, 1963), p. 102; and A. L. Rowse, *The Elizabethan Renaissance: the Cultural Achievement* (London, 1972), pp. 172–3.

88 Byrd published 'Munsers Almaine' in a collection compiled in 1591 and presented to the wife of Sir Henry Neville. See William Byrd, *My Ladye Nevells Booke*, ed. Hilda Andrews (London, 1926), pp. 221–8 for the score. There was also 'The Frog Gailliard' which the lutenist John Dowland later published as a part song, 'Now, oh now I needs must part', in his *First Booke of Songes or Ayres of foure parts* (London, 1597).

89 Of the various rubies, sapphires, diamonds, pendants, and other ornate pieces, surely the most interesting was a gold locket inscribed 'SERVIET ETERNUM DULCIS QUEM TORQUET ELIZA.' BL, Sloane MSS 814, fol. 22, jewels given to Elizabeth by Anjou, January 1582. I wish to thank Dr Simon L. Adams for calling this document to my attention.

90 *CODOIN*, vol. XCII, pp. 171, 200, Mendoza to Philip, 7 November and 4 December 1581. Also see John Bossy, 'English Catholics and the French Marriage', p. 10.

91 PRO/SP 78/10/122/fols. 308–55. The document states that the money was delivered in December 1581. Thus, it probably came over with secretary Claude Pinart.

92 *CSPF*, vol. XV, p. 409. A copy of the contract, in Burghley's hand, is in BL, Harl. MSS 1582, fol. 44.

93 *CSPF*, vol. XV, p. 423, Anjou to Burghley, 31 December 1581; PRO/SP 78/10/122/ fols. 308–35; and BL, Cotton. MSS, Galba E/vi, fol. 113, 'Sums of money paid to the Duke of Anjou ... by Palavicino, £10,000'.

political than an amorous affair, which had blown hot and cold for nearly a decade. The latest episode, apart from the charade of 22 November, was much more dominated by the Dutch revolt than by matrimonial considerations. Although Catherine de Medici protested to Walsingham on 2 January 1582 about Elizabeth's indecision on the marriage, it was clear to most that the match was off.[94] Even Henry III was forced to admit that 'my brother is still in England pursuing his marriage, or so he writes me, but I can have no real hope of it, seeing the delays that are employed there'.[95] Ultimately, Anjou had very little alternative to taking Elizabeth's £10,000 and returning to the Netherlands. Moreover, by January 1582 Orange was beginning to fear that, if Anjou did not return soon, the offer from the States might be in jeopardy.[96] On 1 February 1582, Anjou departed from London. Elizabeth ordered an impressive array of English nobility to escort him to the Netherlands, including Lords Howard and Hunsdon, the earl of Leicester, Francis Walsingham, and Philip Sidney. Although the accompaniment of the most vociferous opponents of the marriage was surely a sign that the wedding was off, it was also an indication to Orange and the States-General that she supported Anjou's enterprise in their service. One week later the entire expedition departed from Sandwich and sailed for Flushing in very rough seas.

Perhaps the most telling example of the English attitude towards Anjou was expressed in an anonymous political cartoon called 'The Milch Cow', which must have been painted shortly after the duke's visit. The cartoon depicted a cow, which represented the provinces of the Netherlands still in revolt against Spain. Philip II sat upon the cow's back, beating it with a stick. Elizabeth was shown feeding the cow as William of Orange milked it. Finally, Anjou was depicted holding the cow's tail and receiving the scorn of all concerned. The caption read as follows:

> Not longe time since I saw a cowe
> Did Flanders represente,
> Upon whose back Kinge Phillip rode
> As being malcontent.
>
> The Queen of England giving hay
> Whereon the cowe did feede,
> As one that was her greatest helpe
> In her distresse and neede.
>
> The Prince of Orange milkt the cowe
> And made his purse the payle.
> The cow did shyt in Monsieur's hand
> While he did hold her tayle.

[94] Catherine de Medici, *Lettres*, vol. VIII, p. 1, Catherine to Francis Walsingham, 2 January 1582.
[95] BN, MSS CCC 368, fols. 392–3, Henry to Arnaud du Ferrier, 2 January 1582.
[96] Muller and Diegerick, *Documents*, vol. IV, pp. 282–3, Orange to Pruneaux, 9 January 1582.

'The Milch Cow' obviously overestimated the contribution of Elizabeth and underestimated the contribution of Orange in the Dutch revolt. Nevertheless, the duke of Anjou could hardly have known as he crossed the North Sea in February 1582 that his own caricature could incorporate such an uncanny degree of reality.[97]

[97] 'The Milch Cow' is in the Rijksmuseum, Amsterdam. It is reproduced in Hugh Trevor-Roper (ed.), *The Age of Expansion* (London, 1968), p. 79.

8

Turmoil in the Netherlands,
February 1582–January 1583

Around noon on Thursday, 8 February 1582, the duke of Anjou departed from England, accompanied by forty or so English gentlemen.[1] Late Friday afternoon his party reached the outer islands off the coast of Zeeland, where they anchored for the night; and the following morning, 10 February, the duke made his official entry into Flushing. The town had been alerted to his impending arrival, and marked the occasion with bonfires and fireworks. As Anjou stepped off his ship, he was greeted by William of Orange and a host of deputies from Brabant, Holland, Flanders, Zeeland, Friesland, and Gelderland, who had been anxiously awaiting his arrival for months. Thus, the prince of Orange and the duke of Anjou, who had been in such close correspondence for so long, finally met for the first time. It was a festive occasion, and one observer remarked upon the 'bonfires of joy which were burning and lasted almost all night'. The following morning Anjou observed mass in his household, the first time mass had been performed in the province of Zeeland in nearly eight years. Later that afternoon the entourage moved on to Middelburg, the principal town of Zeeland, where he sojourned for about a week. Then on Saturday, 17 February, he reboarded his vessel and sailed up the mouth of the Schelde River toward Antwerp. Two days later at ten o'clock in the morning, a volley of cannon and a blast of trumpets announced his arrival. The deputies of the States-General, the nobles and captains of the city, and the combined French and Dutch armies were there to greet him, a gathering that some estimated to be as many as 25,000 men. They had all assembled to witness Anjou swear the oath of the *Blijde Inkomst* and accept his new title as the duke of Brabant. It was a glorious moment for both Anjou and the States. The euphoria, however, was all too brief.[2]

I

Although Anjou was required to swear a loyalty oath and accept a new title in each of the provinces that had contracted with him, his appearance in Antwerp

---

[1] For a list of the English delegation, see *Holinshed's Chronicles of England, Scotland, and Ireland* (6 vols., London, 1807–8), vol. IV, pp. 460–1.

[2] Anjou's arrival in the Netherlands is described in BN, MSS fr. 3296, fols. 100–6, 'Discours sur la venue et honnorable reception de Monsieur fils et frere du Roy, Duc de Brabant, marquis de

before the States-General and his installation as duke of Brabant on 19 February 1582 was recognized as the act that consummated the Dutch rebellion against Philip II. The event was of such importance, in fact, that the States commissioned the Antwerp printer, Christophe Plantin, to record the event in a literary and visual account. Plantin's description offers a clear insight into what the Dutch hoped to gain from Anjou, and the political symbol they hoped he would become. Moreover, it demonstrates that their expectations could not have possibly been fulfilled.[3]

Plantin related that the city of Antwerp had only six days' notice to prepare for Anjou's arrival, and as a result the ceremony, 'did not even approach the sumptuousness of other entries'.[4] Nevertheless, the city managed to use some of the decorations already on hand, and put up triumphal arches, banners, portraits, and other adornments to mark the occasion. Anjou sailed up the Schelde River early on the morning of 19 February and disembarked at the village of Kiel, just outside the citadel of Antwerp. He was greeted by the prince of Orange and the same array of troops and magistrates that had assembled in Flushing, and then led to a covered dais where the ceremony was to take place.[5] The stage had a throne in the center covered with gold cloth, and on the roof of the dais were the arms of the Holy Roman Empire, the province of Brabant, and the city of Antwerp, as well as two banners depicting the *fleur-de-lis* of the arms of Anjou. The duke was then seated on the throne, as several of the leading English and French noblemen gathered around him on the stage. When the rest of his entourage and all the Dutch deputies assembled at the foot of the stage, the sieur de Hessels, a doctor of law and counsellor in the States of Brabant, rose to deliver the oration from the province of Brabant. He thanked the duke for heeding their call for aid and assisting them in their time of need, and recounted the Spanish villainy and treachery of the last two decades. Hessels pointed out that the States were forced to turn to Anjou in order to protect their ancient liberties, 'which could not be better accomplished than by the election which the said States of Brabant, along with the other provinces, had made of His Highness to be their prince and lord'. As Hessels made explicit, 'it seemed as if

Sainct Empire etc.' (although dates are muddled); *CSPV*, vol. VIII, pp. 29–30; and *Holinshed's Chronicles*, vol. IV, pp. 460–5.
[3] Plantin published the work in both French and Dutch: *La ioyeuse & magnifique Entree de Monseigneur Francoys fils de France, et frere unicque du Roy, par la grace de Dieu, duc de Brabant, d'Anjou, Alençon, Berri, etc. en sa tresrenommee ville d'Anvers* (Antwerp, 1582) and *De blijde ende heerlijcke Incomste van mijn Heer Franssois van Vranckrijck, des Conicks eenich broeder, by Gotts ghenade Hertogh van Brabant, van Anjou, Alensson, Berri, etc. in sijne zeer vermaerde stadt van Antwerpen* (Antwerp, 1582). The French edition is superior, as it contains twenty-one double-page engravings, magnificently hand-colored in some editions, which depict important scenes described in the text. A facsimile edition of the French edition has recently appeared: H. M. C. Purkis (ed.), *La magnifique Entrée de François d'Anjou en sa ville d'Anvers* (Amsterdam and New York, 1975). All my references are to the original French edition.
[4] Plantin, *La ioyeuse & magnifique Entree*, p. 13.   [5] Ibid., Plate I, between pp. 14–15.

some ancient duke of Burgundy had been resurrected for them once more'.[6]
Anjou graciously responded that he was resolved 'to protect them and to restore
their ancient liberties, and in doing so, to risk whatever means God placed in his
hands, and whatever it pleased the king his lord and brother and the queen of
England to lend him, even as far as shedding his own blood and losing his life'.[7]

At this point the articles of the *Blijde Inkomst* were read aloud in Dutch, as was
customary, while Anjou followed a French translation. Anjou was then asked if
he was content to swear unto the articles, or if any of them required any further
explanation. He declared that he was satisfied with the articles, having already
studied them on board ship during his journey from Middelburg to Antwerp.
Hessels then read aloud the oath of allegiance, first in Dutch and then French,
after which Anjou repeated it. The prince of Orange then presented him with
the vestments of the duchy of Brabant: a mantle and bonnet of crimson velvet
lined with ermine.[8] Then, still facing his new subjects, Anjou heard the deputies
of the States of Brabant and the magistrates of the city of Antwerp swear an oath
of loyalty to him, after which he was presented a gold key to the city. Here was the
royal ceremonial and personal attention that he had longed for since his early
days at the Valois court. The installation at Antwerp was undoubtedly his finest
hour.

When all the solemnities were finished, heralds shouted 'Long live the duke of
Brabant!' Then, as trumpets blared, they threw coins bearing a likeness of the
duke into the crowd. Anjou mounted a white Italian stallion, which was
bedecked in a drape of embroidered velvet, and moved slowly towards the
principal entrance to the city and citadel known as Kaiser's gate or St George's
gate. In a royal procession befitting a king, he was ushered into his new city by
representatives of the city, and province of Brabant, the States-General,
members of the Dutch, English, and French nobility, his own household, a
company of Swiss guards, and a troop of trumpeters with fife and drum. As the
entire procession entered the city, it passed beneath a shield mounted above the
gate, on which was written a Latin inscription:

To François, son of Henry II and only brother of Henry III, king of France, who was
singularly nominated to the sovereign lordship of the Netherlands, the dukedom of
Brabant, and the marquisate of the Holy Roman Empire, and who was so fortunately
installed as its most desired prince, as he auspiciously enters his most devoted city as he
promised.   The Senate and People of Antwerp.[9]

As the new duke of Brabant passed beneath the gate and into the city, he was
met by six gentlemen bearing a canopy of gold cloth, which they unfurled and

---

[6] Ibid., p. 18.   [7] Ibid., p. 19.   [8] Ibid., p. 20. See also Plate II, between pp. 14–15.
[9] Ibid., p. 25. The inscription read as follows: 'FRANCISCO Henrici II F[ilio] Henrici III
Galliarum Regis Fr[atri] unico, singulari Numinis providentia ad Amplissimum Belgii Principa-
tum vocato atque in Brabantiae Ducem Sacri Imperii Marchionem, quod felix ac faustum sit,

carried over his head as he continued the procession through the city.[10] The entire route was lavishly decorated and adorned with banners, triumphal arches, and decorations of various sorts. Along the processional route were staged numerous pageants and plays depicting classical and biblical scenes, all of which were meant to symbolize the tyranny of Spanish rule and the tolerance and justice of the duke. Moreover, the entire 'joyous entry' symbolized the resurrection of the house of Burgundy, backed by the alliance of the crowns of France and England. Explicit references were made to the good old days under the rule of the Valois dukes, to whom Anjou was distantly related. The earl of Leicester and François de Bourbon, *prince dauphin* of Auvergne, were prominently placed in the procession to represent Elizabeth and Henry III's support.[11] The entire day was a unique experience for Anjou, who revelled in an adoration he never received at home. Even the Frenchmen who accompanied him were astonished to see him dressed in the ancient vestments of the electors of the Holy Roman Empire. 'They were astounded', noted Plantin, 'and the prince seemed to them more magnificent than ever before'.[12] The royal procession lasted most of the day; and when Anjou finally reached the ducal palace, night was approaching. As he retired for the night, thousands of arquebuses were fired in celebration, and bonfires were lit all over the city. 'It seemed as if the entire city was on fire. Torches and bonfires of joy illuminated every street, square, and steeple, in such number and for so long that night resembled day.'[13]

Once the jubilation and euphoria of his installation had worn off, Anjou had to face the daunting task of continuing the war against Parma. As long as some of the elite of the English peerage remained with him, he felt confident of Elizabeth's support. His principal concern was the lukewarm support he received from France. Moreover, the situation in Antwerp, especially his relationship with the States, was not as encouraging as appearances indicated. The day after his installation he wrote to several prominent persons in France, among them the judges of the *parlement* of Paris, in an attempt to garner support for his military venture. He argued that peace in France depended on the outcome of the war in the Netherlands. With some justification, he attested that, until Philip II was defeated, Spanish interference would ensure the continuation of the French civil wars. Moreover, he tried to persuade his fellow countrymen

---

inaugurato Principi suo exoptatiss[imo] hanc urbem sibi devotissimam auspicatissime ingresso votis faventes. S[enatus] P[opulus] Q[ue] A[ntverpiensis].'

[10] Ibid., Plate V, between pp. 26–7.

[11] Ibid., pp. 27–37 (including Plates VII–XIX), 43–7. See also Frances A. Yates, *The Valois Tapestries* (London, 2nd edn. 1975), pp. 34, 94–108. Dr Yates provides a good historical explanation for this symbolism, and how it was also expressed in a set of tapestries that were presented to Anjou and which now hang in the Uffizi gallery in Florence.

[12] Plantin, *La ioyeuse & magnifique Entree*, p. 23.

[13] Ibid., p. 37. For further details of Anjou's entry into Antwerp, see I. L. A. Diegerick, 'Notice sur l'entrée solemnelle du duc d'Anjou dans la ville d'Anvers, le 19 février, 1582', *Annales de l'Académie d'Archéologie de Belgique*, XI (1854), 405–22.

that his enterprise in the Netherlands was the last alternative, 'being certain that of all the means that could be employed to bring about peace in France, the one currently in my hands is all that is left, all the others having proved to be useless and ineffective'.[14]

Even more worrying was the state of affairs in Antwerp. Anjou was shocked to discover that the local magistrates did not permit the free exercise of Catholic worship in the city. He had promised not to interfere in the religious settlement in the Netherlands, but the States had led him to believe that freedom of religion was allowed in Antwerp. Claude de la Châtre related that Anjou was so incensed that he threatened to pack up and leave at once. 'I cannot describe the anger and discontent that seized His Highness over this barbarous humiliation', noted La Châtre. 'This circumstance will be remembered as one of the first and foremost deceptions committed by them [the States], with others following one after another.'[15] Fortunately, cooler heads prevailed. Orange smoothed Anjou's ruffled feathers and persuaded the city council to allow the free worship of Roman Catholicism in one church in the city. Nevertheless, the entire episode revealed the tension in Anjou's relationship with the States and the weak foundation on which his authority rested. Moreover, he understandably complained that he had yet to receive any of the 200,000 *livres* per month that had been promised to him in the treaty of Plessis-lès-Tours. Bernardino de Mendoza reported from London that Anjou was 'like an old hulk run ashore, high and dry without wind and tide, unable to get off the sandbank'. Moreover, he noted, 'the oath of allegiance to the rebel States was nothing but a joke and a hollow mockery'.[16]

Although popular support of Anjou had never been overwhelming, one event triggered massive resentment against him: the attempted assassination of William of Orange on 18 March 1582. The day was also Anjou's twenty-seventh birthday, and Orange had planned a vast celebration in his honor for that evening. Earlier in the day, however, as Orange was leaving the table after his lunch, an intruder suddenly rushed up and fired a pistol point blank in his face. The prince's bodyguards, caught unaware, leaped on the would-be assassin and quickly killed him. At the time no one could identify the intruder; but because he wore French clothes, it was rumored that Anjou had been responsible. Later, two letters written in Spanish were found in his pocket and he was identified as

14 Nevers, *Mémoires*, vol. I, pp. 151–3, Anjou to the *parlement* of Paris, 20 February 1582 (quotation from p. 153); see also BN, MSS fr. 3321, fols. 32–4, Anjou to the duke of Montpensier, 20 February 1582; BN, MSS fr. 3182, fols. 79–81, Anjou to the towns of France, 20 February 1582; and PRO/SP 78/7/29, Anjou to Burghley, 24 February 1582.

15 BN, MSS n.a. fr. 4709, fols. 20–1.

16 *CSPS*, vol. III, p. 310, Mendoza to Philip, 6 March 1582. Also see De Thou, *Histoire universelle*, vol. VI, pp. 175–6; *CSPF*, vol. XV, p. 546, Norris to Walsingham, 11 March 1582; and Gachard (ed.), *Correspondance de Guillaume le Taciturne*, vol. V, pp. 291–8, 'Articles proposés par le Prince d'Orange et le conseil d'état au duc d'Anjou, Anvers, 10 mars 1582'.

Juan Jauréguy, a hireling in the pay of a Portuguese merchant who was trying to collect the bounty of 25,000 *escudos* that Philip II had put on Orange's head. Fortunately, Orange survived the shooting, as the bullet passed cleanly through his cheek. Due to a heavy loss of blood, however, his life hung in the balance for several weeks. The incident exacerbated the hostility toward Anjou. During Orange's convalescence, rumors continually circulated that the prince was dead. Until he finally recovered, Anjou was treated with contempt.[17]

Further complicating Anjou's problems in the Netherlands was his chronic inability to pay his troops. He was not oblivious to the fact that whatever favor he still held with Orange and the States was dependent on the military support that he could provide. Jean Bodin, the famous author of the *Six Livres de la République* who travelled with Anjou to London and then Antwerp, had pointed this out while they were still in England. 'It is true that His Highness is not come to enjoy himself', Bodin wrote to Francis Walsingham in March 1582, 'but for war with a powerful foe. That is why I told him in England that no conquering prince, elected and called in by the subjects of another, had ever gone save with a good and powerful army.'[18] But how was this army to be paid? Obviously, Anjou planned to conduct his campaign with a combination of his own revenues, the two million *livres* per year promised by the States, and the promised support of Henry III and Elizabeth. Anjou had already alienated so much of his *apanage* to raise troops that his revenue was but a trickle of what it had once been.[19] The Dutch States did finally make a grant of 32,528 *livres* to support the companies under Rochepot's command in Middelburg in the spring of 1582, but it was a far cry from the sum that the deputies had promised him.[20] As for Elizabeth, no-one could predict her behavior. Henry III still distrusted her because of her deceit regarding the marriage. He was convinced that she only wanted to foment war in the Netherlands in order to keep Spain and France at each other's throats.[21] Meanwhile, a perplexed duke of Anjou awaited the aid she had promised him before he left England. In the event, Elizabeth did send a further £15,000 (which, because of fluctuations in the rate of exchange, amounted to 111,000 *livres*), which the sieur de la Fougière delivered in April.[22] It was welcome, but hardly enough. Anjou begged Henry to send one of the secretaries with some sorely needed funds, as his situation was becoming desperate. 'I am awaiting the sieur de la Neufville [secretary Villeroy]', he wrote to his brother in April, 'in the

---

17 See Wedgwood, *William the Silent*, pp. 229–35; De Thou, *Histoire universelle*, vol. VI, pp. 178–81; and Buisseret and Barbiche (eds.), *Les Œconomies royales de Sully*, vol. I, p. 108.

18 *CSPF*, vol. XV, p. 532, Bodin to Walsingham, 5 March 1582.

19 See Appendix C below, 'Income from the *apanage* of the duke of Anjou'.

20 PRO/SP 78/10/122/fols. 308–35.

21 BN, MSS CCC 473, fols. 251–4, Henry to Castelnau, 26 March 1582.

22 PRO/SP 78/10/122/fols. 308–35.

hope that Your Majesty will honor me, as much by your response as by an assurance that you have not completely forgotten me'.[23]

Wishing at all costs to avoid a war with Spain, Henry was forced to maintain his public stance of denying any complicity in Anjou's affairs. 'I will continue to do everything that I can', he wrote to Du Ferrier in April, 'to persuade him to leave the Netherlands before he suffers the fickleness of its people'.[24] Few were convinced, however, least of all the Spanish. Cardinal Granvelle wrote to Philip II that Anjou 'does nothing and could do nothing other than what his mother and brother desire, since they are the ones who are paying'.[25] The Venetian ambassador in Paris was equally suspicious, believing that Henry's protestations were just a smoke-screen to cover up the support he gave to his brother.[26] All these suspicions were justified in mid-May, in fact, when Henry despatched Pomponne de Bellièvre to Antwerp with a promise of 100,000 *écus* (300,000 *livres*). He instructed his councillor to tell Anjou that he would like to do more, but this was all he could afford. Bellièvre carried half the money with him and promised the rest by the end of the year.[27]

There is little doubt, then, that Henry aided his brother's enterprise in the Netherlands, occasionally with considerable sums. The motivation for this assistance, however, continued to be the source of speculation among his contemporaries. Henry may have been trying to induce Elizabeth to contribute to Anjou's expedition. If this was his gambit, it failed hopelessly. Elizabeth informed him through the French ambassador in London that she was willing to share Anjou's expenses with him, provided the marriage did not take place.[28] On the other hand, 300,000 *livres* seems far too large a sum just to use as bait to hook Elizabeth. According to the Venetian ambassador, it is more likely that he offered Anjou this amount 'in order not to alienate his brother completely'.[29] Moreover, when Bellièvre returned from Antwerp in late June, he urged Henry to give Anjou even more assistance. He described the pitiful state of Anjou's army, and advised the king to send marshal Biron to assist, 'because Anjou did not have any soldiers with enough experience or such reputation that he could confidently trust with his affairs'.[30] The king's primary motivation for helping his brother, however, seems to be that suggested by Moro:

[23] BN, MSS Dupuy 211, fol. 80, Anjou to Henry III, 2 April [1582]. Anjou also begged Bellièvre to try to persuade the king to send him 60,000 *écus*. BN, MSS fr. 15906, fol. 639, Anjou to Bellièvre, 13 April 1582.

[24] BN, MSS CCC 368, fol. 436, Henry to Du Ferrier, 8 April 1582.

[25] Antoine Perrenot, cardinal of Granvelle, *Correspondance de Granvelle, 1565–1586*, eds. Charles Piot and Edmond Poullet (12 vols., Brussels, 1877–96), vol. IX, pp. 461–2, Granvelle to Philip II, 8 March 1582.

[26] BN, MSS ital. 1732, fols. 304–6, Moro to the Signory, 15 April 1582.

[27] BN, MSS fr. 15906, fol. 666, Instructions of Henry to Bellièvre, 13 May 1582. Also see PRO/SP 78/10/122/fols. 308–35.

[28] BN, MSS fr. 15906, fol. 685, Castelnau to Henry, 18 May 1582.

[29] BN, MSS ital. 1732, fol. 344, Moro to the Signory, 1 June 1582.

[30] Ibid., fol. 351, Moro to the Signory, 29 June 1582.

Not wanting to drive his brother to complete despair, he will aid him with a good sum, which together with the first grant [that Bellièvre delivered], amounts to 100,000 *écus*. And with that plus the 100,000 the States are obliged to pay him every month and whatever aid he receives from the queen of England, it is hoped that he can make some headway in Flanders.[31]

As both Henry and Anjou soon discovered, however, this assistance was not nearly enough to maintain a French army in the Netherlands.

There is also no question that Anjou's inadequacy as a military commander contributed to his problems. And most of his officers (La Châtre excepted) were as young and inexperienced as he. Nevertheless, his principal handicap was that the Dutch States had not paid him the 200,000 *livres* per month that were promised at Plessis-lès-Tours. By the summer of 1582, almost a year after he relieved the siege of Cambrai, the States had provided Anjou with only 32,528 *livres*.[32] Pruneaux had been complaining to the States since April that Anjou's troops were underpaid because of the failure of the deputies to pay the duke his monthly stipend.[33] As a result, his troops began to desert almost immediately after the 'joyous entry' into Antwerp. For all of Anjou's faults, which were legion, he did not reckon that the States would fail to uphold their promise of financial support. Although the Dutch deputies at Plessis-lès-Tours did not really bargain in bad faith, Orange and the States had themselves largely to blame for the inadequacy of Anjou's assistance. For a variety of reasons they were unable to maintain their pledge to support his army. As Claude de la Châtre ruefully remarked, 'all of their promises and empty words were just bait to draw us into the cage'.[34]

II

If Anjou shared La Châtre's disdain for the States-General, he certainly did not show it. He still had high hopes of obtaining the support that they had promised him. He rejoiced openly at the prince of Orange's recovery, and went about his business of strengthening his army. By June 1582 it was estimated that this original force had shrunk to 6,000 foot and 1,000 horse.[35] Anjou had already paid out more than 300,000 *livres* for these regular troops. Moreover, it cost him another 200,000 *livres* to garrison several towns, including Antwerp, with soldiers from the army of the States.[36] Thus, the sums he received from Henry and Elizabeth were quickly swallowed up. Because of his shortage of cash, his only option was to contract with mercenaries. Whereas small bonuses had to be

[31] Ibid., fols. 351–2, Moro to the Signory, 29 June 1582.
[32] PRO/SP 78/10/122/fols. 308–35. See also p. 171, above.
[33] ARA, Staten-Generaal 11096, fols. 65–8.   [34] BN, MSS na fr. 4709, fol. 25.
[35] BN, MSS ital. 1732, fol. 351, Moro to the Signory, 29 June 1582.
[36] PRO/SP 78/10/122/fols. 308–35.

paid in advance to persuade ordinary levies to enlist, mercenaries could be contracted for a short period simply on the promise to pay. Thus, by midsummer of 1582 Anjou was forced to hire a company of 1,500 German *reîtres* and a similar number of Swiss guards to keep his army up to strength.[37] These mercenaries still had to be paid each month or they would desert like the ordinary levies. So, it was really only a temporary remedy to the main problem, which was a complete lack of proper financial resources.

Of course, Anjou might have made better use of the resources that he did have. La Châtre indicated that Rochepot had a difficult task keeping his forces together during the spring and summer of 1582 because of the shortage of food.[38] Meanwhile, Anjou and his household dined extravagantly. An expense sheet for food purchases for one day in April indicates what was served at his table: beef, mutton, veal, pork, rabbits, pigeons, chickens and other fowl, beef tongue, sheep's feet, a variety of fresh fruit and vegetables including oranges and asparagus, and a selection of fresh salads.[39] Admittedly, Anjou had the right to live royally; even the hungriest soldier in his army would not have begrudged him that. Nevertheless, one has the suspicion that he was as hopeless managing his household budget as he was with his other affairs, and that he might have used his meager resources more prudently.

Anjou got on better with Bellièvre than any other of Henry's councillors. The latter had been urging the king to support Anjou's enterprise for some time, and it was no coincidence that he was chosen to deliver the first instalment of the grant of 100,000 *écus* (300,000 *livres*) in May. Anjou kept up a close correspondence with Bellièvre throughout the summer of 1582, hoping that the veteran councillor might be able to persuade his brother and mother to assist him with more money. On 5 June Anjou wrote: 'You know how the charity has been cut short in this country, and if these poor men [in my army] are not paid soon, they will be sorely inconvenienced.' The very next day he informed Bellièvre that his troops were threatening to mutiny. 'If money is not delivered promptly', he lamented, 'I will be ruined'.[40] Several days later he repeated his pleas of indigence to Bellièvre: 'It is upon you, like a father, that I place all my hope.'[41] The second half of Henry's grant had still not been delivered by July, however. Anjou then despatched the receiver-general of his finances to the French court to make a personal plea for the remaining 50,000 *écus* that the king had promised him in May. Anjou informed Bellièvre that he had been requested to assist the

---

37 Ibid. The *reîtres* were contracted at 255,252 *livres* (10s.) and the better disciplined Swiss at 314,456 *livres* (14s. 9d.), both groups apparently for six months (the monthly wage of the Swiss was normally 17,600 *écus*, or 52,800 *livres* according to Anjou (BN, MSS fr. 15906, fol. 713, Anjou to Bellièvre, 20 July 1582).
38 BN, MSS n.a. fr. 4709, fol. 33.
39 AN, K 101, no. 24, expense sheet of purchases for Anjou's household, 29 April 1582.
40 BN, MSS fr. 15906, fols. 694–5, Anjou to Bellièvre, 5 and 6 June 1582.
41 Ibid., fol. 696, Anjou to Bellièvre, 9 June 1582.

town of Audenarde, but a lack of funds prevented any further military action. He chided the counsellor that, unless something were done immediately, he would be unable to pay the *reîtres* for a second month. A fortnight later he wrote that if he did not pay the Swiss guards their monthly wage of 17,600 *écus* (52,800 *livres*) by the 28th, they too would mutiny.[42]

The king apparently sent his brother the remainder of the sum that he had promised later in the summer. Wages were in such arrears, however, that the money provided only a brief respite.[43] In early August Anjou advised Bellièvre that the war in the Netherlands simply could not continue without the means to carry on. He pointed out that the States had completely neglected him, and that his situation was becoming desperate. If the king could send no more money, he pleaded for at least some grain and wine. The overriding fear, however, remained the threat of desertion by the German and Swiss mercenaries. 'The *reîtres* and the Swiss, who make up the backbone of my army (*le principal fondement de mon armee*)', he insisted, 'are unable to continue in their obedient service without regular paychecks month after month, for that is what renders them obedient'.[44] As a result of these pleas, there were rumors in Paris all summer that Henry had decided to furnish large sums of money. Parma informed Philip II that 'he is throwing away the mask and is now openly assisting Anjou'.[45] A week later Giovanni Moro, the Venetian ambassador in Paris, reported that Bellièvre 'has taken His Highness a large sum of money'.[46] Moro was mistaken about Henry's largesse, however. He did despatch Bellièvre to the Netherlands in August, but it was to investigate a far more serious matter: an alleged attempt to poison the duke of Anjou.

Ever since the assassination attempt on the life of William of Orange, Anjou feared an attempt on his own life, almost to the point of paranoia. When several strangers were surprised and seized near his bedchamber on 21 July, his suspicions were immediately aroused. One of the prisoners was an Italian named Francesco Baza. Under torture he confessed that he had been hired by Parma to poison both Anjou and Orange. He also implicated a soldier in Anjou's personal guard, Nicolas Salcedo, who worked with others from the inside. As none of the other prisoners admitted anything, Baza's confession was crucial. Unfortunately, fearing the fate that awaited him, Baza committed suicide in his cell before a trial could take place. This, at least, is the official story of what happened.[47] There

---

[42] Ibid., fols. 706–8, 713, all Anjou to Bellièvre, 6–7 and 20 July 1582.

[43] When the remainder of the money arrived, Anjou thanked Bellièvre with a gift of some timber to build a house in Grignon plus 100 cords of firewood. BN, MSS fr. 15906, fol. 736, Anjou to Fervacques, 18 August 1582.

[44] Ibid., fols. 727–8, Anjou to Bellièvre, 3 August 1582.

[45] Lefèvre (ed.), *Correspondance de Philippe II*, vol. II, p. 325, Parma to Philip II, 15 August 1582. Also see Albèri, *Relazioni*, vol. v, pp. 371–2.

[46] BN, MSS ital. 1732, fols. 377–8, Moro to the Signory, 24 August 1582.

[47] *Discours tragique et véritable de Nicolas Salcedo, sur l'empoisonnement par luy entrepris en la personne de Monseigneur le Duc de Brabant, d'Anjou, et d'Alençon, frère du Roy* (Paris, 1582), reprinted in M. L.

were still so many unanswered questions, however, that when Bellièvre arrived, accompanied by secretary Brulart, he immediately took charge of Salcedo and escorted him back to Paris for trial there. Once safely back in Paris, Salcedo tried to save his own neck with a different story. He claimed (without the threat of torture) that there was a plot to poison the duke of Anjou and prince of Orange, but that it was not really organized by Parma. Instead, Salcedo revealed that the Guises were behind the plot, and that even secretary Villeroy was implicated.[48] This dramatic revelation failed to save his life, and Salcedo was executed in the Place de Grève in October. That there was some plot afoot seems clear, but exactly what was planned and by whom will probably never be known completely.[49] Nevertheless, the entire episode was less remarkable for the dangers and hazards that Anjou was exposed to than for the extreme suspicion and paranoia that he displayed toward those around him. Some concern was natural after the attempt on Orange's life, but after Salcedo's arrest Anjou became even more apprehensive.

The duke of Anjou's paranoia was compounded by bitter frustration with the States. Their treaty specified that he would receive 200,000 *livres* per month to carry out the war. Yet by mid-summer Anjou had received a total of only 32,528 *livres*, and his patience was beginning to wear a bit thin. The States had divided up the responsibility for making these monthly payments to individual provinces and towns, who were supposed to pay their quotas directly to Anjou. It was clear, however, that the States-General had no way of forcing the individual provinces and towns either to levy or to hand over these revenues. And without this money Anjou could pay neither the troops in his own army nor those in the army of the States used to garrison various towns. When an official from Aalst wrote to Anjou in July pleading for munitions and troops to defend that city from the approaching enemy, for example, there was little that Anjou could do.[50]

On 9 July Anjou wrote to the president of the council of Flanders and complained that the city of Ghent had failed to deliver its quota of the 100,000 *livres* allocated to pay his troops.[51] On 21 July similar complaints were made to the States of Brabant about food and artillery that they were supposed to have provided.[52] On the 23rd and 24th of the month Anjou chided the States of

Cimber and F. Danjou (eds.), *Archives curieuses de l'histoire de France depuis Louis IX jusqu'à Louis XVIII*, series i (Paris, 1836), vol. x, pp. 139–53.

[48] 'Copie de la déposition de Salcedo', in Cimber and Danjou (eds.), *Archives curieuses*, series i, vol. x, pp. 154–63. See also Sutherland, *French Secretaries of State*, pp. 238–9.

[49] Jacques-Auguste de Thou, for one, believed Salcedo's story. His father, Christophe de Thou (First President of the *parlement* of Paris and the chancellor of Anjou's household), presided over Salcedo's trial and thought his confession was sound. Moreover, most historians have believed him. One notable exception is N. M. Sutherland (*French Secretaries of State*, pp. 238–9), who refuses to believe that Villeroy could have been implicated.

[50] AGRB, Audience 560, fol. 177, Robert de Merode to Anjou, 17 July 1582.

[51] ARA, Staten-Generaal 11095, 9 July 1582 (this volume is unfoliated, and I have cited the date of each entry).

[52] Ibid., 21 July 1582.

Friesland and the towns of Ieper and Ghent (again!) for failing to remit their designated quotas.[53] By the end of the month the English troops under the command of Sir Henry Norris were already beginning to desert because of lack of pay, and Anjou pleaded with Norris 'to maintain them in the best discipline possible so that they will have no occasion to disband'.[54]

The situation had not improved by the beginning of August, despite the pomp and circumstance of another 'joyous entry', this time at Bruges on 27 July.[55] Anjou's own garrisons in the town of Mechelen were close to mutiny because the States of Brabant had not yet made good on their quota.[56] Indeed, the situation was so desperate that the duke despatched special messengers to Marnix, the States-General, and the States of Brabant on 3 August to inquire why the money, food, provisions, and ammunition that had been promised to him was not forthcoming.[57] By this time even the prince of Orange was becoming frustrated. He pleaded with the treasurer-general of the province of Flanders to turn over the Flemish quota to Anjou immediately. Moreover, he was disturbed that certain towns in Flanders were not letting French garrisons in, as had been agreed at Plessis-lès-Tours.[58] Orange was as helpless as Anjou, however, in getting the individual provinces and towns to execute the treaty. Meanwhile, Anjou's army was starving, as flour and wheat which had been promised from Ieper and Dendermonde respectively was never delivered.[59] Spanish troops were also fast closing in on the town of Lier, just outside Antwerp. Officials there warned Anjou on 14 August that without new troops to fortify their guard, they would fall to the enemy; and they further lamented 'the lack of money in which we find ourselves'.[60] And to make matters worse, the States-General had virtually stopped meeting. Anjou was particularly enraged that the provinces of Friesland, Utrecht, Gelderland, and the Ommelanden were no longer even bothering to send deputies.[61]

Anjou's bleak financial situation brightened somewhat in September. First of all, Elizabeth sent over another £15,000.[62] She had promised him £60,000 when he was in England, and with this sum had lent him a total of £40,000 since his visit. Unfortunately, this was the last money that she ever sent. At Villeroy's urging Henry III decided to provide 193,500 *livres* in September. The money

[53] Ibid., 23 and 24 July 1582.   [54] Ibid., 28 July 1582.

[55] *De Heerlijcke Incomste van onsen ghevadighen Landvorst, mijn Heere Francoys van Franckrijck, des Conings eenich broeder, Hertogh van Brabant, Gelder, Anjou, Alençon etc. Grave van Vlaenderen, Hollandt, Zeelandt, etc. in sijn vermaerde stadt van Brugge, den xxvij dach Julij Anno MDLXXXIJ* (Bruges, 1582). A third 'joyous entry' took place at Ghent on 29 August. See *L'Entrée magnifique de Monseigneur François, filz de France, Frère unique du Roy ... faicte en sa metropolitaine et fameuse ville de Gand, le xx d'Aoust Anno 1582* (Ghent, 1582).

[56] ARA, Staten-Generaal 11095, 1 August 1582.   [57] Ibid., 3 August 1582.

[58] Ibid., 9 August 1582.

[59] Ibid., 11 August 1582.   [60] AGRB, Audience 561, fol. 95, 14 August 1582.

[61] ARA, Staten-Generaal 11095, 25 August 1582.

[62] PRO/SP 78/10/122/fols. 308–35. At the prevailing rate of exchange this grant came to 142,231 *livres* 19s.

was specifically designated to raise several companies of French troops led by marshal Biron and the *prince dauphin* of Auvergne (now duke of Montpensier).[63] Moreover, Orange decided to review Anjou's finances very carefully to see if something could be done to speed up the payments of the States. On 18 September he surveyed the duke's expenses and concluded that, to continue the war, Anjou needed 305,000 *livres* per month for the wages of the combined armies (6,000 German and Swiss, 2,000 English, 2,000 Scots, 8,250 French, and 11,700 Netherlanders), 145,000 *livres* per month to purchase and feed 5,000 new horses, 24,000 *livres* per month for ammunition and artillery, and 10,000 *livres* per month for food. This amounted to nearly half a million *livres* per month. Although the States were only contracted to pay Anjou 200,000 *livres* each month, Orange offered to try to renegotiate the terms of the treaty so that the States would provide a monthly stipend of 320,000 *livres*, with Anjou paying the remainder from his own resources. New quotas were even drawn up to meet these expenses:

Brabant	63,000 *livres*/month
Gelderland	20,000
Flanders	105,000
Holland and Zeeland	93,000
Friesland	23,000
Overijssel	5,500
Utrecht	9,000
Mechelen	1,500
	320,000 *livres*/month[64]

Anjou was naturally skeptical about whether the States would provide him with 320,000 *livres* per month when they had been unable to meet their original quotas. He had already been forced to order his garrisons in Brussels and Vilvoorde to billet themselves on the local inhabitants.[65] And garrisons in the vital ports of Dunkirk, Nieuwpoort, and Oostende were threatening to mutiny if they were not paid soon.[66] Indeed, Anjou warned the States of Flanders and Brabant that they risked losing all their garrisons if they did not submit their quotas to him.[67] The States-General continued to balk, however. On 18 October they proposed a compromise concerning Orange's new quotas and offered 250,000 *livres* per month instead of 320,000 *livres*. Moreover, the States

---

63 Ibid. François de Bourbon, *prince dauphin* d'Auvergne, succeeded his father as duke of Montpensier upon the latter's death in September 1582, and is hereafter referred to as Montpensier.
64 ARA, Staten-Generaal 11096, fols. 29–30.
65 ARA, Staten-Generaal 11095, 4 and 12 September 1582.
66 Ibid., 24 October 1582.   67 Ibid., 23 October and 2 November 1582.

chastised Anjou for the ill discipline of his unpaid troops, who (they claimed) were responsible for 'the infinite calamities done to these miserable people'.[68]

Claude de la Châtre painted such a dire picture of Anjou's army during the autumn of 1582 that one is tempted to think that he was exaggerating. He reported that by late autumn Anjou's army had shrunk to about 3,000 men, who were camped in the fields and suburbs surrounding Antwerp:

All those poor soldiers left in the fields are without any food or supplies. It is so bad that they come into Antwerp in groups of a hundred, thirty, forty, fifty, completely naked on occasion. Every morning on his way to Mass His Highness gives each of them an *écu*. Nevertheless, more than three hundred have died in the fields from hunger and cold . . . Those soldiers inside the town frequently beg for charity door to door, where some, mostly Catholics, show them favor. The others would have sooner given to a dog.[69]

Other sources appear to substantiate La Châtre's description, however. Jacques-Auguste de Thou, for instance, described one of the worst winters on record in the Netherlands. Both Anjou's and Parma's armies suffered more from the elements – chiefly cold and flooding rivers – than from each other. Parma's troops lost large numbers every day to disease and malnutrition. 'The duke of Anjou's troops', De Thou went on, 'suffered the same hardships throughout the entire winter; wages were not paid, epidemic disease broke out among the soldiers, and a large number were reduced to begging for alms, to the shame of every Frenchman'.[70] Thus, Anjou was in complete despair. 'Everything is falling apart in ruin', he wrote to Bellièvre on 9 October, 'and the worst part of it is that I was given hopes which have led me too far to back down now . . . Thus, I say that it would be better to promise me only a little money and keep your word than to promise so much and not send anything at all.'[71]

On 27 November the intensive lobbying of the prince of Orange finally paid off as the States-General gave in and agreed to renegotiate the financial terms of the treaty of Plessis-lès-Tours. Moreover, the prince persuaded them to provide a total of 4,000,000 *livres* per year to finance the war, even more than he had asked for in September.[72] Anjou was still skeptical, however. The towns of Bruges, Du Franc, and Ieper and the provinces of Flanders, Holland, Zeeland, and Friesland had not paid him any of their quotas since the summer.[73] Why would they pay even larger quotas now? He forcefully urged the States to show their goodwill by delivering their quotas to him 'with all diligence'. Moreover, he

---

68 ARA, Staten-Generaal 11096, fols. 47 and 75, 18 October and 17 November 1582.
69 BN, MSS n.a. fr. 4709, fols. 42–4.
70 De Thou, *Histoire universelle*, vol. VI, p. 206.
71 BN, MSS fr. 15906, fol. 745, Anjou to Bellièvre, 9 October 1582. This same sentiment was expressed again in another letter, BN, MSS fr. 15905, fol. 397, Anjou to Bellièvre, 25 October [1582].
72 ARA, Staten-Generaal 11096, fols. 59v.–62v., 27 November 1582.
73 ARA, Staten-Generaal 11095, 6, 11 and 20 November and 2–8 December 1582.

insisted that they do so 'within six weeks, by the beginning of next January'.[74] Neither Orange nor the deputies probably realized that this was an ultimatum.

Thus, Anjou and his dwindling army suffered through the wintry autumn of 1582 until more cash and the reinforcements led by Biron could arrive. Even with royal support, however, Biron and the new duke of Montpensier were unable to overcome the weather or the slowness in getting wages to the soldiers. Moreover, by November it was reported that the reinforcements from France began to suffer the same fate as Anjou's army in the Netherlands: 'Marshal Biron is still on the frontier with little hope of being able to proceed any farther during the inconvenience of winter, since many of his French soldiers have already begun to desert.'[75] Anjou despatched another barrage of letters to the French court pleading for immediate financial and military assistance. 'I find that my expenses amount to some 200,000 *livres* per month, which I cannot meet without the aid of the king', he informed poor Bellièvre on 4 November. 'I beg him ... to assist me as he promised to do.'[76]

Biron and Montpensier's reinforcements finally reached Anjou's suffering army on 1 December 1582. Biron was at the head of 3,300 Swiss guards, 1,500 foot, a company of cavalry, three companies of *gens d'armes* (armored cavalry), and a few volunteers. Montpensier headed the bulk of the reinforcements: 4,500 foot, five companies of *gens d'armes*, five companies of light horse, and 300 volunteers.[77] Biron and Montpensier's arrival did nothing, however, to ameliorate the shortage of food and supplies in the midst of a harsh winter. Moreover, the growing animosity between the Dutch towns and the French troops was exacerbated by the fact that the soldiers were starving, while the townspeople had an abundance to eat. Although his estimate may be an exaggeration, La Châtre claimed that 3,000 French soldiers died of hunger and cold during the winter.[78]

The new sums agreed to by the States in November proved as difficult to levy as the previous ones. By the end of December neither food, powder, and supplies nor the designated quotas had been delivered to the duke of Anjou's army.[79] Henry III and Elizabeth had apparently provided all the aid that they were going to provide, and on 13 January 1583 Anjou made a final plea to the States-General. Before the few deputies who were still meeting in Antwerp, the

---

[74] ARA, Staten-Generaal 11096, fols. 59v.–62v., 27 November 1582.

[75] BN, MSS ital. 1732, fol. 397, Moro to the Signory, 2 November 1582.

[76] BN, MSS fr. 15905, fol. 399, Anjou to Bellièvre, 4 November [1582]. Also see BN, MSS fr. 15906, fols. 747, 758 and 770, all Anjou to Bellièvre, 11 October, 29 November and 31 December 1582; and BN, MSS CCC 337, fols. 91–101, Anjou to Henry III and Catherine de Medici, 3–28 November 1582.

[77] Sidney H. Ehrman and James W. Thompson (eds.), *The Letters and Documents of Armand de Gontaut, baron de Biron, Marshal of France, 1524–1592* (2 vols., Berkeley, 1936), vol. II, pp. 653–7, 'Discours très veritable du passage et arrivée de messeigneurs les duc de Montpensier et mareschal de Biron et de leur armée dans les pais-Bas'.

[78] BN, MSS n.a. fr. 4709, fol. 53. [79] ARA, Staten-Generaal 11095, 30 and 31 December 1582.

duke issued a remonstrance expressing his anger over 'the new delays and stays'. His six-week deadline had expired, and still the States had not paid him what was due. Anjou declared to them that their system of government was remarkably inefficient, and that he had had no idea during the negotiations at Plessis-lès-Tours that the deputies were powerless to act without the approval of the individual States. Moreover, all the delays caused by reporting back to the individual provinces had resulted in great financial cost. He further lamented that each province appeared to be more interested in self-preservation than in the general war effort; but he hoped that the deputies would 'speed up events, suddenly and unexpectedly, and in all things unite to prevent the entire ruin of the provinces'. He ended by reminding the deputies of the 600,000 *livres* in arrears that the States still owed him.[80]

The States replied on 15 January that they were aware that their system of government was imperfect. It had worked under Charles V, however, and they reminded Anjou that 'subjects of the Netherlands must be maintained in all their franchises, liberties, and in security'. Moreover, they had no intention of turning the States-General into an English parliament, as Anjou had suggested in his remonstrance. They did promise to try to work together and more efficiently, however.[81] Anjou nevertheless felt maltreated and deceived, and above all, powerless. Thus, he decided to use his newly reinforced army to remedy the situation.

The attack on Antwerp on 17 January 1583 has long been known as the 'French fury', an allusion to the 'Spanish fury' of November 1576 when Spanish soldiers mutinied and sacked the city. Ironically, the only fury that was aroused during the French attack was that of the Antwerp citizenry. Whereas Spanish troops ravished the city in 1576, the city was forewarned of the French attack and prepared itself.[82] The citizens had armed themselves and barricaded the streets and squares when the French troops entered Antwerp about lunchtime on 17 January. Various reports indicate that the French began shouting as soon as they entered the gates: 'Long live the mass! The city is ours!' The resulting clash was far removed from the 'Spanish fury', however. About a thousand French soldiers were killed outright, and several hundred more were taken prisoner. The Dutch casualties were minimal, and nearly every source indicates that a treacherous duke of Anjou fled the city for his life.[83]

---

80 ARA, Staten-Generaal 11096, fols. 137r.–42r., 'Proposition faicte par son Altesse aux Estats generaux du pays bas assemblez a Anvers le xiiiᵉ jour de janvier 1583'.
81 ARA, Staten-Generaal 11096, fols. 142v.–51v., States to Anjou, 15 January 1584.
82 De Thou, *Histoire universelle*, vol. VI, pp. 268–70. News had also arrived that French troops had tried to seize Bruges and Dunkirk several days before, which further prompted preparations in Antwerp.
83 The fullest and most reliable contemporary account of the 'French fury' is the report of the magistrates of Antwerp, dated 17 January 1583. It is printed in English translation in *CSPF*, vol. XVII, pp. 24–31. Other contemporary sources are the letter from Jean Bodin to his father-in-law (BN, MSS Dupuy 157, fols. 134–5), also printed in Roger Chauviré, *Jean Bodin*,

Because Claude de la Châtre's description of events in Antwerp on 17 January 1583 differs so radically from every other known source, it is necessary to examine his account in some detail.[84] La Châtre claimed that Anjou awoke on the morning of 17 January to discover that the gates of Antwerp were locked, and that guards had been reinforced at all the entrances. Since he and his household resided inside the city rather than with the army, the duke found himself separated from his troops. He was disturbed by the situation, and sent a messenger to the prince of Orange to find out why the gates had been closed. As the sovereign prince of the city, he felt that 'such things should not be undertaken without his knowledge and command, otherwise it was an insult too trying to bear'.[85] Orange informed Anjou that the people were so fearful of a French attack, due to the rumors circulating in the city, that the gates would remain closed all day. Anjou was naturally furious, and declared that 'he was thus a prisoner'. He disliked being separated from his troops, and demanded that the gates be opened, proclaiming that 'he had no other purpose than to dwell with his army'. La Châtre emphasized that there were no evil designs in the air. 'I dare say and vouch before God that he had no other intention that day than simply to leave the city and go to his army.'[86]

La Châtre then revealed that Anjou decided to go unarmed to the Kipdorp gate to try to persuade the guards to let him exit. He was accompanied by about 100 or so gentlemen from his household and some servants, all unarmed. When he reached the gate, he found it guarded by 200 Dutch troops. They agreed to let him pass nevertheless, and planned to close the gate behind him. Unbeknown to the guards inside the city, however, about 800 of Anjou's troops were assembled on the other side. Once the gates were opened, these troops rushed in 'without any resistance'.[87] How did 800 men manage to gather on one side of the gate and remain completely undetected by 200 guards on the other? Moreover, why did the guards not attempt to resist them? These are questions that La Châtre left unanswered, being more concerned with exonerating Anjou:

> It is very clear that His Highness did everything in his power to stop the said soldiers, and being unable to do so and left nearly all alone, he could do nothing else but tell them in passing that if any man did any harm or violence to the citizens, much less to the city, that he would be hanged without remission and that they all would answer for it with their heads.[88]

La Châtre insisted that the French troops only assembled outside the gate because they felt that Anjou's life was in danger. Once inside the city, however,

---

auteur de la République (Paris, 1914), pp. 524–9; the account of the baron de Rosny (future duke of Sully) in Buisseret and Barbiche (eds.), *Les Œconomies royales de Sully*, vol. I, pp. 109–13; and the account of Pruneaux in Muller and Diegerick, *Documents*, vol. IV, pp. 341–6. The most complete secondary work is still Motley, *Rise of the Dutch Republic*, vol. III, pp. 560–72.

[84] This is his 'Relation du voyage du Duc d'Anjou au Pays-Bas, Mal-entendu d'Anvers 1583', BN, MSS n.a. fr. 4709, fols. 1–90.

[85] Ibid., fol. 61.   [86] Ibid., fols. 62–4.   [87] Ibid., fol. 66.   [88] Ibid., fols. 66–7.

their fates were sealed. In graphic terms La Châtre related how a large number of the French nobility were massacred by the citizens of Antwerp 'with the cruelest means possible'. Indeed, bodies were piled up so high at the gate 'one on top of the other, that no-one could possibly pass through'. He concluded that Anjou was in no way responsible for what happened, and that everything 'was contrary to his intention and will'.[89]

How accurate is La Châtre's account? As it is the only account that vindicates Anjou from any responsibility, it is naturally suspect. Moreover, when one considers that he wrote it (as he frankly admitted) as an apology for Anjou's behavior to present to the States-General, it is difficult to be persuaded that the 'French fury' was anything but the duke of Anjou's own scheme. Indeed, considering that both Biron and Montpensier were uninvolved,[90] it has every mark of the type of rash and usually unsuccessful plan for which Anjou was infamous in his younger years. Ultimately, one has to be convinced by all the other sources that Anjou planned the affair on his own with a few younger officers and simply failed to carry it off.

La Châtre's account is nevertheless important, for it reveals some of the external factors which led to Anjou's decision to seize the city by force. Although one cannot trust his conclusions about the 'French fury', his detailed sketches of the French army throughout the autumn and early winter of 1582 are corroborated by other evidence. Above all, his account indicates that all of Anjou's pleas for financial support were grounded in extreme necessity. The state of his army was so poor, in fact, that only the arrival of Biron and Montpensier in December prevented mutiny and desertion. It seems clear, therefore, that Anjou's deteriorating army, the lack of food, and the harsh winter, in addition to his frustration with the States, led to his decision to sack Antwerp. Above all, it was a lack of money – money that was promised by Henry III, Elizabeth, and the States – that forced his hand. Ironically, it was this inability to pay his troops that really marked the 'French fury' as a descendant of the 'Spanish fury'. La Châtre fooled no-one with his whitewash, however. The decision to seize the city was ultimately Anjou's; only he can be held ultimately responsible.

The reaction to the 'French fury' was predictable. Whatever loyalties the citizens of Antwerp had for their sovereign duke 'changed instantly', as Orange informed Anjou on 27 January.[91] Anjou fled from the city and made his way to Berchem, several leagues away, with the remnants of his army. Late in the evening of 17 January, after a hectic day's events, he composed letters to the magistrates of Antwerp, the States-General, and William of Orange. Virtually admitting his guilt in the proceedings, Anjou lamely pleaded that everything was a result of the indignities and unworthy treatment he had been subjected to as

[89] Ibid., fols. 67–9.
[90] De Thou, *Histoire universelle*, vol. VI, pp. 271–2. Biron even lost a son in the fracas.
[91] BN, MSS CCC 450, fols. 119–20, Orange to Anjou, 27 January 1583.

duke of Brabant. Moreover, he emphasized the state of poverty in which his army was now in, and asked if his property still inside the city could be returned to him.[92] His army was down to about 600 men, according to La Châtre, and they were still without food and provisions.[93] In Paris the news of the 'French fury' was greeted with shock. Henry naturally feared for his brother's life, as Anjou was the last Valois heir to the throne. At first, Catherine even refused to believe all the reports. She wrote to Orange and declared that such a bizarre event could not have been led by Anjou.[94] As more details filtered in, however, the reality of the situation became clear. The loss of more than 400 French noblemen was grieved even more than the danger to Anjou.[95] No-one knew what to expect, and secretary Villeroy urged the king to strengthen his army immediately, just to be safe.[96] For the duke of Anjou, however, his world had been turned upside down in less than a year. One wonders, in fact, if he departed from Antwerp through the same gate at which he was so gloriously heralded just eleven months earlier. Perhaps the sign that welcomed him was still mounted above: 'To François . . . who was singularly nominated to the sovereign lordship of the Netherlands . . . and was so fortunately installed as its most desired prince, as he auspiciously enters his most devoted city.'

---

[92] Muller and Diegerick, *Documents*, vol. IV, pp. 299–302, Anjou to the magistrates of Antwerp and to the States, both 17 January 1583; and Gachard (ed.), *Correspondance de Guillaume le Taciturne*, vol. V, p. 78, Anjou to Orange, 17 January 1583.

[93] BN, MSS n.a. fr. 4709, fol. 72.

[94] Groen van Prinsterer, *Archives*, vol. VIII, p. 148, Catherine to Orange, 30 January 1583.

[95] L'Estoile, *Journal*, vol. II, p. 100.

[96] BN, MSS fr. 6629, fol. 3, Villeroy to Henry III, 20 January 1583.

9

'The ruin of France', January 1583–June 1584

I

Whatever else it represented, the 'French fury' of 17 January 1583 was an indication of the widening rift between the duke of Anjou and the States-General. 'The heat of that first welcome quickly cooled', wrote Guido Bentivoglio in his history of the Eighty Years War.[1] Jean Bodin, who travelled with Anjou first to London and then to Antwerp, was one of those taken prisoner on 17 January. A few days later he wrote to his father-in-law that the 'French fury' was inevitable because of the differing concepts of Anjou's role in the Netherlands:

I foresaw and predicted this calamity to MM. de St Aldegonde and des Pruneaux when we were in England. At the time I told them that their negotiations would result in the ruin of our prince and the Netherlands because of the contrary customs and moods of the two, especially concerning the issue of liberty, which they [the States] would never want to give up … Sovereignty, which can never be divided, would be split between the prince and the subjects, which would lead to the ruin of the state.[2]

Anjou was unprepared to accept the role of a figurehead that the States intended for him. Indeed, he lamented to his brother Henry that it was the States-General's attempt 'to make a Matthias of him' that caused the catastrophe on 17 January.[3]

Had it not been for the Herculean efforts of William of Orange, in fact, Anjou and the States would more than likely have parted company at that very moment. Anjou was certainly not prepared to remain in the Netherlands in his present position, and many of the Dutch deputies were willing to negotiate a settlement with Parma before putting their trust in Anjou again. On 26 January, however, Orange outlined to the deputies the options that were open to them. They could make an immediate settlement with Philip II and lose everything that they had fought for during the last two decades. They could continue their battle without

---

[1] Guido Bentivoglio, *The Compleat History of the Warrs of Flanders … Englished by the Right Honourable, Henry, Earl of Monmouth* (London, 1654), p. 205.
[2] BN, MSS Dupuy 157, fols. 134–5, Bodin to Trouillart, 23 January 1583. This letter is printed in Chauviré, *Bodin, auteur de la République*, pp. 524–9.
[3] Motley, *Rise of the Dutch Republic*, vol. III, p. 575.

French aid and try to go it alone (even Orange had given up on Elizabeth by then). Or they could turn to France once again, despite the recent 'French fury'. Orange believed that a settlement with Philip and Parma was out of the question, while the provinces were simply not strong enough to continue the struggle on their own. Should they reject French aid, he reasoned, France would probably join with Spain to defeat them, for they could hardly hope to withstand them both. The only option, Orange argued, was a reconciliation with the duke of Anjou, albeit under new terms. Orange recognized Anjou's failings, and openly admitted that the duke was not the best of allies. He remained their best hope of support, however, provided he was backed by his brother. Despite strong opposition, Orange's advice was too sound to ignore. Reluctantly, the States decided to renegotiate with Anjou.[4]

In the meantime, Anjou fled from the camp at Berchem near Antwerp to the safety of Vilvoorde, one of the few towns that French troops still occupied, just north of Brussels. There, on 25 January, he made a few propositions of his own for a new settlement with the States. First of all, he wanted to exchange the towns he presently held – chiefly Vilvoorde and Dendermonde – for the ports of Oostende and Nieuwpoort on the North Sea. Secondly, he asked the States to give his army free and uninhibited passage to Nieuwpoort. And finally, he wanted food and supplies to be furnished en route to prevent the pillaging of the countryside.[5] Orange responded, however, that Anjou's demands were 'so foreign and so removed from all fairness, that no one dared even mention them', especially as they went far beyond the boundaries of the treaty of Plessis-lès-Tours. Orange urged Anjou to reconsider and to offer more realistic proposals to the States.[6] Meanwhile, the States sent several deputies with some proposals of their own to Anjou, who by this time had moved on to Dendermonde.

It was clear that the Dutch States still mistrusted Anjou. And when their deputies reached Dendermonde on 30 January, they informed him that his proposals had done nothing to restore their faith. They wanted to re-establish the conditions outlined at Plessis-lès-Tours, which meant that all French garrisons had to be replaced with native troops, or at least with other foreign mercenaries. Moreover, they wanted Anjou to make his provisional residence in Brussels, which would be guarded by a Swiss garrison; and all of his guards – foot as well as horse – were required to be native Netherlanders. The deputies also insisted that Anjou would have to disband his private council and conduct all business relating to the Netherlands through the council of state and the States-General. Finally, the States demanded the right to veto his choice of officers in his army, and of a bride, should he decide to marry. The deputies

---

4 Muller and Diegerick, *Documents*, vol. IV, p. 335–41, 'Mémoire délivré de la part du prince d'Orange et du conseil d'état aux états généraux', 26 January 1583.
5 Ibid., pp. 332–3, Anjou to the States, 25 January 1583.
6 Groen van Prinsterer, *Archives*, vol. VIII, pp. 144–5, Orange to Anjou, 27 January 1583.

explained that they were not trying to humiliate him, but that it was mandatory that he accept all of these conditions. If he did so, 'the States are ready to forget everything that has happened and serve him as their prince'.[7] Needless to say, Anjou was taken aback by the Dutch offers, which only served to convince him more than ever that he had been mistreated by the States. One of his household officers noted that the Dutch deputies 'have not brought him anything that pleased him, which has got me very worried'.[8]

Anjou naturally bristled when the deputies scolded him for not adhering to the treaty of Plessis-lès-Tours, for they had failed to provide him with their promised stipends. Perhaps sensing this inequity, Orange persuaded the States to deliver two grants totalling 43,451 *livres* to Anjou, which in all likelihood were handed over by the deputies at Dendermonde.[9] Thus, in late January 1583, the States paid Anjou a larger sum than all the aid they had provided since the relief of Cambrai some eighteen months earlier. Nevertheless, Anjou was reluctant to accept their conditions. His army was still without sufficient money and provisions and was cut off by fortified towns on one side and Parma's army on the other. He wanted to get control of a port on the North Sea, so that he could exit quickly if necessary, and receive assistance from England and France more securely. Above all, however, he refused to be humbled and ordered about like a 'Matthias'. He responded that he was willing to uphold the treaty of Plessis-lès-Tours 'in all its points', an obvious reference to the article granting him financial assistance from the States. He also demanded that his household be allowed the free practice of Roman Catholicism. He agreed to remove the French garrisons from Vilvoorde, Diksmuide, and Bergues, but not from Dendermonde and Dunkirk.[10] Anjou wanted to keep a French garrison of 800 men in Dendermonde for three months and, for obvious reasons, he wanted to keep his French troops in Dunkirk permanently (although he agreed to replace the French garrison currently there with a better-disciplined company). Anjou further agreed to replace his French guards with Dutch soldiers 'as soon as it was practical to do so'. He demanded, however, that all matters concerning the Netherlands should be dealt with in the council of state, as Orange had more influence and control there than in the States. Finally, Anjou requested that his army be provisioned with food and supplies at once.[11] The States still had the upper hand, however. As long as the French army was in such a desperate state, Anjou was in no position to bargain. On 4 February, the States informed him that since so many provinces were of a mind to reject him under any conditions,

7 Muller and Diegerick, *Documents*, vol. IV, pp. 360–9, instructions of the States to their deputies, 29 January 1583.
8 Ibid., p. 371n., Pierre de Castelnau to M. van Dorp [31 January 1583].
9 PRO/SP 78/10/122, fols. 308–35.
10 The towns that Anjou occupied are listed in Muller and Diegerick, *Documents*, vol. IV, p. 335. Diksmuide and Bergues are near Dunkirk.
11 Ibid., pp. 371–3, articles presented to Anjou by the deputies from the States, 31 January 1583.

he ought to accept whatever terms were offered to him. And in order to speed up the delivery of provisions to his army, they asked him to vacate the towns of Dendermonde and Vilvoorde at once.[12]

By this time Henry III and Catherine de Medici were extremely nervous. Henry had already despatched a messenger, the seigneur de Vannes, to Parma in an attempt to ward off any Spanish reprisal. Vannes was instructed to remind Parma of Henry's numerous attempts to dissuade his brother from going to the Netherlands, and of the close relationship that he had always enjoyed with Philip II. Henry promised Parma that he would coax his brother to come home if a free and safe passage across the frontier could be guaranteed.[13] Above all, as he expressed on 14 February, he was still concerned about Anjou's safety:

My said brother ... has gone to Flanders against my advice and counsel, as you well know, and neither I nor the queen mother ever had any knowledge or inkling of that deed in Antwerp, which I swear before God. But seeing my said brother so entangled at present, as I understand that he is, I have decided to do what I can to assist him and to help preserve his life, which is so dear to me, and also to aid and bring home those of my subjects who are with him.[14]

In February Henry despatched the sieur de Mirambeau to the States to express his regret of the 'French fury', and to urge the deputies not to allow Parma to take advantage of the situation.[15] Moreover, he sent Pomponne de Bellièvre to meet with Anjou and Orange that same month, in an effort to repair the duke's relations with the States. Bellièvre, who had already made more visits to the Netherlands because of Anjou than he cared to remember, carried some cash with him: 15,000 *livres* from the queen mother and 150,000 *livres* from Henry.[16] This was a considerable sum and it cheered Anjou immensely.[17]

Meanwhile, the States-General continued to drag their heels. The deputies informed Anjou on 14 February that they were unable to send his troops any provisions, because the deputies from Antwerp and Brussels refused to negotiate with him at all. 'The delay does not proceed from any lack of affection or goodwill', they later told Mirambeau, 'but from the difficulties of our business, being constrained in matters of such importance to obtain the consent of each province, town, and community, so as not to do anything contrary to their

---

[12] Ibid., pp. 376–83, States to Anjou, 4 February 1583. Also see I. L. A. Diegerick, 'Notice sur les négociations qui ont eu lieu entre les états-généraux et le duc d'Anjou après la tentative de ce prince de surprendre Anvers (janvier à avril 1583)', *Annales de l'Académie d'Archéologie de Belgique*, XIII (1856), 5–41, and XVI (1859), 44–72, 289–320.

[13] BN, MSS fr. 3396, fol. 25–7, instructions given to the sieur de Vannes by Henry III, January 1583.

[14] BN, MSS fr. 3308, fol. 64v., Henry to Castelnau, 14 February 1583.

[15] Muller and Diegerick, *Documents*, vol. IV, pp. 390–4, address of Mirambeau to the States, 7 February 1583.

[16] PRO/SP 78/10/122/fols. 308–35.

[17] BN, MSS fr. 15907, fol. 23, Anjou to Bellièvre, 3 March 1583.

customs and privileges'.[18] While this was doubtless true, all this democracy was beginning to wear a bit thin with Anjou. Moreover, the States ordered him to assemble his army and march toward Eindhoven, which was besieged by Parma. By the time Bellièvre arrived in early March with Henry's and Catherine's cash, however, the deputies had still not provided any provisions for Anjou's troops.[19]

Until Bellièvre's arrival, in fact, there was some speculation that Anjou might come to an agreement with Parma in exchange for money and an unmolested journey back to France. Indeed, Parma made an offer to Vannes, Henry's agent in Tournai, and to one of Anjou's agents also there on 4 March. It was so ridiculous, however, that it was never seriously considered.[20] Moreover, on 18 March Anjou agreed to the terms offered by the States and signed a provisional treaty. In return for being able to move his residence to Dunkirk, he agreed to virtually all of their previous demands. He promised to evacuate his troops from Vilvoorde, Dendermonde, and Bergues on the condition that the States provide his army with food and 30,000 *écus* (90,000 *livres*) in back pay. In addition, Anjou was given charge of several hostages – a few deputies of the States, in fact – as a guarantee that all his property confiscated in Antwerp and the prisoners taken on 17 January would be returned. Anjou was allowed to retain up to 500 foot and 300 horse to accompany him to Dunkirk. Finally, it was decided to sign a more lasting agreement once Anjou reached Dunkirk, the prisoners and hostages were exchanged, and his troops were paid.[21]

The States proved that they had been bargaining in good faith by turning over the 90,000 *livres* that Anjou had requested by 1 April. In fact, they paid Anjou 85,000 *livres* and gave marshal Biron, whom Anjou had asked to lead the French army, a further 13,300 *livres*, slightly more than they had promised.[22] The prince of Orange ultimately asked Biron to lead an army composed of Anjou's troops and those levied by the States to relieve the siege of Eindhoven. Although Biron was not very keen to accept the charge, Bellièvre persuaded him to reconsider.[23]

---

18 Muller and Diegerick, *Documents*, vol. IV, pp. 415–20, States to Anjou, 14 February 1583; and ibid., pp. 424–6, States to Mirambeau, 19 February 1583.

19 Ibid., pp. 464–5, States to Anjou, 28 February 1583; and ibid., pp. 473–5, Anjou to the States, 3 March 1583.

20 Ibid., pp. 476–9, proposition of Parma to Anjou, 4 March 1583. In return for food, cash, and supplies plus a free trip home, Parma wanted an immediate suspension of arms, a renunciation of all Anjou's claims in the Netherlands, and immediate occupation of Dendermonde, Vilvoorde, and Cambrai. Although some historians have claimed that an agreement was reached, it is clear that Anjou never followed up Parma's overtures. See Muller and Diegerick, *Documents*, vol. IV, pp. 476–7n; and L. van der Essen, *Alexandre Farnèse* (5 vols., Brussels, 1933–7), vol. III, pp. 118–20.

21 Muller and Diegerick, *Documents*, vol. IV, pp. 506–10, articles agreed upon by Anjou and the States, 18 March 1583. The final document, virtually identical, was signed by Anjou on 24 March and by the States on 26 March.

22 PRO/SP 78/10/122/fols. 308–35.

23 Muller and Diegerick, *Documents*, vol. IV, pp. 536–7, proposition by Orange concerning the relief of Eindhoven, 25 March 1583; and ibid., pp. 550–1, letter of Jean Bodin [March or April 1583].

Thus, Orange outlined a broad plan for the campaign and put Biron in charge of the entire force: 2,500 Swiss guards and 2,000 *arquebusiers* from Anjou's army, 3,500 English, Scots, and Dutch foot, and 1,200 horse hired by the States. Moreover, this force was supported by a company of artillery, consisting of 3 cannons, 2 smaller guns, 25 wagons, 100 armored horse, and 200 pikemen under the command of the States' artillery general, van Cruininghen. Finally, Orange got the States to furnish this army with a daily ration of 2,000 26-ounce loaves of bread, beer, and cheese, and oats for 1,200 horses.[24] For once it appeared that the bureaucracy and administration of the States had been overcome, and that the gigantic and complex machinery of an early modern army would be set in motion. Anjou and the deputies of the States even appeared to trust one another for the first time since the 'French fury'. 'It has been a great pleasure to receive this news', Henry wrote to Bellièvre in early April, 'and the principal success of this conclusion ought to be attributed to your wise and prudent negotiation'.[25] Henry had good reason to be proud of Bellièvre, who, along with Orange, had kept the negotiations going when both Anjou and the States wanted to break them off. When Anjou vacated Dendermonde on 8 April and headed for Dunkirk as promised, the new accord appeared to be working. Almost immediately, however, the same old stumbling blocks surfaced once again.

Although the States presented Biron with his commission on 17 April, the entire operation was too slow getting off the ground.[26] Eindhoven capitulated to Parma on 23 April, before Biron's joint forces could even cross the Schelde. With all the venom of his former attacks and accusations, Anjou laid the blame for the fall of Eindhoven squarely on the shoulders of the States.[27] Orange did his best to speed up the necessary financing, and he urged the deputies to do everything possible to keep the armies of Anjou and the States together. The success of their enterprise against Parma, Orange pleaded, depended on not allowing 'the loss and ruin of such good companies through lack of payment'. And Orange further reiterated that they could not hope to defeat Parma without French aid.[28]

The relations between Anjou and the States became so strained, in fact, that Catherine de Medici decided to make a personal visit to see her youngest son, whom she had not seen for two years. In late April she wrote to Bellièvre and asked him to go to Calais as soon as possible, where she planned to meet Anjou for a lengthy interview.[29] Anjou was pleased to accept the invitation. Not only was he persuaded that money might be more easily obtained from Paris than from

---

[24] Ibid., pp. 536–7. [25] BN, MSS fr. 15907, fol. 54, Henry III to Bellièvre, 4 April 1853.
[26] For Biron's commission see Muller and Diegerick, *Documents*, vol. V, pp. 39–41.
[27] Ibid., pp. 58–62, Anjou to the States, 25 April 1583.
[28] Ibid., pp. 75–9, Advice of Orange to the States, 27 April 1583.
[29] Catherine de Medici, *Lettres*, vol. VIII, p. 99, Catherine to Bellièvre, 23 April 1583.

Antwerp, but he was anxious to vacate Dunkirk, having discovered upon his arrival that the port was infested with plague.[30]

Upon the capitulation of Eindhoven, Biron moved his army northward to Roosendaal, between Bergen-op-Zoom and Breda, where he intended to lay siege to the nearby fortification at Wouw. The chronic problem of paying the troops, however, reared its ugly head as soon as he arrived, as the Swiss threatened to walk out if they were not paid immediately. Moreover, there was dissension within the army. Colonel Norris, the commander of the English regiment, refused to cooperate fully with the marshal, and the Swiss and English troops were causing turmoil by insulting the Catholic troops. Biron was thus faced with a most unpleasant situation, which was exacerbated by the delay in pay.[31] The promised money did not arrive, however. From late April until early June, Biron begged and pleaded almost daily for financial relief. 'If we had been sent what was needed and what was promised to us', he lamented on 5 May, 'we would have already commenced the execution of our orders'.[32] Two weeks later he threw up his hands in resignation, as his troops began to desert:

I can no longer hold out against the constant pleas for money that are made to me. I have been waiting for the gentlemen [of the States] to pay me for over a month. Although they have constantly given me good assurances for the last three weeks, I see that they are without foundation. The Swiss are also screaming that Monseigneur promised to send them 22,000 *écus* as soon as he got to Dunkirk, which is what he still owes them from last January and part of November, and that they were promised pay every month. I sent a gentleman to Monseigneur, who is soliciting him every day … If things continue as they are, both [Anjou and the States] can look for another valet to take my place, because from the end of July you will not find me around here.[33]

By the end of May the situation was desperate, as Biron described to Pruneaux: 'I have discovered severe distress among the regiments, which have only had bread four times in the last ten days … such that it has been necessary to divide one loaf among four soldiers every day. It is so pitiful.'[34] Anjou was well aware of the state of Biron's army, and threatened to leave the country if the States did not send pay and provisions immediately.[35] By the end of May most of Biron's cavalry had deserted, and the army had shrunk to about 4,000 men, while it was estimated that Parma's troops numbered 8,000 foot and 1,500 horse.[36] Another 'French fury', this time abetted by Englishmen, Scots, and even a few

30 Muller and Diegerick, *Documents*, vol. v, p. 107, Anjou to the States, 5 May 1583; and ibid., p. 239, Anjou to Pruneaux, 30 June 1583.
31 Ibid., pp. 70–5, Biron to Pruneaux, 26 April 1583.
32 Ibid., p. 110, Biron to Pruneaux, 5 May 1583.
33 Ibid., p. 169, Biron to Pruneaux, 16 May 1583.
34 Ibid., p. 197, Biron to Pruneaux, 29 May 1583. For similar complaints see ibid., pp. 90–2, 94–5, 96–7, 98–101, 104–7, 116–19, 158, 162–4, 167–8, 200, 201–2, and 203–4, all Biron to Pruneaux, 29 April–4 June 1583.
35 Ibid., pp. 150–3, Anjou to Pruneaux, 13 May 1583.
36 BN, MSS ital. 1733, fols. 86–7, Moro to the Signory, 27 May 1583.

Netherlanders, was a distinct possibility. The States-General did not help matters by disbanding for the summer. Before breaking up, however, they did manage to send Biron 150,000 *livres* in June. It was a welcome sum, but in the circumstances hardly sufficient. Although Anjou managed to raise 72,000 *livres* in Dunkirk to support his garrison there, much more was needed immediately to thwart Parma's advancing army.[37]

Indeed, by June 1583 Parma's troops were on the march southward toward Cambrai and Dunkirk, the last two fortified towns that Anjou held. Meanwhile, Biron's army was still north of the Schelde at Roosendaal, helplessly stranded and unable to stop Parma. In these circumstances, Anjou fled from Dunkirk in late June and hastened toward Calais, hoping to meet the queen mother.[38] Catherine was detained with the king at Mézières, however, and it was not until 12 July that she and secretaries Villeroy and Pinart finally met Anjou in the town of Chaulnes near Péronne.[39] With some justification, Anjou insisted that without further assistance from the king, Dunkirk and Cambrai would inevitably fall to Parma. He begged his mother for 60,000 *écus* (180,000 *livres*) immediately in order to raise new levies in France. Catherine responded that the king was willing to help him, although it would be difficult to forward any money right away. Moreover, any such money would be sent on the condition that it was not used to hire new levies, but was used to bring the French army safely back home.[40]

On 16 July, however, the plague-infested port of Dunkirk fell to Parma after a brief siege.[41] Orange had foreseen the situation, and had desperately tried to transport Biron's army to Dunkirk. The States of Flanders, however, refused to allow the troops to pass through their province or to pay for the costs of transporting the army by sea. Although it is doubtful whether Biron's depleted forces could have stopped Parma in any case, all the delays on the provincial and local level only played into the hands of the enemy, as Orange was fully aware.[42] Biron blamed the States of Flanders for everything. On 21 July he reported to Henry that, once Dunkirk had capitulated, 'they still refused to pay the money that they had promised, and they refused to allow any Frenchmen to enter their towns, claiming that those inside Dunkirk had sold out to the Spanish'.[43] Biron continued to fume, and further blamed the Flemish for the desertion of the Swiss guards and some French troops under his command. 'The fact is', he

[37] PRO/SP 78/10/122/fols. 308–35.
[38] Muller and Diegerick, *Documents*, vol. v, pp. 238–9, Anjou to Pruneaux, 30 June 1583.
[39] BN, MSS fr. 6629, fols. 25 and 29–30, reports of Pinart and Villeroy to Henry III, 12 and 13 July 1583.
[40] Sutherland, *French Secretaries of State*, pp. 240–1; and BN, MSS fr. 15907, fol. 133, Henry III to Bellièvre, 29 June 1583.
[41] See van der Essen, *Alexandre Farnèse*, vol. III, pp. 134–8.
[42] Muller and Diegerick, *Documents*, vol. v, p. 245–8, memoir of Orange, 7 July 1583.
[43] Ibid., pp. 293–7, Biron to Henry III, 21 July 1583 (quotation from p. 296).

lamented to Catherine de Medici, 'Monseigneur your son has been very badly and most unworthily served'.[44]

Orange was equally upset. He reprimanded several towns, notably Bruges and Ghent, for using tax money levied to pay Biron's army for strengthening their own garrisons. He argued that such selfish behavior would only drive Anjou into Parma's arms, and urged them to send representatives to Middelburg, where the States-General would reconvene on 26 July.[45] It was clear, however, that Orange's influence did not extend to the provinces and towns. Even in Holland, where Orange was stadholder, the overwhelming sentiment was against dealing with Anjou at all because of his religion. In Flanders and Brabant, several towns were on the brink of capitulating to Parma or of seeking aid from John Casimir once again, rather than negotiate with Anjou.[46] Thus, popular hostility on the local level counteracted the efforts of Orange and the States-General to fulfill their promises of financial support. Anjou failed to comprehend this fully, however, and continued to blast the deputies of the States for reneging on their promises.[47]

Anjou remained in Picardy throughout the rest of July and August trying to raise new levies in La Fère, St-Quentin, and Chaulnes. The States did forward 21,000 *livres* to him in July, but it was too little, too late. Anjou also managed to collect more than 41,500 *livres* from the citizens of Cambrai to strengthen the garrison there, but it was not enough to save Biron's army.[48] Anjou's efforts to raise new troops in Picardy, however, angered the king, who feared new troubles on the French frontier if still more soldiers were levied.[49] Although the queen mother was ill, she left for Picardy to see Anjou again in early August, accompanied by secretaries Pinart and Brulart. She arrived in La Fère on 9 August and had a second interview with her recalcitrant son, scolding him for disobeying the king's orders to cancel his new levies. She told him that Henry would give him some monetary support if he promised to come home at once. Moreover, she explained that Henry had scheduled a full meeting of his council in September, and wanted both Anjou and Biron to be present to explain the current state of affairs in the Netherlands.[50] Meanwhile, Biron was completely

44 Ibid., pp. 298–301, Biron to Catherine, 21 July 1583 (quotation from pp. 300–1). See also Biron's correspondence with Bellièvre in this period, in Biron, *Letters and Documents*, ed. Ehrman and Thompson, vol. I, pp. 253–339, 11 May–9 August 1583.

45 Muller and Diegerick, *Documents*, vol. V, pp. 279–81, Orange to the city of Bruges, 19 July 1583. Also see Groen van Prinsterer, *Archives*, vol. VIII, pp. 234–7, Orange to the magistrates of Ghent, 20 August 1583.

46 Muller and Diegerick, *Documents*, vol. V, pp. 326–30, States of Holland to Orange, 25 August 1583; and Groen van Prinsterer, *Archives*, vol. VIII, pp. 238–40, Orange to the States of Flanders, 29 August 1583.

47 Groen van Prinsterer, *Archives*, vol. VIII, pp. 230–2, Anjou to the States, 22 July 1583.

48 PRO/SP 78/10/122/fols. 308–35.

49 BN, MSS fr. 3357, fol. 28, Henry to Matignon, 22 July 1583.

50 BN, MSS ital. 1733, fols. 152–4, Moro to the Signory, 19 August 1583; and Sutherland, *French Secretaries of State*, pp. 241–2.

out of money and patience. When he heard that Henry desired his presence at the council meeting in Paris, he wasted no time in arranging his departure from the Netherlands. With the help of Orange, who arranged for a vessel to take his haggard troops from Flushing to Calais by sea, Biron arrived back in France in late August.[51] He was glad to get home, and his last letter from the Netherlands, written from Flushing on 9 August, doubtless represented his deepest feelings. 'Those of these provinces', he quipped, 'cannot trust the French'.[52]

Anjou left La Fère on 2 September for Cambrai, the lone remaining town in the Netherlands still occupied by French troops. Although the seigneur des Pruneaux was still in Middelburg where the States reconvened in late summer, the departure of Biron's army left Anjou virtually alone to bargain for himself. By 1 September, Bellièvre had already arranged for the delivery of the money that Catherine had promised at La Fère. She wisely made certain, however, that the Swiss guards were paid their back pay and that Biron's army was given enough to get back home before the remainder was delivered to Anjou – a sum of only 64,000 *livres*. Although the duke complained profusely to Bellièvre that this did not leave him enough to pay his garrison in Cambrai, it was the last amount he received from Henry, who had supplied him with nearly a million *livres* in the previous two years.[53] Anjou wrote to Pruneaux on 3 September that he was worried about 'the continual stalling and delay of the gentlemen of the States, since it is impossible, as I have informed you, to persuade the king my lord and brother to assist me according to my needs unless the said States give some indication that they desire to have me as their prince and recognize me as such'.[54] But even Orange could not get a consensus in the States now. He had no particular affinity with Anjou, but he argued that the States had proceeded too far with the duke to alienate him now. If the deputies cut him off, Orange argued, Anjou and Henry would retreat to the enemy.[55] But the deputies, finally cognizant of the popular hostility to Anjou in the provinces, made no apparent effort to keep him in their pay.

On 9 October Anjou informed the States that he was returning to France to attend the meeting of the king's council at St-Germain-en-Laye.[56] Although he had been ordered home, he would probably have returned in any case, as his health was beginning to deteriorate badly. The beleaguered Biron, who faithfully stood by Anjou after his army had landed safely at Calais, accompanied him

51 BN, MSS ital. 1733, fol. 154, Moro to the Signory, 19 August 1583; and Muller and Diegerick, *Documents*, vol. v, pp. 330–5, Biron to Pruneaux, 29 August 1583.

52 Biron, *Letters and Documents*, ed. Ehrman and Thompson, vol. I, pp. 335–9, Biron to Bellièvre, 9 August 1583.

53 See Catherine de Medici, *Lettres*, vol. VIII, p. 126, Catherine to Bellièvre, 21 August 1583; BN, MSS fr. 15907, fol. 226, Anjou to Bellièvre, 15 September 1583; and PRO/SP 78/10/122/ fols. 308–35. See also Table 1, p. 196 below.

54 Muller and Diegerick, *Documents*, vol. v, pp. 353–4, Anjou to Pruneaux, 3 September 1583.

55 Ibid., pp. 357–60, Orange to the States of Holland, 6 September 1583.

56 Ibid., pp. 379–81, 395–7, Anjou to the States and to Pruneaux, both 9 October 1583.

southward toward Paris. Anjou's illness was far worse than he realized, however, and he was forced to stop off at Château-Thierry to recuperate before going on to Paris.[57] From Château-Thierry he instructed Pruneaux to keep up his efforts to secure money from the States, no matter how hopeless the situation appeared. While in France, he would do his best to convince the king to assist his enterprise and to lift the ban on levying troops. But, he insisted, the king's support was only a mirage without the money from the States. 'I regret to see', he concluded, 'the miseries and calamities of those provinces multiply because of their own failure and negligence'.[58] Despite his promise to the States to return to Cambrai as soon as possible, however, Anjou's active participation in the revolt of the Netherlands was finished. He was unaware that he had chronic tuberculosis, and had only seven months to live.

II

It is clear from the preceding discussion that the traditional picture of the duke of Anjou's involvement in the Dutch Revolt is in need of some revision. Generations of historians have become far too accustomed to accepting the verdict of John Lothrop Motley that Anjou was 'upon the whole, the most despicable personage who had ever entered the Netherlands'.[59] Although most historians have firmly rejected some of Motley's more prejudiced conclusions, his portraits of the 'French fury' and the duke of Anjou have nevertheless remained. One factor is that most historians who have studied Anjou's enterprise in the Netherlands have tended to be Dutch or Belgians. As such, they are content to view Anjou as one of a string of foreign interlopers, all failures, who used the Revolt for their own ends (Casimir, Matthias, and Leicester usually get the same treatment). Thus, Motley's portrait of Anjou has served them well.[60] And while Motley and others have justly characterized Anjou's shortcomings, theirs is not a complete portrait.

It has been amply documented that Anjou's principal problem throughout his stay in the Netherlands was a lack of sufficient funds to pay his army. This is hardly surprising, as the inability to pay troops regularly during an extended war was a chronic problem that plagued every early modern European state. Even Philip II's famed army of Flanders suffered through long periods without pay, with the inevitable result of mutiny and desertion.[61] Anjou's army was no exception. When the Dutch States-General signed a treaty with him at

---

57 BN, MSS ital. 1733, fols. 205–9, Moro to the Signory, 28 October 1583.
58 Muller and Diegerick, *Documents*, vol. v, pp. 439–45, Anjou to Pruneaux, 9 November 1583 (quotation from p. 444).
59 Motley, *Rise of the Dutch Republic*, vol. iii, p. 339.
60 See, for example, van der Essen, *Alexandre Farnèse*, and Kervijn de Lettenhove, *Huguenots*.
61 Geoffrey Parker, 'Mutiny and discontent in the Spanish army of Flanders, 1572–1607', *Past and Present*, lviii (1973), 38–52.

Table 1. Sources of revenue of the Duke of Anjou for the war in the Netherlands 1 May 1581–31 October 1583 (all figures in 'livres tournois')

Elizabeth	Henry III	Dutch States	Apanage	Other
1. 145,000 (Sept. 1581)	1. 90,000 (Aug. 1581)	1. 32,528 (Feb.–Mar. 1582)	1. 36,000 (May–June 1581)	1. 24,000 (from a sieur de Challopier of Paris, Autumn 1582)
2. 133,340 (Sept. 1581)	2. 150,000 (Dec. 1581)	2. 33,000 (Jan. 1583)	2. 300,000 (May–June 1581)	2. 15,000 (from Catherine de Medici, Feb. 1583)
3. 100,000 (Jan. 1582)	3. 300,000 (May 1582)	3. 10,451 (Jan. 1583)	3. 18,000 (April 1582)	3. 72,000 (collected from Dunkirk, June 1583)
4. 111,700 (April 1582)	4. 193,500 (Sept. 1582)	4. 85,000 (Mar. 1583)	4. 36,000 (Autumn 1582)	4. 41,632 7s. (collected from Cambrai, July 1583)
5. 142,231 19s. (Aug. 1582)	5. 150,000 (Feb. 1583)	5. 13,300 (April 1583)	5. 39,600 (Sept. 1583)	
	6. 64,000 (Aug. 1583)	6. 150,000 (June 1583)	6. 21,000 (Oct. 1583)	
		7. 21,000 (July 1583)		
632,271 19s.	947,500	345,279	450,600	152,632 7s.

Total: 2,528,283 6s.

Source: PRO/SP 78/10/122/fols. 308–35

Plessis-lès-Tours in September 1580, they contracted to pay him 2,400,000 *livres* per year. Even at the time Anjou lamented that this sum was not enough to cover all his expenses. In the two-and-a-half-year period between May 1581 and October 1583, however, Anjou only realized slightly more than that amount from all his sources of revenue (see Table 1).[62] The lack of sufficient revenue explains perhaps more than any other single factor the reasons for Anjou's military failure.

An inspection of his sources of income reveals that his principal paymasters were Henry III and Queen Elizabeth. The income from his *apanage*, the Dutch States, and several sources provided lesser, though not insignificant, amounts. Elizabeth has often been criticized for her irresolute policy toward the Netherlands before 1585.[63] Indeed, she used the bait of marriage to lure Anjou even further into the revolt so that she would not have to commit herself openly. Nevertheless, she provided Anjou with a total of £70,000 (632,271 *livres* 19s.) in less than a year.[64] According to recent estimates, Elizabeth's ordinary revenues probably never amounted to much more than £250,000 per year before 1585.[65] Thus, in less than a year she provided Anjou with more than one-fourth of her total regular annual income. Elizabeth doubtless had other sources to cover such expenditures, but it is remarkable that she managed to provide such a sum.

Henry III gave his brother an even larger amount: 947,500 *livres*. His payments, however, were spread over two years from August 1581 to August 1583. Moreover, his income was vastly larger than Elizabeth's. Because of the lacunæ in the records of the *chambre des comptes*, it is impossible to determine the exact amount of crown revenues during the Wars of Religion. The best estimates, however, indicate that, in the 1580s, Henry's total regular income amounted to 25 or 30 million *livres* per year.[66] Thus, while Elizabeth was financing Anjou with more than 25 per cent of her total regular income, Henry was aiding his brother with only 2 per cent of his. Of course, England was not in the midst of an extended civil war, which severely escalated Henry's expenses. Nevertheless, the contrast is significant. Moreover, despite Henry and Catherine's constant pleas of poverty, they quite frivolously spent larger amounts than they gave to Anjou. Henry paid one of his favourites, the viscomte de Joyeuse, for example, 1,200,000 *livres* in September 1581 simply to marry the sister of Henry's wife. Anjou, who had just relieved the siege of Cambrai and was in dire need of cash to pay off his troops, bitterly rebuked his brother for ignoring him

---

[62] PRO/SP 78/10/122/fols. 308–35. The total revenue for the period amounted to 2,528,283 *livres* 6s. (although in the MSS the total is incorrect).

[63] See, for example, Charles Wilson, *Queen Elizabeth and the Revolt of the Netherlands* (London, 1970).

[64] The conversion rates from sterling to *livres tournois* are explained in Read, *Mr Secretary Walsingham*, vol. II, pp. 99–100n.

[65] Penry Williams, *The Tudor Regime* (Oxford, 1979), pp. 70–3.

[66] Martin Wolfe, *The Fiscal System of Renaissance France* (New Haven and London, 1972), pp. 205–13.

while spending such an incredible sum on one of his *mignons*.[67] 'Everyone was flabbergasted at such luxury and at such enormous and wasted expense by the king and others at the court in a time which was not the best in the world', noted Pierre de l'Estoile after the Joyeuse wedding.[68] The inescapable conclusion is that, had it not been for Henry and Catherine's paranoia concerning Spanish reprisal, they could have provided Anjou with a great deal more money that they did.

Anjou's principal financial headaches, however, were caused by the Dutch States-General. While Henry and Elizabeth never firmly committed themselves to regular subsidies, the States contracted to pay him 200,000 *livres* per month – 2,400,000 *livres* per year – in the treaty signed at Plessis-lès-Tours in September 1580. Almost from the moment of Anjou's installation as duke of Brabant in February 1582, however, it was painfully clear that the States would be unable to fulfill their promise. Indeed, from February 1582 until Anjou departed for France in October 1583, the States provided him with a total amount of only 345,279 *livres*, less than two months' support. Of all his sources of revenue, Anjou depended on the States more than any other. It was upon their pledge of regular subsidies that he levied his troops and hired Swiss and German mercenaries. When this revenue never materialized, his military venture was doomed to failure. The obvious question, then, is why were the States unable to pay Anjou what they had promised him? While it is difficult to estimate the total revenue that was available from the rebellious provinces, it can hardly have been much more than Elizabeth's total income. One wonders, then, how the deputies expected to pay such an amount. Nevertheless, it appears that Orange and the States bargained with Anjou in good faith, and fully expected each province and town to meet its quota of his monthly stipend.

The main excuse that the deputies gave Anjou for the many delays was that it took an inordinate amount of time for all the deputies to consult their constituencies, as required by the constitution, before the necessary taxation could be levied. There was some truth to their argument, and Anjou was doubtless unprepared for the bureaucracy and administration in the Nether-lands on the provincial and local level. In the emergencies of war, however, bureaucracy could usually be overcome to some degree, as the States themselves proved after the 'French fury'. It seems abundantly clear that the principal reason for the States-General's inability to pay was the overwhelming popular hostility to Anjou and his army. Despite the repeated efforts of Orange and some of the leaders in the States, the necessary quotas were either not levied locally or, if they were collected, not delivered to Anjou's army. For instance, the States of Brabant were designated to provide Biron with 10,000 *livres* in April 1583 to pay his French troops. In spite of constant prodding by Orange, however, they

[67] L'Estoile, *Journal*, vol. II, pp. 21–4, 29.   [68] Ibid., p. 23.

198

refused to hand over the money.[69] The States of Holland, commissioned to provide Biron's army with food and provisions, also refused to furnish these.[70] Later in the summer the States of Flanders reneged on their promise to pay the wages of Biron's soldiers.[71] After Dunkirk fell to Parma in July, many towns such as Bruges used funds collected for Anjou's army to strengthen their own garrisons, fearful that they too might be attacked by the Spanish.[72] Moreover, in the provinces where Orange did wield some influence, in Holland and Zeeland, the States were overwhelmingly opposed to Anjou because of his religion.[73] Thus, for a variety of reasons the financial agreements of the treaty of Plessis-lès-Tours were never carried out. It was not so much a case of deception on the part of Orange and the States, but an inability to control the individual provinces. Each province was more interested in self-preservation than in defeating Parma. Not surprisingly, they begrudged every penny that was not earmarked for local purposes. As the States of Brabant lamented in 1584 when Flanders fell to Parma, 'each province, preferring its own particular interest, has scarcely bothered about the fate of its neighbours and allies, thinking it enough to make fine promises on paper without following them up or giving them any effect'.[74] Furthermore, the States-General could not even pay the wages of its own army, which mutinied throughout the 1570s and 1580s.[75] It is hardly surprising, then, that the deputies were unable to meet Anjou's expenses. The fact remains that Anjou signed a treaty with an institution which, despite the revolutionary nature of its constitution and recent behavior, had no control over its individual provinces. 'In the difficult days of its birth', writes Professor Geyl, 'the young Netherlands state had as little control over its limbs as a newborn babe'.[76] Anjou should not, therefore, despite his numerous personal faults, bear total responsibility for his military failure in the Netherlands.

Another item in need of revision is the traditional belief that the 'French fury' ended any interest the States had in Anjou. 'So the French have lost their credit here forever', wrote Thomas Stokes, an English agent in the Netherlands, on 23 January 1583.[77] One glance at the revenues paid to Anjou by the States, however, indicates that of the total of 345,279 *livres* he received by October 1583, all but 32,528 *livres* was paid after the 'French fury' (see Table 1). Moreover, even after Anjou departed for France in October 1583, the States sent ambassadors to Château-Thierry in an attempt to negotiate a new treaty. Up until the very day of Anjou's death, in fact, Orange and the States labored to work out a new

---

[69] Muller and Diegerick, *Documents*, vol. v, pp. 90–2, Biron to Pruneaux, 29 April 1583.
[70] Ibid., p. 98, n.1.
[71] Ibid, pp. 293–7, Biron to Henry III, 21 July 1583.
[72] Ibid., vol. v, pp. 279–80, instructions from Orange to Groeneveld, 19 July 1583.
[73] Ibid., vol. v, pp. 326–30, States of Holland to Orange, 25 August 1583.
[74] Parker, *The Dutch Revolt*, pp. 201, 216 (quotation from p. 216).
[75] Ibid., p. 192; and G. Parker, *Spain and the Netherlands*, p. 101.
[76] Pieter Geyl, *The Revolt of the Netherlands*, 2nd edn (London, 1958), p. 188.
[77] *CSPF*, vol. XVII, p. 37, Stokes to Walsingham, 13/23 January 1583.

agreement.[78] Although the attempted sack of Antwerp did alienate most of the Dutch populace, it was not really the watershed that it has been made out to be.

Perhaps Anjou, even had he received the necessary funding from the States, would still have failed to defeat Parma. With a few singular exceptions, his officers were young and inexperienced like himself. He had little knowledge of tactics and logistics, the 'French fury' being a case in point. Would an experienced commander have attempted a *coup* against a city of 80,000 people with an army made up of several thousand starving and freezing troops, and this without the aid or advice of his most experienced officer, marshal Biron? Moreover, would he have tried to seize one of the main gates of the city with just 200 men, knowing that it was heavily guarded? Even Parma's army – better financed, better equipped, and better commanded – did not capture Antwerp in 1585 without a struggle. One can only conclude that it was utter stupidity to attempt such a venture, and that Anjou thought it might succeed is a sign of gross military incompetence. But the 'French fury' aside, could he have defeated Parma even with the promised revenues from the States? The earl of Leicester could not manage it several years later. Not only was he a cut above Anjou as a military commander, but he had a larger subsidy from Elizabeth as well as her public support. So, when all is said and done, Anjou's own inadequacies would probably have ensured the same result even had he been properly financed. The chancellor of his household admitted as much upon his departure from the Netherlands in October 1583:

Since we left Dunkirk, we have continued to mess up everything, conducting our affairs so badly that we have lost all reputation, and what is worse, the friendship of the common people of these provinces. We have irritated the king so often, that I have no hope that His Majesty will aid us in Flanders, or in any other enterprise for that matter.[79]

Thus, Anjou's deficiencies, which have contributed to the traditional picture of his enterprise in the Netherlands, cannot be ignored. They should, however, be set beside the failure of the States-General to finance his venture as promised at Plessis-lès-Tours.

III

The council meeting to which Henry had recalled both Anjou and Biron was actually an 'assembly of notables', a collection of great nobles, prelates, and government officials who were called together by the king in emergencies or to

---

[78] See Léonel de la Tourasse, 'La négociation pour le duc d'Anjou aux Pays-Bas de 1578 à 1585', *Revue d'histoire diplomatique*, XII (1898), 527–55, which underscores the role of Pruneaux in these negotiations.

[79] Muller and Diegerick, *Documents*, vol. V, p. 400, Guy du Faur de Pibrac to Pruneaux, 14 October 1583 (Pibrac replaced Christophe de Thou as the chancellor of Anjou's household in November 1582 upon De Thou's death).

deal with special issues. The assembly of 1583 was convoked to discuss a set of emergency measures dealing with the financial crisis of the crown, the result to some degree of Henry's spendthrift policies.[80] Anjou did not attend the opening session on 18 November at St-Germain-en-Laye because of his illness. He had developed a high fever, 'a relic, as everyone knows, of a former illness' according to the Venetian ambassador. Catherine de Medici had visited him earlier in the month and reported that doctors were giving him medicine and purging his blood because of 'the great sweat that he had'.[81] Anjou did send a member of his household to represent him at the assembly, Claude Clausse, seigneur de Ponts. Although it has been suggested that Anjou refused to attend because he was trying to foment rebellion in the provinces,[82] it is clear that his health was the principal reason for his absence.

His poor health did not, however, prevent him from staying abreast of the situation in the Netherlands. One of Parma's agents – the sieur de Gougnies, governor of Quesnoy – arrived in Château-Thierry to try to negotiate a settlement with the duke, whose troops still held Cambrai. Gougnies had contacted Anjou earlier on 22 October, and the duke did no more than listen to his proposals. Moreover, Anjou had alerted both Orange and the States to Parma's overtures and kept them informed of the situation.[83] In a confidential letter to Pruneaux, who was still meeting with the States, Anjou made it clear that he had no intention of dealing with Parma. 'I would never do anything that would prejudice them [the States] or the promises and oaths that I made to them', Anjou insisted. 'Moreover, if they are resolved to send some deputies to me when I see the king, you know that I will do everything for their welfare, advancement, and prosperity'.[84] Nevertheless, rumors abounded both in France and in the Netherlands that Anjou was secretly negotiating with Parma and planned to betray the States. The Dutch deputies, even though they were informed of the meeting with Gougnies by Anjou himself, were understandably concerned.[85] When Gougnies arrived in Château-Thierry for a second meeting on 12 November, the rumors intensified. As on the first occasion, however, Anjou informed both Orange and the States of Parma's offers and kept them abreast of the entire negotiation.[86] Nonetheless, some historians remain convinced that

80 Aline Karcher, 'L'Assemblée des Notables de Saint-Germain-en-Laye (1583)', *Bibliothèque de l'Ecole des Chartes*, LXIV (1956), 115–62, esp. pp. 126–7.
81 BN, MSS ital. 1733, fol. 226, Moro to the Signory, 11 November 1583; and Catherine de Medici, *Lettres*, vol. VIII, p. 152, Catherine to madame de Nemours, 4 November 1583.
82 Karcher, 'L'Assemblée des Notables', pp. 128–9. As evidence Karcher cites *CSPF*, vol. XVIII, p. 162, Edward Stafford (new English ambassador to France) to Walsingham, 21 October 1583. Stafford clearly said nothing of the sort, however.
83 Muller and Diegerick, *Documents*, vol. V, pp. 402–3, Anjou to the States, 22 October 1583; and Groen van Prinsterer, *Archives*, vol. VII, pp. 263–4, Anjou to Orange, 22 October 1583.
84 Muller and Diegerick, *Documents*, vol. V, pp. 415–16, Anjou to Pruneaux, 22 October 1583.
85 Ibid., pp. 450–3, the States to Anjou, 15 November 1583.
86 Ibid., pp. 456–8, Anjou to the States, 16 November 1583; and Groen van Prinsterer, *Archives*, vol. VIII, pp. 269–70, Anjou to Orange, 16 November 1583.

Anjou was making a deal with Parma to sell out the States.[87] If that was his intention, why did he immediately inform Orange and the States each time he was contacted by Gougnies and reveal what was being discussed? Even Professor van der Essen is forced to admit that it was Parma whom Anjou betrayed. Indeed, Parma eventually broke off the negotiations altogether, because everything that was proposed was immediately reported to the States by Anjou.[88]

It is possible, however, that Anjou may have been using the talks with Gougnies to extract money from his brother. Catherine de Medici suspected as much, as she confided to Bellièvre. 'Concerning my son', she wrote on 21 November, 'he has been negotiating with the governor of Quesnoy for eight days and we have heard nothing, except that he presses the king every day to pay his garrison in Cambrai. Otherwise, he will be forced to lose it due to a lack of money.'[89] Cambrai was still a vital fortification on the frontier, and Henry and Catherine were obviously concerned about the negotiations with Gougnies. Because they did not wish to see Cambrai fall into Parma's hands, they immediately despatched secretary Pinart to Château-Thierry with 50,000 *écus* (150,000 *livres*) for the French garrison in Cambrai. Catherine informed Bellièvre that this was done so that Anjou 'could not claim that necessity and a lack of means constrained him to accept the offers made to him by the said prince. I wish that he would trust us more in these matters than he has done in the past.'[90] If indeed this was Anjou's ploy, it worked. His garrison in Cambrai was paid, and Gougnies departed from Château-Thierry in a huff in early December, having concluded nothing. Soon thereafter, some deputies from the Dutch States arrived to negotiate a new treaty.[91]

The States had despatched Antoine de Lalaing, seigneur de la Mouillerie and Jean d'Asseliers, first secretary of the States, to inform Anjou that the States desired to retain him as their prince and to remain his loyal subjects. A prerequisite for any reconciliation, however, was a firm commitment from Henry III to support their cause, as 'the States and inhabitants of these provinces are not inclined to make a reconciliation with his said Highness unless the king favors him openly'. They also insisted that Henry close all French ports to Spanish shipping and cease all trade with Spain and her allies. They underscored the necessity of Henry's commitment, because he 'was the only Christian prince who could stand up to the king of Spain'.[92]

While waiting for the arrival of the deputies, Anjou despatched an agent of his

87 See, for example, Kervijn de Lettenhove, *Huguenots*, vol. VI, pp. 489–91; and van der Essen, *Alexandre Farnèse*, vol. III, pp. 159–60.
88 Van der Essen, *Alexandre Farnèse*, vol. III, pp. 159–60.
89 Catherine de Medici, *Lettres*, vol. VIII, p. 156, Catherine to Bellièvre, 21 November 1583.
90 Ibid., p. 157, Catherine to Bellièvre, 22 November 1583. Also see BN, MSS ital. 1733, fol. 241, Moro to the Signory, 25 November 1583.
91 BN, MSS ital. 1733, fols. 271–2, Moro to the Signory, 23 December 1583.
92 Muller and Diegerick, *Documents*, vol. V, pp. 469–75, instructions to the deputies sent to Anjou, 24 November 1583.

own to the States on 8 December. He was instructed to tell them that time was of the essence, 'considering that the king of Spain now has in his grasp the entire army which conquered Turkey and Portugal'. Anjou was willing to lead an army to win back the provinces already lost to Spain, but would need another 450,000 to 600,000 *livres* to do it.[93] When the Dutch deputies finally arrived in Château-Thierry in early December, they made it clear that nothing could be concluded without the backing of Henry III. And they virtually admitted that they were hindered in their efforts to reach a new settlement with Anjou because of the hostility of the people.[94]

The deputies' insistence that Henry be included in any agreement prompted Catherine de Medici to make another journey to Château-Thierry on 31 December. Although she remained a fortnight, she was able to accomplish little without a firm resolution of the king to support his brother openly.[95] Just as at Plessis-lès-Tours in September 1580, Anjou responded that the king could not possibly declare war on Philip II. Moreover, he thought that even to secure an open pledge of support from the king, the States would have to offer him some form of inducement, such as a few fortified towns along the frontier. Because of these conditions, the deputies despatched a messenger to the States-General, informing them that an agreement with Anjou and Henry appeared unlikely.[96]

Because of the stalemate with the States, and also because the queen mother had become seriously ill after her return to Paris, Anjou decided that his own health had improved enough to make a visit to the capital. As he made his belated entry on 10 February 1584, the entire court rejoiced at the return of the prodigal son. Henry warmly received his brother, whom he had not seen in nearly three years, and they both wept openly at the reunion. From 10 to 21 February Anjou and the king paraded publicly throughout Paris and St-Germain-en-Laye in a great show of devotion and affection. 'I praise God from the bottom of my heart', wrote Catherine, 'to see them so happy together, which can only be for the welfare and prosperity of the affairs of this kingdom'.[97] There is no record of what the two royal brothers discussed, although Pierre de l'Estoile reported that Henry gave Anjou 100,000 *écus* (300,000 *livres*). All the accounts make it clear, however, that Anjou and the king were genuinely closer than they had ever been. Such harmony and affection was so unlike their previous behavior that 'a great many' were completely astonished, according to Edward Stafford.[98] The queen

93 Ibid., pp. 506–10, instructions from Anjou to the sieur de Fouquerolles, 8 December 1583.
94 Ibid., pp. 522–8, Dutch deputies to Anjou, 16 January 1584.
95 BN, MSS ital. 1733, fols. 289–91, Moro to the Signory, 6 January 1584; and Catherine de Medici, *Lettres*, vol. VIII, pp. 168–9, Catherine to Villeroy, 2 January 1584.
96 Muller and Diegerick, *Documents*, vol. V, pp. 535–43, instructions sent by Asseliers and Lalaing to the States, 19 January 1584.
97 Catherine de Medici, *Lettres*, vol. VIII, p. 174, Catherine to the sieur de Liverdis, 13 February 1584.
98 See L'Estoile, *Journal*, vol. II, pp. 147–8; BN, MSS ital. 1733, fols. 323–4, Moro to the Signory, 17 February 1584; *CSPF*, vol. XVIII, p. 350, Stafford to Walsingham, 13/23 February 1584; De

mother, who had seen her sons quarrel since childhood, was moved perhaps more than anyone else by their reconciliation. Upon Anjou's departure from Paris on 21 February, she wrote to Bellièvre that her sons were 'so satisfied with each other that I have great occasion to praise God and to hope for peace and contentment for the rest of my days. And I assure you that this has greatly assisted the recovery of my health and the departure of my fever, which was brought on by the worry and sadness that I experienced throughout their separation'.[99]

Upon his return to Château-Thierry, Anjou wrote William of Orange that the king was ready to support his enterprise in the Netherlands once again and was willing to do so publicly. But Anjou also warned that the States would have to act quickly. If Philip II 'collects all his forces together, there will no longer be time to look for a remedy'.[100] There was a new hitch in the negotiations, however. Henry's open support for the Netherlands and his generous offers of money and troops were contingent on French troops replacing Dutch troops in several garrisoned towns along the frontier. Lalaing and Asseliers complained that this demand had never been made in previous negotiations. Moreover, they frankly admitted 'that the abandonment of these places depended on the people, not the States. Even if French troops were allowed in, the inhabitants in concert with the enemy could easily chase them out.' Nevertheless, because of the gravity of the situation and the king's willingness to support his brother openly, the two deputies urged Orange and the States to grant these concessions.[101]

On 14 March the States-General despatched a third envoy to the duke of Anjou – Guillaume de Maude, seigneur de Mansart – with the news that Parma's forces had laid siege to the town of Ieper in southern Flanders, which was on the verge of capitulation. If Ieper fell, they feared for the remainder of the province. The States admitted that their own army of 3,000 foot and 2,000 horse was insufficient to stop Parma's advance, and they pleaded with Anjou to join his forces with theirs before it was too late. Mansart was instructed to tell Anjou that the deputies of the States 'do not deny that the provinces and towns have adopted delays and irresolutions, which have upset and displeased a number of good men in the service of both Anjou and these provinces'. Nevertheless, they hoped that he would not abandon 'the welfare of both France and these provinces'.[102]

By mid-March, however, Anjou's health had deteriorated further. His fever and vomiting of blood became so intense that some doubted that he would

---

Thou, *Histoire universelle*, vol. VI, p. 378; and BN, MSS CCC 140, fol. 222, 'Presens faict du duc d'Anjoue frere du Roy à son arrivée a Paris', 13 February 1584.

[99] Catherine de Medici, *Lettres*, vol. VIII, p. 175, Catherine to Bellièvre, 29 February 1584.

[100] Groen van Prinsterer, *Archives*, vol. VIII, pp. 320–1, Anjou to Orange, 25 February 1584.

[101] Muller and Diegerick, *Documents*, vol. V, pp. 589–93, Lalaing and Asseliers to the States and Orange, 2 and 3 March 1584.

[102] Ibid., pp. 594–9, instructions of the States to Mansart, 14 March 1584 (quotation from p. 598).

recover. Catherine de Medici rushed again to Château-Thierry, as doctors worked frantically to save her son's life. As Villeroy reported on 13 March, some of the sixteenth-century remedies appeared to stabilize Anjou's condition, albeit only temporarily:

For two days since the recurrence of his fierce fever he has been plagued by a flux of blood from the nose and mouth which has greatly impaired his health. If he had not been promptly treated on the same day by means of two bloodlettings, which not only stopped and checked the said flow of blood but also greatly reduced the violence of the said fever, we would have expected the worse. God willing, another accident will not put us in such doubt of his recovery.[103]

Although Anjou experienced less pain and discomfort after this attack, there was little improvement. On 19 March Catherine wrote to Villeroy that 'my son was supposed to be bled this morning, but he slept so late and awoke so refreshed that the doctors decided to take another look at him tomorrow, hoping that he will be better and that maybe they will not have to bleed him'.[104] Instead of improving, however, Anjou's condition only worsened. He had another harsh attack of fever and vomiting at the end of the month, which caused further fears for his survival. On 30 March the Venetian ambassador reported that

Monseigneur's illness increased in such intensity that all hope for his life was nearly given up. In the night he was bled three times, but the process was aided by a more natural loss of blood which flowed freely from his nose and mouth. He seems to be somewhat better now, though he is very weak and sluggish, which will prevent his returning to court until after the [Easter] holidays.[105]

By April, however, there was little improvement. Once the doctors diagnosed that he was suffering from the same lung disorder that had killed Charles IX, they gave up all hope of recovery.[106]

Anjou's illness was watched so attentively because he was the last Valois heir to the throne. Should he die, the crown would pass upon Henry's death to the Bourbon house, a cadet branch of the Capetian dynasty descended directly from Louis IX. This was significant, since the closest Bourbon heir was Henry of Navarre, a Protestant. Even in March there were vague rumors that the Guises might try to prevent the Bourbon succession if the Valois line expired.[107] By mid-April the ageing cardinal of Bourbon, Navarre's uncle, claimed that he should be the first Bourbon heir, as the people of France would never accept a heretic as their monarch. According to the Venetian ambassador, Henry III was forced to send for Navarre and his wife Marguerite 'to confirm and secure the

---

103 BN, MSS fr. 3321, fol. 92, Villeroy to Matignon, 13 March 1584.
104 Catherine de Medici, *Lettres*, vol. VIII, p. 177, Catherine to Villeroy, 19 March 1584.
105 BN, MSS ital. 1733, fol. 351, Moro to the Signory, 30 March 1584.
106 BN, MSS ital. 1733, fols. 358–9, Moro to the Signory, 13 April 1584.
107 BN, MSS fr. 3902, fols. 267–75, anonymous memoir 'sur les desseins de la maiso[n] de Guise ava[nt] la mort de M. le duc danjou', 15 March 1584.

succession of the throne in the event of Monseigneur's death, the king being unable to have children himself'.[108] The crisis escalated further when the Guises openly endorsed the cardinal of Bourbon's claim in May.[109] It was with the realization that his death would precipitate a certain political crisis that most politically minded Frenchmen monitored Anjou's condition closely throughout the spring of 1584.

In mid-April Anjou wrote to his mother and sister that his health had improved somewhat, although his doctors did not consider him out of danger.[110] Nevertheless, he attempted to continue his negotiations with the deputies of the States-General in France because of the growing threat to the towns of Ieper and Cambrai. When he learned that Ghent had been negotiating with Parma for a separate settlement, Anjou immediately despatched a messenger to try to persuade the city to hold out until he and the States could send assistance.[111] The States were becoming more despondent, however. They instructed their deputies in France to tell the king that they would not require him to declare war on Philip II if he would prevent provisions and supplies bound for Parma's army from passing through French ports. Moreover, the States promised to make a better effort to secure the protection of the Catholic religion in the Netherlands. But unless Anjou returned to the Netherlands at once with a French-supported army, the States might be compelled to ignore the treaty of Plessis-lès-Tours altogether, the duke having abandoned them.[112]

Despite his illness, Anjou had no intention of losing the initiative in the Netherlands, and he drew up a new treaty which he sent to Pruneaux to present to the States. It is clear that Anjou took Henry's promises of support at his word, for this new proposal was entirely dependent on the king's largesse. In the twenty-eight articles of the proposed treaty, Anjou promised to provide an army of 17,000 men, for which the king would provide him a subsidy of 1,200,000 *livres* for the remainder of 1584 and 200,000 *livres* per month thereafter. He would ensure that any provisions bound for Parma's army did not pass through France or French ports. For their part, the States would have to raise an army of 6,000 men, for which they would furnish 75,000 *livres* per month. They would have to continue to pay for the garrisons of Dutch troops that they were already financing, and would also have to give him four new fortified towns which would be garrisoned with French troops. Finally, all towns and cities in the Netherlands except Ghent and Antwerp would have to be open to the duke, who could place a French garrison there whenever he was visiting them. Other stipulations provided that the prince of Orange would have a stronger role in the operation of

---

[108] BN, MSS ital. 1733, fols. 358–61, Moro to the Signory, 13 April 1584.

[109] BN, MSS ital. 1733, fols. 378–9, Moro to the Signory, 11 May 1584.

[110] BIF, MSS God. 260, fol. 204, Anjou to Catherine, 20 April 1584; and BN, MSS fr. 20434, fol. 114, Anjou to Marguerite de Valois, 18 April 1584.

[111] Muller and Diegerick, *Documents*, vol. v, pp. 631–3, Anjou to Pruneaux, 29 March 1584.

[112] Ibid., pp. 644–8, instructions from the States to their deputies in France, 5 April 1584.

the central government – certainly to Anjou's advantage – and that, if Anjou died without an heir, the provinces would remain permanently allied to France on the same terms as already contracted.[113]

Due to the gravity of the situation, as well as the continued harangues of Orange, the States were more or less forced to accept Anjou's terms. Orange made it very clear that there was no other alternative:

I confess that I am at a loss because of several towns and provinces of this country, who say (not secretly, but openly, and not in twos or threes, but in full States) that it is necessary to make a reconciliation with the king of Spain, or else look for sufficient aid elsewhere. Having first approached the princes of our own religion, who have left and abandoned us, they desire some other recourse than the king of France and his brother. I declare that I am perplexed when such things are proposed in the States, as they are, and I am unable to respond in any way, although it is necessary to try at least. Even if there is nothing else good about him, we nevertheless overlook the fact that the king of France is not our enemy, and that he will always keep the king of Spain in suspense of his intentions.[114]

Orange's reasoning eventually overcame all opposition, and the States-General signed a treaty with the seigneur des Pruneaux on 25 April at Delft. With a few minor changes, Anjou's earlier proposals were accepted intact. Thus, a new agreement was reached which replaced the treaty of Plessis-lès-Tours and gave the duke of Anjou a much stronger hand in the Netherlands.[115] It was both a remarkable victory for Orange and a reflection of the desperate position that the Dutch provinces were in.

By the end of April, however, Anjou was unable to execute the new treaty. Although he had despatched a company of French guards to Cambrai under the command of Jean de Montluc, seigneur de Balagny, earlier in the month, his declining health precluded any further activity in the Netherlands.[116] On 26 April he suffered another major attack of fever and vomiting of blood which left him very weak.[117] On Sunday, 6 May, the *parlement* of Paris offered a special prayer for the duke in the St-Geneviève monastery, where Pierre de Gondi, the bishop of Paris, offered a prayer of intervention for Anjou's life.[118] But it was all to no avail. Anjou's agents did their best to reassure the States that all was well, in an attempt to downplay the rumors of his illness. 'I assure you that he is completely out of danger', wrote the sieur de Fervacques from Château-Thierry on 12 May.[119] Only the night before, however, Anjou had suffered another

113 Ibid., pp. 657–66, proposed treaty sent to Pruneaux, 8 April 1584.
114 Groen van Prinsterer, *Archives*, vol. VIII, pp. 349–63, Orange to John of Nassau, 18 March 1584 (quotation from p. 355).
115 Muller and Diegerick, *Documents*, vol. V, pp. 686–700, treaty concluded by Pruneaux and the States, 25 April 1584.
116 BIF, MSS God. 260, fol. 194, Anjou to Henry III, 12 May 1584, for the mission of Balagny.
117 BN, MSS ital. 1733, fol. 377, Moro to the Signory, 27 April 1584.
118 BN, MSS CCC 143, fols. 273–4, copy of the registers of the *parlement* of Paris, May 1584.
119 Muller and Diegerick, *Documents*, vol. V, p. 724, Fervacques to Pruneaux, 12 May 1584.

severe loss of blood from his nose and mouth, and for the first time, from his ears as well.[120] The pain continued to increase in his chest, and he became weaker with each successive flux of blood. By the beginning of June his condition was so bad that he could not leave his bed.

One of his followers, the sieur de la Fougière, described the suffering of his final days:

I will tell you, then, that yesterday the ninth of this month he took his medicine, after having a very restful night the night before. He felt well on awakening, and this gave us some hope of his recovery, until eight or nine o'clock in the evening when we began to lose all hope. He had taken to his bed to sleep as was his usual custom, after washing out his mouth, because of his declining condition. Then, he suddenly awoke and began calling for his doctors, complaining that he could not sleep because of the pain on both sides of his chest and the extreme difficulty he had in breathing. A little while later, after he was relieved somewhat ... he wanted to go back to sleep. He lay there without being able to sleep until the following afternoon, with incredible pain and a cold, deadly sweat which left him dying. Realizing his failing condition and feeling the end approaching, he asked the sieurs de Tigor and Botal, the doctors who were watching over him that night, if anything could be done to ease his difficulty in breathing and the intense pain in his chest ... I cannot tell you how much sorrow I saw there in that room. I cannot explain it in any language.[121]

That same night Anjou called for his priest, Jacques Berson, who also left a record of the duke's last hours.[122] He begged forgiveness of all his sins and said, 'I am fully resolved to God's will.' Berson tried to acknowledge the duke's confession, but as he related, 'I was left speechless. In truth, he was still belching up blood very freely into the basin that I held in one hand, while with a handkerchief in the other I wiped from his face and chest a heavy, cold sweat which even smelled of death.'[123]

After a sleepless night Anjou asked to hear mass, which Berson dutifully performed. Afterwards, he tried to sleep a little, which was his first rest since the preceding Friday evening. He awoke shortly, however, at about eleven o'clock in the morning, and requested that Berson give him the sacrament of extreme unction. After one last confession he tried to sleep again. Although he never managed to doze off, he rested comfortably after the pain of the night before. Then, about an hour and a half later, he died just before one o'clock in the afternoon on Sunday, 10 June. As Berson recollected, Anjou 'expired so sweetly that it almost went unnoticed. Indeed, several persons who did not believe that he was dead (his eyes were still open and clear and his expression was

---

[120] BN, MSS ital. 1733, fols. 378–9, Moro to the Signory, 11 May 1584.

[121] BN, MSS fr. 3902, fols. 283–8, memoir of La Fougière, 10 June 1584.

[122] Jacques Berson, *Regret funèbre contenant les actions et derniers propos de Monseigneur, fils de France, frère unique du Roy, depuis sa maladie iusques à son trespas* (Paris, 1584) reprinted in Cimber and Danjou (eds.), *Archives curieuses*, series i, vol. x, pp. 201–18.

[123] Ibid, p. 207.

unchanged) placed a mirror in front of his mouth. But there was no sign of life.'[124] The king, who was residing at St-Maur-des-Fossès southeast of Paris, did not receive the news until very late that evening. He immediately asked marshal Biron to go to Château-Thierry to accompany his brother's body back to Paris.[125]

The following morning, 11 June, Anjou's surgeons opened up the body in the presence of the king's doctors. The report of their findings indicates the extent of the duke's suffering: peritonitis, a spleenic abscess, an enlarged liver with a subdiaphragmatic abscess, pneumonia, empyema, meningitis, and a calcified brain lesion consistent with a tuberculoma. This report, written in Latin, was very brief, as a sixteenth-century autopsy only extended to an examination of the skull and abdomen.[126] It is nevertheless clear from these observations and his medical history that Anjou almost certainly died from chronic disseminated tuberculosis, in all likelihood contracted during childhood.[127] Moreover, if one were to hazard a guess, Anjou's contraction of the disease could probably be traced to the court's grand tour of the provinces in 1564. In July of that year he had suffered his first serious illness as the court travelled from Lyon to Valence. Because he was periodically ill thereafter, it is reasonable to assume that he contracted the disease in July 1564, at the age of nine. In any case, the autopsy performed on 11 June clearly indicates that Anjou had been infected with the disease for a long time. Later that evening the body was embalmed, wrapped in black velvet and white satin, and placed in a lead coffin. His heart had previously been removed and placed in a small leaden box in the shape of a heart.[128]

Marshal Biron did not arrive at Château-Thierry until Thursday, 14 June. Because the members of Anjou's household wished to accompany the body back to Paris, it was Tuesday, 19 June before the funeral train finally departed for the capital. When Biron arrived in Paris late in the evening of 21 June, he took the body to the church of St-Magloire in the *faubourg* St-Jacques, where the bishop of Paris blessed it and offered prayers of salvation for the duke's soul. The following day, Friday, 22 June, the bishop celebrated high mass with the royal family, which was followed by numerous orations and prayers from some of Anjou's household officers and several nobles of the court. The body lay in state over the weekend at the church, and was transferred to Notre Dame the

---

[124] Ibid., p. 215.
[125] Théodore Godefroy, *Le Cérémonial de France, ou description des cérémonies, ranges, et séances observées aux couronnemens, entrées, et enterremens des Roys et Roynes de France, et autres actes et assemblées solennelles* (Paris, 1619), p. 549. The description of Anjou's funeral and burial is on pp. 548–96.
[126] BN, MSS fr. 3902, fol. 289r.-v., 'Quae observata sunt in corpore integro & dissecto defuncti principio Illustrissimi Andem Ducis die 11 Junij 1584 praesentib. sublignatis Medicis Regis e. principis Illustrissimi defuncti e. Chirurgis.'
[127] I wish to thank my brother, Dr Philip J. Holt, for this diagnosis.
[128] Godefroy, *Cérémonial de France*, p. 550.

following Monday.[129] On Tuesday, 26 June, Renaud de Beaune, archbishop of Bourges – Anjou's former chancellor who had been sacked for embezzlement – conducted the funeral ceremony at Notre Dame. According to Pierre de l'Estoile, the archbishop gave a boring funeral oration and tugged at his beard throughout the entire proceedings. 'He said nothing worth listening to', L'Estoile went on, 'and he never did so badly in his whole life'.[130] After the funeral the body was conducted in a formal parade of mourning to the basilica at St-Denis, where the duke was to be buried with his ancestors. The covered casket lay in the nave of the basilica overnight, and the following morning the body was buried, after a brief sermon by Jacques Berson. Before he died, Anjou had requested that he be buried as 'the duke of Brabant and lord of the Netherlands'. Henry, not wishing to annoy Philip II, preferred otherwise, and the duke was buried in a white pall bearing the arms of Anjou and Alençon.[131]

Unable to write, the duke of Anjou had dictated his last will and testament on 8 June at Château-Thierry, which was in the form of a harangue to the king:

One of the greatest regrets I have, my Lord, is that I have irritated and displeased you by my actions and undertakings. So many of them were from a desire to pacify your kingdom and to protect it from foreign invasion more than any other single ambition. This is the principal reason why I beseech you to forgive me, as I requested the last time I had the good fortune to see you. I feel sure that you will do so out of your generosity. I was born your brother and subject, and I have possessed a fine and vast *apanage* by your consent and liberality. You have augmented my means by your kindness, and what is more, you have allowed me to assist myself from the revenues of my domain, and to secure a portion of it with my creditors. I have been gratuitously assisted, however, by many lords and gentlemen, your subjects, most of whom have inconvenienced, impoverished, and nearly ruined themselves in my service. My servants have served me faithfully, each in his own charge, and I have not had the means to repay them as I would like and as reason dictates. Even the majority of them have not been paid. I owe around 300,000 *écus* to many different subjects of your kingdom, and I carry to the grave their earnings, their tears, and their wailing, without having the means to discharge myself to God and men ... I beg you to continue my revenues for four more years and to employ them to this effect, that is to say, to acquit my debts and to pay my servants' wages, whom I ask you to employ for two further years ... Finally, the Netherlands have bestowed upon me most dearly the titles of duke and count, which they still owe me. And if I have any power in their behalf, I pray them to transfer everything to you, to whom (and equally to your successors) I leave and give all rights and pretensions that I have been able to acquire in this respect, by virtue of the official treaties that I have made with them. Moreover, Cambrai can serve as a bulwark, acquired and won by the means you have given me. I remain obliged to defend its citizens, who with such affection and devotion threw themselves into my arms. I beg you in God's name, my Lord, to accept what I

---

[129] Ibid., pp. 553–62.   [130] L'Estoile, *Journal*, vol. II, p. 157.
[131] Godefroy, *Cérémonial de France*, pp. 585–92; De Thou, *Histoire universelle*, vol. VI, p. 379; and L'Estoile, *Journal*, vol. II, p. 156.

possess by right and authority in this place, and to put an end to the oppression and desolation of such good people.[132]

It is clear from his testament that Anjou felt responsible for his many faithful servants, to whom he was heavily in debt. Moreover, he did not forget the people of the Netherlands, and he asked his brother to continue in the same capacity in which he had served. He spent the last six years of his life occupied as much by the revolt of the Netherlands as by the French civil wars. His testament, as well as his request to be buried as 'lord of the Netherlands', is a firm indication of what he felt was his principal accomplishment. Due to possible repercussions from Spain, however, Henry refused to accept the sovereignty either of the city of Cambrai or of the Netherlands as a whole. Because of the unhealthy fiscal state of the crown, he also declined to honor his brother's debts. Nevertheless, the death of the duke of Anjou did not go unnoticed. Henry, perhaps more than anyone else, was fully aware of its significance. 'Their Majesties and all of France are saddened, and with good reason', wrote secretary Villeroy on 12 June, 'since the king has no children'.[133]

IV

Upon the assassination of Henry, duke of Guise at Blois in December 1588, the Florentine ambassador in France ruefully reflected on the preceding four years of civil war. 'One can say with good reason', he wrote, 'that the death of the duke of Anjou was the ruin of France'.[134] It was equally clear upon Anjou's death, however, that a struggle would develop for the throne. As early as March 1584 the Guises had announced their intention to prevent a heretic from succeeding Henry III. When the cardinal of Bourbon announced his own claim, again while Anjou was still alive, they supported his candidacy. It was not too difficult to foresee the inevitable struggle between the Protestant Henry of Navarre and the Catholic Guises, though surely no-one could have predicted the severity of the suffering that such a conflict ultimately produced. Pierre de l'Estoile recorded that the Guises 'took great heart' from Anjou's death. 'It came at a very opportune time for them, facilitating and advancing the designs of their League, which from that moment began to grow stronger as France grew weaker.'[135] Marshal Biron was equally disturbed by Anjou's death. 'This loss has caused a great deal of sorrow', he wrote, '[and] those who understand politics predict that this death could bring harm to our France'.[136] It is clear, then, that Anjou's

---

132 Nevers, *Mémoires*, vol. I, pp. 601–3.
133 BN, MSS fr. 16092, fol. 239, Villeroy to the sieur de Maisse, 12 June 1584.
134 Desjardins, vol. IV, p. 850, Cavriana to Serguidi, 31 December 1588.
135 L'Estoile, *Journal*, vol. II, p. 158.
136 Biron, *Letters and Documents*, ed. Ehrman and Thompson, vol. I, p. 363, Biron to the abbé de Blaisemont, 30 June 1584.

contemporaries were well aware of the significance of his death. 'The tenth of June will forever bear witness to our misfortune', concluded Jacques Berson's *Regret funèbre*, 'the year 1584 is indeed a year of revolution'.[137]

Coupled with the assassination of William of Orange at Delft one month later, Anjou's death also had a great impact on international politics. 'My son the duke of Anjou being deceased and the prince of Orange also dead', wrote Catherine de Medici in July 1584, 'it is necessary to believe that the king of Spain will soon reduce the Netherlands in his obedience'.[138] Even before Orange's assassination, the Dutch States had begged Henry III to accept the title of defender and protector and to continue French assistance in their struggle against Parma. Left completely leaderless after Orange's murder, the States then asked Henry to accept the title of duke of Brabant, and to succeed Anjou as their titular sovereign.[139] The growing strength of the League (which was openly backed by Spain after December 1584), however, forced Henry to decline. The Dutch then turned to Elizabeth one last time. As William Camden recorded, Elizabeth sent a special agent to France upon hearing of Anjou's death 'to give the King to understand how heavily shee tooke the Duke of Anjou's death, whom she had found to be a most faithfull and deere friend unto her; and withal to put him in minde how miserable was the state of the Netherlanders, the Prince of Orange being slaine, and how dreadfull was the overgrowing power of the Spanyard'.[140] Thus, Anjou's death led indirectly to English intervention in the Dutch revolt, which culminated a year later in the treaty of Nonsuch between Elizabeth and the States-General. Far more important, however, was the domestic scene in France, where Anjou's death precipitated the last and bloodiest of the Wars of Religion: that tripartite struggle between Henry III, Henry of Navarre, and Henry, duke of Guise. No-one who survived the horrendous siege of Paris in 1590 would have disputed the Florentine ambassador's claim that the duke of Anjou's death in June 1584 was 'the ruin of France'.

V

What is the final verdict on François de Valois, duke of Alençon and Anjou? Just that he was a troublemaker and a failure? In dealing with the first of these charges it is clear that Anjou (then duke of Alençon) undoubtedly posed a serious threat to the French crown and to his brother Charles in the spring of 1574 by participating in multiple plots with the French Protestants. This threat became

---

[137] Cimber and Danjou (eds.), *Archives curieuses* series i, vol. x, p. 217. For similar reactions, see the memoirs of Jacques-Auguste de Thou in Michaud and Poujoulat, *Mémoires*, vol. xi, p. 319; and Pasquier, *Lettres familières*, ed. Thickett, pp. 442–3.

[138] BN, MSS CCC 473, fol. 589, Catherine to Castelnau, 25 July 1584.

[139] Groen van Prinsterer, *Archives*, vol. viii, pp. 405–7, 24 June 1584; and BN, MSS fr. 3284, fols. 55–6, 11 October 1584.

[140] Camden, *Historie*, book iii, p. 42.

graver still in late 1575 and early 1576, when the duke fled from court to join with Navarre, Casimir, and Condé in a military assault upon the crown. As the Huguenots were already advancing theories of resistance to the monarchy, Anjou's mere association with them – whatever his actual role or participation – was ample cause for Henry III, the queen mother, and most French Catholics to doubt his loyalty to the crown and the church. But the heir to the throne had been the traditional focus for royal opposition ever since the Middle Ages. Can Anjou really be justly compared, for example, with Gaston d'Orléans, the recalcitrant brother of Louis XIII?[141] Orléans, also known as the duke of Anjou in his early years, was involved in numerous conspiracies to murder cardinal Richelieu, and was one of the ringleaders of the 'Cinq-Mars affair', when a treasonous band of rebels signed a pact in 1642 with the count-duke of Olivares, first minister of Philip IV of Spain, to bring Spanish troops across the Pyrenees to help steal the French crown. After May 1576, when Anjou was rewarded with the titles and recognition that he had long sought, was he ever again a direct threat to his brother's crown? His intervention in the Netherlands obviously upset Henry and did provide cause for possible Spanish retaliation. In this sense, perhaps, Anjou was a threat to the crown. But never again was he implicated in any plot or attempted *coup* against his brother. Moreover, he served faithfully in the French army thereafter (too faithfully to suit most Protestants) and helped negotiate the peace settlements of 1577 and 1580. His loyalty to his brother and to the French crown cannot really be questioned after 1576.

That Anjou was a failure, however, is less easy to dismiss. None of the schemes in his early years ever came off, nor did he appear to learn from his mistakes. He never led a great military victory (unless one counts the pathetic victory at Cambrai in 1581), and is best remembered for the fiasco at Antwerp in January 1583. Above all, he never succeeded in wearing the 'three crowns' of France, England, and the Netherlands. Thus, every major enterprise in his life failed to achieve success. His incompetence doubtless contributed to these failures, but how much could someone like Anjou really expect to achieve? Was he not really the epitome of that forgotten and disparaged class of early modern figure: the Overmighty Subject? With an inadequate power base in both government and the army, his ambitions were clearly greater than his capabilities (not to mention even his copious financial resources). But was this not also true of far more talented and accomplished figures like Coligny? Guise? Leicester? Even Orange?

Perhaps Anjou's greatest failures were really missed opportunities. In France he had the chance to help close the festering sore of civil war immediately after the edict of pacification of May 1576. With close contacts in both camps, he could have helped diffuse the religious turmoil that shattered the peace and soon led to the renewal of the civil wars. Rather than speaking out in the council and

141 A recent example of such a comparison is Sutherland, *The Massacre of St Bartholomew*, p. 49.

supporting the *politique* factions within the second and third estates at Blois in 1576–7, Anjou did nothing, and thereby condoned Henry's decision to break the peace edict. The Catholic reaction against the settlement was so overwhelming, of course, that his participation in the *politique* struggle might not have mattered. He forced them to look elsewhere for someone to champion their cause, however, when he was in a unique position to dissipate the religious and political tensions. As this study has demonstrated throughout, Anjou never really joined the *politique* struggle, much less became its leader.

His situation in the Netherlands produced much the same story. With overtures from both the Calvinist-dominated provinces of Holland and Zeeland in 1576 and the Catholic provinces of the south in 1578, Anjou was in a unique position to help arbitrate the disputes that divided the provinces. Although it was beyond him to prevent the break with Spain, he could have made an attempt to diffuse the one issue that ultimately split the provinces apart: religion. When the 'Spanish fury' caused the revolt to expand outside Holland and Zeeland once again in late 1576, Anjou was the one figure that the Calvinist maritime provinces and the Catholic southern provinces (who distrusted Orange) were willing to trust, albeit temporarily. When his troops arrived in the Netherlands in the summer of 1578, however, they exacerbated rather than healed the internal divisions within the revolt. Once the agreements made at Arras and Utrecht were signed in 1579, these divisions became permanent. As in France, Anjou's cause in the Netherlands was not the *politique* cause of Orange and others in the States-General. His was a more personal crusade. And although he obviously could not have prevented the split between the Dutch provinces, perhaps he could have made it less painful.

Thus, the duke of Anjou's greatest failure was his unwillingness to become part of the *politique* struggle. Perhaps, had his career not been cut short by tuberculosis, things might have altered. He was on better terms with his brother and mother than ever before in 1584. As the only Valois heir, he had much to look forward to, and every reason to want to preserve the state and end the religious division. In the Netherlands, the States had just offered him new terms which ameliorated the deficiencies of the treaty of Plessis-lès-Tours and helped repair the damage of the 'French fury'. 'He dyed, when together with his years his hopes did most flourish', noted the Italian chronicler, Guido Bentivoglio. 'For the King having no hopes of Issue, he did not only promise to himself to enjoy the Principality of Flanders, but by a greater fortune to succeed to the Crown of France.'[142] Both states were doomed, however, to suffer over a decade more of civil war.

---

[142] Bentivoglio, *History of the Warrs of Flanders*, p. 214.

Appendix A: The household of the duke of Anjou, 1572–84

(Average salaries are given in *livres tournois*)

Office	1572 No.	1572 Average Salary	1575 No.	1575 Average Salary	1576 No.	1576 Average Salary	1578 No.	1578 Average Salary	1584 No.	1584 Average Salary[k]
Aumôniers	6	153	9	103	15	110	23	76	8	445
Prédicateur	1	200	1	400	1	400	1	600	1	600
Chapelains	3	120	4	120	6[a]	153	11	160	7	160
Clercs de chapelle	3	100	4	100	6[b]	110	7[e]	109	8	100
Officiers spéciaux	4	1,150	—	—	1	4,000	14	1,943	2	11,000
Chambellans	8	650	18	778	118	575	111	600	50[g]	1,170
Gentilshommes de la bouche	—	—	—	—	—	—	21	800	—	—
Gentilshommes de la chambre	22	448	57	399	147	388	157	500	23	391
Maîtres de la garderobe	1	500	1	600	2	600	—	—	—	—
Maîtres d'hôtel	6	442	6	483	16	428	20	510	12[h]	500
Gentilshommes des panetiers et écuyers	20	320	32	294	75	309	83	405	10	600
Ecuyers	7	343	10	380	13	431	15	453	8	588
Contrôleurs généraux	1	1,000	1	1,000	1	1,000	1	1,200	2	600
Contrôleurs et clercs	4	200	5	200	13	218	11	249	4	280
Médecins	2	400	4	120	16	97	23	100	8	450
Chirurgiens	3	133	—	—	11	180	10	180	6	203
Apothécaires	1	200	1	200	1	400	1	400	2	400
Valets de chambre	16	163	39	174	66[c]	196	79[f]	204	19[i]	221
Valets de garderobe	9	111	18	133	40[d]	172	45	166	19	180
Marchands fournissans	—	—	—	—	—	—	—	—	6	60
Barbiers	3	140	4	180	6	200	6	203	3	367

Appendix A (cont.)

Office	1572		1575		1576		1578		1584	
	No.	Average Salary	No.	Average Salary	No.	Average Salary	No.	Average Salary	No.	Average Salary
Portemanteaux	3	200	6	233	10	220	11	218	5	240
Portemalle	—	—	1	200	1	200	1	200	1	200
Huissiers de chambre	4	150	3	120	6	233	6	233	5	240
Huissiers de salle	3	120	—	—	6	120	6	120	4	140
Portiers	1	80	1	80	9	244	11	300	10	240
Tapissiers	3	100	4	100	4	120	4	120	5	120
Aides de tapissiers	1	60	1	60	2	60	4	60	—	—
Maréchaux des logis	4	350	4	350	10	480	10	480	5	560
Fourriers	7	140	9	140	15	160	16	160	12	160
Sommeliers de paneterie	3	160	3	160	6	180	7	180	7	206
Aides de paneterie	3	120	3	120	6	140	7	140	5	152
Sommeliers de l'échansonnerie	3	160	3	160	6	180	7	180	9	193
Aides de l'échansonnerie	3	120	4	140	6	140	6	140	4	140
Coureurs des vins	—	—	—	—	1	200	1	200	2	87
Serdeau	1	50	1	50	1	70	1	70	1	100
Ecuyers de cuisine	3	180	3	180	3	200	4	200	3	200
Maîtres queux	3	160	3	160	6	180	7	180	6	200
Hasteurs	3	120	3	120	3	140	3	140	4	140
Potagers	3	120	3	120	6	140	7	140	5	156
Enfants de cuisine	3	60	3	60	3	70	3	70	3	100
Galopins	3	25	3	25	3	30	3	30	3	37
Porteurs en cuisine	4	70	4	70	5	80	5	144	6	85
Verduriers	1	50	1	50	1	60	1	60	2	60
Huissiers de cuisine	2	60	2	60	2	70	4	70	2	100

Gardes de vaisselle	1	200	1	300	1	300	1	300	2	300
Huissiers du bureau	2	100	2	100	3	120	6	120	4	120
Fruitiers	3	100	3	100	3	120	3	147	4	200
Aides des fruitiers	3	57	3	60	3	70	3	70	5	70
Valets des fourriers	3	100	3	100	3	120	4	120	4	120
Aides des fourriers	3	60	3	60	3	70	4	70	4	70
Menuisier	1	60	1	60	—	—	—	—	—	—
Serrurier	1	10	1	10	—	—	—	—	—	—
Lavandiers	2	60	2	60	2	120	2	120	2	120
Boulangers	1	120	1	120	1	120	1	120	2	60
Pâtissiers	1	40	1	40	2	50	2	50	2	50
Aides des pâtissiers	1	30	1	30	1	35	1	35	2	35
Boucher	1	25	1	25	1	25	1	25	—	—
Poissonier	1	25	1	25	1	25	1	25	—	—
Gens de métier	4	11	5	11	12	30	15	35	—	—
Sommiers	10	180	10	180	14	200	15	200	17	188
Chancelier	1	1,200	1	4,000	1	4,000	1	6,000	1	12,000
Secrétaires des finances	2	600	2	600	2	1,000	11	764	4	1,200
Maîtres de requêtes et gens du conseil	20	29	30	35	87	146	126	107	14[j]	764
Secrétaires ordinaires	13	125	57	97	122	123	144	110	34	178
Généraux des finances	1	1,000	1	1,000	1	1,500	2	4,000	4	1,000
Receveur général des finances	1	2,500	1	2,500	1	3,000	3	3,333	1	7,000
Trésorier général	1	1,500	1	1,500	1	2,000	1	2,000	2	4,000
Maître de la chambre	—	—	1	600	1	600	1	600	—	—
Argentier	—	—	1	600	1	600	1	600	—	—

Appendix A (cont.)

Office	1572		1575		1576		1578		1584	
	No.	Average Salary	No.	Average Salary	No.	Average Salary	No.	Average Salary	No.	Average Salary
Agent près du roi	—	—	—	—	—	—	—	—	1	6,000
Secrétaire d'état	—	—	—	—	—	—	—	—	1	7,200
Conducteur d'ambassadeurs	—	—	—	—	—	—	—	—	1	800
Totals[m]	262 persons 77,990 livres		415 persons 115,640 livres		942 persons 263,710 livres		1,123 persons 351,880 livres		418 persons 251,510 livres	

[a] This figure does not include one paid at 5 livres.
[b] This figure does not include one paid at 5 livres.
[c] This figure does not include one paid at 10 livres and three paid at 5 livres.
[d] This figure does not include one paid at 10 livres.
[e] This figure does not include one paid at 5 livres.
[f] This figure does not include three paid at 5 livres and three paid at 10 livres.
[g] This figure does not include two at no salary.
[h] This figure does not include one paid at 20 livres.
[i] This figure does not include one paid at 20 livres.
[j] This figure does not include one at no salary.
[k] The figures for 1584 are given in écus in the MSS, and I have converted them to livres tournois at the rate of 3 livres or 60 sous = 1 écu.
[m] All the MSS distinguish between the cuisine de bouche and the cuisine de commun, which I combined. Also the total wage figure for each year may not always tally with the sum of the average salaries, as the totals include several pensions not shown in the table. For a full analysis of Anjou's household, see my article, 'Patterns of clientèle and economic opportunity at court during the Wars of Religion: the household of François, duke of Anjou', French Historical Studies, XIII (1984), 305–22.

Sources: For 1572, BN, MSS Clair. 1216, fols. 112–20; for 1575, BN, MSS fr. 23029, fols. 137–45; for 1576, Marin le Roy, seigneur de Gomberville (ed.), Les Mémoires de monsieur le duc de Nevers (2 vols., Paris, 1665), vol. I, pp. 577–99; for 1578, BN, MSS fr. 20614, fols. 47–70; and for 1584, BN, MSS fr. 20614, fols. 73–83.

Appendix B: The *apanage* of the duke of Anjou

Date of grant	Territories included
February 1566	Alençon, Château-Thierry, Châtillon-sur-Marne, Epernay, Perche, Gisors, Mantes, Meulan, Vernon, Les Andelys
October 1569	Dreux, Beaumont-le-Roger, Couches, Breteuil, Orbec, Passy, Sézanne, Evreux[a]
October 1570	Caen, Falaise, Bayeux, Dives, Valognes, Avranches, Coutances, Chaumont-en-Vexin, St-Saveur-le-Vicomte, Pontoise, Beaumont-sur-Oise, La Ferté-Alais
June 1573	Maine, Meaux, Montfort-l'Amaury
May 1576	Anjou, Touraine, Berry

[a] In October 1569 Charles IX granted the *comté* of Evreux to the duke to replace the seigneuries of Gisors, Vernon, and Les Andelys, which were desired by the duchess of Ferrara. See BN, MSS fr. 5944, fols. 23–7.
Source: BN, MSS fr. 5944, fols. 1–78.

Appendix C: Income from the *apanage* of the duke of Anjou

Source: For 1579, AN, KK 237, fols. 1–62. 'Recepte generalle des finan[ces] de Monseigneur pour l'annee finie le dernier jour de decembre mil v^c soixante dixneuf. M. Mathieu Marcel receveur g[é]n[ér]al'. For 1583, PRO/SP 78/10/fols. 287–93, 'Estat de la Recepte des finances de Monseigneur frere unicque du Roy de la presente annee mil cinq cens quatre vingtz trois ensemble des despenses ordinaries de sa maison et parties que son Altesse entend estre paiees des deniers de sad[ite] Recepte de lad[ite] annee'.^{a}

Domain	1579	1583
Alençon	25,617 *livres* 14s. 3d.	12,545 *livres* 15s.
St-Sylvin	—^{b}	636 *livres* 18s.
Argentain et Exienne	—^{c}	16,167 *livres*
Domfront	—^{d}	5,908 *livres* 12s.
Verneuil	3,480 *livres*	1,290 *livres* 15s. 6d.
Château-Thierry	6,273 *livres* 3s. 8d.	—^{n}
Evreux	3,270 *livres*	2,523 *livres* 13s.
Breteuil	3,600 *livres*	—^{p}
Beaumont-le-Roger	1,880 *livres* 1s.	4,002 *livres*
Orbec	19,000 *livres*	—^{q}
Dreux	5,922 *livres* 12s.	7,500 *livres*
Perche	2,511 *livres* 10s. 6d.	1,998 *livres* 2s.
Mantes and Meulan	10,674 *livres*	—^{r}
Sézanne	2,750 *livres*	—^{s}
Pontoise	—^{e}	—
Chaumont-en-Vexin	—^{f}	—
Aleps	—^{g}	—
Beaumont-sur-Oise	—^{h}	—
Montfort-l'Amaury	5,213 *livres* 7s. 2d.	1,977 *livres*
Meaux	—^{i}	—
Le Mans	—^{j}	—
Château-du-Loir	2,494 *livres*	—^{t}
Touraine	—^{k}	—
Couches	—^{m}	6,462 *livres* 18s.
Montrichard	990 *livres*	—^{u}
Anjou	80,809 *livres* 7s.	89,200 *livres*
Berry	157,962 *livres* 10s. 1d.	—^{v}
Caen	147,387 *livres* 9s. 1d.	147,387 *livres* 5s.
Bourges	100,000 *livres*	100,000 *livres*
Tours	75,000 *livres* 4s. 6d.	75,000 *livres*
Total	654,835 *livres* 19s. 3d.	472,599 *livres* 18s. 6d.

[a] I have converted all figures from both MSS from *écus* to *livres tournois* at a rate of 1 *écu* = 3 *livres* or 60 *sous*.

[b] Not yet collected.

[c] Not yet collected.

[d] Not yet collected.

[e] Rights to income sold to Nicolas Aubelin, sieur de Favelles, amount not specified.

[f] Rights to income sold to madame de Longueville, amount not specified.

[g] Rights to income sold to M. Guillaume Bailly, president in the *chambre des comptes*, amount not specified.

[h] Rights to income sold to M. Elausse for the sum of 24,000 *écus* (72,000 *livres tournois*) 'de laquelle recepte est faicte au compte de lextraordin[aire] de la guerre de flandres' (quotation from AN, KK 237, fol. 36r).

[i] Not yet collected.

[j] Not yet collected.

[k] Rights to income sold, neither purchaser nor amount specified.

[m] Not yet collected.

[n] Rights to income sold, neither purchaser nor amount specified.

[p] Rights to income sold, neither purchaser nor amount specified.

[q] Rights to income sold, neither purchaser nor amount specified.

[r] Rights to income sold, neither purchaser nor amount specified.

[s] Rights to income sold, neither purchaser nor amount specified.

[t] Rights to income sold, neither purchaser nor amount specified.

[u] Rights to income sold, neither purchaser nor amount specified.

[v] Rights to income sold, neither purchaser nor amount specified.

The only years for which complete information is available concerning the income from the duke of Anjou's *apanage* are 1579 and 1583. It is clear from this limited information, however, that much of Anjou's regular annual income from his domains had already been alienated by 1579 to help pay for the costs of his enterprise in the Netherlands (see the entry for Beaumont-sur-Oise above). This trend continued through 1583, with the result that his domains actually brought in less revenue in 1583 than in 1579, as more and more of his *apanage* was alienated. All of the annual income from his *apanage*, as well as the revenue derived from alienations, was still not enough to cover his expenses in the Netherlands, moreover, and Anjou died in 1584 deeply in debt (see pp. 210–11 above).

Select bibliography

The following list is only a guide to the most significant sources used in the preparation of this book, and is not a complete list of sources consulted.

I. MANUSCRIPTS

A. PARIS

Bibliothèque Nationale

The largest collection of Anjou's correspondence and papers is located here, primarily in the *Fonds français*. The most useful volumes in the various collections (though by no means the only ones cited) are as follows:

Fonds français 3177–8: Miscellaneous correspondence of Anjou, 1569–82

3181–4: Miscellaneous correspondence of Anjou, 1570–6

3201–8: Correspondence of Anjou to François de Montmorency and Henri de Montmorency-Damvillé, 1569–76

3226–9: Miscellaneous correspondence of Anjou, 1569–70

3239: Papers of Damville, 1574

3245–8: Correspondence of Anjou and Henry III to Damville, 1572–6

3277–91: Correspondence between Anjou and William of Orange, the Dutch States-General, the provincial States of the Netherlands and their agents, 1575–84; correspondence between Anjou and his agent in the Netherlands, the seigneur des Pruneaux, 1576–84. Much, though not all, from these volumes is printed in Muller and Diegerick, *Documents*.

3296: Anjou's reception in the Netherlands, 1582

3300–1: Correspondence between Anjou and Henry III and Catherine de Medici, 1577–80

3306–8: Miscellaneous papers relating to Anjou's marriage negotiations, including correspondence between Henry III and Michel de Castelnau, Henry's ambassador in England, 1580–2

3316–17: Correspondence of Henry III to Jacques d'Humières, 1575–7

3321–33: Miscellaneous papers of Anjou, 1574–84

3336–50: Miscellaneous papers of Anjou and Henry III, 1575–81

3357: Correspondence of Henry III, July 1583

3383–8: Miscellaneous correspondence of Anjou and Henry III, 1575–84

3410: Anjou to Anne de Montmorency and François de Montmorency, 1564–7

3420: Correspondence of Anjou to Damville and the prince of Condé, 1578

3902: Anonymous memoir on the designs of the house of Guise on the French throne, April 1584; eye-witness account of Anjou's death by M. de la Fougière, 10 June 1584; and an autopsy report by the king's doctors, 11 June 1584

3952: Harangue by Barnabé Brisson on Anjou's proposed marriage, April 1581

3956–61: Correspondence between Anjou and Henry III and Catherine de Medici, 1575–6

3969: Documents concerning the uprisings at court, March and April 1574

4505: Papers relating to Anjou's proposed marriage, 1581

4554: Expenses of the royal army at La Rochelle, 1573

4632: Correspondence between Anjou and Gaspard de Saulx, 1570

5067: Papers relating to Anjou's proposed marriage, 1581–2

5138: Treaty between Anjou and the Dutch States-General, 13 August 1578

5140: Papers relating to Anjou's proposed marriage, 1581

5944: Financial documents concerning Anjou's *apanage*, 1566–84

6547: Correspondence between Anjou and Henry III, 1575–84

6623–9: Correspondence of Anjou to Henry III and Catherine de Medici, 1575–84

15536: Documents on the augmentation of Anjou's finances, July 1580 (in Villeroy's hand)

15560–4: Papers of secretary Villeroy, 1578–82

15886: Papers relating to Anjou's proposed marriage, 1581–2

15904–7: Papers of Pomponne de Bellièvre, including correspondence with Anjou and Henry III, 1576–84

15973: Papers of Michel de Castelnau, 1579

16092: Report by Villeroy on Anjou's death, June 1584

17199: Correspondence of the sieur de Maisonfleur to Charles IX from the Netherlands, 1573

17306: Papers concerning Anjou's *apanage*, 1566–84

18582–4: Papers concerning Anjou's *apanage*, 1566–84

20434: Correspondence between Anjou and Marguerite de Valois, April 1584

20614: Anjou's household expenses and wage lists, 1578–84

23029: Anjou's household expenses and wage lists, 1571–8

26156: Receipt for payment by Anjou to G. Corbinelli, his Italian teacher, 1574

Fonds nouvelles acquisitions françaises 4709: Diary of Claude de la Châtre in the Netherlands, 1581–3

7738: Protestant complaints to the crown, 1576

Collection Cinq Cents de Colbert 7–8: Miscellaneous papers of Anjou, Henry III, and Catherine de Medici, 1569–77

24: Correspondence between Anjou and Henry III, 1569

29: Miscellaneous correspondence of Anjou, Navarre, and Condé, 1575–7

81: Papers relating to Anjou's *apanage*

82: Papers relating to Anjou's proposed marriage, 1581–2

87: Letter from Anjou to the *parlement* of Paris, May 1581

140: Description of Anjou's arrival in Paris, February 1584

337: Correspondence from Anjou in Antwerp, mainly to Henry III, 1582

366–8: Correspondence of Henry III to Arnaud du Ferrier, French ambassador in
  Italy 1574–84

473: Papers of Michel de Castelnau, 1580–82

Collection Clairambault 357: Organization of justice in the duchy of Anjou, 1576

  633: Declaration of Anjou at Moulins, April 1576

  1216: Anjou's household expenses and wage lists, 1572

Fonds italien 1727–33: Despatches of the Venetian ambassadors in France, 1569–85
  (in Italian)

Collection Dupuy 137: Correspondence from Anjou to Villeroy, 1579

  157: Letter from Jean Bodin in Antwerp, January 1583

  211: Correspondence from Anjou in Antwerp, April 1582

  500: Documents relating to the siege of La Rochelle, 1573

  537–8: Papers of Henry III, 1578–9

  569: Correspondence from Anjou to Christophe de Thou, sieur de Cély, 1581

  590: Papers concerning the uprisings at court, March and April 1574

  755: Papers concerning the uprisings at court, March and April 1574

  832: Concerning Anjou's powers to fill vacant offices in the domains of his *apanage*,
  1580

Archives Nationales

Although the French national archives are generally disappointing for materials relating
to the duke of Anjou, there are some very useful financial papers here pertaining to the
duke's *apanage* and household expenses. Also of interest are the papers of Juan de Vargas
Mexia, Spanish resident ambassador in France in the 1570s, now available only on
microfilm (the originals having been returned to Simancas).

Série K: Cartons des rois

  K 98: Accounts of Anjou's annual pension, 1571

  K 100: Donation of 600 *écus* from Henry III to Anjou, July 1579

  K 101: Expense sheet of purchases made for Anjou's household, April 1582

  K 1544: Papers of Juan de Vargas Mexia

  K 1548: Patents issued to the captains of Anjou's army, 1578

Série KK: Comptes royaux

  KK 237: Receipts from Anjou's *apanage*, 1579

  KK 279: Receipts from the city of Angers, 1582

Bibliothèque de l'Institut

Housed in the rear of the Académie Française, this private collection contains in the
famous *Collection Godefroy* a number of important sixteenth-century manuscripts. Some
of the most significant are those pertaining to the edict of pacification of May 1576.

Collection Godefroy 71: Papers relating to the peace edict of May 1576

  74: Declaration of Anjou in London, November 1581

  94: The 'secret articles' not published in the general peace edict of May 1576, drawn
  up by Catherine de Medici to placate Condé, Navarre, and Damville

  95: Papers of Anjou on negotiations leading to the peace edict of May 1576

Select bibliography

96: Documents pertaining to the Peace of Fleix, November 1580
256: Correspondence of Charles IX pertaining to the siege of La Rochelle, 1573
259: Correspondence to Henry III to Anjou, 1578–9
260: Correspondence of Henry III to Anjou, 1580
291: Papers relating to the uprisings at court, March and April 1574
316: Patent letters of Henry III, May 1576
327: Papers of Henry III relating to Anjou's proposed scheme to relieve the siege of Cambrai, December 1580

B. ANGERS

Archives Communales

(These are housed in the *Bibliothèque Municipale*.) Although the duke of Anjou was almost never resident in the most important domain of his *apanage*, this collection contains some useful material on Anjou's attempts to raise funds from his duchy to support his military campaign in the Netherlands.

Série BB 34–40: Registers of the *Hôtel-de-ville*, 1576–84

C. BLOIS

Bibliothèque Municipale

The important private diary of Pierre de Blanchefort, noble deputy from Nivernais and Donsiais at the meeting of the Estates-General in 1576–7 at Blois, is located here.

MSS 89: Diary of Pierre de Blanchefort

D. BRUSSELS

Archives Générales du Royaume

The papers of the rebel government in the Netherlands are located here in the *Papiers d'Etat et de l'Audience*. As the duke of Anjou was just a figurehead and not really a part of the governing process, he does not figure prominently in the proceedings. The process by which the rebels made decisions and the influence of William of Orange are clearly revealed, however.

Etat et l'Audience 550–5: Correspondence of the government of Archduke Matthias, 7 December 1577–31 October 1581

556–63: Correspondence of the government of the duke of Anjou, 1 November 1581–30 May 1583

564–79: Correspondence addressed to the rebel government and to the States-General, and patent letters issued by the rebel government, 1577–83

E. THE HAGUE

Algemeen Rijksarchief

Anjou's personal correspondence while in the Netherlands during 1582–3, none of which has been published to my knowledge, is located here. The duke's negotiations with

Select bibliography

individual provincial States, and their reluctance to pay him their respective quotas of the sums approved by the States-General, are clearly indicated in the record of his correspondence kept by the secretary assigned to him by the States-General, Johan van Asseliers.

Eerste Afdeling, Staten-Generaal 11095: Letter-book of the duke of Anjou while in the Netherlands, 1582 (in the hand of Johan van Asseliers; this volume is unfoliated, but letters are arranged chronologically)

11096: Miscellaneous papers of the duke of Anjou, 1582–3

11098–104: Correspondence between the States-General and France, 1577–85

11105–11: Correspondence between the States-General and England, 1576–89

F. LONDON

The British Library

The Cottonian Collection and the series of Additional MSS both contain some useful unpublished material pertaining to Anjou's proposed marriage to Queen Elizabeth.

Additional MSS: 5753, 19398, 20850, 30342, 33594, 34216

Cottonian Collection: Caligula E/v–vii, Galba C/vi, Galba E/vi, Vespasian F/v–vi, Cleopatra F/vi, Titus B/ii, Titus C/xviii

Harleian Collection: 253, 260

Sloane Collection: 814

Public Record Office

All of the papers of England's foreign agents and resident ambassadors abroad are located here. For the reign of Elizabeth I, all the foreign papers to 1577 are contained in the vast SP 70. After 1577, the papers are arranged by country. A selection from the entire collection of state papers has been calendared and published in the *Calendar of State Papers, Foreign Series*, yet much of importance has been omitted from the published *Calendar*. Moreover, some of the documents that have been included have been either poorly transcribed or improperly translated. There is thus a great deal in this collection of state papers that pertains to the duke of Anjou that is not available elsewhere. The important list of Anjou's military expenses in the Netherlands and his sources of revenue, for example (SP 78/10/122/fols. 308–35), a list that was provided for Lord Burghley, is not published in the *Calendar* and is apparently not available, even in copy, in any of the continental collections.

State Papers 70 (Foreign)/130 to 145: All foreign papers from diverse English agents and ambassadors abroad, January 1574–June 1577

State Papers 78 (France)/1 to 12: Papers of English agents and ambassadors in France, July 1577–December 1584

State Papers 83 (Holland and Flanders)/1 to 22: Papers of English agents and ambassadors in the Netherlands, June 1577–August 1584

II. PRINTED PRIMARY SOURCES

Acta Nuntiaturae Gallicae:

II *Correspondance du nonce en France Girolamo Ragazzioni, 1583–86*, ed. Pierre Blet (Rome, 1962)

Select bibliography

VII *Correspondance du nonce en France Giovanni Battista Castelli, 1581–83*, ed. Robert Toupin (Rome, 1967)

VIII *Correspondance du nonce en France Anselmo Dandino, 1578–81*, ed. Ivan Cloulas (Rome, 1970)

XIII *Correspondance du nonce en France Antonio Maria Salviati, 1572–8*, ed. Pierre Hurtubise and Robert Toupin (Rome, 1975)

Albèri, Eugenio, ed., *Le Relazioni degli ambasciatori veneti al senato durante il secolo decimosesto*, 1st series (6 vols., Florence, 1839–62)

Aubigné, Agrippa d', *Histoire universelle*, ed. A. de Ruble (10 vols., Paris, 1886–1909)

Bentivoglio, Guido, *The Compleat History of the Warrs of Flanders . . . Englished by the Right Honourable Henry, Earl of Monmouth* (London, 1654)

Biron, Armand de Gontaut, baron de, *The Letters and Documents of Armand de Gontaut, baron de Biron, Marshal of France (1524–1592)*, ed. S. H. Ehrman and James W. Thompson (2 vols., Berkeley, 1936)

Blaes, J. B., ed., *Mémoires anonymes sur les troubles des Pays-Bas, 1565–1580* (5 vols., Brussels, 1859–66)

Bodin, Jean, *Les Six Livres de la République* (Paris, 1576); translated into English by Richard Knolles, *The Six Bookes of a Commonweale*, ed. Kenneth D. McRae (Cambridge, Mass., 1962)

Cabié, Edmond, ed., *Guerres de religion dans le sud-ouest de la France, et principalement dans le Quercy, d'après les papiers des seigneurs de Saint-Sulpice de 1561 à 1590* (Paris and Albi, 1906)

Calendar of Letters and State Papers relating to English Affairs of the Reign of Elizabeth, preserved principally in the Archives of Simancas, ed. M. A. S. Hume, vols. II–III (London, 1895): vol. II, 1568–79; vol. III, 1580–86

Calendar of State Papers and Manuscripts relating to English Affairs existing in the Archives and Collections of Venice and in other Libraries of Northern Italy, ed. H. F. Brown *et al.*, vols. VII–VIII (London, 1890–94): vol. VII, 1558–80; vol. VIII, 1581–91

Calendar of State Papers, Foreign Series, of the Reign of Elizabeth, preserved in the Public Record Office, ed. S. C. Lomas *et al.*, vols. VIII–XVIII (London, 1871–1914): vol. VIII, 1566–8; vol. IX, 1569–71; vol. X, 1572–4; vol. XI, 1575–7; vol. XII, 1577–8; vol. XIII, 1578–9; vol. XIV, 1579–80; vol. XV, 1581–2; vol. XVI, 1582; vol. XVII, 1583; vol. XVIII, 1583–4

Calendar of State Papers relating to English Affairs preserved principally at Rome in the Vatican Archives and Library, ed. J. M. Riggs, vols. I–II (London, 1916–26): vol. I, 1558–71; vol. II, 1572–8

Camden, William, *The Historie of the Most Renowned and Victorious Princesse Elizabeth, Late Queen of England* (London, 1630)

Charrière, E., ed., *Négociations de la France dans le Levant*, vol. III (Paris, 1853)

Cimber, M. L. and F. Danjou, eds., *Archives curieuses de l'histoire de France depuis Louis XI jusqu'à Louis XVIII*, 1st series (12 vols., Paris, 1834–6)

Colección de documentos inéditos para la historia de España, ed. Don Martín Fernandez Navarrete *et al.* (112 vols., Madrid, 1842–95)

Desjardins, Abel and Giuseppe Canestrini, eds., *Négociations diplomatiques de la France avec la Toscane* (6 vols., Paris, 1859–86)

De Thou, Jacques-Auguste, *Histoire universelle* (11 vols., Basel, 1742 edn)

Select bibliography

A Dialogue or Speaking Together of two Personages of the which, the one is the Well willing Comminalitie, and the other the Noble and moste puissant Prince, my Lorde the Duke of Anjou, Our Most Redoubted Lord, &c. (London, 1582)

Digges, Dudley, *The Compleat Ambassador* (London, 1665)

'Documents originaux relatifs au rôle du duc d'Alençon, sous les règnes des rois Charles IX et Henri III, ses frères, et à l'histoire du tiers-parti', *Revue rétrospective*, 2nd series, v (1836), 226–92, 321–66; vi (1836), 113–44, 349–405

Du Mont, Jean, ed., *Corps universel diplomatique du droit des gens*, vol. v, part i (Amsterdam and The Hague, 1728)

Du Plessis-Mornay, Philippe, *Mémoires et correspondance pour servir à l'histoire de la Réformation et des guerres civiles et religieuses en France, sous les règnes de Charles IX, de Henri III, de Henri IV et de Louis XIII, depuis l'an 1571 jusqu'en 1623* (12 vols., Paris, 1824–5)

Frederick III, elector of the Palatinate, *Briefe Friedrichs des Frommen, Kurfürsten von der Pfalz*, ed. August Kluckhohn (2 vols., Brunswick, 1868–72)

Gachard, Louis P., ed., *Actes des Etats-Généraux des Pays-Bas, 1576–1585* (2 vols., Brussels, 1861–6)

[Gentillet, Innocent], *Brieve remonstrance à la noblesse de France sur le parct de la declaration de Monseigneur le duc d'Alençon* (Paris, 1576)

Godefroy, Théodore, *Le Cérémonial de France, ou description des cérémonies, ranges, et séances observées aux couronnemens, entrées, et enterremens des Roys et Roynes de France, et autres actes et assemblées solemnelles* (Paris, 1619)

Gomberville, Marin le Roy, seigneur de, ed., *Les Mémoires de monsieur le duc de Nevers* (2 vols., Paris, 1665)

[Goulart, Simon], ed., *Les Mémoires de la Ligue sous Henri III et Henri IV, Rois de France* (6 vols., s.l., 1598–1604)

Mémoires de l'estat de France sous Charles Neufiesme (3 vols., s.l., 1577)

Granvelle, Antoine Perrenot, cardinal of, *Correspondance du cardinal de Granvelle, 1565–1586*, ed. Charles Piot and Edmond Poullet (12 vols., Brussels, 1877–96)

Griffiths, Gordon, ed., *Representative Government in Western Europe in the Sixteenth Century: Commentary and Documents for the Study of Comparative Constitutional History* (Oxford, 1968)

Groen van Prinsterer, G., ed., *Archives ou correspondance inédite de la maison d'Orange-Nassau*, 1st series (8 vols., Leiden, 1835–47)

Henry III, *Lettres de Henri III*, ed. Michel François (3 vols. to date, Paris, 1959–72)

Henry IV, *Recueil des lettres missives de Henri IV*, ed. Berger de Xivrey and Joseph Gaudet (9 vols., Paris, 1843–76)

Historical Manuscripts Commission, *Calendar of the Manuscripts of the Most Hon. the Marquis of Salisbury, K.G., preserved at Hatfield House*, vols. I–III (London, 1883–90)

Holinshed, Raphael, *Holinshed's Chronicles of England, Scotland, and Ireland* (6 vols., London, 1807–8)

Japikse, N., ed., *Resolutiën der Staten-Generaal van 1576 tot 1609* (14 vols., 's-Graven-hage, 1915–70)

Kervijn de Lettenhove, J. M. B. C. and L. Gilliodts van Severen, eds., *Relations politiques des Pays-Bas et de l'Angleterre sous le règne de Philippe II* (11 vols., Brussels, 1882–1900)

Select bibliography

Kossmann, E. H. and A. H. Mellink, eds., *Texts concerning the Revolt of the Netherlands* (Cambridge, 1974)

Lalourcé and Duval, eds., *Recueil des cahiers généraux des Trois ordres aux Etats-Généraux* (4 vols., Paris, 1789)

Recueil des pièces originales et authentiques concernant la tenue des Etats-Généraux (9 vols., Paris, 1789)

La Mothe-Fénelon, Bertrand de Salignac, sieur de, *Correspondance diplomatique*, ed. A. Teulet (7 vols., Paris and London, 1838–40)

La Noue, François de, *Discours politiques et militaires*, ed. F. E. Sutcliffe (Geneva, 1967)

L'Estoile, Pierre de, *Journal pour le règne de Henri III (1574–1589)*, ed. L.-R. Lefèvre (Paris, 1943)

Mémoires-journaux de Pierre de l'Estoile, ed. MM. Brunet *et al.*, vols. I–II (Paris, 1888)

Medici, Catherine de, *Lettres de Catherine de Médicis*, eds. Hector de la Ferrière and Gustave Baguenault de Puchesse (10 vols., Paris, 1880–1905)

Michaud, J. F. and J. J. F. Poujoulat, eds., *Nouvelle collection des mémoires relatifs à l'histoire de France depuis le XIIIe siècle jusqu'à la fin du XVIIIe siècle*, 1st series (Paris, 1838)

Muller, P. L. and I. L. A. Diegerick, eds., *Documents concernant les relations entre le duc d'Anjou et les Pays-Bas, 1576–1584* (5 vols., Amsterdam and The Hague, 1889–99)

Orange, William of Nassau, prince of, *The Apologie of Prince William of Orange against the Proclamation of the King of Spaine* (ed. H. Wansink, Leiden, 1959)

Correspondance de Guillaume le Taciturne, ed. Louis P. Gachard (6 vols., Brussels, 1850–7)

Parma, Alexander Farnese, prince of, *Correspondance d'Alexandre Farnèse, prince de Parme, gouverneur général des Pays-Bas, avec Philippe II, dans les années 1578, 1579, 1580 et 1581*, ed. Louis P. Gachard (Brussels and Ghent, 1853)

Pasquier, Etienne, *Lettres familières*, ed. Dorothy Thickett (Geneva, 1974)

Lettres historiques pour les années 1556–1594, ed. Dorothy Thickett (Geneva, 1966)

Pears, S. A., ed., *The Correspondence of Sir Philip Sidney and Hubert Languet* (London, 1845)

Petitot, C. B., ed., *Collection complète des mémoires relatifs à l'histoire de la France*, 1st series (Paris, 1819–27)

Philip II, *Correspondance de Philippe II sur les affaires des Pays-Bas (1558–1577)*, ed. Louis P. Gachard (5 vols., Brussels, 1848–79)

Correspondance de Philippe II sur les affaires des Pays-Bas (1577–1598), ed. Joseph Lefèvre (4 vols., Brussels, 1940–60)

Plantin, Christophe, *De blijde ende heerlijcke Incomste van mijn Heer Franssois van Vranckrijck, des Conicks eenich broeder, by Gotts ghenade Hertogh van Brabant, van Anjou, Alensson, Berri, etc. in sijne zeer vermaerde stadt van Antwerpen* (Antwerp, 1582)

La Ioyeuse et magnifique Entree de Monseigneur Francoys fils de France, et frere unicque du Roy par la grace de Dieu, Duc de Brabant, d'Anjou, Alencon, Berri, etc. en sa tresrenommee ville d'Anvers (Antwerp, 1582)

La magnifique Entrée de François d'Anjou en sa ville d'Anvers, ed. H. M. C. Purkis (Amsterdam and New York, 1975)

Rowen, Herbert, ed., *The Low Countries in Early Modern Times* (New York, 1972)

Sidney, Philip, *Miscellaneous Prose of Sir Philip Sidney*, ed. Katherine Duncan-Jones and Jan van Dorsten (Oxford, 1973)

Select bibliography

Stubbs, John, *The Discoverie of a Gaping Gulf whereinto England is like to be swallowed by an other French marriage, if the Lord forbid not the banes, by letting Her Maiestie see the sin and punishment thereof* (London, 1579)
John Stubbs's Gaping Gulf, ed. Lloyd E. Berry (Charlottesville, 1968)
Sully, baron de Rosny, duke of, *Les Œconomies royales de Sully*, vol. I, ed. David Buisseret and Bernard Barbiche (Paris, 1970)

III. SECONDARY SOURCES: BOOKS

Actes du colloque l'Amiral de Coligny et son temps (Paris, 1974)
Beame, E. M., 'The development of Politique thought during the French religious wars (1560–1595)' (unpub. Ph.D. dissertation, University of Illinois, 1957)
Benedict, Philip, *Rouen during the Wars of Religion* (Cambridge, 1981)
Bergevin, L. and A. Dupré, *Histoire de Blois* (2 vols., Blois, 1847)
Bodin, Jean-Félix, *Recherches historiques sur l'Anjou* (2 vols., Angers, 1847)
Boucher, Jacqueline, *Société et mentalités autour de Henri III* (4 vols., Lille and Paris, 1981)
Brimont, le vicomte de, *Le XVIᵉ siècle et les guerres de la Réforme en Berry* (2 vols., Paris, 1905)
Buisseret, David, *Sully and the Growth of Centralized Government in France, 1598–1610* (London, 1968)
Champion, Pierre, *Catherine de Médicis présente à Charles IX son royaume* (Paris, 1937)
Charles IX, la France et le contrôle de l'Espagne (2 vols., Paris, 1939)
Charleville, Edmond, *Les Etats-Généraux de 1576* (Paris, 1901)
Chauviré, Roger, *Jean Bodin, auteur de la République* (Paris, 1914)
Cloulas, Ivan, *Catherine de Médicis* (Paris, 1980)
Corvisier, André, *Armées et sociétés en Europe de 1494 à 1789* (Paris, 1976)
Croze, Joseph de, *Les Guises, les Valois et Philippe II* (2 vols., Paris, 1866)
Davies, Joan M., 'Languedoc and its *gouverneur*: Henri de Montmorency-Damville, 1563–1589' (unpub. Ph.D. thesis, University of London, 1974)
Decrue, Francis, *Anne, duc de Montmorency, connétable et pair de France sous les rois Henri II, François II et Charles IX* (Paris, 1889)
Le parti des politiques au lendemain de la Saint-Barthélemy (Paris, 1892)
Deshoulières, M. F., *Un gouverneur de la province de Berry: le maréchal de la Châtre, 1536–1614* (2 vols., Bourges, 1906–7)
Dewald, Jonathan, *The Formation of a Provincial Nobility: The Magistrates of the Parlement of Rouen, 1499–1610* (Princeton, 1980)
Dickerman, Edmund H., *Bellièvre and Villeroy: Power in France under Henry III and Henry IV* (Providence, 1971)
Dictionnaire de biographie française (11 vols. to date, Paris, 1933–82)
Diefendorf, Barbara B., *Paris City Councillors in the Sixteenth Century: The Politics of Patrimony* (Princeton, 1983)
Doucet, Roger, *Les Institutions de la France au XVIᵉ siècle* (2 vols., Paris, 1948)
Filhol, René, *Le premier Président Christofle de Thou et la réformation des coutumes* (Paris, 1937)
Franklin, Julian H., *Jean Bodin and the Rise of Absolutist Theory* (Cambridge, 1973)

Select bibliography

Freer, Martha Walker, *Henry III, King of France and Poland, his Court and Times* (3 vols., London, 1858)

Frémy, Edouard, *Un ambassadeur libéral sous Charles IX et Henri III: ambassades à Venise d'Arnaud du Ferrier d'après sa correspondance inédite (1563–1582)* (Paris, 1880)

Garrisson-Estèbe, Janine, *Protestants du Midi, 1559–1598* (Toulouse, 1980)

Tocsain pour un massacre: la saison de Saint-Barthélemy (Paris, 1968)

Geyl, Pieter, *The Revolt of the Netherlands, 1555–1609* (London, 1932)

Graham, Victor E. and W. McAllister Johnson, *The Royal Tour of France by Charles IX and Catherine de Medici: Festivals and Entries, 1564–66* (Toronto, 1979)

Griffiths, Gordon, *William of Hornes, Lord of Hèze and the Revolt of the Netherlands, 1576–1580* (Berkeley, 1954)

Haag, E., *La France Protestante* (10 vols., Paris, 1846–59)

Harding, Robert R., *Anatomy of a Power Elite: The Provincial Governors of Early Modern France* (New Haven and London, 1978)

Hauser, Henri, *François de la Noue, 1531–1591* (Paris, 1892)

Héritier, Jean, *Catherine de' Medici*, tr. Charlotte Haldane (London, 1963)

Howell, Roger, *Sir Philip Sidney, the Shepherd Knight* (London, 1968)

Joubert, André, *Un mignon de la cour de Henri III: Louis de Clermont, sieur de Bussy d'Amboise, gouverneur d'Anjou* (Paris and Angers, 1855)

Kervijn de Lettenhove, J. M. B. C., *Les Huguenots et les Gueux* (6 vols., Bruges, 1883–5)

Kierstead, Raymond F., *Pomponne de Bellièvre: A Study of the King's Men in the Age of Henry IV* (Evanston, 1968)

Kingdon, Robert M., *Geneva and the Consolidation of the French Protestant Movement, 1564–1572* (Madison and Geneva, 1967)

La Chenaye-Desbois, F. A. A. de and Badier, eds., *Dictionnaire de la noblesse*, 3rd edn (19 vols., Paris, 1863–76)

La Ferrière, Hector de, *Le XVIᵉ siècle et les Valois* (Paris, 1879)

Lavin, Michael O. H., 'Franco-Spanish Rivalry from the Treaty of Cateau-Cambrésis to the Death of Charles IX' (unpub. Ph.D. dissertation, Stanford University, 1956)

Lebrun, François, *Histoire d'Angers* (Toulouse, 1975)

Lecler, Joseph, *Histoire de la tolérance au siècle de la Réforme* (2 vols., Paris, 1955)

Lowenstein, Steven M., 'Resistance to Absolutism: Huguenot organization in Languedoc, 1621–22' (unpub. Ph.D. dissertation, Princeton University, 1972)

MacCaffrey, Wallace T., *Queen Elizabeth and the Making of Policy, 1572–1588* (Princeton, 1981)

Major, J. Russell, *Representative Government in Early Modern France* (New Haven and London, 1980)

Malengreau, Guy, *L'Esprit particulariste et la révolution des Pays-Bas au XVIᵉ siècle, 1578–1584* (Leuven, 1936)

Mariéjol, J. H., *La Réforme et la Ligue, l'Edit de Nantes, 1559–1598* (Paris, 1911)

Mayer, Charles, ed., *Des Etats-Généraux et autres assemblées nationales*, vol. XIII (Paris and The Hague, 1789)

Motley, John Lothrop, *The Rise of the Dutch Republic* (3 vols., New York, 1858)

Mourin, Ernest, *La Réforme et la Ligue en Anjou* (Paris and Angers, 1856)

Mousnier, Roland, *Les Institutions de la France sous la monarchie absolue, 1598–1789* (2 vols., Paris, 1974–80)

Select bibliography

La Vénalité des offices sous Henri IV et Louis XIII, 2nd edn (Paris, 1971)

Mouton, Léo, *Bussy d'Amboise et madame de Montsoreau* (Paris, 1912)

Muller, P. L., *Geschiedenis der regeering in de Nader geunieerde provincien tot aan de komst van Leicester (1579–1585)* (Leiden, 1868)

Parker, Geoffrey, *The Army of Flanders and the Spanish Road: The Logistics of Spanish Victory and Defeat in the Low Countries Wars, 1567–1659* (Cambridge, 1972)

    The Dutch Revolt (London, 1977)

    Spain and the Netherlands, 1559–1659 (London, 1979)

Pater, J. C. H. de, *De Raad van State nevens Matthias, 1578–1581* ('s-Gravenhage, 1917)

Picot, E., *Les Italiens en France au XVI⁰ siècle* (Bordeaux, 1901)

Picot, Georges, *Histoire des Etats-Généraux de 1355 à 1614* (4 vols., Paris, 1872)

Ranke, Leopold von, *Civil Wars and Monarchy in France in the Sixteenth and Seventeenth Centuries*, trs. M. A. Garvey (2 vols., London, 1852)

Read, Conyers, *Lord Burghley and Queen Elizabeth* (London, 1960)

    Mr Secretary Walsingham and the Policy of Queen Elizabeth (3 vols., Oxford, 1925)

Rocquain, Félix, *La France et Rome pendant les guerres de religion* (Paris, 1924)

Roelker, Nancy L., *Queen of Navarre: Jeanne d'Albret, 1528–1572* (Cambridge, Mass., 1968)

Romier, Lucien, *Le Royaume de Catherine de Médicis: la France à la veille des guerres de religion*, 2nd edn (2 vols., Paris, 1922)

Salmon, J. H. M., *Society in Crisis: France in the Sixteenth Century* (New York, 1975)

Shimizu, J., *Conflict of Loyalties: Politics and Religion in the Career of Gaspard de Coligny, Admiral of France, 1519–1572* (Geneva, 1970)

Soman, Alfred, ed., *The Massacre of St. Bartholomew: Reappraisals and Documents* (The Hague, 1974)

Strong, Roy C., *Portraits of Queen Elizabeth I* (Oxford, 1963)

Sutherland, N. M., *French Secretaries of State in the Age of Catherine de Medici* (London, 1962)

    The Massacre of St Bartholomew and the European Conflict, 1559–1572 (London, 1973)

    The Huguenot Struggle for Recognition (New Haven and London, 1980)

Swart, K. W., *William the Silent and the Revolt of the Netherlands* (London, 1978)

Thompson, I. A. A., *War and Government in Habsburg Spain* (London, 1976)

Thompson, James W., *The Wars of Religion in France, 1559–1576*, 2nd edn (New York, 1958)

Van der Essen, Léon, *Alexandre Farnèse, prince de Parme, gouverneur général des Pays-Bas (1545–1592)* (5 vols., Brussels, 1933–7)

Wedgwood, C. V., *William the Silent: William of Nassau, Prince of Orange, 1533–1584* (London, 1944)

Weill, Georges, *Les Théories sur le pouvoir royal en France pendant les guerres de religion* (Paris, 1891)

Wernham, R. B., *Before the Armada* (New York, 1966)

Wilson, Charles, *Queen Elizabeth and the Revolt of the Netherlands* (London, 1970)

Wolfe, Martin, *The Fiscal System of Renaissance France* (New Haven and London, 1972)

Woudhuysen, H. R., 'Leicester's literary patronage: a study of the English court, 1578–1582' (unpub. D.Phil. thesis, University of Oxford, 1980)

Select bibliography

Yardeni, Myriam, *Conscience nationale en France pendant les guerres de religion (1559–1598)* (Paris, 1971)
Yates, Frances A., *The Valois Tapestries*, 2nd edn (London, 1975)
Zeller, Gaston, *Les Institutions de la France au XVIᵉ siècle* (Paris, 1948)
Zupco, Ronald E., *French Weights and Measures before the Revolution* (Bloomington, 1978)

IV. SECONDARY SOURCES: ARTICLES

Baguenault de Puchesse, Gustave, 'La politique de Philippe II dans les affaires de France, 1559–1598', *Revue des questions historiques*, XXV (1879), 1–66
Baumgartner, Frederic J., 'Renaud de Beaune, Politique prelate', *Sixteenth Century Journal*, IX (1978), 99–114
Bossy, John, 'English Catholics and the French marriage', *Recusant History*, V (1959), 2–16
Boucher, Jacqueline, 'L'évolution de la maison du roi des derniers Valois aux premiers Bourbons', *XVIIᵉ siècle*, XXXIV (1982), 359–79
Cloulas, Ivan, 'Les aliénations du temporel ecclésiastique sous Charles IX et Henri III, 1563–1587', *Revue d'histoire de l'église de France*, XLIV (1958), 5–56
Decrue, Francis, 'La Molle et Coconat et les négociations du parti des politiques', *Revue d'histoire diplomatique*, VI (1892), 375–94
Diegerick, I. L. A., 'Notice sur l'entrée solemnelle du duc d'Anjou dans la ville d'Anvers, le 19 février 1582', *Annales de l'Académie d'Archéologie de Belgique*, XI (1854), 405–22
'Notice sur les négociations qui ont eu lieu entre les etats-généraux et le duc d'Anjou après la tentative de ce prince de surprendre Anvers (janvier à avril 1583)', *Annales de l'Académie d'Archéologie de Belgique*, XIII (1856), 5–41; XVI (1859), 47–72, 289–320
Duke, Alistair and Rosemary Jones, 'Towards a reformed polity in Holand, 1572–1578', *Tijdschrift voor geschiedenis*, LXXXIX (1976), 373–93
Holt, Mack P., 'Patterns of *clientèle* and economic opportunity at court during the Wars of Religion: the household of François, duke of Anjou', *French Historical Studies*, XIII (Spring 1984), 305–22
Jackson, Richard A., 'Peers of France and princes of the blood', *French Historical Studies*, VII (1971), 27–46
Karcher, Aline, 'L'assemblée des notables de Saint-Germain-en-Laye (1583)', *Bibliothèque de l'Ecole des Chartes*, LXIV (1956), 115–62
Koenigsberger, H. G., 'The organization of revolutionary parties in France and the Netherlands in the sixteenth century', *Journal of Modern History*, XXVII (1955), 335–51
'Why did the States General of the Netherlands become revolutionary in the sixteenth century?', *Parliaments, Estates and Representation*, II (1982), 103–11
La Ferrière, Hector de, 'Catherine de Médicis et les politiques', *Revue des questions historiques*, LVI (1894), 404–39
'Les derniers conspirations du règne de Charles IX', *Revue des questions historiques*, XLVIII (1890), 421–70
La Tourasse, Léonel de, 'La négociation pour le duc d'Anjou aux Pays-Bas de 1578 à 1585', *Revue d'histoire diplomatique*, XII (1898), 527–55

Select bibliography

Lovett, A. W., 'Some Spanish attitudes to the Netherlands, 1572–1578', *Tijdschrift voor geschiedenis*, LXXXV (1972), 17–30

MacCaffrey, Wallace T., 'The Anjou match and the making of Elizabethan foreign policy', *The English Commonwealth, 1547–1640*, ed. P. Clark *et al.* (New York and Leicester, 1979)

Major, J. Russell, 'Noble income, inflation, and the Wars of Religion in France', *American Historical Review*, LXXXVI (1981), 21–48

Neuschel, Kristen, 'The Picard nobility in the sixteenth century: anatomy and power', *Proceedings of the Western Society for French History*, IX (1981), 42–9

Parker, Geoffrey, 'Spain, her enemies and the Revolt of the Netherlands', *Past & Present*, XLIX (1970), 72–95

'Why did the Dutch Revolt last eighty years?', *Transactions of the Royal Historical Society*, 5th series, XXVI (1976), 53–72

Powis, Jonathan, 'Gallican liberties and the politics of later sixteenth-century France', *Historical Journal*, XXVI (1983), 515–30

Sutherland, N. M., 'Antoine de Bourbon, king of Navarre and the French crisis of authority, 1559–1562', *French Government and Society, 1500–1800*, ed. J. F. Bosher (London, 1973)

'Catherine de Medici: the legend of the wicked Italian queen', *Sixteenth Century Journal*, IX (1978), 45–56

'William of Orange and the Revolt of the Netherlands: a missing dimension', *Archiv für Reformationsgeschichte*, LXXIV (1983), 201–30

Vogler, Bernard, 'Le rôle des électeurs palatins dans les guerres de religion en France (1559–1592)', *Cahiers d'histoire*, X (1965), 51–85

Index

Index